Buy It Now

Buy It Now

Lessons from eBay

MICHELE WHITE

DUKE UNIVERSITY PRESS   DURHAM AND LONDON 2012

© 2012 Duke University Press

All rights reserved

Printed in the United States of America on acid-free paper ∞

Designed by Amy Ruth Buchanan

Typeset in Minion by Tseng Information Systems, Inc.

Library of Congress Cataloging-in-Publication Data appear

on the last printed page of this book.

CONTENTS

FIGURES

PREFACE AND ACKNOWLEDGMENTS

A small painting of a postcard of the Statue of Liberty and Staten Island Ferry, which is listed in the "Postcards" category, highlights a series of lessons and methods from eBay.[1] It is difficult to understand what is being auctioned because the shape and color of the ferry depicted in the postcard is similar to the yellow ruler that is at the top of the image. Such rulers are a typical part of eBay auctions and illustrate the problems conveying the aspects of objects. In this case, the ruler is difficult to read because the numbers are upside down, almost cropped from the image, begin before the six-inch mark instead of at zero, and are part of a painting of an eBay listing rather than a postcard. The artist Conrad Bakker, who uses the eBay ID untitledprojects, auctioned a series of these paintings at the "original" listing price of the postcard.[2] He titled the listing "Staten Island Ferry Statue Liberty 1980'scolor postcard: an UNTITLED PROJECT: eBay/POSTCARDS/INDIANA" to reference the quirky spelling, uppercase and lowercase typefaces, punctuation, and spacing that eBay sellers deploy. Typographical errors and eccentric textual elements are common and conceptually important aspects of Internet content and are thus referenced by people like Bakker and quoted in this book. Through his project, Bakker proposes methods for thinking about Internet texts, consumerism, the ways things are categorized, the aspects and limits of the objects that are listed on eBay, and the terms of eBay selling. Images like Bakker's series, the people who produce them, and colleagues and friends have helped me understand the processes and critiques of eBay.

I began using and thinking about eBay in 1997. This was about the same time that I was considering dissertation research on "virtual museums," which provide views and accounts of museums rather than physical structures. While this book is not part of that early project, eBay also produces shifts between different representational and material versions of objects and can be understood through collecting and related literature. I therefore appreciate the grounding in collecting and critical understandings of visual objects that were provided by Bill Agee, Carol Armstrong, Rosemarie Haag Bletter, William Boddy, Patricia Clough, Setha Low, Linda Nochlin, Jane Roos, Eve Kosofsky Sedgwick, Ella Shohat, Chris Straayer, Michelle Wallace, and Sharon Zukin.

In a series of extremely productive conversations at the Console-ing Passions Conference in 2004, Mary Desjardins, Ken Hillis, Mark Williams, and I began to think collaboratively about eBay. During the same period, Ken Wissoker and I started discussing eBay. His intellectual and editorial assistance have been invaluable in conceptualizing this project. These conversations encouraged me to write about the ways vintage photography sellers use terms such as "gay" and "gay interest" to constitute a viewing public, sell items, and forward gay politics. This research appears in the *Everyday eBay: Culture, Collecting, and Desire* anthology that Hillis, Michael Petit, and Nathan Scott Epley edited.[3] Some research on the critical use of these terms in underwear and swimwear auctions, which is expanded and developed in chapter 4 of this book, was graciously supported by Blu Tirohl and published in the *Journal of Gender Studies*.[4] Work on heterosexuality, including the means through which the company and members profit from their wedding narratives, received enthusiastic support from Lisa McLaughlin and Cynthia Carter and has appeared in *Feminist Media Studies*.[5] David Beer and Roger Burrows edited a special issue of the *Journal of Consumer Culture* that includes my study of how eBay's heteronormative focus is challenged by the disorder of the site and messes of members.[6]

Colleagues also have invited me to present parts of this book and provided invaluable commentary. Caren Kaplan graciously included me in the Cultural Studies Colloquium Series at the University of California, Davis. Susanna Paasonen involved me in her provocative conference on identity and sexuality at the Collegium for Advanced Studies at the University of Helsinki. Ann Cvetkovich, Ann Reynolds, and Janet Staiger encouraged some research on how doll producers render themselves as artists and mothers on eBay. I spoke at their rigorous Political Emotions Conference, and Staiger's thoughtful commentary improved the chapter that appears in their anthology.[7] I also owe thanks to Batya Friedman, Gilly Leshed, Carman Neustaedter, Helen Nissenbaum, and Phoebe Sengers for including my consideration of eBay and free labor in their busyness symposium, which was sponsored by the National Science Foundation at the University of Washington. Early versions of some chapters were also considered in the Seminar on Historical Change and Social Theory at Tulane University. Emily Clark, Joel Dinerstein, Kate Drabinski, Marline Otte, Anthony Pereira, Allison Truitt, Edith Wolfe, and Justin Wolfe were among the many participants who provided careful readings and bibliographic suggestions at the seminar.

My ability to spend time researching eBay has also been facilitated by generous grants from a number of institutions. The National Endowment for the Humanities funded the very important summer seminar on literature and information technologies that Kate Hayles led at the University of California, Los Angeles. Kate is an amazing mentor and colleague and an astute scholar with a wide knowledge of new media practices. Other seminar participants, including Kathleen Fitzpatrick, William Gardner, Tara McPherson, and David Silver, continue to contribute to my intellectual inquiries. Colleagues at my current and previous academic institutions have also supported expenses for technology and travel and included me in their scholarly conversations. Tulane University and its School of Liberal Arts have funded this project with Committee on Research (COR) Summer Fellowships, Lurcy Grants, and a Research Enhancement Grant. The Newcomb College Institute offered me a number of research grants, and the Newcomb College Center for Research on Women provided a reading group grant that has been key to my intellectual development. I am particularly grateful to George Bernstein, Michael Bernstein, Carole Haber, Tara Hamburg, Sally Kenney, Rebecca Mark, Brian Mitchell, Jan Mulvihill, Molly Travis, and Laura Wolford for their support through these grant opportunities. I also thank the students who considered eBay in the classroom and Michael Garrett, Julie Schwartzwald, and Megan Weinlein for their research on eBay. My departmental colleagues, including Connie Balides, Kai-man Chang, Kukhee Choo, Carole Daruna, Marie Davis, Ana Lopez, Jim Mackin, Vicki Mayer, Mauro Porto, Beretta Smith-Shomade, Frank Ukadike, and Ferruh Yilmaz, have been encouraging. While evacuated from Tulane for Hurricane Katrina and just starting to work on this book, the University of California, Santa Cruz—especially the Center for Cultural Studies—offered me an intellectual home. I owe particular thanks to Stephanie Casher, Chris Connery, Dana Frank, and Gail Hershatter for their kindness and intellectual support.

I also greatly appreciate the friends, including the people already mentioned, who commented on drafts and presentations, critically considered eBay with me, and helped envision other uses for Internet sites and engagements. I extend heartfelt appreciation to Mark Anderson, Margy Avery, Megan Boler, Elizabeth Hill Boone, Mary Bryson, Jean Dangler, Carolyn Dean, Ken Gonzales Day, Greg Elmer, Anna Everett, Joan Fujimura, Joy Fuqua, Radhika Gajjala, Tarleton Gillespie, Ellis Hanson, Barbara Hayley, Steve Jones, Maggie Morse, Nance Maveety, Supriya Nair, Lisa Nakamura, Erica Rand, Alan Rosenberg, Ellen Fernandez Sacco, Mimi Schippers, Leslie Regan Shade, Carol Stabile, Jenny Sundén, Mike Syrimis, Karen Taylor, Fred Turner, and John Willinsky. I also owe a great deal to Courtney Berger, Leigh Barnwell, and Chris Dahlin at Duke University Press for their support, enthusiasm, and thoughtful questions during the writing and editing process. Finally, I thank my family. This book would never have been completed without the intellectual mentorship of Stephanie White and Pauline Farbman.

Lessons and Methods from eBay

twingles33 uses listings, profiles, and additional features in a manner similar to other eBay members and helps construct the site, participants, and consumerism. Her narrative reflects how eBay markets and facilitates community, links families and corporations, uses categories to control what can be seen and sold, organizes gender and sexuality on the site, and mandates work from members. twingles33 asks the viewer, "Got to have that Barbie?!" and answers her own inquiry by self-presenting as a Barbie collector.[1] As with "most Barbie? collectors," her "collection grew to" its "very own room," which her three boys call "Barbie? Blvd." and they "tell their friends 'don't go in there'" or she will make them "dress Barbie." Her narrative about the interlinked pleasures of identity production and consumption, which can be accessed through eBay, are problematized by the untraditional gender and sexuality positions that get culturally associated with collecting and the question marks that are sprinkled through the commentary. These punctuation marks probe her statements even though they are probably an HTML misreading of the Barbie trademark sign. Such nascent evaluations indicate some of the ways eBay functions and help me study members' listing and posting practices.

The question marks and descriptions of out-of-control collecting in twingles33's description trouble cultural mandates for women to order their lives and bodies and indicate that her feminine doll spaces jeopardize her sons' masculinity. Her sons fear being made to dress Barbie up and being clothed like the doll. Since her Barbie Boulevard has become a "highway under constuction," she is going to sell her "items on the Internet highway" and connect these sites. twingles33's listing is a version of eBay's community because members can solve her sons' panic, commit to her products, be good community members, and extend her family and its functions. eBay describes such connections between buyers, sellers, and the company as "community" and "social selling," since members' consumerism is based on shared interests. For instance, eBay's WorldofGood.com, a "multi-seller marketplace for socially and environmentally responsible shopping," uses the tagline, "Join a community of those who care."[2] eBay continues to employ the term "community" to render the values of the company and members and to get people to connect more often, assist individuals, and do the work that otherwise would be performed by customer-service representatives.

twingles33's "Got to have that Barbie" is conflicted. She addresses everyone as Barbie collectors, calls a community of doll collectors with particular attributes into being, justifies the auctioning and removal of Barbies from the home, still has to "have" dolls, and establishes gendered populations who pleasurably remember and fear Barbie play.[3] eBay also shifts between attending to everyone and constituting the normative identities that are most welcome on the site. eBay claims, "Whatever it is, you can get it on eBay," the company and its executives "recognize and respect everyone as a unique individual," and "Everyone has something to contribute."[4] eBay assures viewers about the openness of the site while, whether desired or uninvited, constituting normative subjects and consumerism. For instance, eBay uses the marriage of the site's founder, Pierre Omidyar, to Pam Wesley and other consumer-oriented weddings to stand in for the setting, encourages members to mirror these consumer practices and values, and regulates gay men's self-representations and descriptions of erotic interests.

eBay's "Whatever it is" campaign and featuring of the word "it" throughout the site are exemplary instances of the ways in which the company figures the setting as a diverse community. Through such slogans, eBay promises that the site connects everyone, fulfills all desires, delivers any object, and acknowledges a multitude of consumer identities. eBay's many deployments of the term "it," and the many appearances of the phrase "you can get it on" as part of the company's advertising slogan, relate the passionate aspects of collecting to sexual activity. eBay also tries to stabilize the unknowable aspects of Internet consuming and unrecognizable features of computer-represented objects and people—the "Whatever it is"—by assuring individuals that eBay is a compendium of everything and a logical frame. eBay and members such as twingles33 use such tactics to indicate and then control the messy and erotic elements of collecting. eBay's indications of profusion and tolerance are actively disingenuous because, as I have started to suggest, eBay regulates listings. eBay also functions as an instructional text and offers members lessons and guidelines.

eBay is a useful model for thinking about and advancing Internet and new media studies because other sites also deploy these operations. For instance, the developers of marketplace-oriented sites such as Etsy and craigslist have set rules and "community" links for participants.[5] There are thus many lessons researchers and designers can learn from examining eBay, including the problems with constituting virtual communities, the identity functions of brand communities and conferences, how rules and principles can be critically remediated, and the informative aspects of members' complaints and resistance. Popular discourses and Internet studies research often make it seem as if members are in support of such sites and practices. However, my study provides examples of the production of mainstream identities and corporate power in Internet settings, how members' values and positions are associated with sites, and the ways members make other identities and desires visible. I engage with these issues by focusing on ebay.com—the English-language site. In this introduction, I outline the concepts of brand community, configuring the user, organizational logic, sexual citizenship, and consumer citizenship; explain eBay's visual culture and the methodologies employed; and provide a chapter breakdown.

Brand Community Formation

eBay uses the concept of community as a way to structure the opening parts of the setting, categories, profiles, advertising campaigns, and newsletters. Early versions of eBay offered a "welcome" to the "community."[6] eBay continues to render this idea through "Community" forums that focus on members' collections and identities, accounts of individuals doing good deeds, opportunities to email sellers, and occasions to socialize at physical eBay conventions. Members support, and sometimes undermine, eBay's rendering of a community with their descriptions of shared interests, rituals, and values. They promote the site, post about their attachments to other participants, create elaborate eBay-branded outfits, provide economic and emotional support to members, critique the setting's functions, and produce the kinds of social selling strategies eBay encourages while depicting the kinds of bodies and desires eBay has tried to ban. eBay and other sites and spheres use community as a structuring device because it appears to accept everyone while articulating rules and values.

eBay also makes it seem as if members' engagements in the brand and community are empowering. For instance, joining "eBay Main Street" and "eBay Government Relations" will "make your voice heard."[7] Participating means being notified about "legislative matters that may affect E-commerce," being asked to communicate with "elected officials on crucial issues," and eBay directing members' engagements and politics.[8] Such options configure participants' opinions and constitute brands as shared cultural property rather than individually or corporately owned intellectual property.[9] They promote the formation of brand communities—cohorts of fans, creative producers, and consumer critics who collect around these arrangements. For the marketing scholars Albert M. Muñiz Jr. and Thomas C. O'Guinn, a brand community "is a specialized, non-geographically bound community, based on a structured set of social relations among admirers of a brand."[10] There are communities arranged around such brands as Apple, Coca-Cola, Saab, and *Star Wars*.[11] The eBay brand community is called into being by the company, facilitated on the site, supported and materialized by the work of productive members, and interrogated and further highlighted by consumer critics. The brand community literature explains how community is deployed on eBay, how the company organizes members, and how participants envision the company and site as their own. Yet I am critical of some aspects of the literature and brand community formation because individuals are used to produce value for corporations.

Popular and academic considerations of brand communities tend to identify participants as co-producers and even owners of brands who are willing to work for corporations. For the marketing-focused researchers C. K. Prahalad and Venkat Ramaswamy, consumers "want to interact with firms" and "co-create" the value of the brand and products.[12] Scott Cook, a member of eBay's board of directors, goes even further than this when he notes that "millions of people make all kinds of voluntary contributions to companies—from informed opinions to computing resources."[13] He advises companies to use "volunteers" to build their businesses. These brand managers, marketers, and academic researchers, according to the marketing scholarship of Detlev Zwick, Samuel K. Bonsu, and Aron Darmody, tend to celebrate "collaborative value creation as a moment of consumer empowerment and transfiguration."[14] However, they are interested in delivering "the customer over to the corporation." Members of a brand community are inclined to celebrate and buy the brand's products and to identify with the associated corporation, although the company's abandonment or mishandling of the brand can lead to alienation and critique.[15] For example, members of the eBay anti-brand community are a noticeable part of the site. Whether engaged for social, affective, identity-building, or even critical reasons (since resistance facilitates new commercial opportunities and value), people's engagement with brand communities supports corporations, consumerism, and the market.[16]

Jeff Skoll, Meg Whitman, John Donahoe, and others in eBay's leadership continue to be part of this brand community along with performing for a time as presidents and chief executives.[17] During their appearances at eBay community conferences, they shift between being brand celebrities and everyday members by wandering among the crowds, signing autographs, wearing the same outfit as other employees, and hosting events. Whitman "makes a point of being self-effacing" at such proceedings, says the reporter Chris Taylor, and "her first words to adoring online auctioneers are, 'This is about you.'"[18] This makes members feel like co-producers or even owners of eBay and has helped shift engagements with the site: in 1996, the year after the setting was developed, it had 41,000 registered members; in 2010, it had 94.5 million active members.[19] However, drops in the value of eBay's stock, growing member disenfranchisement, decreases in site traffic, a desire to "simplify and streamline" the organization, and a global economic downturn contributed to eBay's firing of more than one thousand full-time employees and six hundred temporary workers in 2008.[20] These changes also challenge Whitman's recognition of members, which does not extend to giving them significant site input, keeping auction fees low, or allowing GLBTQ sexual representations.

eBay identifies the setting as a community and site of co-production while supplying members with texts that describe their obligations and values.[21] For instance, readers of eBay's history section are told that "Omidyar built eBay around what remain the company's core values; a belief that: People are basically good, Everyone has something to contribute," and "An open environment brings out the best in people."[22] Omidyar and the company connect goodness to a community where people "contribute," or labor, without economic compensation from eBay. Members are encouraged to train new members, provide help with listings, moderate and resolve problems, and make individuals feel connected to the setting and the company. Yet the site also uses conceptions of goodness and the screen of diversity to articulate a normative setting ethos. For instance, eBay's "Community Values" narrative is accompanied by an image of heterosexual couples.[23] eBay's deployment of community encourages critical considerations of the values it and other Internet sites facilitate and the ways members are configured.

Configuring the User

eBay portrays community members as collectors, binary gendered and heterosexual subjects, and good moral people. It also uses a variety of tactics to get members to adopt these roles. Thus, eBay produces a version of members or "configures" them as this concept is delineated in science and technology studies. Steve Woolgar, who is informed by social theory and the philosophy of science, argues that individuals who design personal computers also define, delineate, and facilitate the appearance of the user.[24] He considers how different sectors of companies speak for users, teach users what to want, and incorporate conceptions of users into products.[25] eBay speaks for members when it offers a list of "Community Values" that are produced by the company.[26] In a related manner, Woolgar describes how warning labels and other elements of computer systems direct individuals to keep the computer case sealed and provide messages about the skill level, nationality, and other features of users. Nigel Thrift extends Woolgar's thesis and how eBay configuration can be understood. According to Thrift, electronic toys introduce children to interfaces, technologies, and worldviews and thereby configure them for future interactive environments.[27] eBay configures members through instructional texts, rule systems, advertisements that indicate how the site is supposed to function, and features that articulate identities and goods. Configuration therefore defines users' identities, delimits their actions, and challenges the cultural association of the term "user" with agency and an unmediated and unmarked engagement.

A number of researchers in feminist science and technology studies nuance Woolgar's conception of configuring the user and consider the introduction of technologies to consumers as a process of mutual adaptation in which gender and technology are shaped.[28] They study the consumption junction where consumers choose between competing technologies, individuals are co-producers, and technological diffusion happens. Identifying people as co-producers, who in the broadest sense help design technologies, acknowledges the complicated ways mechanisms and social practices are developed. Models of co-production challenge narratives about miraculous discoveries and scientific genius. They avoid replicating histories of white male inventors, such as focusing on Omidyar's role as the "founder" of eBay, and displacing members' participation. Microsoft renders a form of co-production in commercials where individuals describe how they influenced the operating system's design and declare, "I'm a PC and Windows 7 was my idea."[29] However, the generic aspects of these ideas perpetuate Microsoft's authorship. In my study of eBay, I recognize how groups of people assist in the production, marketing, and diffusion of technologies and processes *and* how users are socially constructed, encouraged to work because of their position as co-producers, and directed to adopt certain notions of technologies and roles.

Equating co-production and agency can be politically troubling. After all, eBay uses conceptions of co-production, as I suggest in chapters 1 and 2, to get members to identify with the site and brand and work for free. In a manner similar to computer warning labels, eBay functions as an instructional text. For instance, "Buy It Now," an eBay shopping option with a fixed cost and expectation that individuals will immediately pay for purchases, is also a directive that encourages specific types of consumerism and commands members to accept the company's terms. A critical attention to these processes and the claims made by Internet and new media studies researchers, including the tendency to identify hypertexts, fan cultures, and virtual communities as empowering, is imperative. Notions of users' agency discourage research on how sites regulate and configure individuals and the ways governments and other political forces deploy settings and technologies in support of their platforms and policies.

Gender and the Company's Organizational Logic

Most aspects of the eBay interface are designed to configure viewers. The "Magic Snow Globe" helps individuals "find the perfect gift" during the holiday season. It encourages people to "Wish for it," using a gender-neutral pronoun to acknowledge everyone and everything, and accidentally suggests the desire for non-binary gender positions.[30] However, the gift finder divides all eBay shopping into items "For Him" or "For Her." Gender is further differentiated and hierarchized by associating masculinity with the "Brainiac," "Mr. Fix It," and intelligence and technical skill and by associating women with traditional feminine labor and the "Domestic Goddess."[31] In a similar manner, the shopping search engine TheFind asks, "What can we find for you?" and associates consumerism with women by offering "short prom dresses, cameo jewelry, layered necklace, stackable rings, prom dress," and "diamond earrings."[32] These articulations of gendered identities, objects, and forms of shopping are antithetical to selling to the widest number of consumers. In such cases, user-articulated searching is replaced with cultural instructions and the configuration of users as gendered subjects with particular buying interests.

eBay's varied lists and categories create a set of objects and relationships between objects; articulate what is recognizable and purchasable; structure how things can be viewed; help to articulate collecting; and produce gender, race, and sexuality classifications. For example, the "Baby" category has links for "Girl Clothes," illustrated by a dress, and "Boy Clothes."[33] Dads and parents are not mentioned in the "More Info About Baby" section, but the viewer is informed, "You can also find great gear for mom."[34] Through such frameworks, eBay connects ideal items to traditional roles and extends the organizational logic of the site. Gender and sexuality, according to the sociologist Joan Acker, are constitutive elements in the "organizational logic, or the underlying assumptions and practices that construct most contemporary work organizations."[35] These beliefs and behaviors, and understandings of individuals and companies, are instituted through abstract conceptions of workers, written and computerized work rules, managerial directives, and other methods for running organizations. The concept of organizational logic—and I am using this term to describe such things as eBay's categories, feedback reviews, menu options, narratives, and principles—allows me to interrogate the underlying structures and ideologies of businesses and the larger ways things are classified according to gender and heterosexual norms. Critiques of such corporate and social arrangements are needed because society often views companies and their policies and practices as gender-neutral and considerations of gender and sexuality as imposed on or peripheral to the systems.[36]

Buyers are introduced to eBay's organizational logic when they find listings by using the menu-driven category system, search function, or previously saved searches. Buyers who search by using a particular term receive results that specify how many items are in each category; they are provided with contextualizing images and statements and have the option to continue to view through eBay's specific categories and users' terms. Buyers and, especially, sellers must accept eBay's categories and configuration, think like the structure, allow its organizational logic, and view in particular ways to engage successfully. For instance, people buy and then resell things on eBay and make a profit by changing categories so interested buyers are more likely to view listings.[37] eBay's categories suggest a whole system of knowledge and an organizational logic because they have links to subcategories and a set of titles and listings written by sellers.

eBay connects the organizational aspects of the site and its technologies to binary gender and heteronormativity. This correlation occurs on an ideological and structural level. Binary gender supports and produces hierarchical social relations and power by mapping a dyadic system and values onto individuals, bodies, organizations, and other things. Heteronormativity, which is the assertion of heterosexual privilege and pervasive ordering of existence through inflexible sexual standards, is also an organizational logic.[38] eBay seems to renounce this structure with such features as the "Gift Spot" holiday search engine, which, according to the company, provides "Something for everyone" and references the "G-Spot" and overt sexuality.[39] However, the Gift Spot functions in a manner similar to eBay's other references to everyone. It places heterosexual relationships at the forefront with "gifts that are just right for your husband, wife, kids, family, fashionista, techie, sports fan—everybody on your list." In such instances traditional positions, and terms such as "techie" are gender-coded by establishing a relationship between the men's gifts and technology categories, are equated to everybody. eBay promises an infinite array while supporting organizing principles that naturalize binary gender and heterosexuality.

Sexual Citizenship

eBay's organizational logic recognizes and verifies particular subjects. Its interrelated conceptions of citizenship and community, which emphasize the obligations that come with membership, are also related to binary gender and heterosexual positions.[40] This "normal citizen," according to the social-policy scholar Diane Richardson, "has largely been constituted as heterosexual."[41] David Bell, Jon Binnie, Beverley Skeggs, and David Trevor Evans indicate that sexual minorities are excluded from full citizenship by criminalizing nonnormative sexualities, preventing anyone who is not most narrowly paired into a male-and-female couple from marrying, and enacting other exclusionary policies.[42] For instance, the eBay brand produced heterosexual citizenship by linking Omidyar's marriage to the invention and continuation of the site.

Omidyar began AuctionWeb in 1995 with the sale of a broken laser pointer and first called the setting eBay in 1997.[43] However, eBay's apocryphal and often repeated origin story indicates that Omidyar started the site so his fiancée, Wesley, could trade plastic dispensers for Pez candy.[44] Mary Lou Song, who initiated this myth when she was eBay's public relations chief, has stated that the site began "as kind of a love token."[45] According to Kevin Pursglove, who was a company spokesperson, Omidyar designed eBay to resolve his fiancée's experience of "frustration that many collectors have experienced" because geography limited her ability to buy, sell, and trade.[46] This scripts men as technological producers, facilitates a founding story about family and community work, and renders women as men's support and inspiration. A large number of members extend this brand story and heterosexual citizenship by indicating how eBay has helped initiate their relationships, narrating marriages on the site, and using eBay to buy and sell wedding items. These representations of weddings are not inherent or politically neutral aspects of the site and company. By highlighting eBay's apocryphal stories throughout this book, I demonstrate how the company crafts accounts to sustain its relationship to normative gender and sexuality positions and configure the site. Such normative gender and sexuality structures are often ignored but critical considerations of heteronormativity indicate how heterosexual privilege is incorporated into society and the ways it pervasively and cunningly orders the everyday.[47]

eBay continues to promise "you can get it on" and that the site provides an open sexual setting and marketplace. However, in 1999, there was press coverage of unlawful activities on the site, and the company began using software and other devices to search for illegal and infringing items.[48] Kenneth Walton received a U.S. federal felony conviction for his use of shill bidding to drive up auction prices, marketing of forgeries, and other criminal activities.[49] eBay also removed the firearms category and no longer allows sellers to list legally saleable guns and ammunition. In another regulatory move, eBay forces many erotic materials into its "Adult Only" category, which requires special registration and cannot be searched from the main part of the site. Buyers who use the search terms "gay" and "lesbian" on the main site are asked, "Are you looking for... the Adult Only login page or help about the Adult Only category?"[50] eBay associates gay and lesbian identities with illicit sexualities, discourages gay and lesbian members from using the main part of the site, and articulates undesirable forms of consumerism and sexual citizenship. Although eBay offers this preprogrammed proviso, sellers use the terms "gay" and "lesbian" in listings and assert the presence of gay, lesbian, and queer sexualities; the marketability of these terms; the errors of this search prompt; and consumer citizenship. The eBay setting even foils its own disciplinary mechanisms and produces more defiant consumer and sexual citizens when members adopt the site's sexual narratives about being able to "get it on" eBay.

Consumer Citizens

Consumption is linked to sexual citizenship when companies advertise directly to gay men and eBay members list photographic documents as "gay interest" and "lesbian interest." Consumption and citizenship, according to academics like Sonia Livingstone and Peter Lunt, Margaret Scammell, Verónica Schild, and Michael Schudson, are interrelated.[51] The history of politically oriented consumer activities includes the American Revolution and people resisting Britain's promotion of goods; the bus boycott in Montgomery, Alabama, to protest racial segregation in the United States; and the Stonewall Riots, in which gay men, lesbians, and drag queens resisted police raids and harassment at bars.[52] People also act as consumer citizens when they organize health food store collectives, establish brand boycotts and buycotts, recraft media and other texts so they function as cultural critiques, and select objects to signal their subcultural identities.[53]

eBay connects consumerism, citizenship, co-production, and moral behavior in its WorldofGood.com site, "Where your shopping shapes the world."[54] Members also act as consumer citizens when they use listings and other practices to critique the system and company. These forms of consumerism point to methods for holding companies and governments responsible for environmental, health, human rights, labor, and sustainable development issues.[55] Consumer critique, as Scammell argues, is fundamental to citizenship.[56] It highlights the otherwise invisible political power of corporations. With eBay, consumer critiques and theoretical models for research are particularly important because the setting claims to be transparent, is vetted by a cohort of individuals, deploys a founding mythos that indicates preferred identities, and is supported by many of the concepts of Internet and new media studies. The deployment of these consumer-citizenship processes in Internet settings, including craigslist's links to U.S. President Barack Obama, promises of sexual freedom, removal of advertisements, and control of members' sexuality and angry commentary, make Internet studies the examination of governmentality, social regulation, and resistance.

Whitman extends eBay's sexual- and consumer-citizenship processes by participating in U.S. politics. She was the national co-chair for finance for Mitt Romney's campaign, and she co-chaired John McCain's presidential bid in 2008. Whitman also ran for governor of California in 2009. While doing this, she managed the gendered aspects of her citizenship, and how her position as a top executive might influence her political aspirations, by identifying as "a wife and mother who raised two boys" during interviews and at her address to the U.S. Republican National Convention in 2008.[57] She supported California's Proposition 8, an initiative that eliminated the rights of same-sex couples to marry, and conceptually continued eBay's regulation of gay sexual representations. Her fame among eBay members and her political ambitions are related to Ronald Reagan's and Arnold Schwarzenegger's Hollywood-facilitated celebrity status and political careers. As Internet interfaces continue to produce familiar cultural figures, including the designers and executives associated with these settings, their social influence and political power, and the values of their Internet sites, are amplified. Of course, members' alienation, which in the case of eBay increased during Whitman's last few years as president and CEO and has escalated with Donahoe's leadership, also creates a ready group of commentators who practice more critical forms of consumer citizenship.

Whitman uses eBay's economic history as a way to represent her readiness for political office and her position as a good citizen. Other U.S. politicians employ eBay as a way to indicate the possibilities for American innovation and economic recovery.[58] eBay therefore functions as a resonant cultural symbol, as well as an interface. Former U.S. President George W. Bush compared eBay to the development of "new medicines to treat diseases," new security measures "in Americans' airports," and "new jet engines" and argued that eBay "extended the frontiers of knowledge," "inspired a wave of innovation," and "helped create a global marketplace."[59] McCain proclaimed that "1.3 million people in the world make a living off eBay," and "most of those are in the United States of America."[60] McCain, according to his senior economic adviser, has used eBay to signal that he is "fundamentally optimistic about the capacity of the U.S. economy to innovate"; this will lead to "new opportunities for jobs," and residents "shouldn't be obsessed with looking backwards all the time, and saying, 'Gee, where did those jobs go?'"[61] Of course, eBay was firing employees and members were being asked to work for free around the time this statement was made.[62] These politicians identify eBay as good for Americans and a worldwide community, and code the company as a kind of citizen, but the site's distinctive contributions to global welfare and technological advancement are not explained.

Politicians have not addressed indications that the company's fees and policies are ruining sellers' chances to make money; that some members are selling off their belongings because of unemployment, escalating bills, and foreclosures; and that selling personal goods may not be economically productive over the long term. A number of economists argue that reselling things cannot improve the economy.[63] The 2006 ACNielsen study, which generated McCain's figures, identified eBay as a "primary" or "secondary" source of money for members.[64] McCain has also repeatedly referred to Whitman as the founder of eBay even though she was hired around the time of the initial public stock offering.[65] Sarah Palin failed to sell an Alaskan state jet through eBay, but she and McCain presented the sale as a testament to her consumer-citizenship skills and the economic possibilities of the interface.[66] As this suggests, McCain's presidential campaign frequently misrepresented eBay's history, position, and sales figures. These politicians use eBay to stand in for a series of values, citizenship processes, and possibilities that are largely fictional. Such narratives have proved troublesome because the Internet makes it possible for political bloggers and angry eBay members to reply quickly, sometimes reaching enormous audiences. For instance, Omidyar used the Twitter micro-blogging interface to respond to McCain's misidentification of Whitman. Numerous individuals repeated Omidyar's critique.[67] The Internet provides methods for challenging erroneous information, but eBay also reshapes its history, status, and values through corporate mythos, including its narrative about the invention of the company.

eBay's Visual Culture

Visual images are an important part of the site and the ways eBay produces its mythos, brand community, users, organizational logic, sexual citizenship, and consumer citizens. For example, eBay conveys its investment in weddings and traditional unions by using images of paired Pez dispensers that stand in for Omidyar and Wesley's marriage (see figure 1), advertisements for engagement rings, and commercials that feature heterosexual couples (see figure 2).[68] Other central aspects of the eBay site include depictions of members and listed objects, icons, logos, grids, bands and blocks of color, and colored typefaces. Individuals become fans of these eBay images and their underlying values when they repost them on image-sharing sites and wear their own versions at conferences. These representations and engagements can be productively analyzed through visual culture studies because it examines what happens when people look at and produce visual objects, the conceptions that emerge from

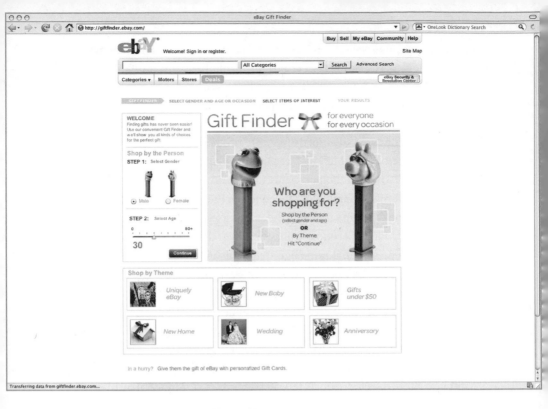

1. eBay, "eBay Gift Finder," 29 March 2009

these acts, and how visuality operates in particular cultures and periods.[69] Visual culture studies scholars such as Lisa Cartwright and Nicholas Mirzoeff link visual analysis (the study of objects and sites) and visual cultures (the societies in which these things are produced) to new media.[70]

eBay uses visual devices to assert its reliability, the more general dependability of new media, and the materiality of objects. This is related to the ways politicians employ eBay to represent their trustworthiness. For example, eBay advises members that producing and trusting legible images of listed objects is an essential part of the interface. Jim Griffith, eBay's "official Dean of Education," argues that buyers like to "see what they are buying" and sellers should therefore provide pictures that are "clear, focused, uncluttered, and as close a representation of your item as possible."[71] According to Dennis L. Prince, Sarah Manongdo, and Dan Joya's how-to book, the "opportunity to sell an item is almost entirely dependent upon whether or not you've provided good images for prospective bidders to see."[72] These claims that objects can be seen through photography and digital imaging are related to the identification of photography as light's direct transcription of objects, which were once in front of the camera, onto a surface. For instance, Roland Barthes argues in his theoretical and affective study of viewing that the "photograph is always invisible: it is not it that we see" and photographs are not fully distinguished from the objects they represent.[73] Susan Sontag's study also identifies photography as a "trace, something directly stenciled off the real, like a footprint or a death mask."[74] On some level, the association of photography with material objects persists in settings like eBay. However, the processes of buyers and sellers and functions of listing images also compromise visual representations.

Many eBay sellers use digital images and digitized photographs to portray unique items and once-in-a-lifetime events. Nevertheless, the framing structures and functions of these images have the tendency, as the philosopher and cultural critic Walter Benjamin argues, of substituting "a plurality of copies for a unique existence."[75] The photographic copy, according to the art histo-

2. eBay, "eBay," 11 August 2007

rian Rosalind E. Krauss, facilitates the "quotation of the original" and splinters "the unity of the original 'itself' into nothing but a series of quotations."[76] When objects function as a series of quotations, which are facilitated and mirrored by the representations in listings, there are fewer reasons to buy them. This suggests that eBay, sellers, and other institutions and individuals need to contain and monitor the truth claims of photography and related imaging processes in order to support larger investments in the authenticity of the material world.

Sellers specify in numerous listings that their images do not do objects "justice," have flaws, and lack in detail and thus highlight the referential aspects of digital images and photographs that are digitally conveyed. At the same time, these sellers seem to destabilize cultural conceptions of photography and eBay's values by identifying imaging failures in clear depictions. The common phrase "pictures do not do it justice" suggests that images do not honor objects or represent them fairly.[77] It also renders eBay as less visual because certain things cannot be seen. This statement is part of sellers' attempts to contain how depictions disturb the unity and authenticity of listed objects. Sellers describe the imperfections of images to specify that objects have a greater value than representations imply and individuals can only fully experience things by buying, touching, wearing, and living with them. For instance, recherche-gallery's listings provide an affective experience that "cannot be justified by pictures." The artworks only show their "best qualities in person," where they "'move' as you walk past" them and leave "guests speechless!!"[78] In such cases, the distinctness and experiential aspects of material artifacts, the things that complement visual seeing, displace the images of objects that accompany listings.

Sellers encourage viewers to see the features of photo-like representations and read images differently from experiences with objects. novelty.star's photographs cannot convey the object's "finely detailed" surface.[79] "eBay's reduced resolution . . . may appear grainy (particularly linen postcards) or blurry," according to dwells00collectibles, "but not in the real world! They will look much better in your hand."[80] These sellers point to the aspects of digital imaging, which include visible pixels, the appearance of code or icons instead of images, and distorted depictions. They distinguish between images and objects and hint that you can "get it on eBay" but that experiences with things ordinarily cannot be sustained by eBay or remain on the site. The changing aspects of the eBay interface, especially the opening part of the site, and the impermanence of listings are important to the setting's functioning.

Depictions of reliable and good sellers rather than images are sometimes the deciding factor in buying. People's basic auction "fears," according to Josh Boyd, "are compounded by the fact that bidders cannot examine and touch the items they are bidding on; they must trust descriptions and photographs. They cannot see the people they are bidding against; they can only see letters on a screen."[81] cburnscrx believes that one "of the flaws" in eBay's functioning as a selling platform "is the unknown" and the inability to "look at, or touch the items you are buying."[82] Buyers and sellers "rely on people's honesty and their integrity" because of these issues. While some scholars in visual culture studies identify the Internet as an exemplary instance of contemporary society's visual emphasis, Boyd, cburnscrx, and other eBay members indicate instances in which specific features of the visual are not delivered or fail. In such cases, successful transactions, social engagements, and links between participants, which are still conveyed through representations, replace an interaction with images of objects.

Methods for eBay and Internet Settings

The visual and textual aspects of Internet settings are an important part of this book and help me to understand eBay. I use the humanities methods of close visual, textual, and theoretical analysis to study eBay's site texts, category system, forums, advertising campaigns, and listings from the English-language setting. Some of the examples provided in the book were obtained by using the site's search function. However, the related tendencies emerged through an examination of individual categories and large sets of listings. Accounts by eBay executives, other employees, and members; reporters; and how-to book authors also provide detailed explanations of how the site is produced and culturally understood. For instance, posts from enthusiastic and critical members in eBay-facilitated forums and other settings convey participants' experiences and sentiments. My understanding of eBay and its members is further informed by information about the eBay Live! conferences, forum posts that describe these conventions, listings for eBay-ana convention collectibles, and my attendance at eBay Live! and the Developers Conference in Boston in 2007. These diverse texts highlight the varied individuals who contribute to understandings of eBay, the divergent narratives about the site, and the widescale reach of the setting. They show how Internet sites can be redeployed as critical strategies.

As part of this examination, I quote the kinds of texts that are commonly available in Internet settings. The quoted texts include typographical errors and unconventional forms of spelling, uppercase and lowercase typefaces, punctuation, and spacing. These elements are typical aspects of Internet content, which nevertheless change or become unavailable, and are cited without such qualifications as "intentionally so written" or "sic." Such references provide a more comprehensive account of eBay and the Internet, support my arguments, offer references, and enable researchers to consider these sites. This method also helps me interrogate how stereotyped notions are rendered across multiple sites and made to appear inherent, natural, and real. I try to be sensitive to individuals' investments in Internet settings while being critical about the problems and cultural conceptions that are instituted. A variety of methods and ethical models have been proposed for studying the Internet.[83] As I have suggested elsewhere, ethics texts that insist that all Internet research is human subject research and that sources should be elided fail to acknowledge the deeply produced aspects of Internet settings and the humanities methods that apply when writing about Internet and computer-facilitated representations.[84] Internet research methods can critically interrogate how representations are understood as places and people or support the naturalization of these conventions. In this project, I understand eBay and related sites as interfaces, purveyors of information, producers of depictions, and cultural processes.

Academic studies of eBay also inform this book and indicate what still needs to be researched. For instance, identity issues, including the ways gender, race, and sexuality are produced and regulated, often remain under-addressed in critical literature about eBay. Economists and business scholars consider the relationship between game theory and eBay's auction system; buy it now, reserve price, and other auction and sales models; and the means through which price is determined.[85] While some of this literature focuses on the ways reputation enhances final auction prices, it does not provide related studies of how sellers produce their standing or the sorts of social engagements and self-presentations that are encouraged by eBay and other companies. There is significant writing about eBay's production of trust among members, eBay's and other companies' feedback systems, and how reputation contributes to positive auction outcomes and prices.[86] These texts veer away from studying sellers and their connections through events like eBay Live! conferences. There is also increasing academic interest in eBay and consumerism, including research on the collecting cultures that operate through the site and how business strategies and characteristics are influenced by the interface.[87] Most of these texts support eBay's positive accounts about members' empowerment.

Adam Cohen's popular ethnography is a largely enthusiastic account of eBay, the site, and the company's early history.[88] Like that of the academic literature, Cohen's intent is different from my goals in this book. He does not provide critical strategies for looking at eBay, a detailed study of the interface, considerations of members' engagements, or an analysis of the means through which site design and advertising are interrelated. The *Everyday eBay: Culture, Collecting, and Desire* anthology provides the most rigorous critical engagement with eBay (and, as an ethical addendum, I have a chapter in that text).[89] Jon Lillie's and Kylie Jarrett's chapters in *Everyday eBay* and Josh Boyd's "In Community We Trust: Online Security Communication at eBay" are useful for my consideration because they address the ways eBay deploys community as a trust-building mechanism that gets individuals to contribute.[90] Yet I also consider issues that do not appear in these works, including how eBay promises to support diverse objects and desires while producing normative gender, race, and sexuality conventions; how buyers and sellers work with and against the site's principles; and how members render brand communities in eBay's bulletin boards and conference cultures.

Chapter Summaries

eBay uses notions of community to tie members to the site, to articulate values and norms, and to get individuals to work for free. In chapter 1, I describe how eBay positions the corporation and site as a community rather than as profit-motivated. eBay's narratives about community offer the opportunity to reflect on academic and popular accounts of virtual communities and to calls for the dismantling of community because of the intolerance such groups can perpetuate.[91] The concepts of community and virtual community are connected to the related notions of brand communities and social networking settings. My assessment addresses the ways eBay participants are made to labor for their standing in the system, support company positions, resistantly respond to changes in the site, and constitute their own versions of community.

In chapter 2, I reflect on the ways members identify and how community and cultural identities are shaped through the company's asynchronous conference forum, its conferences (including the eBay Live! that I attended in 2007), and the collecting and sale of eBay-ana (branded objects that are produced for conventions and given to sellers and employees). These engagements teach people how to be members of the fan and brand community, support eBay's normalizing and economic goals, and work for the company.[92] Nevertheless, when the company and brand do not fulfill promises, connected members are more likely to critique the setting, rupture the concept of eBay community, and pose a threat to the ideological and economic values of the brand. eBay uses the conference board, conferences, and branded items as ways to keep members enthralled and working for the company, but this structure is not always successful.

eBay also employs representations of heteronormativity as a way to sustain its values and configure members. For instance, eBay features engagement rings and wedding dresses on the main parts of the site, in press releases, and in advertising. It connects these items to binary gender, heterosexuality, and conceptions of shopping for "the one" and suggests they are key elements of eBay and of women's lives and identities. In chapter 3, I analyze how eBay interlinks its heteronormative narratives with the organizational logic of the site. Sellers repeat these narratives and support eBay when they use images of their weddings to sell dresses, mandate perfect bodies and gowns, and describe the perfect dress and mate. While some members portray perfect weddings, others display dirty and crushed dresses that do not fit into their homes and mention they are selling dresses because of weight gains or the ending of relationships. I use literature on weddings, dirt, and collecting to consider eBay's narratives and the ways sellers destabilize the notion of ideal weddings and heteronormativity.[93]

Most sellers, encouraged by eBay's normalizing texts, provide narratives about heterosexual marriages and traditional gender identities. I reflect on the oppositional strategies of buyers and sellers of "gay" and "gay interest" underwear, swimwear, and vintage photography in chapter 4. These members portray unconventional male bodies, emphasize gay desires, constitute gay communities, perform a consumer critique of the eBay setting and its values, and sometimes garner high prices. In doing this, they achieve the combination of personalization and successful selling eBay encourages but manage this through the kinds of erotic representations eBay has tried to prohibit. Literature on gay identities, consumerism, and masculinity assists me in studying the ways these practices undermine eBay's normalizing discourses and larger conceptions of identity and embodiment.[94]

Members do not always uphold eBay's viewing positions, which support binary gendered consumers and straight desires. As I argue in chapter 5, sellers of vintage mass-produced erotic photographs of women list materials as "lesbian" and "lesbian interest" and make heterosexual male buyers, who are their target consumer, seem less straight. Sellers of vernacular photography further complicate these viewing and desiring positions by listing images of note to lesbians, documentation of lesbian pasts, women performing masculinities, and drag weddings under the "lesbian" and "lesbian interest" search terms. The inclusion of these varied texts means that these images cannot be consolidated into a homogenous category, men are not the entitled viewers, the relationship between men and masculinity is challenged, and eBay's organizational logic at least temporarily fails. The production of men with lesbian interests and portrayal of women performing masculinities, particularly when combined with critical literature about drag and the cultural construction of genitals, promote continued examinations of how gender, sex, and sexuality are identified.[95]

Some eBay sellers assert alternative gender and sexuality positions, but eBay still produces stereotypes. In chapter 6, I show how eBay's "Black Americana" category renders stereotyped black identities and disempowered African Americans. In this category, sellers use racist terms, equate stereotyped representations to African Americans' histories and characteristics, promote reprehensible reproductions, displace stereotypes by calling items "cute," and invoke slave auctions. These racist practices are encouraged by eBay's organizational logic. I interrogate these listings and their logic by relating them to the histories and critiques of nineteenth-century and twentieth-century representations of African Americans and critical work on the commodification of identities.[96] eBay's terms and sellers' listings promise to deliver black cultures, collectibles, and history while listing racist representations that empower whites, providing apocryphal narratives that excuse slavery, and constructing an eBay community that appears to be good while reproducing intolerance.

The afterword continues to emphasize the lessons that can be learned from eBay and the ways literature on brand communities, configuring the user, organizational logic, and sexual citizenship can be deployed. I focus on craigslist where members' posts, sales of items, and searches for relationships are also envisioned as a community. The site appears to have a sexually tolerant and liberal ethos. However, the numerous women who have had dating listings removed through "community flagging" find the site to be deeply disciplining. In the craigslist boards that are dedicated to helping individuals with flagged and removed posts, volunteers claim to convey the community's values while instructing women in traditional conceptions of femininity. Yet the resistant comments from flagged women point to models for consumer critique. Internet and new media scholars can look to such disgruntled customers and their assessments as ways of understanding the problematic aspects of Internet settings.

Conclusion: The Costs of Internet Lessons

The costs of the Internet's organizational and cultural logics are too rarely considered. For instance, women who do not meet cultural norms or interrogate Internet and computer conventions have their commentary, actions, and bodies mercilessly critiqued. They also receive violent threats from anonymous and copious posters, who usually self-identify as men. Kathy Sierra, an acknowledged expert on the Java language and author of programming texts, stopped blogging and speaking publicly after death threats and her home address were posted in Internet settings. She noted, "I'm at home, with the doors locked, terrified."[97] In the posts that worried Sierra, critiques of her skills were commingled with insults about her physiognomy, a "digitally altered photo of Sierra being strangled in women's panties," and an image of Sierra positioned next to a noose.[98] Discussions about how to prevent such threats, including suggestions that blog owners take responsibility for posted content, largely have been rejected as censorship and the misrecognition of how open commenting is central to the principles of new media.[99] In these cases, the organizational and cultural logics of Internet settings are associated with righteousness even when they oppress and efface some people and positions. Of course, editing and deleting extraneous and uninvited texts are familiar parts of computer and Internet use.[100]

Many feminists have encountered regulatory and threatening behavior in Internet settings. craigslist's best-of postings, which are nominated by the community and vetted as significant, provide instructional "dictionaries" for women's personal ads. These lexicons, which equate "Feminist" with "Fat" and "Professional" with "Bitch," propose a language of intolerance and encourage women to enact extremely traditional forms of femininity.[101] Joan Walsh, who writes for the news and commentary site *Salon*, considers such regulating behaviors, including the harassment of Sierra and her own experiences with vicious emails. Walsh finds it "hard to ignore that the criticisms of women writers are much more brutal and vicious than those about men" and that this is supported by the ethos and design features of Internet settings.[102] I was stunned at the reactions to a post in a *Forbes* forum, in which I casually noted that a poll about identifying with imaginary characters should include empowered positions for women.[103] According to readers, my discussion was not relevant; I should stop interrogating gender issues; and I should die from breast cancer or vaginitis because I was a "whore." In this and other cases, members make it clear that they will continue to discipline people for performing gender and other critiques that they consider unrelated to the setting. They employ the organizational logic of sites to support their controlling positions. Writing about such initially anonymous engagements in academic or news venues can cause further problems because it allows individuals, who are invested in regulating sites and behaviors, to identify authors and continue harassing them. It also produces a setting in which commentators are forced to repetitively justify their interpretations, and critical work is kept at the most basic level.

It may be possible, and it is certainly understandable, for women, gay men, lesbians, queers, people of color, and other dismissed sexual citizens to stop engaging with Internet settings where they are configured, scorned, and threatened. However, ostracized individuals who ignore dismissals, and the associated settings, leave abuse unchallenged and support the coding of technologies as white heterosexual men's terrain. Walsh argues that the misogynist "self-righteous fury" directed at female writers makes them "reflexively compose" their "own hate mail," "type and retype to try to avoid it," and write more cautiously and produce less.[104] Thus, the technologies that are credited with enabling faster production methods and greater audience attention constrain some opinions and subjects.[105] As Internet settings and related technologies are becoming expected aspects of daily life — and in many ways, educators, employers, peers, and local and national governments already mandate their use — the power of such configurations and the costs of detaching are increasing. This means that we need to incorporate critical methods for thinking about the sexist, racist, and heteronormative aspects of organizational and cultural logics into Internet and new media studies and settings. To deflate current narratives and versions of empowered masculinity, we also require more detailed considerations of site design, analysis of how dialogue occurs in Internet settings, and collaborative feminist support and responses. My intent is not to identify a recipe for resistance, if such a thing is even possible. However, I hope that my outline of the ways gendered, raced, and sexualized subjects are imbricated in Internet settings, and considerations of consumer critiques, encourage the continued development of critical research in Internet and new media studies.

chapter one

Between Security and Distrust

EBAY'S BRAND, FAN, AND VIRTUAL COMMUNITIES

eBay uses narratives about community to transform its visual and textual representations into people and spaces, connect members, provide reasons for participants to invest and work for the site, and turn the company into a neighbor and friend. eBay labels parts of the site with the term "community" and makes it a key structural and emotive feature. For instance, notions of community are conveyed through eBay's "Group Gifts" feature. With this option, people make partial payments and "Give bigger, give better, give it together."[1] The Group Gifts site depicts members in eBay's color scheme collaboratively supporting a large gift box and underscores the power of eBay groups, caring, and that this is a site-based community practice. These characteristics are emphasized in eBay's newsletter when an employee, Nino, describes lildivasboutique*com giving minimaxshow an extra item along with a listing, getting a gift in response, and the two women becoming friends and business partners.[2] Two other female members featured in the newsletter, raglebagle and unique-find, form a vital connection that incorporates social selling, "a special friendship," and "countless emails every day" until raglebagle "cannot imagine living life without unique-find." While there is an image of "raglebagle with husband" and assertion of heteronormativity, the article also describes people "meeting their future spouse on eBay," the women knowing "exactly what to say to each other on good days and bad," and plans for "the two friends" to "finally meet in person – after three years of waiting" at eBay Live! The newsletter thus evokes intense eBay-facilitated female friendships, or even queer romances.

eBay references passionate attachments and uses accounts of community to constitute members as normative citizens—individuals who freely give to each other, take an active part in society, do good work, and perform traditional roles. The concept of the eBay citizen and the company's relationship to citizenship, sexuality, and governmentality should be examined in depth. eBay's linking of these social structures includes eBay-facilitated weddings and Meg Whitman's campaign to become governor of California. By rendering community, relationships, and citizenship, eBay makes the setting matter, addresses everyone, coaxes individuals to invest and work for free, and institutes a series of norms that are productive for the company's profile and profitmaking capabilities. Members' engagements, whether they are fans of the site, outcome-oriented shoppers, or critics of the company and its interface—are always filtered through eBay's community discourse and establishment of norms. Members are envisioned, and sometimes act, as co-producers of the technology and community, especially when their own positions match that of eBay. Therefore, a full understanding of eBay is not possible without considering how the company and members deploy the term "community" and related features.

In this chapter, I consider eBay's rendering of community, consumer citizenship, and sexual citizenship; the importance of consumer and organizational critique; and how members support and resist these configurations. According to Margaret Scammell, "Consumer critique is fundamental to citizenship in the age of globalization. It brings into the daylight the dangerously hidden issue of the political power of corporations."[3] Such critiques are vital because organizations such as eBay and their values get attached to contemporary behavior, discourses, and politics. The journalist John C. Abell connects Whitman's gubernatorial candidacy to eBay's auction processes by titling an article "'Buy It Now' FAIL: Former eBay CEO Whitman Is the Biggest Loser."[4] leapord420 continued the company's investment in heteronormative unions when commenting on a wedding at the convention and asking, "Does anyone know what I have to do to get married at Ebay live?"[5] The literature on sexual citizenship, brand communities, and configuring the user provides powerful methods for examining the ways organizations such as eBay produce and engage members. eBay's production of community and norms informs my studies of members throughout this book. My analysis also offers methods for reconsidering the critical literature about community and discourses about virtual communities, which were common in early Internet studies research and continue in slightly reorganized versions. A reassessment of this literature is vital because popular culture often accepts that communities are essential and inherently good. However, the eBay company's community, when it works, transforms individuals into privileged insiders, enforcers of norms, unpaid workers for the company, and promoters of the brand. eBay's managing of members and profiting from community, which can be conceived as the company's community, is sometimes different from and a threat to members' community structures and reasons for engaging.

Producing eBay Community

eBay uses the term "community" to articulate connections among members, participants and employees, people and consumption, users and the site, and constituents and the brand. The term informed initial conceptions of the site and continues to be an important structuring feature.[6] Early versions of the setting, when Pierre Omidyar was still calling it AuctionWeb, encouraged individuals to "join our community."[7] The setting was "dedicated to bringing together buyers and sellers in an honest and open marketplace." Omidyar added the "AuctionWeb Bulletin Board" asynchronous message system in 1996, which allowed people "to communicate with the rest of the AuctionWeb community."[8] eBay thus produces community by informing people that they are part of it, suggesting that individuals have a responsibility to their community, providing asynchronous text-based boards where participants can communicate, establishing stable identities and consumer records so members have a recognizable position within the setting, and giving buyers and sellers the opportunity to evaluate transactions and establish trust among members.

The menus of ebay.com and many of eBay's country-specific sites contain a "Community" link. The menu usually remains constant and suggests that people are a part of the eBay community as they view different parts of the site. eBay also commits to individuals and personalized features by including a "My eBay" link before the Community link. Yet the My eBay link provides individuals with ways to track items, bids, and purchases rather than an array of methods for structuring the site around personal interests. Jon Lillie explains that eBay "was one of the first to successfully apply the principles and technologies of online community toward the dominant regime of commerce and consumption."[9] These practices and features establish community as an organizational aspect of the site. Individuals are thereby made into a collective and citizenry with shared values and obligations to the site and company. At the same time, the tendency to associate community with people and sentiments minimizes the technological and organizational aspects of the site, encourages participants to feel comfortable, and assuages concerns about engaging in transactions with unknown individuals. A related series of community narratives are a part of other Internet settings, including Dell computers, craigslist, Second Life, Weight Watchers, and YouTube.

Omidyar and Whitman use the phrase "Dear eBay Community" and further the idea that the site facilitates intimate connections between members, executives, and the setting.[10] Members' engagements are characterized as "social selling" and "social commerce"—"a powerful combination of commerce, communication and community that enhances traditional buying and selling."[11] The concept of social selling, which is conveyed through accounts about sellers such as raglebagle and unique-find, emphasizes friendly connections between people rather than profit, market forces, and isolated viewing.[12] It remakes the work members perform while selling products into a communal dialogue and commitment to the site and participants. Social-selling principles include providing personal descriptions that bond people, emailing prospective buyers with special notes about items, identifying as stay-at-home mothers and encouraging buyers to support this role, marketing listings by communicating in the bulletin boards, and passing out items at eBay Live! imprinted with the sellers' IDs. eBay's notion of social selling is connected to its production of brand community and attempts to link people to the company and get them to work for the site because of shared forms of identity and collecting. Members, as I show in more detail in chapter 2, assist eBay in producing this community engagement. They do such things as reshape eBay's text-based board engagements into tea parties, plan events at conferences, and offer assistance to other members.

eBay encourages members to help each other. The options and social contracts in other early Internet settings, such as Usenet, influenced this model of community work.[13] Omidyar included forums and provided members' contact email addresses because he was unable to maintain the site alone. For a period of time, many individuals used email addresses as eBay IDs, and their availability and willingness to engage were thereby a part of their system identities. Community is thus articulated so Omidyar and other employees can detach, disinvest, and transfer a lot of the work to unpaid members. This results in community having different personal and economic meanings or even being an altogether different structure and discourse, for different constituencies. All of this suggests that co-production and brand community opportunities include decreased rather than amplified commitments from corporations. This is certainly the case with brand communities for the Apple Newton personal digital assistant and Radio Shack TRS-80 computer, because the initiating companies stopped supporting the products.[14] However, it is also likely to be the case with commodities that are available on the market and garnering increased value from brand community members.

Virtual Communities

eBay's community, as Adam Cohen argues, is one of the company's "greatest assets."[15] The records individuals provide to consumer communities, which includes demographic data, shopping habits, detailed reviews of products, critiques of the company, and indications of how site design facilitates connections, are highly valuable. This information allows companies to understand consumers better, meet their needs, sell individuals more products, and encourage customer loyalty.[16] Jay Marathe, who works with startups and corporate ventures, identifies Internet-facilitated communities as "central to a sustainable business model," because they bring people to the site, keep them engaged, provide assurances that companies meet individuals' needs, lower the costs of customer support, and pinpoint successful strategies.[17] The detailed information members provide allows companies to mirror people's interests and constitute stronger brand community ties.

People sometimes use the term "community" to resist the idea, which persisted through the 1990s and still occasionally appears today, that only poorly socialized individuals choose to communicate without physical co-presence and use the Internet to shop. When people portray Internet settings as communities, they emphasize the complex and important activities that occur in these settings and make them seem more spatial and real. For instance, "The Power of All of Us" campaign portrays eBay as a physical location, community, and "a place where people love the things you love."[18] Part of this advertising site depicts a rural landscape where an eBay "neighborhood," and brand community with shared attributes, is being constructed from very similar houses. eBay also situates people in community spaces by naming the discussion boards "The Front Porch," "The Homestead," "The Park," and

"The eBay Town Square."[19] Members support this spatialization and materi-alization of the setting when they perform popcorn parties and group teas in the forums.

eBay's rendering of community, which is envisioned as collaborative and intermeshed because of common desires and values, is related to larger so-cial drives to resuscitate preindustrial communities. Robert Putnam argues that a variety of technological and social factors have destroyed community.[20] With eBay, old-time community is supposed to be remade from porches, unlocked doors, and communitywide celebrations, features that are simul-taneously virtual and material.[21] eBay's rendering of small-town values and trust are related to its marketing of sentimental goods. eBay's "The Power of All of Us" campaign asks, "What if nothing was ever forgotten? What if noth-ing was ever lost?" The campaign promises that a community incorporating the power of all of us, including the labor of participants, can replace these purportedly lost emotive states. eBay remakes people's economically moti-vated sale of goods and casting off of mementos, which could mark items as valueless, into the community's maintenance of history. Everything thus has value, and sellers are doing good work by looking for the right owners. For example, eBay's *Toy Boat* advertisement depicts a ship's crew finding a boy's plaything and using the eBay interface to return it to the adult who is still longing for it.[22] In a similar manner, sellers of antiquarian photographs try to remake people's family albums by matching individuals with the photographs they have lost or through "instant ancestor" replacements.[23] All of this sug-gests that everything is loved, saved, remembered, and saleable within the community.

eBay also represents harmony and concord as attributes of the site and community. For the theorist Alphonso Lingis, community mandates that "each one, in facing the other, faces an imperative that he formulate all his en-counters and insights in universal terms, in forms that could be the informa-tion belonging to everyone."[24] Images of eBay's community of cookie-cutter homes, figured in "The Power of All of Us" campaign, and its string of hand-holding paper-doll-like members insistently evoke a community in which all members are the same. This is in line with community investments, includ-ing the community's alignment with "unity, commonality, and agreement," that the social philosopher and political theorist Linnell Secomb describes.[25] Community is associated with consciousness of a kind, but disagreements and discrepancies are also inherent and important aspects of communities.

A number of theorists have come to question the philosophy of community with its bias toward sameness and tendency to distinguish between self and other, or even to expulse the other.[26]

Many texts about Internet communities describe the utopian possibilities of collectivity and caring that happen in these settings. At the same time, theoretical writings declare that community, as we know it, has or should end. Such theorists as Benedict Anderson and Jean-Luc Nancy chronicle the regional conflicts that are spurred by conceptions of community and how purportedly supportive groups ostracize individuals who are identified as not belonging because of ethnic, racial, religious, or other identities.[27] Brand communities are also usually described as supportive structures that enable individuals to identify and engage, but participants articulate norms and position themselves as opposed to other products and cohorts.[28] For instance, consumer research by Thomas Hickman and James Ward describes how members have a "tendency to seek information that positively discriminates" their "own brand community from others" and "either seek or accept negative information" about other groups.[29] In a related manner, eBay's discourse about community gets members to do such patrolling and ostracizing work as questioning the legitimacy of listings and directing participants to value eBay that would otherwise be associated with the company. Community seems to be an Internet structure that gets people to do the corporate and state work of rejection and hate.

These issues are not addressed in most of the literature about virtual communities. For Howard Rheingold, an early and often referenced writer on the subject, virtual communities are usually positive "social aggregations that emerge from the Net when enough people carry on those public discussions long enough, with sufficient human feeling, to form webs of personal relationships in cyberspace."[30] For him, the WELL (Whole Earth 'Lectronic Link) became a community because of social contracts and collaborative negotiations: "Norms were established, challenged, changed, reestablished, rechallenged, in a kind of speeded-up social evolution."[31] In a similar manner, Michael and Ronda Hauben wrote an early book about "Netizens" and describe "people who care about Usenet and the bigger Net and work towards building the cooperative."[32] Omidyar's and other setting designers' narratives about care and cooperative work are often influenced by these early conceptions of virtual communities.

There are also analyses of how virtual communities can enhance businesses. According to John Hagel and Arthur Armstrong, who promote ecommerce communities within the business sector, the "rise of virtual communities in on-line networks has set in motion an unprecedented shift in power from vendors of goods and services to the customers who buy them."[33] We are therefore, writes Tom Murphy, a technology journalist, "witnessing the greatest transition of power in history, one that will take power away from the mightiest corporations and social institutions and give it to . . . consumers."[34] However, these authors focus on how businesses can profit rather than on how individuals can gain power and change corporations and governments. There is also research in new media studies on the ways Internet social networking sites and virtual communities offer modes of resistance through digitally facilitated protests, email updates about corporate behavior, culture jamming (subverting mainstream institutions and corporations), and the redeployment of corporate logos.[35] Given that the commercial and academic cohorts find empowering aspects of Internet settings, but the business writers tend to identify corporate advantages in providing consumers with a form of authority, the relationship between virtual communities, brand communities, and agency needs further investigation.

Omidyar's People Are Basically Good Ethos, Free Work, and the Value of Fun

eBay's community discourse gets members to work for free. Work is often identified as an expected aspect of community. Lingis has noted that "rationalists perceive the reality of being members of a community in the reality of works undertaken and realized; we perceive the community itself as a work."[36] Community is produced, its features are determined by the work of controlling members of the group, and the benefits of community are ordinarily provided to this cohort. Community is a successful model for Omidyar to deploy because it requires people "to participate in the market," "political structure," and "laws."[37] Nevertheless, working should be distinguished from having a significant amount of control. eBay members do not have a great deal of power over site design, security issues, or fee structures. The marketing scholars Bernard Cova and Stefano Pace believe that brand communities allow consumers to have more control over their relationships with "beloved" brands, but the inability of eBay members to change things points to some problems with brand community research models and eBay's promises.[38]

Omidyar and eBay deploy brand community in similar ways to what the marketing researchers Scott Cook, C. K. Prahalad, and Venkat Ramaswamy envision.[39] They get enthusiasts to work for free on improving the value of corporations and products. eBay encourages members to coach new participants, provide information about HTML, and patrol listings for scams and infractions of the rules. For instance, Omidyar's SafeHarbor 2.0 security message of 1999 reminds members that "community participation is the foundation upon which eBay was built. It is our history of participation that helped eBay grow with unparalleled success."[40] Omidyar establishes work as vital to the eBay community's development and traditions. However, he does not acknowledge the many buyers and sellers whose revenues have decreased and have been forced to give up eBay businesses as the company has continued to raise fees and sellers have lowered prices to beat the competition. In 2004, janica-online pointed to the "thousands of people on ebay that have been doing this full time for a number of years and are now basically unemployed due to the changes ebay has made."[41] eBay instituted another series of rate hikes, and members were "evenly split," according to the reporter Gary Rivlin, "over whether" to use "'FeeBay' or 'GreedBay'" as "the most apt epithet" for the company.[42] More recently, as I show later in this chapter, sellers have escalated their use of community narratives to critique eBay.

Omidyar and eBay encourage buyers, sellers, and viewers to help with site security, to engage deeply, and to become more affiliated brand community members. There are many instances of members following these directives. Board regulars work together to find people who use the site for scams and, as the eBay seller Steven Phillips notes, make "their lives miserable."[43] Ina Steiner, a reporter for *AuctionBytes*, describes the rise of eBay vigilantism, which is encouraged by the company, and the large amount of time people spend on these projects.[44] For instance, Karen Christian, who set up a site to publish information about a fraudulent seller, worked "about 5–6 hours a day keeping the Web site up to date, contacting law-enforcement officials, and talking to reporters."[45] Other sellers spend hours every day reviewing competitors' listings and informing eBay about terms of service violations.[46] Evading fees and regulations allows sellers to lower their prices and thereby ruin the businesses of those who follow the rules. Deeply engaged members also regulate other settings because of their commitment to brand communities and interest in garnering a kind of validation from the interface. For instance, rather than offering assistance, self-appointed advisers to craigslist admonish and discourage sexually active women and sex workers when they seek help with their flagged and removed ads.

eBay and other Internet companies are able to keep their salaried workforces small by directing members to function as unpaid customer-support representatives, advocates, and marketers of the brand. An important element of eBay's business model, according to Lillie, is to "train" individuals to "do much of the company's work."[47] Yet these behaviors are widely understood as brand community participation rather than labor. Some immaterial labor researchers, as Lillie also suggests, consider how these underacknowledged and undercompensated forms of work render and support Internet settings and other spheres. For the activists and theorists Michael Hardt and Antonio Negri, immaterial labor "produces immaterial products, such as information, knowledges, ideas, images, relationships, and affects."[48] These things are often byproducts of daily life and cultural participation and therefore are undervalued. This devaluation is likely to be intensified when the products and emotional performances are collaborative, including shared work done by brand community members and corporations, rather than individually created.

Brand community researchers classify co-production opportunities as empowering, but the activist and academic Maurizio Lazzarato identifies the precarious and hyperexploitative features of this labor.[49] Networks and new communication technologies enable employers to use temporary and mobile laborers rather than committing to long-term employment and material infrastructures. This suggests that Internet technologies and their social structures diminish the stability of work while signaling users, expecting responses, and keeping conceptions of individuals enmeshed with the infrastructure even when people are not logged on. People are increasingly tied to digital systems that intensify their precarity—an existence with limited material and emotional predictability and security.[50] The Internet complicates such careers as journalism with blogging and is unpredictable and insecure because of software failures and data leaks. Unfortunately, as the philosopher George Caffentzis argues, the term "immaterial," with its allusions to intangibility and evanescence, can dismiss the personal costs of labor as well as critique these structures.[51] This vocabulary mirrors the ways Internet settings are coded as immaterial, or less substantive, with terms such as "virtual." The phrase "immaterial labor" is also out of sync with the feminist struggle to make "'housework', 'reproductive' work and the body . . . central to the analysis of capitalism."[52] The concept of immaterial labor thus provides useful ways to interrogate eBay's affective forms of social selling and community and, if not managed, can elide the work mandates and gender and sexuality distinctions that the company and members deploy.

A cohort of Internet studies scholars also considers the functions of free labor.[53] For instance, Tiziana Terranova describes how in 1996, "at the peak of the volunteer moment, over thirty thousand 'community leaders' were helping AOL to generate at least $7 million a month."[54] At about this time, Omidyar was adding features to eBay that would get members to do site labor. This free labor is "a trait of cultural economy at large, and an important, and yet undervalued force in advanced capitalist societies."[55] According to the game studies researcher Julian Kücklich, modders employ game companies' authoring tools to produce new or modified products and offer them for free.[56] This generates profits for the companies that make digital games because the people playing mods must buy the original game, but it provides few economic rewards to the modders. In researching the same population, Hector Postigo argues that game companies can sell modders' work as a new product or addition and "harness a skilled labour force for little or no initial cost," and that this "represents an emerging form of labour exploitation on the Internet."[57] Whether they are employees of game companies or participants in eBay, individuals are coaxed into excessive hours of engaging with new media because their work is supposed to be social communication and play. This is related to Hardt and Negri's identification of how immaterial labor practices tend "to blur the distinction between work time and nonwork time, extending the working day indefinitely to fill all of life."[58] Internet representations and calls for users to respond also weave through daily activities and constitute seemingly alive data images that support the presence and functions of individuals, brands, and systems.

People are directed to "spend" time coding and beta testing open source browsers and operating systems, tagging articles and images, writing encyclopedia entries and reviews, leaving feedback, and creating other content without economic remuneration. For example, academic proposals for new settings often include plans to design structures and then have scholars generate all the content. eBay sellers also design the listings, and therefore most of the content, on the site. These plans for user-generated content rarely address the costs of participants' labor and how it will continue as the number of sites increases and existent settings require more content and editing. In the case of academe, all of this is drastically reorganizing commitments and work demands. However, there is no accompanying rethinking of such academic labor issues as the amount of time people are expected to spend with students, teaching, and providing service for their institutions and only a slight reformulation of the forms of research that are believed to indicate academic success. eBay has also not addressed the increased content and programming requirements that accompany site changes. Such projects have radically skewed when many people are working as well as the relationship between corporations, organizations, and individuals. Nevertheless, individuals may be unaware of their time expenditures. The design features of the computer and the Internet, including the scrolling of instant messaging sessions and documents, encourage people to "space out," deeply engage, and ignore the time unfolding.

Some individuals enjoy the design of mobile computing devices, which are often manufactured with rounded and smooth edges that encourage tactile engagements, and delight in the features of operating systems and software.[59] Modders, community leaders, and eBay members also take pleasure in performing some kinds of immaterial labor. However, this should not prevent critical considerations of the ways companies can provide participants with control, economic rewards, and physical and psychic comforts. When the eBay site and its membership structure function properly, individuals do not interrogate how the company encourages free work; the work requirements individuals have to fulfill to be recognized members of the community; and the many ways buyers, sellers, and viewers support the site. This may not be surprising since, according to Terranova, certain forms of labor, which include advice, "chat, real-life stories, mailing lists, amateur newsletters," and fan activities, are not ordinarily recognized as work.[60] They are often feminized and devalued, like the association of women with housework and child care. By incorporating humor and play into work, companies elide the personal costs of long-term and demanding Internet engagements.

eBay jokes about its poor compensation for immaterial labor in the "About Me" site it produced for one of its imaginary characters. elf, or elfie, is a mascot and invented figure that "posts" in the boards and other parts of the site. Readers of the boards engage with elfie, provide images and props for his activities, and make his board presence and placement within the eBay setting real. In his About Me site, elfie complains that he works for the company, but "it isn't as though they PAY me or anything or that I can actually BUY anything. Okay, they gave me a cave under the Gazebo in the Park" (one of eBay's boards).[61] He goes on to provide a "Big whoop" about these accommodations and argue that the company does not "think elves NEED money." In a similar manner to Terranova, elfie indicates how participants' activities are valuable aspects of eBay's cultural economy but result in few economic rewards for laborers. The inequity of not paying elfie—and, by implication, members who support the setting—is diffused because elfie is portrayed as a nuisance who plays pranks and steals socks and other insignificant items.[62] Through this narrative, eBay suggests that members need to pay for their errant leisure and validates its immaterial labor practices. People support the site to engage with elfie's performances, and through his antics they have contact with employees. This echoes eBay's emphasis on the social aspects of social selling rather than economic rewards. Within eBay's social economy, individuals can elevate their status by working for free and getting employees to recognize and favor them. Individuals who do not engage risk being ignored and having no network in times of crisis. This makes immaterial labor a tactical practice for people who rely on the site.

eBay directs members to work while conveying the idea that the site and its community features are fun and therefore a form of leisure. During the eBay Developers Conference and eBay Live! in 2007, executives expressed interest in recapturing the fun and amusing aspects of eBay as a method of attracting new people and keeping current members attached to the site. The "New to eBay Board" invites readers: "Come on in and join the fun."[63] eBay engages collectors, who are more likely to want experiential shopping experiences, by conveying how fun it is to buy, sell, and help other members. According to the consumer researchers Peter H. Bloch and Grady D. Bruce, collectors tend to demonstrate "product enthusiasm" and "enduring involvement."[64] Fervor and commitment are also key aspects of brand community formation. It is likely that individuals will buy more items and purchase things with greater frequency when eBay renders fun and playful activities. The site's narratives and promises of pleasure, if they bring individuals to purchase more goods, may also turn members into collectors. All of this suggests how fun can be used as a controlling sentiment. This is certainly the case with the ways fun is deployed in work environments to generate greater commitment to the company, a better organizational culture, and increased work output.[65] Fun can also turn into displeasure and resistance. This is highlighted by eBay members' negative responses to site changes and gamers' descriptions of how gaming is "more like work than fun" and goes "from enjoyable to just work."[66] In these cases, some of the absorbing aspects of Internet engagements, collecting, and brand community identifications are unpleasant but still continue, with people unwilling to give up their established identities and commitments.

Community Values and Norms

eBay is similar to Apple, Coca-Cola, Saab, and other brand communities and offers such traditional community features as "we-ness," "rituals and traditions," and the establishment of morals and a "sense of obligation to the community and its members."[67] For example, active eBay Live! attendees identify as a cohort, wear branded items on their way to the conference so other people can identify them, and assist participants with planning their attendance and collecting conference collectibles. As Cohen notes, Omidyar wanted eBay to "operate according to the moral values he subscribed to in his own life: that people are basically good, and given the chance to do right, they generally will."[68] Readers of eBay's "Community Values" statement are informed that

> eBay is a community that encourages open and honest communication among all its members. Our community is guided by five fundamental values: We believe people are basically good. We believe everyone has something to contribute. We believe that an honest, open environment can bring out the best in people. We recognize and respect everyone as a unique individual. We encourage you to treat others the way you want to be treated.[69]

A cohort of eBay members uses the values statement in listings, About Me sites, and forum posts. Members thereby constitute their moral character, attract customers, identify with the brand, and provide support for eBay's standards of conduct.

A line drawing that accompanies the Community Values statement represents people as outlines and suggests that anyone can fit into the community. However, eBay also marks these people as heterosexual couples by grouping them into pairs and using gendered gestures, gender-specific clothing items, and height differences. For instance, a man steers a woman in a skirt by pressing his hand into her back. Another man, with a significant genital bulge, points and directs a woman who wears heels and has a scarf tied around her neck. In each of these gendered images, the man directs the conversation and is in power. The woman acknowledges his purported authority by leaning in or bending her head. With this portrayal, eBay continues to use narratives about acceptance as a lure and as a way to get people to engage in the gender-specific behaviors and normative sexualities that, as I argue in the introduction and chapter 3, articulate its organizational logic.

eBay's production of values is related to the larger corporate trend for brands to assert emotional and social ethos. For example, the Body Shop emphasizes fair trade and ecological responsibility in its sourcing of items, and MAC Cosmetics donates to AIDS causes. In an advertisement for a tartan-themed VIVA GLAM Christmas product, where all proceeds are donated, MAC asks the potential buyer to "Keep the VIVA GLAM clan alive & thriving"; "Keep the MAC AIDS Fund flowing!"; "Keep the coffers confident"; and "'Tis Noble to Give!"[70] Through the advertisement, MAC constitutes a clan of community members that will enliven the brand and do good deeds by supporting the cause. It and other companies attract and configure customers by highlighting such values.[71] Members are also at an advantage because their consumerism, which could otherwise be understood as passive and self-involved, is melded with active and righteous citizenship. In a related manner, eBay members are constituted as socially conscious on its WorldofGood.com site, "where every purchase makes a positive impact."[72]

eBay represents its consumer system as a community- and citizenry-based model, in which all members produce aspects of the system. Nevertheless, belonging to a community implies that others do not.[73] Most academic and popular texts about virtual and brand communities do not consider what happens when the ostensibly inclusive community rejects some people, cultures, and ideologies. The sociologist Kenneth E. Pigg suggests that the best way for corporations to facilitate community is by providing members with means of collaboratively thinking about values and standards.[74] However, there is no established mechanism for the ideals of eBay buyers, sellers, and viewers; the principles members articulate in boards; or the standards sellers express in their listings to be acknowledged by eBay or integrated into the company's values statement. Forum writers have wondered about their community engagements since critiques receive no response from the company. craigslist members who identify problems also note that the company does not respond. In these cases, the company is not good to members, disallows their attempts at co-production, and fails to meet its own promises about accepting everyone.

eBay members who want to be approved of and remain acceptable citizens must strive for system validation because some individuals are removed from the system, evaluated negatively by other members, and commodified against their will. These forms of normativity filter through society, according to the political philosopher Onora O'Neill.[75] "Good" is a normative word that refers to behavior and success—in the case of eBay, coding selected members as ethical, encouraging other people to follow these examples, and guaranteeing that eBay fulfills commercial and economic functions.[76] eBay uses "good" and its heteronormative representations to produce the acceptable sexual citizen. This citizen is coded as doing and being good and becomes even more productive for the company when helping other members and performing site-specific labor.

Socially Conscious Consumerism and Critique

eBay's narratives about doing good are important to its position as a resale platform because other forms of reselling and exchanging are socially conscious. According to Gretchen M. Herrmann, a researcher, garage sales provide a sense of community, and gift giving is as common as "simple recommodification" in these situations.[77] Garage sales provide a place for people to congregate, allow friends and groups to buy and sell together, create ties between buyers and sellers through the exchange of items, enable people to connect by sharing personal histories, let individuals do good work by selling items at a low cost or giving them away, and promote neighborhood solidarity. Omidyar and some other eBay executives envision eBay as a worldwide garage sale. However, the "outright acts of giving" at garage sales, which accompany or even displace the sale of objects, evoke the Freecycle movement and its location-based listservs rather than eBay.

Popular and academic writers associate Freecycle with certain individuals' desires to decrease their possessions and the work required to support consumption.[78] Freecycle's motto is "changing the world one gift at a time," which figures participants as consumer citizens who do political work by giving (rather than getting rid of unwanted items).[79] It has 5,007 local groups, which are ordinarily organized through listservs, and 8,869,534 global members. Freecycle identifies as "a grassroots and entirely nonprofit movement of people who are giving (& getting) stuff for free in their own towns. It's all about reuse and keeping good stuff out of landfills." Volunteers, who are also envisioned by Freecycle as "good people," moderate local groups. Freecycle describes its listservs as a political movement and community, but most product exchanges happen between individuals. Like other forms of consumer citizenship and political consumerism, Freecycle enables a degree of environmental and social assistance. Nevertheless, it also threatens to make it appear as if people are facilitating significant social change when they are moving consumer goods from one place to another.

eBay's facilitation of recycling is less proactive and ambitious than Freecycle and, as I suggest later in this section, eBay often regulates the kinds of recycling it claims to enable. eBay's Green Team site, introduced in 2009, provides information about how the company has installed solar panels on its new headquarters and invested in varied methods to reduce its carbon emissions.[80] Many of eBay's green initiatives have economic underpinnings. eBay encourages people to employ its local classified site, which is "Inspiring the world to buy, sell and think green every day."[81] During an address at the Developers Conference that was remediated in video form, the early eBay investor Bob Kagle described Omidyar as green because of his vision of reselling.[82] Some eBay members also assert that reselling goods is inherently green. For msklusa, "BUYING VINTAGE JEWELRY IS A GREAT WAY TO BE GREEN AND HELP OUT LOCALLY AND GLOBALLY."[83] However, such indications do not explain who is helped or the manner of socially conscious consumerism that occurs. Shipping requires a great deal of material that often is new and not biodegradable and fuel to transport goods. eBay tries to resolve these problems with its "simple green shipping" program in which 100,000 reusable boxes were given to sellers.[84] Of course, the project requires receiving buyers to be, or become, sellers for the boxes to be reused and the project to continue. It also deploys buyers and sellers as brand community workers by offering "plenty of space on the boxes . . . to write a personal message to the next person in the chain" and "a virtual community where buyers and sellers can connect" and track boxes. Through such tactics, eBay, Freecycle, and some other social networking settings intertwine notions of socially conscious individuals and consumerism, produce versions of the consumer citizen, and further narratives about community belonging.

eBay's community values are linked to and influence the perceived exchange value of objects. eBay buyers are assured of an equitable trading platform and that they will receive the listed item because sellers are "basically good." The corollary to this is that the values represented by objects and listings support or undermine eBay's community ethos. For David A. Crocker and Toby Linden, who consider the ethical impact of consumption, personal and collective purchasing decisions are connected to values.[85] One reason people become involved with a product, according to Bloch and Bruce, is "the congruence of product usage and meaning with the individual's values, self, and reference group-imposed role expectations."[86] Brands and objects, including paintings of morality tales, soap wrappers testifying to purity, advertisements portraying gender norms, and signs directing individuals to line up or be quiet, are designed to direct people's behavior and configure them. The connection between consumerism and eBay's principles is particularly strong when it is eBay collectibles, materials that document the company's values and histories, that are being bought and sold. Individuals are conceptually buying and selling eBay in the form of shirts once owned by employees, items signed by Omidyar and Whitman, and representations of eBay community. Through these goods, members declare their alliance to the brand community and work as advertisements for the company.

Other values are also represented on the eBay site. In chapter 4, I study how gay interest listings of underwear and swimwear constitute a form of gay community and desire that is not acceptable to the company. In a different manner, sellers' narratives about deception and marketing of tools for committing crimes undermine eBay's ethos and belief in good people. For example, tankdriver7753 scorns eBay's "stupid firearms, weapons and knives policy," which prohibits the sale of firearms and many firearm-related items.[87] tankdriver7753 admits to violating the rules that "keep throwing off listings for cloth backpack sets" because of the regulating algorithms that are designed to find illegal items. tamotol challenges eBay's values by describing how the company prevents the sale of previously worn and clean cloth diapers and diaper covers and ecologically oriented mothering.[88] Such conflicts and consumer critiques are more likely to occur because brand community structures are designed to get individuals to connect, believe the brand belongs to enthusiastic consumers, and identify the company as a reflection of their lives and values.

The different ways the eBay company and brand community members use the concepts of community and goodness, while perpetuating ideas about normative sexual citizenship, are exemplified in the conflict over reselling diapers and diaper covers. In her reaction to eBay's banning of listings for recycled diapers and diaper covers, tamotol expresses brand alienation rather than attachment. She argues that eBay prevents women's choice because it "is owned by a vicious huggies loving megalomaniac who decided that mothers across the world cannot make their own decision when it comes to buying gently used Aristocrats" (a form of diaper cover).[89] The company pulled her "offer off of Egay. So now this young, sensitive, doe eyed mother" is "attempting to thwart Egay by doing some snazzy evasive" maneuvers.[90] In this commentary, tamotol portrays herself as a delicate mother who is fighting a large and unjust corporation. She equates goodness with straight sexuality and sexual citizenship, a tactic eBay also deploys, by calling eBay "eGay" because of its policy about recycled cloth diapers and related clothing. Thus, tamoto1 performs a consumer critique while unfortunately establishing cultural norms and associating gay identities with stupidity.

A cohort of diaper sellers has used the PetitionOnline site to encourage eBay to adopt better community values: "Help save the planet" and "do your part to help us help the environment by using reusable diapers!"[91] Louise Pendry employs PetitionOnline and identifies this group of eBay sellers as "parents trying to do our best for our babies" by recycling diapers, which "is a wonderful, green act."[92] Pendry identifies as "we" and constitutes parents rather than eBay as the community. eBay's ban, tamoto1 also suggests, is about community and "the integrity of the whole human race" because such decisions embody values. Sellers of recycled diapers and diaper covers portray themselves as the good mothers and eBay as the bad mother rather than as the benevolent nurturer of community. These sellers, in processes that are related to oppressed cohorts striving for citizenship, convey the moral and social features that demonstrate they are good and worthy of inclusion.[93] They go even further and position their behavior above that of the company and challenge eBay's claims that it is good, green, and pro-recycling. Diaper sellers' critiques are one outcome of the melding of consumerism with citizenship. Such consumers are demanding further social responsibility and ethical behavior from corporations.[94]

Sellers of recycled cloth diapers believe that the children who would benefit from ecological consuming are victimized by adult sexualities, members who sell used underwear, adults who buy used diapers for erotic purposes, and eBay. It "seems silly to group cloth diapees" with used "adult skivvies," writes tamoto1, but that is "the world we live in." For tamoto1, it is a world in which mothers' livelihood and claims to normative sexuality are at risk. She challenges eBay's standards and sexuality, which she suggests are inextricably intertwined. Unfortunately, tamoto1's association of unconventional sexualities with disaffection is apt on eBay since the company cancels some listings for adult items and overt representations of queer sexualities. Nevertheless, GLBTQ listings, including "gay interest" vintage photographs of men romantically engaged with other men and images of sellers' visible penis lines in underwear and swimwear, can allow men to engage erotically through the site, generate higher sale prices in some cases, and challenge the conflation of the site with heteronormative culture. Gay connections, attachments, and the forms of sexual citizenship that move beyond proscribed norms are encouraged by Lingis's community, which is formed "when sexual excitement spreads among us."[95]

Mothers who sell diapers, eBay, Freecycle, and other Internet sites and participants render narratives about goodness but sometimes have radically different visions of what is good. The ways diaper sellers and eBay use cultural conceptions of community to articulate good people and condemn the sexualities of other groups encourages a further assessment of the value of community discourses and the violence such beliefs support. For the women's studies scholar Donna Jowett, what "could be good about community, good in a way that is not just about me getting what I want out of one, requires that we not even assume community, never mind its goodness."[96] eBay's and tamotol's consumer interventions and critiques could facilitate Jowett's proposal by considering how organizational and individual decisions affect other people rather than imagining a generic goodness and community that holds the same beliefs. While eBay now allows the sale of diapers and diaper covers, it does not mention the petitioners in its new policy statement and avoids acknowledging different opinions and the work of resistant members.[97] In fact, eBay's change was so under-advertised that auntava posted the announcement to the forums, and other sellers of diapers and diaper covers expressed surprise about the new policy.[98] eBay's challenge, if it wants to render normative positions, and its critical failing are producing a cohesive notion of goodness and community.

The Feedback Forum

eBay uses the feedback forum to constitute a good and trustworthy community. Omidyar started the feedback forum in 1996 so members could communicate about transactions instead of depending on him to mediate them.[99] Readers of eBay forums are informed, "Feedback is an essential part of what makes eBay a successful community" and are encouraged to write about transactions.[100] The system adds informational value to the site, creates trust, keeps people engaged, and furthers brand community identification because IDs are linked to feedback reviews and active members tend to identify with their feedback. Amazon, Froogle, Hotels.com, OpenTable, and countless other sites have feedback systems and prompt consumers to contribute. For Chrysanthos Dellarocas, who researches information technologies, these Internet feedback systems have changed individuals' "behavior in subtle but important ways" because people used to base their consumer "decisions on advertisements or professional advice" but are now increasingly relying on the opinions that are available through such systems.[101] Consumers develop a certain level of prominence and authority through feedback systems, but they have also taken over much of the responsibility for researching products and manufacturers, providing advice and assistance, and making decisions. The relationship between this consumer labor, which is often a form of review, and more detailed consumer critiques of settings and policies could use further research and theorizing.

Omidyar's 1996 letter about implementing the feedback forum, which is supposed to reflect eBay's "founding values," is included on the site.[102] In it, Omidyar reiterates that eBay is "an open market that encourages honest dealings" and that "Most people are honest." Of course, noting that most people are honest is a different claim, and allows for a more variable member base, than his indications that people are basically good. Omidyar also admits that "some people are dishonest. Or deceptive." But they "can't hide. We'll drive them away. Protect others from them. This grand hope depends on your active participation." Omidyar and the company thereby indicate that the feedback system will make people behave and encourage them to work for the community. They admit that basing eBay's functioning on good people has some problems. This conceptual flaw is evoked in the many ways feedback is manipulated and the posts on varied sites that describe bad eBay members.

Feedback originally enabled eBay buyers, sellers, and viewers to leave comments and "positive," "neutral," or "negative" evaluations for any reason. In 2001, eBay restricted feedback to individuals who were in transactions because evaluations were sometimes manipulated.[103] In 2007, eBay added options for buyers to evaluate transactions with Detailed Seller Ratings (DSRs). This system provides buyers with more nuanced ratings but makes it even less equitable and collaborative. Sellers cannot see the DSR stars that individual buyers assign to them and cannot reply. In 2008, eBay adjusted the system so sellers cannot leave neutral or negative feedback for buyers. This change further destabilizes the promise of open communication, lowers final sale prices for sellers whose scores decrease, and puts businesses at risk because eBay removes sellers with low scores from the system. eBay's new feedback model implies that buyers are basically good and sellers are bad and need to be regulated. Numerous sellers, as I suggest in more detail at the end of this chapter, have greeted these changes with anger. eBay's redesign of the system, which purportedly facilitates consumer critiques because buyers no longer need to fear retaliatory negatives, has encouraged members' resistance to the setting and company.

eBay still uses the feedback system to make the setting appear safe and encourage individuals to employ it for transactions. For instance, the member's "star" often appears next to the ID, represents the amount of feedback received, and is intended to function as "your symbol of trust and experience in the eBay Community."[104] Trust, according to Lingis, "binds one ever more deeply to another; it is an energy that becomes ever stronger and more intoxicated."[105] With eBay, this binding and intoxication includes brand community identification and allows the company to retain members. Intoxication may also prevent members from evaluating trust and the feedback system's consequences. Individuals are invested because the system testifies to their dependability and facilitates sales, and they become their feedback. In his instructional book about using eBay, Michael Lewis describes feedback as "a spotlight on how you do business, and the first impression you are giving to the eBay community, following you around wherever you go on the site. You are your feedback."[106] During eBay Live! keynote addresses, executives get attendees to rise, go through the feedback increments, and have people who have not reached benchmark feedback numbers sit down until only individuals with a large amount of feedback are standing.[107] Through this ritual, eBay emphasizes the large-scale selling that the site facilitates, vast amount of feedback behind the company's trust mechanism, and relationship between people and feedback.

Some sellers identify the value of feedback and use feedback numbers to indicate their reliability. Such reputation building, according to the business scholars Jennifer Brown and John Morgan, affects "prices and the probability of a sale."[108] baseballsteve123 emphasizes his reputation, writing that his "FEEDBACK STAND AT 100% BECAUSE" he is "AN HONEST SELLER SELLING QUALITY CARDS."[109] Other sellers claim, "You can trust us based on our Feedback Rating."[110] Sellers market feedback numbers, but their comments can be misleading. For example, itrimming advertises as the "Globally ranked #2 eBay Seller with over 520,000 feedback!" but has a 98.3 percent feedback score because 9,837 members left negative reviews.[111] jayandmarie proclaim they are "eBay's HIGHEST RATED DEALER with a big red 'Shooting Star' and over 250,000 unique satisfied customers."[112] They have a "celebrity status" in the eBay community, and the company has honored them, but 3,979 members had already given them negative reviews by 2007.[113] eBay uses feedback to constitute a reliable community *and* includes members that trouble its notion of trust.

Feedback auctions, where individuals pay for positive reviews, are common, and sellers are willing to lose money on listing fees to increase their feedback scores, enhance their ability to sell high-priced items, and strengthen their ability to engage in auction fraud.[114] The technologist Alan Williamson describes individuals selling items for pennies and promising that positive feedback is always provided.[115] There are also listings for manuals that will enable members to "Get 100 Feedback in ONE Week!"[116] Participants in forums such as "Ebay Sucks" perform a consumer critique and sell eBay accounts with positive feedback.[117] zarkid lists an auction to "Obtain Feedback for 99 cents" because the seller is "taking a trip to Europe during Thanksgiving" and needs "money to hand out 100 soccer jerseys to the poor children. All this money will be going to a great cause. Plus it is a great way to get feedback."[118] This auction violates eBay's policies and positions zarkid as bad. However, the seller is trying to constitute the kinds of good community behavior eBay encourages. Oddly enough, feedback sales and sellers' attempts to avoid negative reviews, and consumer critiques, attest to people's investment in the system. These people identify the value of feedback as they problematize its functions. Widespread knowledge of the feedback market should destroy the system's value and community, but this has not occurred.[119] This is because feedback is inextricably intertwined with active members' identities and community investments, and they are unwilling to give up these positions and structures.

Conclusion: Critiquing Community

Some previously engaged brand community members now organize protests against eBay. Such behavior is related to the two phases of consumer and brand community development that Bernard Cova and Daniele Dalli research.[120] For a period of time, consumers enjoy their articulated role as co-producers and are happy to be recognized by the company and other participants. At a certain point, usually after trust has been eroded through policy changes or other incidents, consumers feel unacknowledged, that the connection between company and participants is inequitable, and their labor is exploited. Participants' anger and alienation can lead to consumer critiques, boycotts, and buycotts. For instance, sellers attempted to get eBay to lower fees by listing items on other Internet auction sites during the "million auction march."[121] At eBay Live! 2008, many members booed during the keynote address and highlighted their disaffection in other ways.

People also comment critically about eBay in blogs and forums. For example, Ed "DOC" Koon operates a site that interrogates eBay's policies. He conveys the two phases of consumer and brand community engagement with companies. It used to be rare, according to Koon, "to get ripped by a bad seller and eBay booted the bad element out right away" but now "it's all about collecting those $$$ And hiding behind the disclaimer 'we are only a venue' eBay is NOT Liable for any transaction."[122] Koon also started a petition to let eBay investors know members are "tired" of how the company "is currently being managed" because eBay has become "infested with dead beat bidders, scammers, con artists, fences selling stolen property, internal pharming links, porn used in listing thumb nails, etc. Buying and selling on eBay is no longer safe."[123] Petition signers believe that eBay should be "directly accountable for the fraud they allow"; that "ebay has gone downhill concerning security to the point that one can no longer trust trades due to hijacked accounts, scams and lax ebay security"; and that members "need a better and safer marketplace."[124] In writing these posts, members assert their alienation and argue against positive accounts of eBay's community.

The name of another blog—"FireMeg.com: THE anti-eBay management website!"—also functions as a form of consumer critique, although it asks for the removal of a retired executive.[125] In it, Firemeg questions the ways brand community members are supposed to give to the community. He directs readers to the user agreement that makes "eBay look a lot more like Big Brother, if not a full blown communist regime where your thoughts belong to the 'community' and where those with bad thoughts may be disappeared."[126] eBay includes a proviso in which members give the company "a non-exclusive, worldwide, perpetual, irrevocable, royalty-free, sublicensable (through multiple tiers) right to exercise any and all copyright, trademark, publicity, and database rights (but no other rights) you have in the content."[127] The eBay member nonnie*mouse*posting*id expresses concern about this policy, which "basically means that Ebay is giving itself license to steal from all its users."[128] Firemeg is also concerned about the mandate for members to "report problems, offensive content, and policy violations" to the company, which seems to be a "call to arms for the collective community gestapo to quash anything from listing violations to dissent among users . . .

with no financial incentives for users." In addition, Firemeg uses "the fact that eBay reports only 80 million of its 300 million users were active over the past year" to deduce that "something is making masses of online shoppers upset."[129] This critique is similar to Secomb's description of how communities, in striving for unity and coherence, ignore different opinions and regulate members.[130]

Numerous eBay members perform consumer critiques and articulate a community that is resistant to eBay's policies. They are motivated by changes to the feedback forum, increases in fees, insistence that sellers accept PayPal, holding of money on some transactions, temporary freezing of accounts, and removal of sellers with low feedback. In some of these cases, the thwarting of consumer reviews has led to consumer critique of the system and its policies. The term "consumer critique" may seem to apply best to buyers, but many sellers purchase items on the site and services from eBay. Sellers' expressions of political consumerism through timed boycotts, the closing of eBay stores, the canceling of accounts, the choosing of different auction interfaces, the posting of critical comments, and communicating with corporate employees have been widely reported in the popular press. Detailed critiques of the company's unfair decisions and disruption of community accompany Internet news reports and other eBay commentary. Rick Aristotle Munarriz has been covering "eBay since the 1990s" and now finds it "rare to put out an article and not have a faction of disgruntled sellers—or ex-Power Sellers—chime in with complaints."[131] For the reporter Alexander Wolfe, members' anger is foregrounded by how articles about eBay receive comments long after the news is posted.[132] This is very unusual, since comments usually stop after a few days. These reporters indicate how eBay produces active and critical consumers. Members engage, but not in the ways encouraged by the site and the company.

eBay removes listings and posts that criticize the site.[133] When Chris Johnston supported a boycott in his listings, he was informed that "sellers aren't permitted to state their personal opinions and views in their listings" and that the behavior might result in the suspension of his account.[134] Yet disagreements, as Secomb explains, are important aspects of community. They may disrupt the "formation of totalizing identity, or commonality," but there are few ways to include such diversity in the eBay setting and establish viable dialogues.[135] eBay sellers and other business owners, according to the reporter Karen E. Klein, are some of "the hardest-working, most creative members of our society."[136] However, they "too often lack a voice in both corporate and government policy." This powerlessness is antithetical to eBay's claims that everyone has something to contribute. It also threatens to foil eBay's community structures and management of public perceptions. Since eBay makes a profit from getting individuals to work for the site and the company, it is worth considering how members and the company could benefit from allowing participants greater influence.

eBay has convinced many members that they produce the site and its community. Whitman used to greet cheering members at eBay events with, "This is about you."[137] This duplicitous promise has increased participants' anger. For instance, Brian D. asserts, "WE MADE EBAY WHAT IT IS."[138] Justice For All, whose forum ID poses an alienated and demanding citizenry, describes how members "gave their all into a business opportunity only to be sent through a slaughter house as a reward for their years of hard work and investment."[139] Another poster uses "One of many" as an ID, has "been selling on Ebay for over 9 years," and is one of the community members and "pioneers" who "helped BUILD THEM UP between buying and selling on Ebay."[140] One of many is now alienated and looking for another auction site. eBay and other brand communities promise participants agency and co-production opportunities and can therefore encounter increased forms of resistance, critique, and alienation when these assurances are not fulfilled.

Some brand community members use eBay's rituals and values as a way to critique the company and the site. The company treats members "like criminals," notes chatanooga, despite its assertion "that people are basically good."[141] For KD, when eBay "betrays the trust the trusting freely gave, then a moral and ethical crime has been committed and a break in a precious bond is broken forever."[142] By writing, "You cant find 'it on ebay' anymore," lessthenavrgjoe inverts eBay's slogan.[143] Members rework eBay's themes as a means of highlighting their estrangement and problems with the company's brand formation. Their critiques are more potent because contemporary society also associates eBay with its community. Such critiques by brand community members can therefore endanger companies. For instance, the Coca-Cola brand community vociferously resisted the modification of "its" drink and brand when the company replaced the original beverage with what is now New Coke.[144] This decision alienated fans and thus threatened the stability of the brand and economic position of the company. eBay faces similar hurdles in having noticeably alienated the community it claims as its family and supporters. In accounts about Whitman's run for governor, reporters have highlighted members' angry comments in news stories, forums, blogs, and dedicated Internet settings. The visibility of this conflict gives members increased opportunities to critique the company and foil the political and social aspirations of eBay executives.

Alienated eBay members interrogate their relationship with the corporation and identify the limits of the eBay community. However, many of them are still drawn to the concept of brand and consumer communities. Even after becoming aware of the discrepant relationship between corporations and brand community members, they seek more satisfying brand communities and better companies.[145] For instance, Karen believes that everyone who uses the OnlineAuction site (ola.com) is "part of a community. There are REAL people who answer your questions and solve any problems; not canned responses like at eBay. We ALL encourage each other in every single way we can and help each other out where we can."[146] cabanalolita closed her eBay store and "moved" to the Bonanzle selling site; she loves "the friendly community and the Bonanzle guys are great!"[147] This interface is different, according to cabanalolita, because it offers the opportunity to "Chat live with Bonanzle neighbors. eBay never had that option!" In a similar manner, Bonanzle self-identifies as an interface where people can buy and "sell unique items with the friendliest community online" and figures site usage as a collaborative project.[148] These brand community members, in comparable ways to the arrangements Hickman and Ward describe, choose to declare their allegiance to new brands and position themselves as opposed to eBay.[149] Rather than investing in another brand community, which is likely to economically fail or alienate members, individuals might highlight the troubling aspects of community and problematize the use of the term in Internet settings.

In the next chapter, I continue to study how members engage with eBay's community and ethos. Such structures are profitable for companies such as eBay because they get consumers to work for the company and invest in its products. Members initiate individuals into the culture, regulate those who do not conform, and try to meet the mandates for selflessness by providing assistance. My analysis of eBay's asynchronous conference forum, eBay Live! conferences, and collecting and sale of eBay-ana demonstrates how companies use Internet technologies to produce brand enthusiasts and company supporters. I also point to the advantages for members, which include acknowledgments of their interests, increased sales opportunities, and support from the company and other invested participants. Settings such as eBay should be carefully considered and critical strategies proposed because they tend to produce members who enthusiastically support site codes and normalized and regulated bodies. Yet fan and brand attachments can also put companies at risk.

chapter two

Pins, Cards, and Griffith's Jacket

PRODUCING IDENTITY AND BRAND COMMUNITIES THROUGH

EBAY LIVE! CONFERENCES AND COLLECTING

Individuals who are planning to attend eBay Live! conferences express excitement in the conference forum, make plans to socialize with other members at events, strategize about attending classes, arrange elaborate branded outfits, and envision the eBay-ana they can collect. For instance, mattie-lily-rose posts that she is "excited, really excited, no really really really excited" about the convention.[1] surfsilicon1 is "so excited about eBay Live!" that the poster "started to literally dream about it."[2] Both raglebagle and unique-find eagerly anticipate eBay Live! because it will allow them to finally meet.[3] These individuals share similar stories about eBay and the conferences as ways to articulate eBay identities, connect with other members, engage the company and its employees, and support the brand community. Such collaborative conference practices are important for deeply engaged members and the company. They explain, justify, and extend attachments to the site.

eBay promotes this enthusiasm and community through its conferences. eBay Live! conventions have been held in Anaheim, California (2002); Orlando (2003); New Orleans (2004); San Jose, California (2005); Las Vegas (2006); Boston (2007); and Chicago (2008). Versions have also occurred in Berlin (2003) and Düsseldorf (2006). The eBay Live! conference for 2009 was canceled. In 2010, eBay began making the conferences over into eBay: On Location, holding them in varied U.S. cities throughout the year and promising to reach more interested members.[4] eBay describes these conferences as "Live" and "On Location" and indicates that they incorporate physical people and locales and are more than computer mediation. Members also use the conferences to produce material spaces and experiences that bolster eBay's representations. eBay Live! provides raglebagle with the opportunity to "actually hug unique-find and thank her for her precious friendship."[5] Yet surfsilicon1's account of dreaming about the conference evokes connections, as well as ruptures, between the immaterial (including dreamscapes) and the physical. The conferences thereby represent and trouble the realness of eBay's goods, identities, and participants.

Studying eBay Live! and its limits allows me to reflect on the ways members identify and how the asynchronous conference forum, conferences, eBay Live! I attended in 2007, and sale of eBay-branded objects shape larger fan, community, collecting, and cultural identities (figures 3 and 4).[6] Such processes of individual and group identity construction are always in tension and should be considered together. Social identification, as the anthropologist and sociologist Richard Jenkins comments, is not only about "knowing who we are" and "what we think about ourselves" but also "what people think about us" and how they render our identity and position.[7] Internet settings and their physical manifestations (such as eBay Live!) offer powerful opportunities for individuals to identify and companies to engage members, constitute brand communities of like-minded people, and get individuals to do more work for the company and brand.

Events such as eBay Live! and eBay: On Location have a significant value for participants and the associated corporations. However, there has been a dearth of critical literature about conferences. Technology-oriented convention cultures determine what products we see on the market; how technologies are understood; and the relationship between hardware, software, and identity positions. These events play a considerable part in configuring users. Studies of conferences should be further incorporated into research on blogging, computers and peripherals, fan cultures, gaming, social networking, and software, because they have active conference cultures. Since eBay features classes and a trade show, I use the terms "conference" and "convention" somewhat interchangeably. Literature on brand, fan, and Internet communities and collecting helps explain these conventions and the ways the identities and values of individuals, the company, and branded objects become intertwined. Connecting brand community and fan processes and literature allows me to further analyze how these structures function and some of the limits of these research models.

3. eBay Shop, eBay Live! 2007, Boston

4. Susanna Millman, "Photos From eBay Live! 2008 So Far," *Chatter*, 20 June 2008

Fans and Brand Communities

Brand community members tend to be active fans of particular companies, products, logos, sites, virtual communities, and media texts. Engaged eBay members and brand community participants demonstrate a kind of media and console fandom.[8] They are proponents of such eBay texts as the forums, advertisements, logo, listings, and narratives about values and how these features are supported by the interface. eBay fans meet Roger Blackwell and Tina Stephan's criteria for consumer fans and "invest time, attention, energy, emotion, and money into building and maintaining a relationship to a brand."[9] Their book, which is directed at businesses, indicates the distinctive ways brands encourage and support fan identifications. Brand communities attach fans to branded products, companies, and community members. They articulate objects and ethos individuals can identify with, settings and rituals where participants can connect, and cultures of fannish enthusiasm that embrace engaged people. This suggests how media fans, whether they participate in collaborative engagements or are solely attached to the text, are also brand community members.

The sociologists Denise D. Bielby, C. Lee Harrington, and William T. Bielby distinguish between media viewers, who "engage in a relatively private behavior," and fans, whose activities include "purchasing or subscribing to fan magazines," "writing letters to actors, producers, writers, or fan publications," engaging with other fans in Internet forums, "joining fan clubs," and attending conventions and other fan events.[10] eBay fans are also distinct from people who casually deploy the site and individuals who actively buy and sell but do not participate in such fan practices as identifying with the company, reading eBay newsletters and magazines, engaging with members through forums and other site features, attending convention parties, and wearing or collecting eBay-branded items. These eBay enthusiasts and fans, as my analysis in this chapter demonstrates, tend to repeat the company's discourse. This encourages a closer analysis of fan practices and of how individuals support the values of corporations. It also points to some limitations in the canonical fan studies literature by, among others, Camille Bacon-Smith, John Fiske, and Henry Jenkins because they identify fans as active producers who are resistant to mainstream media and corporate structures.[11]

Canonical fan studies texts, according to Jonathan Gray, Cornel Sandvoss, and C. Lee Harrington's research, associate fandom with "a collective strategy, a communal effort to form interpretive communities that in their subcultural cohesion evaded the preferred and intended meanings of the 'power bloc.'"[12] For instance, Jenkins identifies Internet-based fan communities as being "focused around the collective production, debate, and circulation of meanings, interpretations and fantasies in response to various artifacts of contemporary culture."[13] Fiske argues that fans oppose and rework dominant culture.[14] These researchers are interested in the productive and creative aspects of fandom. They rightly resist notions that fans are foolish and their engagements valueless. Instead, as Jenkins notes, the intent is to portray fans as "active, critically engaged," "creative," and "rogue readers."[15] These fan studies researchers emphasize the importance of fandom and may overstate the oppositional aspects of these cultures. I hope to enrich this literature by further highlighting how fans are related to brands. For instance, eBay brand community members also act as fans when they narrate and extend the history of the site, wait for company executives to sign eBay-ana, and indicate that they have crushes on employees.

There is some research that interrogates how fans support the values and products of media producers and corporations, regulate what can be included in fan cultures, and perpetuate media products by completing missing parts of texts. Yngvar Kjus, who studies cross-media events, describes how the "television industry is actually strengthening its grip" on fans and other viewers "to reduce costs and risks while increasing revenues."[16] In his study of alternate reality gaming, Henrik Örnebring argues that convergence culture facilitates increased opportunities to market texts in ways that support the hierarchies and values of producers rather than dissolving the boundaries between authors and texts.[17] While there are opportunities for interactivity, many texts position audiences as consumers. These researchers acknowledge the importance of fan practices while identifying how engagements with loved objects and representations can be personally pleasurable, resistant to some mainstream cultures and positions, and support corporations and their values. Such active and complicit fan engagements are key to the functioning and productivity of the eBay Live! forum and conventions.

eBay's Community Discussion Boards

The community discussion boards or forums, which are available from the Community link, are an important part of eBay's and members' identity production. Pierre Omidyar started the community board in 1996 to engage members in a collaborative dialogue and disengage himself from requests for assistance. Jim Griffith was employed as the first customer service representative and to maintain a board presence because his textual drag performances engaged members and helped resolve conflicts. Some individuals would email Griffith and indicate they were so upset about board disputes that they "had cried all night, sometimes all week."[18] Such intimate connections and attachments to settings, including representations of crying participants, are associated with fandom. They point to the value these texts have for some viewers and the combined pleasures and frustrations that are implicit aspects of these kinds of engagements. eBay members' passionate and agitated responses suggest the centrality of conflict in computer-mediated settings.[19] Varied disputes occur in eBay forums. They are vital features of this setting and community, pointing to the ways difference operates, but individuals often associate sites like eBay with agreement, support, and shared values and tend to mandate affinity from members.[20]

Individuals articulate their identity and are identified as members of the community by being board participants. In the Internet forum that Anne-Laure Fayard and Gerardine DeSanctis study, identity "occurs as speakers define themselves in relation to the group. Identity can be found in surface language features that convey intimacy with others, such as reference to 'we,' 'us,' or 'our group' and in references to a common, larger community."[21] In a related manner, brand community researchers identify consciousness of a kind and brand stories as important aspects of community formation.[22] For Steven P. Westly, who collected toy soldiers as an eBay employee, eBay's and members' identifications of shared interests are connected to collecting. eBay sells collecting as well as goods, so consciousness of a kind is related to eBay's commercial intents. Westly believes that collectors "have a passion about something that makes them feel a little left out. And at eBay, they are immediately connected to someone else. eBay represents a community of people who deeply understand one another."[23] eBay is also a community of people who know about collecting and whose identities are partially organized through particular kinds of consumption. For instance, the opening part of the site often features antiques and curios and offers links to "Collectibles" categories. The apocryphal reason Omidyar developed the site was so that Pam Wesley, his fiancée, could collect Pez dispensers. Thus, eBay emphasizes collecting, provides individuals with a setting in which they can connect with other collectors, and supports individuals' identities as collectors.

eBay offers varied features that facilitate consciousness of a kind, including participants' recognition of other collectors and social selling, in which individuals market goods by communicating about personal interests. Members provide detailed personal information in listings, eBay-facilitated blogs, "About Me" and "My World" sites, and forums. Boards make readers and posters into buyers and sellers by including links to feedback reviews, About Me sites, stores, and listings. Interestingly, some participants choose to use posting IDs rather than selling IDs in forums because their outspoken comments make them unpopular and cause people to bid on items they have no intention of paying for. The community's disruption of some listings, even if these behaviors are not corporately sanctioned, articulates acceptable forms of engaging, the identities that are most welcome, and the individuals who are invited to take part or discouraged from participating. In such instances, brand communities employ and reject difference as a way to articulate and extend consciousness of a kind.

Board postings also tend to render connections between individuals and make the setting matter, both affectively and physically, by transforming textual features into shared spaces. For instance, an individual may post the word "pop" and people reply with "pop, pop, pop" to turn the site into a popcorn party.[24] People post detailed images of tea and cookies to convey their hospitality and bond with other readers. These renderings of the site as a community and detailed setting are supported only when others engage. As Nancy Baym's Internet studies research indicates, computer networks become meaningful when "they are invoked by participants in ongoing interaction."[25] Omidyar called community into being, but the company needs members to support his narratives with their practices, investments, and identification of consciousness of a kind. eBay encourages members to work. Yet it is buyers and sellers who decide to produce much of eBay's content, perform as fans of the setting, and activate the site.

The eBay Live! Community Conference Board

Members' fan and brand practices galvanize and sustain the conferences and conference board. This forum is focused on eBay's yearly convention, includes all of the messages about the conference that were posted since the event was first announced in 2002, and is still available in a read-only format. This allows eBay to feature brand enthusiasts while preventing critical debate about the shift to eBay: On Location. Individuals are directed to use the forum to make "arrangements to meet your friends, talk about travel and accommodations," "discuss what you would like to see during the event," "find out about the Pink Lounge" (a meeting area run by "pinks," or employees whose posts are demarcated with a pink stripe), and learn about "other activities that are planned."[26] They are also advised that before "posting, please read and familiarize yourself with the eBay Board Usage Policies," and people unfamiliar with the discussion forums can select a "tutorial." Such notices and instructional texts accompany many Internet sites. They provide individuals with provisos and warnings, indicate the kinds of engagements that are expected, offer further lessons, and configure people. Through the board and conferences, eBay works with members to extend the company's notion of community.

Most posts to the eBay Live! forum are concerned with problems registering for the conference, inquiries about the usefulness of going, attempts to convince uninitiated readers to attend, plans to meet people, indications of members' physical locations, and enthusiastic posts about the conference. eBay promises to connect all people in a global market. This idea is related to popular and academic narratives about the Internet, such as R. B. Driskell and L. Lyon's virtual community research and description of how "cyberspace has been liberated from the confines and constraints of place."[27] However, members' eBay Live! forum threads convey their interest in engaging with people from the same cohort and geographic place. For instance, board threads inquire, "Anyone from Oklahoma going to ebay live?"; "Any Canadians Going?"; "Owner or interested in an Ebay CONSIGNMENT BIZ? LET'S MEET at Ebay Live!!!!"; and "Any Asian wanna hang out together?"[28] These brand community members, and many other people who use Internet settings, produce traditional geographic and identity positions as part of their fan and brand allegiances. Their interests are addressed in the shift from the nationally, or even internationally, coded eBay Live! conferences to the more regional focus of On Location.

The company presents the conference as its way to thank engaged members. However, the event also enables eBay to get members to work. According to scooch, a pink who posts official messages to the site, eBay believes "everyone has something to contribute. eBay Live gives us an opportunity to meet and thank you."[29] Yet scooch frames the conference experience and prefaces the possibility of being thanked with the common eBay directive that members should "contribute" and work. A cohort of members contributes by expressing enthusiasm for the site and conference, helping other individuals to join and engage, and promoting the convention and company by selling branded items. In this manner, members respond to eBay's mandates for immaterial labor and replicate eBay's configuration of consumer identities.

On the eBay Live! board, members offer brand stories and reiterate eBay's ideas about community and values. This is not surprising since learning and sharing brand stories, as Albert M. Muñiz Jr. and Thomas C. O'Guinn indicate, also assists members in "learning communal values."[30] A key eBay brand story, as structured by Omidyar and perpetuated by forum participants, is that the site provides access to good people and a community. artful. seller supports this notion and describes eBay as "a wonderful gift" that "has given so much to so many."[31] eBay creates "this amazing, growing mass of goodwill around the world." For danse, eBay Live! is "a wonderful small community of people from all over the world. It didn't take long" for her "to get to know many of them by name and feel . . . part of a greater good."[32] Relating the conference to Omidyar's values, misswigglesemporium writes, "Everyone was super nice proving Pierre's thought that 'People are basically good.'"[33] These members provide reasons for being attached, encourage others to work selflessly for the company and community good, and do good work for eBay by perpetuating brand stories.

Individuals also redeploy brand stories as a means of telling more personal accounts and increasing their visibility. In some of these cases, sellers support and extend brand stories for personal profit. beachbadge, who often signs her posts "Anita / beachbadge," has an eBay site "guide" that transforms her individual behavior into a brand story and part of eBay's history.[34] According to beachbadge's guide, board members loved her virtual rum balls (a version of the tea and cookie ritual that is common on the forums). She was "able to share the real ones with everyone" at the conference, people searched for her in order to try the rum balls, and her "husband was even using the rumballs to barter" for collectible convention pins.[35] beachbadge uses her identity, practices, and brand story to stand in for eBay's processes and its interlocking of representations and material objects. She emphasizes the shifts from textual to material rum balls and from the forum to the corporeal relationships of the conferences.

This is a brand story because the "rumballs made eBay history" when Meg Whitman mentioned them while giving beachbadge a community award. beachbadge's claims to exemplariness operate along with traditional identity positions. Her self-presentation is similar to the managing of Whitman's corporate position with portrayals of the executive as a wife and mother. beachbadge emphasizes her femaleness, femininity, and heteronormativity by including her real name in posts, connecting her eBay identity to cooking and hospitality, and indicating that cooking facilitates her husband's collecting desires. Members are not required to link eBay IDs to binary gender positions but many forum participants create identities that are gendered and perform stereotyped roles. This tendency is encouraged by eBay's directive to provide personal information, cultural expectations that physical and virtual identities are connected to gender positions, and the requirement on such sites as MSN/Hotmail, MySpace, and Yahoo! that individuals provide gender identifications in order to get accounts. Since telling brand stories, including beachbadge's narratives about rum balls, assists members in learning communal values, these practices contribute to eBay's binary gender and heterosexual organizational logic.

Participants and Identity

Popular and academic literature often indicates that Internet sites and technologies empower everyone while popular representations, including some of the aforementioned texts, associate advanced computer processes with white heterosexual men. For instance, eBay configured the gender of attendees at its 2007 conference for software developers, which happened before eBay Live!, with signage that almost always depicted men. In doing this, eBay establishes third-party software development, and knowledge of advanced technologies, as a male terrain. Racial and other identity positions are not infallibly determined. Nevertheless, whether through years of encouragement and acknowledgment or for other reasons, most third-party developers in attendance at eBay developer conferences appear to be young, male, and white. eBay Live! employees range from young and newly hired individuals to established executives, but they are, with some variance, usually white men. Buyers and sellers are also likely to be white, although there is a broader range of racial identifications in this group. Thus, eBay references everyone while remaining a fairly homogeneous culture.

eBay associates men with site design and programming. Women are more apt to be identified as sellers in advertisements, listings, and About Me sites. For instance, the banners for the 2003 eBay Live! convention depicted an engaged female member hugging a feedback star. This is not surprising since women are still associated with such activities as shopping, sales work, and running yard sales.[36] Women are the most visible group at eBay Live! conferences. Middle-aged and retired heterosexual couples, networks of friends, and extended family groups also have a significant presence at eBay Live! conferences and sell on the site. Individuals with other identifications and sales strategies, such as the gay men who sell underwear and swimwear, are not visible within the convention culture. This may be because eBay and members tend to configure attendees as heteronormative and encourage heterosexual couples to go to the convention as a nuclear-family vacation. kathryn states that "the idea is to have a city suitable for a family vacation, so dad can take the kids to entertainment while mom attends the convention."[37] The company chooses tourist destinations and describes the conference as fun, a community, a family, and a reunion.

Some members use eBay as a way to change careers, make extra money, retire, or leave jobs that are difficult to maintain because of health or family issues, while still operating within a kind of traditional role.[38] For instance, tradrmom "got onto Ebay (in addition to not having to wear pantyhose)" because it is "flexible," it "provides time for family and other responsibilities," and going back to "the regular office," "the clothes," "and/or the politics would kill" her.[39] tradertif started her own business so that she would "never have to wear 'business attire' EVER AGAIN!!!"[40] These women have their own businesses, although many of them present as professionalized without being professionals and businesslike without being businesspeople. They are "motivated and inspired" by Whitman heading such a large corporation.[41] They reject aspects of corporate femininity, such as pantyhose, in favor of a hybrid identity that combines conventional women's roles and self-directed work and careers. In doing this, they reference Whitman's own self-portrayals as traditional and family-oriented.

Attendees range from pre-teens to individuals who are more than eighty. Many board participants identify as older than forty, but varied concerns about being "old" are conveyed in threads. axzar3000 assures a member that "at 35 you will be the life of the party": "Most people at eBay Live are like 300 years old!"[42] The participant www-internetishop-com worries about not having "fun because" of being "really young compared to the general" attendees, and people older than forty are boring and staid.[43] Members highlight their concerns about aging and desire to be with individuals in their age range when they ask, "Any older folks who don't party going?"; Any party people going who are younger than 30?"; and "ebay live- What's your age?"[44] These posts reproduce traditional divisions and feelings of unworthiness rather than providing the supportive setting eBay promises. Such ageism, according to Todd D. Nelson, "is one of the most socially-condoned and institutionalized forms of prejudice" in the United States.[45]

eBay posters represent their social value by indicating that they look and act younger than their numerical age. For instance, acmeusa self-identifies as "a single 43 year old that is very young at heart and is accused of looking and living like someone much younger."[46] According to the ageism research of Victor Minichiello, Jan Browne, and Hal Kendig, individuals detach themselves from "the 'old' group" by doing such things as indicating they have "a positive attitude, not looking old," and "not acting old."[47] craftypetstuff critiques such attempts to belong, which require individuals to detach from and dismiss people, by identifying as "young at heart, but wrinkled and much older in other places."[48] She has "just ordered a t/shirt that says not getting older-becoming more valuable"; performatively worries that the "mind isn't what it used to be either....now what were we talking about?"; considers "tips on how to blend in"; and realizes she does not "have enough time to do a total makeover" and is just going to be herself. She proposes a way to accept different identities and forms of embodiment, but posts to the conference board collaboratively establish age, gender, and sexuality norms. These stories about age incorporate prejudice—and, occasionally, resistant identifications—into the company and site.

Queer Performances and Values

Forum participants who are asked about their age discuss weddings and long-term marriages and thereby relate eBay to normative sexuality. For example, susiecraft identifies as "59 and dh" (dear husband) "is 61."[49] deco2mod4u is "47F, 3rd Ebay live," and her husband is attending because it is their thirty-first wedding anniversary.[50] theimpus is a "25 year old female, First time" at "Ebay Live, Just got Married in Vegas 3 Months ago."[51] These narratives encourage members to mirror traditional identifications and are widely embraced within the setting. This is because "what tends to be valorized as 'normative'" in society, according to the feminist and sexuality studies researcher Stevi Jackson, "is a very particular form founded on traditional gender arrangements and lifelong monogamy."[52] These forms of heterogender—a gender system that asserts heterosexuality because of its coupling of male with female—and monogamy are incorporated into eBay's brand community identifications, stories, and organizational logics. Members' interlocking of heterosexuality and age also point to the cultural functions of heteroage, where individuals equate "growing up" to heteronormativity.

eBay and many of its members configure the site with traditional narratives about age, gender, race, and sexuality. Other people work against this production of normativity. For instance, fiberwireguy performs his gay identity and asserts a queer series of meanings for eBay and for members' brand identifications in the forum. In response to a question about the appropriate attire for the conference, fiberwireguy insists that "there is a strict dress code. For women you must wear a hoop skirt and bustle and carry a parasol with you at all times. No colors will be allowed that are not in the eBay logo."[53] When queen-ebabe responds that she is planning to wear "overalls" and a "cowboy hat and be done with it," fiberwireguy uses the opportunity to queer her.[54] He advises, "That's mighty butch."[55] unique_finds93 supports fiberwireguy's performances and flirts with him by inquiring, "Can I wear a hoop skirt? I have one with the gay rainbow colors, so if I just take out two of the colors, I will be good to go."[56] He also finds gay content in eBay's portrayals. When fiberwireguy asks unique_finds93 to go to the eBay Live! gala as his date, he argues that "you can't say 'gala' without saying 'gay.'"[57] fiberwireguy's reading of the gala as a gay event and the indication that it supports his proposed rendezvous is not something most members would accept. Yet it does evoke the company's own references to multiform desires. The self-declared positions of fiberwireguy and unique_finds93 as an "institution on this board" kept the gay identities and queer aspects of eBay highlighted in the forum for a period of time.[58]

Both fiberwireguy and unique_finds93 playfully destabilize the categories within which other members operate. For example, one-gr8-deal expresses confusion and asks, Are "fiber and unique two guys, one girl and one guy, or two girls?"[59] He associates their eBay engagement with the unidentifiable and "Whatever it is." In response, fiberwireguy, whose name provides a gender reference, says he "can't speak" for unique_finds93, but he is "all man."[60] unique_finds93 "*looks down there*" and asserts, "Man here too!!!!"[61] Nevertheless, stable and knowable gender is problematized because, as fiberwireguy suggests, "Some of us didn't need to check."[62] One may be, according to Baym, "anyone he or she wants to be online, but if one wants to be admired or even liked, then he or she would be wise to attend to the very real social constraints that groups develop."[63] Even Baym does not offer a model that goes beyond the dyadic gender distinctions of "he" and "she." Those who support the "communal values" of sites such as eBay "are likely to be praised, quoted, and otherwise supported, while those who try to present other identities are likely to be disregarded."[64]

In a manner similar to other individuals who interrogate the codes of Internet settings, fiberwireguy and unique_finds93 are opposed and ignored. For example, extraordinary-ellie says she wants fiberwireguy and unique_finds93, or you "two boys," to "give it a rest": It is "tiresome to open just about any thread on this board and find your hijinks."[65] She evokes heteroage by stating that they are not properly normed and engaged in age-appropriate work. Whether because of such negative assessments or for other reasons, unique_finds93 stopped participating in the forum, and fiberwireguy adopted a much more conventional way to engage. Then curiously-strong-ellie-mint (extraordinary-ellie's posting ID) noted that "Fiberwireguy annoyed the heck out of" her "a few months before the convention when he was such a goofball with another poster and kept veering off topic."[66] But now, she is "fond of him." Of course, fiberwireguy was supporting communal values at this juncture. He could be tamed and made into a kind of quirky but adorable pet without his inclusion of overtly gay content. When fiberwireguy reproduces the processes and codes of the forum, he is allowed to become a full sexual citizen.

Group Identification and Community in the eBay Live! Board

eBay tries to use pinks and other employees to sustain the site's identities, values, sexual citizens, and organizational logic. Pinks act as handlers and cheerleaders for individuals who are positively identified with the company and its positions. Active members respond to them. For instance, women reply by creating threads about male pinks. They also compromise expectations about female members' "proper" femininity by marveling at the physical attributes of male pinks and imagining having relationships with favorite employees. When individuals manipulate images of male pinks in the forum, *queen*cheese* wonders, "Did someone say it was hot in here??"[67] She also jokes, "That's a mighty big gun you got there" as a way to comment on a male pink's genitals. been_there*done_that humorously plans her wedding with a pink.[68] These posters connect brand enthusiasm to the historical processes of fan cultures and accounts of female fans desiring and swooning over male stars. At the same time, they assert some control over the company, men, and male employees by converting male pinks into erotic objects. Male pinks are already associated with some level of gender confusion and disempowerment because the color pink is culturally linked with femininity. Yet even women's playful desires for male employees and assertion of sexual power are managed when pinks tell them to "stay within the realm of good taste."[69] In these cases, eBay maintains a precarious balance between values and enthusiasm.

Pinks have a special status in the forum, and members can increase their status by communicating with them. It is therefore not surprising that individuals often respond to pinks with mannerly agreement and even fannish enthusiasm. For instance, a number of members positively repeat scooch's language when he inquires, "Is everyone getting excited" about the conference?[70] **christymj** replies, "excited yet???? how about STILL!!! Can't wait."[71] suebeany says she "can't wait!"; she is "Counting the days!" and is "looking forward to meeting all you nice folks and absorbing info and tips like a sponge."[72] abovethemall is "SO ready!!!" and "looking forward to meeting" everyone.[73] This repetitive language extends the insider references that Fayard and DeSanctis find in Internet forums.[74] eBay board participants employ similar expressions and writing styles, render agreement about the event, and produce a group identity.

This group identity is often associated with family. For instance, bobals_wife, whose ID attaches her to the better-known bobal and highlights her position as married and family-identified, writes about the conference that she "went to a FAMILY REUNION" that "was the most fantastic and rewarding time of" her "life. Over five thousand relatives showed up."[75] valentinemcgee "was so happy to be spending" her birthday with "ebay family" at the conference.[76] A "very sweet lady" recognized funfindsfromsuz because of her eBay-specific clothing and invited her to ride to an eBay Live! event from the hotel.[77] They "laughed about how anyone else would think" she "was crazy for taking a ride with a carload of strangers, but that as ebayers," they "were ALL family!" In these narratives, members' engagements and feelings of security exceed the kinds of trust produced by the feedback system. Their attachments are related to corporations' references to family. For example, when eBay acquired a new shopping search engine, it shared the "Great news" that "Milo has joined the eBay family!"[78] These structures, according to the organizational research of Catherine Casey, render caring employers and familial colleagues. Companies' promises of greater "involvement, commitment, and 'empowerment'" attract employees and consumers while including a built-in disciplinary mechanism that enforces businesses' internal rules and values.[79] Critiques of such cultures are also difficult because they challenge members' caring families and the values that appear to be in the best of interest of this kinship structure.

eBay's conference materials continue these narratives about intimacy and connections by depicting members holding hands and promising participants that they will bond. In a related manner, community members tell brand stories about being connected to people who understand one another. cuties4u appreciates how attendees accept and understand eccentric selling and brand community practices: "If you pull your wallet out of your purse and packing peanuts fall out ... NO ONE thinks a thing about it"; "If you use words such as eeek ,erk or snort ... EVERYONE gets it"; and "If you have to fix a broken purse strap to get you thru the day and use priority tape ... EVERYONE understands."[80] For ion_treasures, the conference population includes "1000s of people whose eyes don't glaze over when you start talking about eBay."[81] Fan conventions also provide assurances "that there are others out there just like oneself," according to the American studies scholar Joe Sartelle.[82] cuties4u and ion_treasures emphasize the otherness of active members and the ways their differences are embraced in eBay's conference cultures. However, a group of participants on the eBay Live! board, as I suggest later in the chapter, also make it clear that some posters and attendees do not belong. Their methods of creating a common culture should be cause for concern, even though the outcomes are not as extreme as those addressed by Benedict Anderson's and Jean-Luc Nancy's community research.[83] Participants use their shared differences to articulate norms that should be followed by others.

Attendees are encouraged to identify with the group by creating visually recognizable brand community identities. "Dawn's Top Ten Tips for eBay Live" pushes members to "'show your eBay spirit.' Dress in a creative way using the eBay colors."[84] Upon registering at the conference, everyone receives branded bags to carry their logo-covered programs and is made over into fans, a brand community, and an advertisement for the site. Media fans also identify with T-shirts that are legible only to insiders, jewelry that replicates symbols and items from television shows or films, media-specific language, and elaborate replications of clothing and settings from texts. In the case of eBay, members who display company logos and colors are rewarded by receiving gift certificates from pinks, being depicted in issues of eBay's *Chatter* (e.g., the wearer of eBay-branded socks and sneakers in figure 4), and getting represented in slide shows of attendees that appear before sessions.[85] For some members, eBay's recognition, transformation of them into model members, and facilitation of their fame within the community lead to personal pride, acknowledgment from peers, and increases in sales.

A number of members convey their membership even before they arrive at the conference. For example, sanda-girls_closet purchased stickers that declared her love of eBay and her husband "bought some kind of 'spirit foam' to 'paint' the car" in eBay colors.[86] She wants members who see them driving to the conference to "honk or wave," acknowledge their presence and spirit, and connect. frednmag encourages members "to wear something that reflects ebay" while flying so people can recognize each other and "sit together and get pumped up."[87] Sports fans also decorate cars with flags and stickers so their enthusiasm is extended out from the game and engages a larger public sphere. Academic and business conferences tend to hand out bags with the event name and logo; they presume people will need something to carry conference materials and thereby get attendees to show spirit and allegiance on the way home. By creating and wearing branded items, eBay and other fan and brand community members render a marketplace and sphere of sociality that exceed the site and conferences, extend the brand and products, and support their investments. Such brand community objects and stories suggest that members' alliances and brand community structures are global and constant. Nevertheless, even a resistant or disgruntled patron who carries a bag with a company's name on it performs some version of this role and labor.

Community Work

Attendees specify that they are good community members and situate themselves at conferences by posting images to the board, describing events, and gathering souvenirs for individuals who cannot participate. eBay encourages attendees to post images in the forum and suggests that photographs situate viewers at the event. For instance, katy, who is a pink, announces that the "party has started," coaxes readers to "gather here to see all of those great images the nice folks can post for us from eBay Live so we can join in the fun with them," and thanks participants for "helping us 'be' there with you!"[88] In a similar manner, rizal, another pink, asks individuals to share photographs and give "the entire Community the chance to see and experience eBay Live! 2005, as it happens."[89] Events as diverse as the Association of Internet Researchers Conference (AoIR) and regional furry conventions, where individuals wear carefully crafted outfits made out of fake fur, include forums where members ask for and post images and sites with numerous images of the event.

In response to requests for images in the eBay Live! forum, beadhappys presents a visual tour of the conference that moves the viewer into the space. It shows the banners that are "all over the streets around the convention center," "the front of the convention center," and "inside the Village" an "incredible sand castle."[90] Viewers reply with requests for particular views, look for images that portray them, express regrets about not attending, and thank posters for depictions. wigglzzzz offers a "Thank you TIEDYEJOHN!!!!" for taking pictures and bringing "eBay Live as it was happening" to individuals who could not attend.[91] beachbadge describes "all those back at home who eagerly awaited news of EBAY LIVE!"[92] Images make viewers feel as if they are "there with you!!"[93] In these cases, images exceed the function of listing depictions, which I describe in the introduction, by adequately conveying sites and providing materializing views. While objects must be distinguished from representations to further Internet selling, participants and the company code conference images as versions of the physical experience and thus incorporate more people into the brand community and experience.

Individuals documenting the conference work at eBay's and members' requests. They have to take images, locate or deploy image-hosting sites, resize pictures, find Internet access, and upload images during the convention. Other members also labor for the company. Adam Cohen describes members sharing information about births, marriages, and deaths and getting favorite participants computers so they can post from home.[94] The popular messageboard poster bobal found it financially and physically difficult to travel to the conference but was brought to the event through the active work of other members until he died.[95] They appreciated the specialized knowledge that he shared with members on the eBay boards. According to Jeff, an eBay employee, bobal had "a cult following, and his unparalleled eBay enthusiasm at past eBay Live! events have made him a star."[96] Members believed "eBay Live! wasn't eBay Live! without bobal," and raising enough funds for his attendance was a "thank you for the years of help he'd given in the past." While economic, health, and family issues are identified as factors that prevent individuals from attending conferences, attendees ordinarily do not work to fund their presence.[97] Yet funding bobal's trips and guaranteeing his presence was deemed important, as bobal and his wife, daughter, and granddaughter, with their hand-crafted vests and matching hats in eBay's color scheme, acted as visual examples of fan and brand enthusiasm and loyalty. By bringing bobal and his family to the conferences, participants produced an event populated by model members and bolstered eBay's claims that people are basically good. They supported eBay's rendering of heteronormative families and sexual citizens.

Forum participants who are unable to attend post to the board, sip virtual margaritas, and try to find someone to collect pins and additional eBay-ana for them. When the eBay employee Jackie ran a trivia contest about eBay Live! for people who could not attend, it made winners "feel closer to the action," and some of them decided to attend the following year.[98] The temporary cancellation of eBay's conventions pointed to problems with this structure, focused attention on members' longing for these events, and has now been replaced with video of eBay: On Location that promises to make you "feel like you were there."[99] This experience of being present at rituals, which is sometimes delivered by representations, is important. sanda-girls_closet was "practically crying" about not being able to attend the conference in Boston.[100] For her, there were "No pins and cards," "No pictures with Bobal and Griff," and "No Gala with Kool and the Gang." She associates the conference experience with the ability to physically collect materials, attend the gala, and demonstrate her attendance through depictions. Popular posters such as beachbadge work to assuage feelings of detachment by providing collectibles to individuals who cannot attend.[101] beachbadge does not need anything in return and instead hopes people will "Pay It Forward" and "help another person complete their set." These members work to increase their personal position, the attendance at future conferences, the collecting of branded convention items, the materialization of events, and the notion of eBay community.

Most of the labor performed by forum members is done without monetary compensation, but eBay occasionally offers incentives like "Skippy bucks," coupons that can be used to pay for listings. eBay uses such tactics to make it seem as if payment may occur at any time and encourages participants to freely provide listing advice, moderate problems, and create positive representations of the eBay community. In a forum thread, bamajl argues that eBay should reinstitute Skippy bucks because they are "a darn fine incentive to keep eBay heppers heppin'."[102] However, other members believe the desire for small forms of payments is selfish and a betrayal of eBay's values. They extend mandates for uncompensated immaterial labor. For example, bobal chided bamajl: "do you really need to get paid to help your fellow user?"[103]

Helping others made bobal "feel good." cherbear likes "to help people" and does not "expect skippy bucks."[104] Both bobal and cherbear reference the positive emotional experiences that are associated with immaterial labor. These members also elevate their status by indicating they are willing to help without reward. In doing this, they justify eBay's methods of getting members to labor without economic compensation. Nevertheless, it is not clear how such helpers are supposed to make a living, although favored sellers can garner more sales because of their free work.

bamajl did not appreciate being interrogated about his Skippy bucks proposal and worked to identify with the values of the unreservedly laboring members. The "lack of tangible reward in the form of skippies" would not stop bamajl from helping but might "entice others with knowledge in" esoteric "areas to come forward and share their knowledge."[105] Individuals in brand communities are expected to be responsible, support the product, and solve problems.[106] eBay brand enthusiasts are likelier than other members to enforce the brand's values and are more resistant to critiques and complaints about "their" company and community. René Algesheimer, Utpal M. Dholakia, and Andreas Herrmann have stated that "identification with the brand community leads to positive consequences, such as greater community engagement, and negative consequences, such as normative community pressure."[107] Engaged members tend to internalize brand norms, perform as good sexual citizens, and understand their actions as stemming from an overlap between their values and that of the brand.

eBay Live! and the Conference Culture

eBay Live!, like other trade shows, is designed to enhance the company's brand and corporate image.[108] The eBay Live! conference in 2006, the company's largest, sold out, with nearly 15,000 registered individuals.[109] Nevertheless, eBay elides its marketing intentions, the size of the venues, and the number of attendees when it calls eBay Live! "part family reunion, part classroom, part trade show, and all fun!"[110] eBay Live! thereby supports and extends the coding of the site as pleasurable, recreational, and communal rather than as an impersonal market. Yet many of eBay Live!'s offerings reflect the features of other conferences. eBay conferences include such activities as classes, category roundtables, book signings, "town hall" meetings, keynotes, networking meals, and galas. There is also a bookstore, an eBay Shop for collectibles, an expo hall, and an "eBay Community Lounge" where pinks socialize with members and pins and other collectibles are traded. These features are designed to articulate the brand and connect attendees to other members, the site, and the company.

eBay's conference practices emphasize the presence and reach of the company and site. eBay recodes cities and meeting places as eBay-identified by branding interior convention spaces, areas around convention centers, and convention cities with the site logo and other identifiers. The company also makes employees, buyers, sellers, and press into advertisements by distributing branded lanyards, T-shirts, conference bags, and temporary tattoos. Wearing logos conveys enthusiasm and attachment to the company and, according to the English scholar Herbert Smith, turns the individual into a "walking billboard."[111] All of the 655 employees working at the conference in 2007, from new hires to Whitman, were identifiable by their blue polo shirts with the eBay logo and khaki pants.[112] In previous years, eBay had also used shirts with the logo to identify employees, emphasize their presence, and make them available to attendees. Companies such as Hammertap, which provide services to eBay sellers, further distinguish their workers and articulate binary gender distinctions by having different branded shirts for women and men.

The culture of similitude and brand affiliation that these items render seems antithetical to the unique individuals eBay portrays and the ethos of computer programmers and designers. Technologists, particularly individuals engaged in startups and technology innovation companies, distinguish between their work life and the structures and wardrobes mandated by corporations. The Jargon File, which illuminates "many aspects of hackish tradition," describes corporate cultures that require "Ugly and uncomfortable 'business clothing' often worn by non-hackers."[113] The text claims that "it is not uncommon for hackers to quit a job rather than conform to a dress code," but eBay employees and many of the third-party developers wear identical branded clothing at conferences.[114] Other hackers and computer workers also eagerly don T-shirts and denim shirts given out by technology companies. At the conference, everyone is reconceptualized as a team of workers who display the same logo and participate in the culture of fan and brand enthusiasm. Emphasizing the presence of employees is important, because board posters often indicate eBay staff is unavailable.

Many members are eager to wear branded items and advertise eBay and its third-party vendors. eBay "understands that many of their users are collectors by nature," writes Micah Alpern, a former eBay employee, "so they provided a number of things for attendees to collect."[115] The company gets people to collect eBay and embrace the company by providing branded promotional items. This increases the value of the brand and people's attachment to the company and its objects. Other companies also offer free items at the conferences to connect their products and services to eBay, memorialize the event and significance of their brand, and link their businesses to collecting cultures. Attendees are presented with such things as branded enamel pins, Frisbees, magnets, packing tape, pens, stress balls, trading cards, and shopping bags in the exposition hall. These related objects help create a collecting culture in which eBay and eBay-generated items are central. Many attendees respond to these materials and decorate lanyards and clothing with dozens of branded, blinking, and enamel eBay pins and other collectibles. eBay's conference culture is similar to *Star Trek* conventions, where, according to Sartelle, "opportunities for identity-oriented consumption; attending the event and buying Trek products are ways of confirming one's membership in the larger 'community' of fans."[116] Product manufacturers also extend "brands into lines of collectible merchandise," which, as the research of John Philip Jones and Jan S. Slater suggests, heightens brand loyalty, "extends exposure to the brand message," and articulates the identity of consumers in relationship to the brand.[117] These individuals function as collecting consumers and connect brand communities to collecting cultures.

eBay's self-promotion and loyalty production through branded pins and other collectibles are part of larger corporate trends, including the Walt Disney Company's sponsorship of pin trading at its theme parks.[118] Disney has always offered collectible pins, but since 1999 it has created trading areas, rules for how visitors may trade pins with workers, seminars, and pin-trading conventions.[119] Disney's sponsorship of these activities makes attendees into collectors and fans, further connects people to the company and brand, and brings individuals to the parks more often. My own institution and its members use collecting to declare their organizational affinity, constitute a value for souvenirs, and validate the places and ideologies represented by these items. Tulane University dispenses free Mardi Gras beads, collectible enamel pins, and other items with its logo during academic rituals. Branded items thereby become a visible part of the institutional body and enable faculty to designate their current affiliation rather than just wearing robes that declare their graduate institutions. Newcomb, the women's coordinate college that was associated with Tulane, was disbanded after Hurricane Katrina and the flooding of New Orleans. However, it remains visible, and individuals' attachment to it is declared by the enamel pins, sashes, and embroidered patches with the Newcomb colors and logo that are displayed during graduation ceremonies. These items are designed for specialized markets, make some individuals into fans, and articulate brand communities and resisters.

These events, like eBay's conferences, assert the centrality and value of collecting. eBay's first conference guide describes "one-of-a-kind" trading cards that are "exclusively designed for eBay Live attendees to collect" and encourages individuals to "collect the entire set."[120] At the 2003 conference, some pins and cards were less available because, as Alpern explains, a market is only interesting if "there is scarcity, so some pins were harder to come by."[121] In a similar manner, the 2007 conference guide advises that "pins are some of the hottest collectibles at eBay Live! because you can only get them at certain times during the event."[122] eBay uses terms like "one-of-a-kind" and "exclusively designed" to render items as collectible, valuable, and significant rather than allowing collectors' tastes and market forces determine their long-term appeal. This creates a culture in which enthusiasts strive for items, worry about not being able to find things, and declare passion for the brand. ah6tyfour finds it "kind of scary to think that the pins are only" available "for a little while."[123] toys2keep likes to play games at the conference and win "the elusive special category pins and Limited Edition Hot Wheels car."[124] Collectors of such mass-produced goods, according to Russell W. Belk's consumer research, "value rarity in collected objects because it provides both more challenge and a greater feeling of accomplishment and a higher status."[125] The discourse about rarity encourages collectors to find value in objects and the brand and obtain things as soon as possible. Yet, as David Burton indicates in his analysis of souvenirs, these conceptions can be duplicitous when used to sell large production runs of collectible plates and related items.[126] eBay and other Internet-based collecting sites deploy conceptions of uniqueness and rarity even as they make it easier to obtain objects.

eBay codes its giveaways as limited editions to motivate collecting. However, eBay and employees are also aware that too much scarcity can frustrate members. In 2007, employees regularly carried gigantic bags of pins onto the convention floor, "96,500 pins were handed out," and numerous pins decorated most attendees' lanyards.[127] Each collectible pin was supposed to be distributed only during a short, predetermined period, but employees offered all of the collectible pins, coins, and cards to attendees during the last day of the event. Some employees helped attendees complete their sets, but others eagerly and indiscriminately distributed large numbers of branded items to members. Providing attendees with numerous versions of the same item encourages members to sell collectibles on the eBay site or share them and their enthusiasm and testament to eBay loyalty with friends. People "didn't grab and hoard as much as possible for their own collecting and souvenirs," argues stmmcmanus; "they did that so they could come back home and sell it."[128] Attendees sell extra items to make a profit and because culture mandates that collections, and individual objects within each compilation, should be unique. As the collecting research of Brenda Danet and Tamar Katriel suggests, for an "assemblage of objects to be considered a collection, each item must be *different* from all others in some way discernible to the collector."[129] Since eBay items are often given away in gray plastic wrappings that prevent individuals from seeing what they are acquiring, the only way to sustain one-of-a-kind collections is by getting rid of redundant items.

In 2007, attendees could get pins and other giveaways from eBay employees when Kool & the Gang's song "Celebration" played in the exhibition area and throughout the conference facility. eBay's themes of gathering and community are evoked by the band's invitation to join the party and share good times.[130] A frenzy of activity, perhaps encouraged by Kool & the Gang's encouragement to "celebrate," occurred on the exhibition floor during pin giveaways. According to the reporter Julia Wilkinson, whenever "Celebration" played, the crowd started "moving like lemmings towards eBay booths and employees blessed with bags of the sacred pins."[131] She identifies collecting as part of an uncritical and ecstatic process of transcendence with the brand and eBay. Her narrative also perpetuates the association of collecting with addictive and obsessive behavior.[132]

Attendees' values have also been questioned. People at the conferences gather and even steal unconventional items. In Las Vegas, the "IT" sign, which was featured in television campaigns, was taken from an eBay display. Employees advertised without success on the eBay Live! board in order to try and recover it.[133] Attendees have been pickpocketed; bags of collectible pins have been stolen from employees; and people have tricked other members out of more collectible items.[134] According to the eBay pink johnjohn, the "eBay Live team has watched centerpieces disappear from every eBay Live Gala" and therefore "designed the centerpieces to be taken."[135] However, the team was surprised that "several of the 8 foot towers decorating the buffet tables also disappeared (even though they were weighted down with sandbags) and one of the CHOCOLATE FOUNTAINS." chix_nuggets was amused "that someone climbed onto the chocolate fountain tables to steal the huge balls on top of the displays."[136] For giraffer, taking such things as personal mementos is more justified than acquiring things for resale. She hates "when they put them up on auction! If you take a memory, then keep it as a memory!"[137] People are respected within collecting subcultures when their accumulation is not economically motivated.[138] Nevertheless, these tales render crafty and avaricious eBay collectors who are happy to beat out other individuals and steal from their purported family and community.

eBay encourages a culture of enthusiastic collecting, but some attendees interrogate such behavior and identify it as unproductive. coniemiller hopes "people won't be so crazy for pins" at future conferences.[139] To critique members' attachments to the company and its products, phreaky2 initiated a thread titled "Pins, Cards, Get a Life People."[140] In doing so, phreaky2 also referenced the performance on *Saturday Night Live* in which William Shatner advised *Star Trek* fans to "get a life."[141] Shatner's comment has become an often referenced joke within fan communities. Nevertheless, eBay members diffuse these critiques and differences by providing conversion narratives about becoming fans and embracing the brand. For instance, skip555 initially dismissed people who were "groveling and begging for cards and pins" and then started to collect enthusiastically.[142] The eBay Live! thread that began with phreaky2 asserting people should keep collecting in perspective ended with people trading cards. These shifts emphasize the important functions of convention items. eBay-ana stands in for the company and its processes, further attaches members to the brand, marks the identities of fans and brand community members, offers reasons for members to communicate and engage in trading, provides ways for attendees to make money, and creates a market on the eBay site.

Buying and Selling eBay Live!, Community, and Presence in the eBay-ana Category

eBay extends consumer identities and fan and brand communities by linking the eBay Live! board, conferences, and eBay-ana category. This system is interactive and responsive because items from the convention are listed while the conference is still occurring. There is an eBay-ana category under "Collectibles > Advertising" on the ebay.com site. There are also eBay-ana categories on the German and United Kingdom sites. eBay did not offer the eBay-ana category in the United States until 2005, even though sellers have been listing convention materials since 2002.[143] Before the advent of the category, Barbara

Shaugnessy advised readers to "simply search eBay with the key words, eBay Live, and you'll get a sense of the collecting and trading frenzy associated with these items."[144] Expressions of excitement about eBay: On Location suggest these processes will continue. People who engage with eBay items by acquiring them at conferences or buying, selling, and producing them are connected to the site and to collectors of the brand. eBay increases the absorbing kinds of consumption that occur with collecting and are facilitated by the setting because eBay-ana objects represent aspects of eBay and thus stand in for fandom and collecting.[145]

eBay facilitates the eBay-ana market by offering large amounts of swag at conferences. Employees then counsel individuals to find materials on the site.[146] The company also provides employees with many eBay-specific products and sanctions selling them. While a personal gift from Whitman or another executive is expected to have a personal value and be displayed in the employee's office or cubicle, the overproduction and distribution of products make it difficult to retain everything. In addition, individuals sell eBay-ana after leaving the company because they no longer need to display company spirit in the form of branded items. For instance, denverain offers a "huge assortment of eBay collectibles" amassed while working for eBay and argues that "it's time to get rid of all the stuff collecting dust."[147] After working at eBay for five and a half years, arubadubis "collected a lot of wonderful and rare eBay memorabilia" and wants "it out of" the "house."[148] These former employees no longer have to be eBay-identified and discard objects and the accompanying brand community associations. Such processes offer members of the eBay brand community opportunities to get closer conceptually to their beloved brand and company, but they offer this tie while suggesting the limits of employees' investments and the ways they opt out of the system when they are not being paid to identify. In these cases, identification and detachment are interlocked.

Most eBay-ana buyers and sellers indicate the value of collections and importance of completing the set. For example, dottie, who bid on the "ONLY eBay Live pinback" she "didn't collect during the convention," "Won it for $42.00 and some change," and completed her collection.[149] Attendees work as intermediaries for eBay collectors who are invested in extending their collection but cannot obtain all the material or go to the conferences. The seller lllo80551g4rwb, who already had a "set," coaxed prospective buyers that "now it's time to get yours."[150] aleegold advertised an auction for a "lanyard PLUS all the pins" that the seller is "here collecting for you."[151] Sellers emphasize owning collections, but the buyer's work in constituting it is depicted as less important. This is distinctly different from the majority of collecting cultures in which individuals respect collectors who work to find, organize, and maintain items and groups. According to Susan Stewart, "It is not acceptable to simply purchase a collection *in toto*, the collection must be acquired in a serial manner."[152] The cultural move away from appreciating the work in forming a collection is partially due to the changes facilitated by sites like eBay.[153]

Buying and owning items, rather than being located in a particular place, are associated with eBay collectors' experiences. Sellers promise that listings and collections situate buyers at the conference. gailcat1 offered "a deluxe package of collectibles from the convention" for individuals who "weren't able to attend Ebay Live 2007."[154] Like the tourist souvenirs Danielle M. Lasusa studies, eBay-ana collectibles "are thought of as an extension of that experience or location, and play the important role of serving as empirical evidence that one has actually visited."[155] For instance, possessions_ recycled, who "spent 3 days of touring booths and speaking and enjoying the experience," says that buyers "can feel" like they "were there" by buying the items.[156] eBay assists in these narratives about "being there" by depicting sites and historical events from Boston on its pins and cards for the 2007 eBay Live! conference. eBay-ana items thus function as mementos of experiences that buyers have not inherently had and as souvenirs they have not directly collected. These selling practices extend the aspects of virtual settings where visceral experiences and notions of being in specific spaces have flexible relationships with situated materialities. This is related to "on-demand" sculptural castings of people's game avatars, which can be ordered on a variety of Internet sites and provide a concretized record of individuals' virtual identities.[157]

Buyers are also offered a form of access to eBay employees through collecting. Sellers indicate that signatures, clothing, and images deliver traces of employees' embodiment. This is similar to the ways fans collect materials and even bodily matter from favorite media and music stars. For instance, a cohort of eBay sellers presented a residue of Britney Spears in the form of gum that she purportedly chewed and spit out.[158] In a related manner, Griffith offered a version of himself constituted from artifacts when he listed "Griff's Cool Mylar Blazer From eBay Live 2007."[159] The "high winning bidder not only gets the blazer," he wrote, but "they will also receive . . . a signed full color photo" of him "in the jacket taken during the keynote." This glittering jacket stands in for Griffith but also represents his sexuality in more acceptable ways. It associates his sexual citizenship with fashion, consumerism, and his labor for the company rather than with male partners and sex acts. He has not "autographed the jacket but the high bidder can request a signature to be placed in a location of their choice (on the blazer silly . . . lapel or inside the collar for example)." With this comment, Griffith acknowledges people's visual and tactile interests in his body and slightly averts the gaze. Women engage with Griffith as if he is sexually available and work to situate him in a form of closet. For instance, a female fan asked him to marry her at a 2007 keynote address.[160]

Griffith is not the only employee who has eBay fans. Cards signed by Whitman and Omidyar that were listed on "the same day" as the 2003 keynote sold "for a 'Buy It Now' price of $124.95."[161] jenuinelyjill offered "an Officially Autographed Meg Whitman Collector Card" that she "stood in line waiting for Meg to sign," suggesting that her personal engagement and Whitman's mark increased the value of the card.[162] Another seller, toys2keep, described the frenzy generated by Omidyar's presence at the conference and the importance of celebrity executives. In "the confusion," Omidyar "started signing Meg's card instead of his own" and toys2keep "inadvertently ended up with the ever-so-rare 'Pierre Sig on Meg Card' . . . any takers? LOL."[163] Members joke about their belief that signed eBay-ana items are unique, rare, and valuable. At the same time, they testify to their investments in these objects and conviction that autographed items further connect them to the executives and brand.

eBay-ana is envisioned as enriching owners' lives by invoking or even replicating conference experiences and as something that can fund eBay attendance. For instance, postalrainey3 asks potential buyers to "HELP ME PAY FOR MY TRIP TO EBAY LIVE! BOSTON."[164] ion_treasures advises that "you can probably resell some/all of your pins/trading cards after the show and make back more than the registration cost."[165] The "freebies will be worth more packaged away and brought out in 10 years," biggbill believes.[166] These sellers identify collecting as an investment, a tactical process, and a way of connecting to eBay. Nevertheless, wmack2 identifies the pins as valueless and pin collecting as a base activity by asking, "WHAT THE HELL ARE YOU SUPPOSED TO DO WITH THEM??? WEAR THEM??? HOW VALUABLE DO YOU HONESTLY THINK THEY WILL BE???"[167] These critiques and anti-fan positions have some validity. Autographed cards used to sell for more than 100

U.S. dollars, but a trading card signed by Omidyar sold for only $3.99 in 2007.[168] This shift in the market reflects negatively on eBay and the brand community. It points to waning enthusiasm for the site and its community.

Disgruntled Fan, Anti-fan, and Anti-brand Community Critiques

There are disgruntled fan, anti-fan, and anti-brand community engagements with eBay. In Candice R. Hollenbeck and George M. Zinkhan's consumer activism research, they identify anti-brand communities that "typically focus on one dominant brand or corporation," "are nongeographically bound communities based on a structured set of social relationships," and voice "opposition to corporate domination."[169] For the fan studies scholar Jonathan Gray, "fans' apparent opposites," or anti-fans, are "those who refuse to let their family watch a show, who campaign against a text, or who spend considerable time discussing why a given text makes them angry to the core."[170] Derek Johnson develops this model and distinguishes between "anti-fans who hate a program (without necessarily viewing it)" and "disgruntled fan factions who hate episodes, eras, or producers because they perceive a violation of the larger text they still love."[171] There is a dearth of research on these critical positions but such notions help elaborate individuals' resistances to eBay and the functions of criticism.

Negative assessments are visible aspects of eBay listings, About Me sites, feedback reviews, and forum posts. Ina Steiner critiques eBay because she expects a noncommercial setting and more authentic community. Her disgruntled fan critiques, like the interrogations in news forums, are based on perceived conflicts between eBay's ethos and practices. The convention, she suggests, "was all about hype" (including the deployment of "the word 'community'"), "was a made-for-TV event," and the "words 'Mary Kay' and 'Amway'" were used "more than a few times to describe the spirit of the event."[172] howtooster also resists eBay's culture of community and enthusiasm and positions himself somewhere between a disgruntled fan and an anti-fan. He plans to "be the guy" at the conference "wearing a t-shirt, one side will say 'I HATE EBAY' and the other will say 'I WAS SCAMMED BY EBAY.'"[173] Thus, howtooster proposes anti-fan and anti-brand items that provide a counterpoint to positively branded people.

Disgruntled fans, anti-fans, and anti-brand community members are part of eBay rather than articulating separate spheres, but forum members ordinarily dismiss their critical commentary. Although fiberwireguy began his own participation on the board as an opponent of eBay's normalizing tendencies, he notes that howtooster's "T-shirt will catch everyone's eye. Especially" if standing "at the buffet next to the sour grapes."[174] creations1106 feels that howtooster has "a sorry attitude," is "looking for someone to blame," should "stay away and leave the room for the business minded folks," and instead "try www.Ifeelsorryformyself.com."[175] In these instances, members work to protect the company's brand and reputation by trying to erase critical participants from the setting. Even after individuals in other settings were widely critiquing the company, many members in the eBay Live! forum mandated positive comments.

Members protect their enthusiastic positions and reasons for being attached by blaming consumer critics rather than the company. They become evaluators of the critics, or anti-anti-fans. There are cycles and levels of critique and resistance rather than a clear dyadic structure. For instance, creations1106 interrogates howtooster's critique by examining one of the seller's listings. creations1106 determines that his "problem" is that the listing is "a non creative auction with no thought or concern behind it."[176] dennis2kang notes that howtooster's "44 negatives" explain his comments.[177] Of course, some of the popular, enthusiastic, and award-winning members, as I suggested in chapter 1, have more negative reviews than howtooster and therefore have their own anti-fans. When wjkski lists reasons for not attending the conference, other posters wonder, if "Ebay makes you so upset, why do you still use it?"[178] chainmaillady gleefully replies that those who do not attend because of problems provide "MORE ROOM FOR THE REST OF US!"[179] Such posters do not admit that eBay controls a great deal of the Internet auction trade, and sellers are not always economically able to abandon their positive feedback and other labor. They imagine fans and brand community members to be expendable. However, howtooster rightly critiques such behavior by commenting that the "optimists don't allow room to hear anything negative without getting upset. What happened to their good attitude?"[180] Active eBay members, like the brand community members considered by Algesheimer, Dholakia, and Herrmann, believe that "belonging" requires "compliance and an obligation to think and act in certain ways."[181] These forms of ostracizing and controlling participants provide consumer critics with sites from which to interrogate eBay and its ethos. eBay's and its members' assertions about goodness structure the site and are flaws in the system that disgruntled fans, anti-fans, and anti-brand community members exploit.

Conclusion: Seasonal Products, Brands, and Fans

eBay Live! has produced seasonal fans and unintentionally highlighted ambivalent and resistant engagements. Most comments to the forum appear
around the time of the conference. The trade in eBay-ana during and after
the conference is also brisk, but fewer items are listed or sold a few months
after the convention. eBay-ana, which invokes the conference for people who
cannot attend and articulates members as fans, is a seasonal product. Members become less eBay-identified and adopt other attachments and passions
when the conference is not occurring. This may make the more frequent eBay:
On Location conferences productive. Yet eBay has not dedicated a forum
to eBay: On Location or related events. The shifting forms of fan engagement that happen with eBay also occur in media fandoms, according to the
research of Matt Hills, because individuals change the texts to which they
are attached.[182] Cyclical fandoms, disgruntled fans, anti-fandoms, and anti-
brand communities are related to the ways members disidentify. While eBay
wants to keep members endlessly attached and investing more—whether by
purchasing goods, listing items, or working on the boards—the company
now appears to recognize that eBay Live! is not fully adequate to this task.[183]

Some commentators propose that the shift from eBay Live! to eBay:
On Location will lessen critiques of the company and the site. However,
funboy1227 humorously relates the change to the possibilities and problems
of political consumerism. According to him, "Ebay Live was cancelled because
there was concern that the local farmers would be unable to supply enough
tomatoes to be thrown at Ebay Manglement. Chilean & Peruvian Farmers are
protesting this decision, as they feel that they would have been able to profit
by" supplying "Ebayers with the needed tomatoes."[184] In funboy1227's critical account, the company foils possible markets. eBay members raise similar
concerns about the ways the company prevents an array of sellers and selling
strategies. eBay's refusal to engage such critiques and change its policies reveals its corporate rather than community structure. There is no established
method through which to address these conflicts or allow members to participate in site decisions.

The more communicative members of consumer communities become,
according to Robert V. Kozinets's marketing research, "the more activist their
activity."[185] eBay fans are highly communicative. Many of them participate in
forums and produce narratives, identities, and objects that have significant
value and meanings within eBay fan and brand communities. Some eBay

members perform consumer critiques, but participants tend to replicate the corporate brand and its meanings. eBay fandoms thus work through connections and consensus with the company and its values. As Marc Andrejevic argues in his study of fan sites, "*All* audiences are active, although perhaps not in the progressive sense the term has come to imply."[186] Internet settings facilitate "strategies for promoting, harnessing, and exploiting the productivity" of fans. eBay, craigslist, and other Internet settings have methods to tap into and control members' attachments. eBay manages members through its discourse about community, work, and goodness and such structures as the conferences and forums. craigslist uses similar narratives about belonging. In the next chapter, I provide a detailed account of how eBay addresses everyone and configures members as heteronormative individuals. Sellers of wedding dresses repeat and extend eBay's mainstream narratives about weddings and heterosexual relationships. Through these practices, members connect and align themselves with eBay's brand stories and principles. The flaws in these practices also point to possible methods of resistance.

chapter three

You Can "Get It On" eBay

SELLING GENDER, SEXUALITY, AND ORGANIZATIONAL

LOGIC THROUGH THE INTERFACE

Many eBay advertisements indicate that the site supports all identities and realizes all desires. However, eBay uses traditional representations, including depictions of heterosexual couples, to sustain the values of the setting and company. For instance, eBay features engagement rings and wedding dresses on the main parts of its site, in press releases, and in advertisements. It connects these items to gender, heterosexuality, and conceptions of shopping for "the one" and suggests they are key elements of eBay and women's identities and lives. Women repeat these conceptions when using images and narratives about their weddings to sell dresses, mandating perfect bodies and gowns, and describing the wonderful qualities of their husbands. eBay's connection of its site, company, and values to heterosexual marriages has a social and economic influence on members. Its ethos also exceeds the setting as the company and site are further incorporated into the contemporary cultural and political sphere through such things as Meg Whitman's engaging in U.S. politics.

eBay's narratives about engagement rings and wedding dresses do more than distinguish gender and sexuality. eBay links such organizational aspects of its site as the category system, feedback ratings, digital imaging and digitized photography, and color coding to binary gender and heteronormativity. This is even more effective since binary gender and heteronormativity are also organizational, and sometimes institutional and business, logics. Binary gender maintains and produces social stratification and power by mapping a dyadic system onto people, bodies, companies, groups, and other things. Heteronormativity is the assertion of heterosexual privilege and pervasive ordering of existence through inflexible sexual standards.[1] By using the concept of organizational logic, I interrogate the underlying structures of businesses, which assert gender and heterosexual norms, and the larger ways things are categorized in Internet settings and other spheres. eBay's gendered and heterosexual organizational logic includes the methods through which the company structures individuals, the ways it organizes things into men's and women's categories, the deployment of engagements and marriages in its founding mythos and advertising, and its claims to equally honor everyone. Critiques of such corporate and social structures are imperative. As Joan Acker and other feminist academics note, society often views companies and their rules and procedures as gender-neutral, equally acknowledging everyone, and considerations of gender and sexuality as forced on or tangential to the organization and analysis.[2]

eBay configures buyers, sellers, and viewers as heterosexuals and supports its organizational logic when featuring engagement rings and wedding dresses on the main parts of the site, in press releases, and in advertising. eBay thereby produces members, technologies, and the site. In a related manner, Steve Woolgar demonstrates how technology designs set constraints upon users' actions.[3] Technologies are imagined to be unbiased tools and to equally serve everyone, and in the case of eBay to enable "Whatever it is," while providing clear messages about the identity of users. eBay's and members' portrayals, as I suggest in the remaining chapters, work with and against each other in configuring the gender, race, and sexuality of participants and constraining their positions and roles. Advertising is an important aspect of this process. It asserts corporate logics; links objects and cultural roles to specific consumer groups; articulates gender, race, and sexuality positions; and coaxes categorized consumers to buy particular goods.[4] Advertising has "consistently reflected prevailing views of appropriate gender relations and heterosexual norms," argues the media studies scholar Katherine Sender, "both endorsing 'proper' femininity and masculinity and yoking these to the heterosexual dyad."[5] In doing this, advertising and related institutions affirm heterogender—a gender system that couples male with female and thereby asserts heterosexuality.[6]

Engagements and weddings, with their normative, moral, and consumerist mandates, are an obvious structure for eBay to deploy. Ramona Faith Oswald, who studies lesbian and gay family structures, describes how "society privileges heterosexual marriages, and thus weddings link the personal decision to marry with an institutional heterosexual privilege carrying profound social, legal, financial, and religious benefits."[7] Critical considerations of heteronormativity and heterogender are important because they show the means through which heterosexual privilege is incorporated into society and the ways these advantages pervasively and insidiously order everyday existence.[8] In this chapter, I address how eBay asserts its organizational logic and configures members by using representations of engagements and weddings. Literature on weddings and sexuality suggests how the company and its members ordinarily work together in instituting stable and traditional women's roles.[9] eBay's reliance on members can also undermine its organizational logic. For instance, eBay's linking of social selling to normative bliss is disturbed by sellers' depictions of grimy objects and failed relationships. The critical literature on dirt and disorder points to some of the ways eBay's normative assertions break down. Sellers' descriptions of weight gains, dirty dresses, broken marriages, and images that do not do objects justice articulate expected conventions and remind members that normative narratives are connected to failed and resistant activities.

Imaging eBay Weddings

eBay's apocryphal founding story, and the concept that configures the site and company's notion of community, is that Pierre Omidyar started eBay as a kind of love token so his fiancée, Pam Wesley, could trade Pez dispensers. His design proved to be economically profitable and purportedly successful in facilitating his marriage. eBay continues this founding narrative in its Valentine's Day gift finder, which associates shopping and the site's functions with Pez dispensers depicting Kermit the Frog and Miss Piggy that stand in for Omidyar, Wesley, and the desire for Pez trading (figure 1 on p. 14).[10] Through the paired dispensers, which are correlated to "Male" and "Female" gift options, eBay interlinks consumerism, the eBay community, heterosexuality, and Omidyar and Wesley's romance. Members retell the founding story, connect their participation and romantic relationships to his design, and make the myth more real. By employing such practices, the eBay company and many members collaboratively configure the site as having a heterosexual lineage and being heterosexual.

Whitman supports the relationship between eBay and traditional gender and sexuality positions by identifying as a wife and mother.[11] For instance, while running for governor of California, Whitman explained her poor voting record to constituents by arguing that she "was focused on raising a family" and on her "husband's career."[12] She configures eBay as a community that supports family and prescribed particularities of boyhood when she describes buying and selling "old sporting equipment on eBay, especially when the boys were younger. They would outgrow hockey skates, they would outgrow skis, they'd outgrow sneakers, they'd outgrow everything. You know how boys grow so fast."[13] Such gender and sexuality narratives are part of early conceptions of virtual community. Indeed, Howard Rheingold situates virtual community in relationship to his home life, wife, and child.[14]

eBay regularly depicts wedding rings in site advertisements. These citations support eBay's association of the site with heterosexual engagements, weddings, and marriages. NetLingo dictionary and a variety of newspapers quote eBay's promotional material about how many "diamond rings" are sold on the site every hour.[15] Jim Griffith notes that a "diamond ring is purchased every two minutes," even though the site has higher sales numbers.[16] eBay's "Build Your Bling" competition enables members to vote on the engagement-ring and wedding-ring designs submitted by participants, viewers to buy material versions of the sketches, and the winning designer to get the "dream ring."[17] Through this contest, eBay gets members to generate, vet, and invest in brand community products. On the main part of the site, eBay furthers its connection to heteronormativity and inquires, "Getting engaged? Let eBay's Wedding Jewelry page help you."[18] The related links offer "Testimonials" about how sellers of engagement rings provide reliability, quality, and reasonable prices.[19] In this narrative, buying reinforces a man's relationship with a woman, so that she "loves the ring and she loves him." eBay's pink "banner" advertisements for engagement rings, which address women by using a gender-specific color, also link the site and auctions to future marriages. Women are assured that eBay can resolve their fears that they will "be single forever" by enabling couples to reasonably acquire the accoutrements of heteronormative relationships.[20] All of this positions eBay and its sellers as good community members, supporters of Omidyar's site ethos, and matchmakers.

The issue of *eBay Magazine* from June 2000, which is culturally marked as the time of year when marriages occur, includes a section on the "bridal wave." The reporter Theresa Howard argues that, in addition to "being a marketplace, eBay has spawned marriages, collectors' clubs and even help in tracing family genealogies."[21] Maggy Wolfe and Brad Aspling—a white heterosexual couple who used the site to get engaged—were featured in company announcements and married in front of thousands of attendees during the eBay Live! conference in 2004.[22] Conference participants could "attend the wedding of two people who met on the community boards. (Now that's doing it eBay.)."[23] Through this text, eBay asserts, as it indicates in other venues, that individuals should be heterosexual and in a monogamous relationship to perform eBay culture correctly. eBay's use of the term "it" in these announcements and notion of "doing it eBay" are related to the company's "Whatever it is, you can get it on eBay" and "Come to think of it, eBay" slogans. However, this text immediately relates sex to sanctified heterosexual unions rather than a variety of sexualities. eBay argues that it makes sense to situate the wedding at the convention, to "do it eBay," and for the couple to be "be married within the Community that brought them together," because the "two met on eBay, and Brad sniped Maggy's engagement ring on eBay."[24] According to Aspling, getting married at the conference gave them the "chance to get married in front of" their "friends in the community" where they "met."[25] In these instances, eBay's community and ethos are equated to the processes of heterosexual marriages, and members are committed to the site through the brand community activities of reading about and attending the wedding.

eBay uses weddings to personalize and individualize eBay and further its community appeal, even though contemporary weddings are consumerist structures and ordinarily require a significant monetary investment. Weddings are thereby a successful way for eBay to emphasize its community-oriented and non-corporate profile while supporting its underlying economic motivations. However, eBay's and Aspling's claims that the site facilitates marriages are disputable. eBay states that Aspling and Wolfe met on eBay, but Wolfe provides a different story, which troubles another one of eBay's origin myths. According to Wolfe, they "met on match.com and he proposed in an auction."[26] By highlighting eBay's apocryphal stories, I hope to demonstrate how the company crafts narratives to sustain its relationship to normative gender and sexuality, configure the site, and support its organizational logic. eBay's wedding narratives are therefore not inherent or politically neutral aspects of the site and company.

eBay's advertising campaigns reference diverse desires and perpetuate heterosexuality and normative sexual citizenship. *Dress*, a television commercial from the "Come to think of it, eBay" campaign that began in 2009, uses a green putting range and red bedroom to articulate separate gendered spheres and shopping experiences.[27] In the commercial, the comic Kevin Hart indicates that his wife should have spent less money on a dress. She provocatively lounges on the bed while hearing his critique, directs him to feed the children, and expels him from the room. By dismissing his partner's eBay purchase, Hart foils their romantic evening. An approving relationship to eBay is thereby coded as good for "it" and erotic heterosexual relationships. The commercial *Camera*, from the same campaign, presents a more queer reading and associates eBay with traditional masculinity and heterosexuality. In it, the comics Michael Showalter and Michael Ian Black are in a tattoo parlor. One of them has wisely and inexpensively bought his camera on eBay. The bad shopper spent more, attempts to get a shark tattoo and remain masculine, and is foiled. As the successful eBay shopper advises, the tattoo is of a dolphin rather than a shark, and he is "going to look so good in a half shirt" because "it is just so feminine." Shopping is thus coded as something that can lead to masculine norms or, if improperly handled, mistaken sexualities and queerness.

Some of eBay's "Whatever it is, you can get it on eBay" television spots, from a campaign that started in 2005, also frame the site's promises of bountiful objects and collections with heterosexual unions. This is necessary if eBay wants to maintain its relationship to heteronormativity. The art historian Michael Camille indicates that the boundlessness of collectors' desires, their interest in possessing an ever increasing web of desirable things, "strain the limits of the heterosexual matrix" and "problematize the logic of oppositions structuring it."[28] The eBay television advertisements manage this boundlessness by connecting everyone and "it" to engagement rings and heterosexual unions. In one of the spots, a woman is wearing a diamond engagement ring that spells out the word "it." She mistakenly drops her ring down the drain as her male partner watches (figure 2 on p. 15).[29] The viewer hears the ring hitting varied parts of the drainpipe and sees the apartments that the ring falls through; each is populated by people who own "it"-shaped items. Their shared engagement with "it," and thereby the site, means they live together in an eBay community. In the final sequence, the heterosexual couple is eating an "it"-shaped fish. When the woman puts a bite of fish into her mouth and pulls out the ring, her male partner is delighted. The ring and their looks of wonder connect the couple into a kind of second engagement proposal. In this advertisement, the many desires and community arrangements articulated as being available through eBay are prefaced by and returned to a normative and sanctified heterosexual union.

In another ad, a cloud of pink smoke forming the word "it" and a sultry musical track lure a man from the refrigerator to the bedroom. The narrative frames the man's masculinity in relationship to a shopping platform that is sometimes coded as feminine and to a sequence where the man is lured by a diaphanous pink cloud, or "Whatever it is," but ends up getting "it on." He follows the cloud into the bedroom, where his female partner is clad in a white slip, spraying herself from a perfume flacon shaped like the word "it" and getting ready for a seduction scene. At the end of the commercial, the tagline reads, "Give in to temptation." However, temptation has already been framed in very limited terms. In these spots, the profusion of objects, community arrangements, and desires, which give the individual a variety of collecting choices, are bracketed by normative gender and heterosexual roles and monogamous relationships.

The Power of All of Us site, which is associated with eBay's 2004 campaign, also emphasizes community and heteronormative positions. The site begins with an outlined image of the community and then provides the viewer with a "Welcome to the eBay Community. The Power of All of Us."[30] This is another stand in for everyone. According to an article in the *Chatter* newsletter, eBay "is about millions of human connections," but the company uses a "special effects technique called 'green screen' to create thousands of sellers" in the advertisement.[31] eBay thus figures community where there literally is none. The Power of All of Us site also configures the gender, race, and sexuality of members. It represents the "future of eBay" as a light-skinned mother, father, and two children who are about to travel toward a "community" of architecturally similar houses and desires.[32] While the site's generic outlines of people begin as a stand in for everyone, they are subsequently filled in with gendered and raced individuals. Members are thereby encouraged to occupy specific roles.

eBay's *Clocks* and *Maze* television spots, from the "Power of All of Us" campaign, also render buyers and sellers moving from fields of everyone to heterosexual unions. The *Clocks* advertisement begins and ends with a man standing in front of his collection. As the commercial unfolds, the prospective buyer is presented with everyone as his home, street, neighborhood, and landscape are filled with potential sellers and clocks. Selecting an item from the eBay community allows the buyer to meet a woman, briefly join hands with her, and obtain the object from her hands.[33] In *Maze*, a woman's confused search through an incomprehensible labyrinth of everything is resolved when she finds "the one thing" she wants "from the one person who has it" and is united with a man across a bundled rug.[34] eBay uses these advertisements to relate individual and community engagements with objects to heteronormative romances between people, make a connection between the "thousands of people who love what you love" and "the one" partner who is right for an individual, and indicate that eBay can enable the individual to "find them." The arrangement between buyers and sellers is even referred to as "trading partners."[35] The company uses these texts to support its narratives about eBay being a community of everyone, constitute the normal citizen as heterosexual, and institute heterosexuality as a necessary condition for full eBay citizenship.[36]

Gender and Sexuality Conventions in Other Settings

eBay's allusions to everyone and production of normative positions encourage evaluations of the ways other Internet sites generate conventions. For instance, early writings about the Internet tend to claim that everyone can connect equitably because of Internet-facilitated anonymity. According to Virginia Shea's often quoted "Netiquette" guidelines, individuals are not judged according to their age, body size, class, and race in Internet settings.[37] The Jargon File attributes hackers' gender and racial tolerance to their engagement with text-based communication.[38] More recent work identifies Internet-based production opportunities as democratizing and providing young adults, women, and people of color with the same chances as those who have traditionally been able to express their opinions.[39] Such indications incorrectly make it seem as if power discrepancies are the fault of individual engagements rather than cultural and structural inequities. Scholarship on GLBTQ consumerism, sexual citizenship, and configuring users provides methods for analyzing such promises and representations. For instance, Sender demonstrates that advertising—and I would argue that most websites function as a form of self-advertising—support and continue normative conceptions of gender and heterosexual relationships.[40]

Adesso, which sells input devices, uses three digital images to advertise its products, represent the company, and configure individuals (figure 5).[41] In the middle image, a young white woman and man are dressed in a wedding gown and tuxedo, surrounded by family, engaged in normative forms of connectivity, and getting married. Since the depicted wedding is a union

5. Adesso, "Adesso --> Home," 29 March 2009

between a man and woman and facilitator of familial connectivity, it evokes and stands in for technological connectivity. The image therefore associates heterosexual relationships with technologies. As Sender's analysis and my critique of eBay indicate, company advertisements tend to support normative roles and link people's binary gender position to their presumed place in a heterosexual couple. On either side of the Adesso wedding image, parents are teaching their children how to use computers as the representation instructs consumers in heterosexuality. Adesso establishes technology as part of the normative family, or even constituting it, and literalizes the notion of a "family" of products. Adesso provides a genesis legend for technologies and gender and heterosexual lessons for consumers. This is similar to eBay's founding mythos.

Many other companies also code individuals who use technologies as family-oriented and occupying traditional roles. For instance, Logitech advertises its WiLife Video Security system, which allows individuals to "Make sure 'all is well,'" with an image of a man in an office monitoring a computer screen.[42] Via the monitor, he watches his home and, most important, as emphasized by their size and position on the monitor, his wife and child. The image establishes a difference between men who skillfully use technologies and women and young children who are protected and watched through technologies. By featuring this image and conveying the idea that the technology allows individuals to make sure "all is well," Logitech references everyone and everything but articulates the heterosexual family as "all" and everything. Such claims to address everyone are related to eBay's assertion, "Whatever it is, you can get it on eBay," references to profusion and varied sexualities, underlying coding of "it" as heterosexuality, and indication that everyone gets/is trained in heterosexuality on the site. In the afterword about craigslist, I continue to consider how the concept of everyone is associated with sexual freedom and the ways it is used to justify rules and regulate members.

eBay and other companies use color coding to configure viewers—directing them to appropriate parts of sites and instructing them. Colors help to articulate the purportedly different behaviors of individuals and organize them into pairs. For instance, the Geni site deploys color coding to establish heterogender. Geni offers a variety of web-based tools to produce family trees; claims to be a place "for your family to build your family tree, preserve history and share your lives"; and advertises with the tagline "everyone's related."[43] Despite Geni's assertion of universal delivery and applicability, the login depiction prevents some individuals from being related and constituting family. The login provides an image of a blue rectangle, which is labeled "Your Father," joined to a pink rectangle, which is labeled "Your Mother." Viewers are provided with a registration box that derives from this union and are told, "You – Start Here." They are also required to choose "male" or "female" for their identity position. By telling individuals that they "Start" from heterosexual arrangements, the site informs viewers that they begin with and are produced from heterosexuality. The log-in diagram and other site mechanisms thereby assert an organizational logic that includes binary gender and heterosexuality. Geni associates relationships with reproduction.

Flickr claims to enable "new ways of organizing photos and video," because once people "switch to digital, it is all too easy to get overwhelmed."[44] In indicating this, Flickr distinguishes itself from the sorts of photographic and organizational logics, fixed in albums, scrapbooks, wallets, and photo frames, that produce developmental histories where children are transformed into heterosexual couples, get married, and have families of their own. From its "inception in daguerreotypy," according to Shawn Michelle Smith, a photography historian and theorist, "the photographic image has been conceptualized as a means of preserving family history and of documenting family genealogy."[45] Flickr indicates its difference from traditional photography but uses the tagline "flickr loves you," links members to the site, and equates this engagement to a relationship or romance. Flickr, in a manner similar to eBay, relates personal connections between the company and members to normative gender and sexuality roles. Its "favicon," the specially designed icon that appears in the browser's URL bar and stands in for the site, further ties photo organizing to heterosexual pairing. It features a blue dot and a pink dot, or a man and a woman, paired together. This reference to heterosexuality also appears in Flickr's blue and pink logo and other texts. In a related way, Phanfare, a photo and "video sharing network for families," connects its setting and photography to heteronormativity.[46] It states, "From wedding bells to the arrival of a new baby, phanfare has the perfect album style to showcase all of your treasured photos and videos." Photographs and photography may be digitally reconfigured. However, these sites still connect photo-like objects and digital processes to families and weddings and thereby assert their role in producing traditional gender and sexuality positions. These unreliable addresses to everyone encourage further critical analysis of the politics of these texts.

Selling Values and Norms

Technology companies use narratives about everyone to stand in for heterosexual relationships and conventional forms of identity and desire. We generally agree that there has been a change in values and norms relating to women's roles since the second wave of the women's movement. Nevertheless, Sherril Horowitz Schuster argues, the increase in bridal magazines (and now websites), consumer shows, and wedding-themed films and advertising indicate "that the traditional bridal ritual and its myths are still salient," and we are collaboratively producing the most traditional roles.[47] eBay's popular narratives and Adesso's images can be added to Schuster's list and her research concerns. They perpetuate traditional roles while claiming to deliver new interfaces and technologies.

eBay chose the wedding as one of its key structuring devices because weddings, as Dawn H. Currie's research on the subject indicates, are "a good example of the increasing commodification of ritual elements of social life in western culture" and "big business."[48] The consumer researchers Cele Otnes and Tina M. Lowrey describe weddings as "significant consumption rituals within American culture."[49] Weddings manage to "'marry' the tenets of consumer culture and romantic love." Weddings are also moments where family and community are constituted as consumers. These families, and the forms of buying they facilitate, are ordinarily envisioned as good and supporting traditional values. This is important to eBay's design, because, as Cohen indicates, Omidyar wanted the site to function in the same manner as his personal values, including his belief in goodness.[50] Through such organizational logics, Omidyar's discourse about community is related to his articulation of the setting's values, establishment of normative beliefs, and the model of trust that is needed for people to participate in economic transactions without physically engaging items or sellers.

Computer designers and marketers, as demonstrated by my analysis of the Adesso and Logitech campaigns, connect the organizational logic of the heterosexual imaginary and its wedding myths to the structures of Internet settings. The heterosexual imaginary, as Chrys Ingraham's feminist and sexuality studies research indicates, is "that way of thinking which conceals the operation of heterosexuality in structuring gender and closes off any critical analysis of heterosexuality as an organizing institution."[51] eBay's heterosexual imaginary, its purported representation of reality and everyone, relies on romantic conceptions of heterosexuality to render the illusion of well-being and mask the specific conditions of the site and its members. The heterosexual imaginary and romance are therefore important to eBay, especially as members become disenfranchised with the site and its rules. eBay justifies consumerism by equating it with heteronormative love and heterosexually infused caring behaviors, including Omidyar's supposed design of the site as a love token. At the same time, as the sociologist Amy L. Best argues, "romance carries tremendous ideological force; it naturalizes and normalizes" heterosexuality and gender and "shapes and organizes modern constructions of self."[52] Normative romance is a key aspect of eBay's advertising structures, as well as a larger thematic in Internet settings, and has a significant impact on eBay's organizational logic, the meaning of the site, and the ways members understand themselves and their position in the setting.

The Wedding Dresses Category

eBay's wedding category and "Wedding Dresses" subcategory, which is listed under "Clothing, Shoes & Accessories > Wedding Apparel & Accessories," repeat the site's normative narratives.[53] The category claims to have "everything a bride needs from wedding dresses, veils, tiaras and garters to flower girl dresses and ring bearer pillows. You can even outfit your whole bridal party with our tuxedos, bridesmaid dresses and ring bearer outfits."[54] Through this text, eBay codes wedding shopping, including outfits for men and children, as the bride's job, constituting the "bridal party," and as fulfilling feminine desires. At the same time, the category offers the opportunity to conceptually connect members' weddings to Omidyar's marriage. Wolfe's and Aspling's searches of the site to shop for wedding items and their eBay Live! wedding further the idea that the setting facilitates marriages and intimate connections to eBay.

In the rest of this chapter, I study the ways individuals list wedding gowns rather than the methods used by Chinese gown producers and U.S. bridal shops, which are significant vendors in this category. This allows me to analyze how people sell items that are culturally coded as deeply intimate and conceptually related to the eBay site. Sellers often use the wedding dresses category to present virtual photographic albums of their wedding ceremonies and families. In these instances, the listings have a personal function. Sellers also personalize items to further social selling and promise potential buyers a connection to community and romantic history. These listings provide traditional social scripts about what weddings look like and how women are supposed to perform and thereby normalize future shoppers and brides. For example, sellers indicate that dresses can be part of a "dream wedding," are "ready for your Special Day," "will make you feel like a princess," and are examples "of bridal romance and femininity!"[55] Sellers' commentary about fantasy weddings and feeling like a princess continue the representations in wedding-dress advertisements, children's toys, and popular films about weddings.

Sellers also convey traditional conceptions of weddings and gendered roles through digital images. Bridal photographs, as Schuster states, have an impact on women by instructing them in how to enact the portrayed role.[56] In doing this, they configure the user. For instance, carolineprezzano helps women envision the bridal role, and the sorts of femininity women are supposed to embody, by presenting an image of her thin form articulated and shaped by a fitted wedding gown and contrasting sash.[57] She holds a bouquet of white flowers and stands fixedly with the train arranged behind her. In such depictions, women emphasize their femaleness and purported connection to nature with sprays of flowers and position in green park settings. An image of carolineprezzano's partner helping her enter the limousine further highlights her limited mobility and need for assistance. Of course, it is the gown rather than any aspect of her psyche or physiognomy that produces this confinement. A similar feminine role is conveyed in emelias2242's dressing-room scene.[58] She demurely and submissively looks down, with her dress, sash, and pose emphasizing her delicateness. Women and listings work to replicate these positions. For instance, carolineprezzano "would love nothing more than for someone else to experience their special day in this memorable gown" and to thereby enact the portrayed role.

Sellers accompany representations of traditional weddings with accounts of guests complimenting brides and dresses. carolineprezzano has "not stopped hearing about how stunning this dress was." Such narratives act as reminders of the commentary and evaluations that brides experience. According to the research of Jeffery Sobal, Caron Bove, and Barbara Rauschenbach, "The role of the bride especially involves observations and scrutiny in the central spotlight of the wedding."[59] Personal and family remembrances of weddings, which are aided by photographic "documentation" of women's bodies, include recollections of the brides' weight. Professional photographers have also "developed strategies to manage their subjects' presentations of their weight, with camera angles, lighting, and posing used to create stylized pictures that portray the weights of people at weddings in socially desirable ways."[60] For instance, carolineprezzano's three-quarter pose and the contrasting background emphasize her slenderness. Charles Lewis's research on wedding photography points to how such images "are nearly always constructing the conventional: it is more or less the same fairy tale for each couple."[61] Sellers reinstitute conventional gender and sexuality scripts when reusing wedding advertisements and photographs in listings.

Sellers also produce normative conceptions of bodies by advertising dresses with a "flair" that "will hide any hip area that you might think is 'fat'" and "GOOD AT HIDING MIDSECTION FLAWS. VERY SEXY DRESS!"[62] cowboyssting "was so frustrated with" her "size, and evil dress designers," but she "put this dress on and started crying" because she was "beautiful."[63] Nevertheless, encouragements to be beautiful include provisos to hide, constrain, or manage "fat." Sellers' texts are reminders, as indicated by Sobal,

Bove, and Rauschenbach, that many "women would like to lose weight to meet cultural expectations about slimness at their wedding."[64] While these researchers also assert that the process of losing weight before weddings is not discussed, eBay sellers unfortunately connect weddings and dieting. For instance, twopickerz wrote that her "MOST BEAUTIFUL dress" would "not fit" and if she "hadn't already had the invitations printed" she "would've post-poned" the "wedding and dieted until this fit!!"[65] Other women get "too fat to wear" their gown.[66] The size of wedding gowns and the body of brides are an issue in wedding-dress selection because of narratives about the perfect day and because, as the fat studies researcher Rachel Colls indicates, "Obesity and bodily bignesses are associated with particular versions of morality."[67] The people involved in weddings try to articulate a set of values that are different from the cultural coding of obesity because it is associated with a lack of control, messiness, dirtiness, and unreliability. Such attributes endanger the reputation of sellers and eBay.

The wedding-dress industry is fixated on the bodies and weight of future brides and their ability to maintain and manage their weight through the wedding-planning process. Weight shifts mark what is purported to be women's lack of control as well as the imperfectness of the planning period. According to Laura Sloan Patterson, who researches brides and body image, "The actual wedding-dress shopping day (or weekend, or month) causes bouts of depression, followed by unreasonable attempts to shrink oneself into a tiny size."[68] The many dresses that are being offered on eBay because they no longer fit are a record of women's weight gains, dieting, and imperfect relationship with bridal workers and shops. Marisa Corrado's study points to how women's weight gains are "a constant problem for bridal workers."[69] Women "order dresses months in advance" and "seem to gain significant amounts of weight between the time of their first measurements and when the dresses arrive." Corrado also states, "Changing shape is such a widespread problem that most bridal shops make clients sign a contract" that the "shop is not responsible for a new dress." The purported irresponsibility of sellers and brides, who are not able to control bodies, threaten to problematize their roles.

Weight gains — or, in some cases, losses — are not the only unruly behavior women exhibit while planning weddings and listing their dresses on eBay. Women also write about their passionate, and fan-like, desire to obtain the perfect dress. princesa052607 "was obsessed with this dress and wanted it no matter how much it was."[70] autumn_gunnels was listing an "ABSOLUTELY

GORGEOUS WEDDING DRESS!!" that she "fell in love with" and was "so upset" to "only wear it once" because she "worked so hard to buy it."[71] Some women get rid of a dress in favor of another gown because they "decided to go with a renaissance faire theme and this gown is much too formal" or changed their "MIND ON THE DRESS" and are "STUCK WITH THIS ONE."[72] Women get caught up in dress buying, or collecting, and invest both economically and emotionally in their gowns. Women's purportedly obsessive wedding-dress desires and collecting are economically productive for sites like eBay, but they also connect negative cultural conceptions of fans to the positively coded and value-producing aspects of brand cultures.

eBay does not always support these emotional investments in dresses. Its site title offers "Wedding Dresses, cheap wedding dresses and discount wedding dresses items on eBay.com. Find IT on eBay."[73] This title assures women that items are a bargain. However, it thereby challenges sellers' promises that the site will facilitate sumptuous fantasies. eBay's conveyance of cheapness and mass-produced abundance, which is evoked by the reuse of the word "wedding dresses" in the title, is mirrored by the large number of visually similar dresses on the site. Individuals and bridal shops often sell new, sample, and gently worn wedding dresses for less than 50 U.S. dollars, which does not economically communicate their personal value or the special aspects of the event. Of course, dresses are also available in much higher price ranges. The repetitive aspects of the text and images, low prices, and frequent failed auctions do not correlate with women's desires for authenticity and uniqueness. In this category, "IT" literally means normativity and wedding apparel and represents much more complicated unions and arrangements between people. The title and overwhelming number of dresses available in the category represent the problems in moving from the many to "IT."

Searches to find "the one"—both a husband and wedding dress—do not always work so smoothly. The "Power of All of Us" campaign addresses the problem of moving from the many to "IT," or the one item, in *Clocks*, but the man ends up back with his abundant collection. His past and future selections only lead to more searching. In collecting, each item must be unique, part of a group, and that which constitutes the idea of whole. Traditional brides need to find and then wear one dress at the ceremony, but a number of sellers articulate wedding-dress shopping as a form of collecting. For instance, corrieandmike "couldn't decide on only one dress."[74] maileib "went a little crazy shopping" and "ended up buying THREE."[75] julieann4him described herself as "a multiple dress bride (10!) who had to make some very difficult choices!"[76] She was "willing to take the chance and resell if they didn't work out" because she was looking for her "dream dress" and could not "pass up these amazing deals!"[77] In these cases, eBay increases the "intensely involving forms of consumption" that Belk associates with collecting.[78] Bridal magazines and other sources advise women to consult multiple sources for the best price and make personal choices. This results in extensive shopping and collecting. Collections, as Susan Stewart describes the process, are usually acquired sequentially and amassed, but the processes and experiences of eBay wedding-dress shoppers—and, indeed, all shoppers for such garments—do not mesh well with neverending dress collecting and items. The process of buying multiple wedding dresses suggests numerous rather than individual weddings and challenges the conception of "the one."[79]

The wedding dress and rings are usually the most precious material parts of the marriage ritual.[80] As Susanne Friese argues in her wedding dress research, many women's wardrobes include "one piece of clothing that, having been worn once, is seldom worn again but is often highly treasured and especially cared for. This piece of clothing is her wedding dress."[81] Nevertheless, eBay becomes a mechanism in which these treasured dresses regularly circulate. For example, 25chanelgirl's "dress is amazingly stunning."[82] She "got it for a steal," "was kinda skeptical about buying a wedding dress on ebay but this dress was perfect," and now wants "to pass it on to another bride who will love it!!!!" eBay's advertisement about the lost wedding ring, in which the object travels through a system of pipes, represents the flow of goods on eBay. This circulation, particularly in the case of wedding dresses, indicates a cultural shift away from investments in family heirlooms. These relinquished items are a part of Daniel Nissanoff's "new auction culture" that, according to him, will "revolutionize the way we buy, sell, and get the things we really want."[83] In his book on secondary market economies, he advises people to adopt the resale model and assess value in other ways. Wedding-dress sellers evaluate value in a different manner. Dresses are no longer kept because they represent meaningful memories or because they are being saved for children, who are envisioned as mirroring their mothers' commitment. Instead, the "heirloom" may be transformed into what the reporter Paysha Stockton Rhone describes as "just another piece of post-wedding detritus" when wedding dresses are sold on eBay.[84]

For the site to function economically, eBay must support listings of personal items. However, eBay must resist the negative coding that accompanies the unsentimental sale of goods for the company's brand community narratives and values to stand. eBay therefore represents cultural nostalgia and asserts that lost or sold-off items can always be regained. In the *Toy Boat* advertisement, a man uses the eBay interface to recover the plaything he lost as a child. The company's commercial about the engagement ring also assures individuals that everything is retrievable. eBay's corporate display cases in San Jose, California, include the timepiece that the man selected from the female seller in the *Clocks* advertisement. The retention and display of such items conveys the idea that the eBay community maintains and preserves the past. Individuals sell off wedding dresses and other items, but the site's narratives and community features assure individuals that these objects are kept within the eBay community, preserved, and loved.

White Weddings and the Problem of Dirt and Disorder

eBay's wedding-dresses category includes a seemingly neverending series of white gowns, which are usually portrayed on white women. By the turn of the nineteenth century, as Ingraham notes, "White had not only become the standard but had also become laden with symbolism—it stood for purity, virginity, innocence, and promise, as well as power and privilege," and for the conception that women had one partner.[85] Wedding-dress photographers tend to perpetuate these traditional conceptions of families, reproduction, and rituals. However, their images also reveal some problems with attempts to configure members and brides. One of jackool78's images shows her in a white wedding gown with a full skirt and train.[86] Two young girls in full-skirted white outfits smile happily, hold the back of her train, and mirror her garb. The arrangement of the figures, with the girls connected to the bride by a swath of white, evokes the transference of normative gender and sexuality positions from one generation to the next. Nevertheless, these images also reveal the messy and imperfect sets where these actions occur. jackool78's position in a parking lot, with a series of vans in the background and her train dragging along the filthy ground, challenges the "perfect wedding dress" and event she describes.

Sellers risk negatively coding their practices, auctions, and weddings when they associate wedding dresses with dirt and consumer clutter. For example, sport222's "dress was not professionally cleaned" after her wedding.[87] Her long list of dirt and damage includes "three pink lines of discoloration along bust," "two small spots on side of bodice," "under the chiffon layer is a dirt spot," "along bottom hem on back is a brown spot," "a few tiny specks on bottom back," "back bottom hem is dirty," "the inside of the straps" have "some dirty spots," and there "are two rips along the hem." The slip on pinkpinkiesmom's wedding gown "could use cleaning" but she advises prospective buyers not to bother and to get married in a soiled dress because "it will be dirty as soon as you walk outside."[88] These sellers promise to make buyers into prominent and beautiful brides, but they also present imperfect events in which staying clean is an impossible fantasy. This is a problem, since, as the wedding photographer Lori Adalsteinsson notes, the mandate for the bride is "Don't step on the dress; don't get dirt on the dress."[89]

Wedding dresses that are filthy and shown in cluttered surroundings are notable. This is especially the case because eBay uses heterosexual marriages and relationships to stand in for the site's values and organizational logic. Critical theorists argue that dirt and disorder challenge approved identities and stable categories. For instance the feminist philosopher Elizabeth Grosz describes how dirt "signals a site of possible danger to social and individual systems, a site of vulnerability."[90] This is because the pure, as the theorist and psychoanalyst Julia Kristeva notes, is associated with "that which conforms to an established taxonomy; the impure, that which unsettles it, establishes intermixture and disorder."[91] In a similar manner, the anthropologist Mary Douglas identifies dirt as "a kind of compendium category for all events which blur, smudge, contradict, or otherwise confuse accepted classifications. The underlying feeling is that a system of values which is habitually expressed in a given arrangement of things has been violated."[92] Thus, sellers' representations of dirty wedding dresses and other sorts of mess diverge from cultural expectations and threaten to unsettle eBay's systems.

Disorder and boundary disruptions challenge normative standards and organizational structures, but many dresses appear crushed, ungainly, and incongruously situated within obsessive collecting cultures. The dresses literally and figuratively do not fit into sellers' homes. For instance, aquarius12960 poses in a small space between the coffee table, door, and fireplace.[93] The wedding dress is difficult to distinguish and is presented as unimportant, because a large-screen television, fireplace, and drape are all depicted behind it. racefanou812 presents her dress in a cramped family room. The uniqueness of this "perfect" dress is hard to accept.[94] It is depicted along with other accumulation, becoming just another item the seller wants to expulse, and is surrounded by a large-screen television, sports paraphernalia, cosmetics, cat carrier, and gerbil cage. roslynn portrays the wedding dress in front of a television cabinet. Christmas cards hang from the cabinet; Christmas toys are

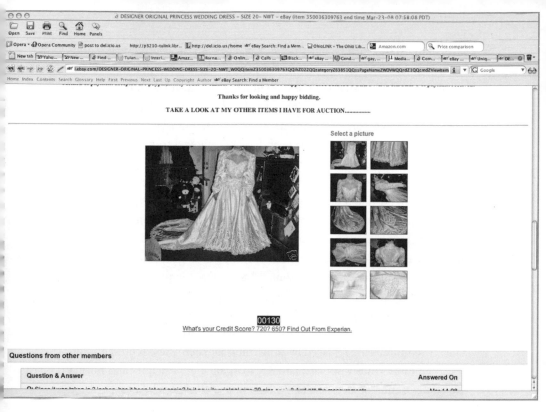

Thanks for looking and happy bidding.

TAKE A LOOK AT MY OTHER ITEMS I HAVE FOR AUCTION...............

Select a picture

00130

Questions from other members

Question & Answer	Answered On

6. roslynn, "DESIGNER ORIGINAL PRINCESS WEDDING DRESS - SIZE 20- NWT," eBay, 13 March 2008

perched above the cabinet and on additional shelves; and such figures as a Santa Claus, a snowman, and a Christmas bear stand on the floor in front of a heavily bedecked tree (figure 6).[95] Such images of clutter and out-of-control collecting challenge eBay's assertion of structure and categories. They also threaten to defile the whiteness and uniqueness of the dress and bride. Clutter is "symbolic dirt or feces," according to Russell W. Belk, Joon Yong Seo, and Eric Li, who conduct research on home chaos: it "provokes disgust and precipitates guilt, shame, and embarrassment."[96] The related cultural condemnation and personal humiliation are more likely to affect women on eBay. Cleaning and organizing are perceived as women's work and used to judge their skills, morals, and identities.[97]

Dresses are visually tainted in other ways. Reflections from objects and physical stains make the dresses look gray, yellowed, or grubby. This undermines their ritual status because, as Nicky Gregson, Kate Brooks, and Louise Crewe's study of used goods shows, certain kinds of secondhand clothing, particularly underwear, stained items, objects with an overpowering odor, and things from the estates of deceased people, threaten to pollute and contaminate physical spaces and the individuals who engage with them.[98] eBay is motivated to control such notions of pollution and requires individuals to clean used items before selling them. The sellers of unwashed gay underwear that I mention in chapter 4 have been largely removed from the site. However, wedding-dress sellers ignore eBay's rules and disrupt the association of the site and members with goodness. Some dresses only have "some dirt on the hem from the floors" but there are also records of women's performances that include more overt forms of failed femininity.[99] For instance, pipoca13's dress "NEEDS TO BE DRY-CLEANED!!!!!!!!!!!!"[100] The dress listed by nuttytoys "needs a cleaning" because it "has stains from walking on train and on base also has wedding cake stains on front."[101] Sellers' accounts of stains and rips show that they did not walk gracefully, eat carefully, and engage in the mannerly behaviors that are expected of brides, and of women more broadly. At such moments, sellers' and photographers' visions of perfect weddings and delicate femininity are replaced by something messier. These representations of dirt and mess thus work against eBay's organizing principles and normative configuration of members and offer some critical possibilities.

The Wedding Dress Guy, eBay, and the Organization of Heterosexuality

eBay also troubles its deployment of normative engagements and weddings when referencing the "Wedding Dress Guy," Larry Star, who depicts himself in a listing wearing what is purported to be his ex-wife's wedding dress.[102] eBay's collectible trading cards include a representation of Star that highlights his sister's involvement in the listing, her indication that "some lucky girl would be glad to have" the wedding dress, and her proposal that "he could make at least enough money for a couple of mariners tickets and some beer."[103] These cards, which also memorialize a seller's attempts to sell one of his kidneys and a child's efforts to get rid of his grandfather's ghost, are designed to represent the quirky aspects of eBay and its social history. At the same time, they strain eBay's moral and organizational limits when not managed. eBay responds to the destabilizing aspects of the wedding-dress narrative, and tries to reaffirm traditional gender positions, by associating Star's sister with the sale of the dress and the male seller with sports and beer. Nevertheless, eBay's production of the site through such narratives is threatened because parts of Star's story, including the statement that his sister helped with the listing and that he has no children with his former spouse, are untrue.[104]

Other male sellers have portrayed themselves in wedding dresses. ajp1999 says he is wearing his ex-wife's dress because "AFTER A 28 YEAR MARRIAGE, THIS WAS ONE OF THE ONLY ITEMS THE JERK DIDN'T STEAL ON HER WAY OUT."[105] He adds, "IT'S A SIZE 6 OR 8 BY THE WAY, WHICH OF COURSE SHE COULDN'T POSSIBLY FIT IN ANYMORE." In his wedding-dress listing, andersonorganization references Star and asserts his normative masculinity. He re-performs large parts of Star's story, offers a "thanks to Larry for help with this auction," labels Star a "hero," and makes fun of his own "'alternative lifestyle' ex."[106] He provides an account of his wife's lesbian relationship and his own cluelessness about the gown, even as he wears it. andersonorganization identifies a world in which he must model the gown and risk the condemnation of his "bar buddies and co-workers" to transform his bad relationship into sports tickets and beer and reassert dyadic gender and sexuality distinctions. The misogyny of Star, andersonorganization, and other male wedding-dress sellers, which takes the form of making fun of the size, hairstyle, or greed of partners, is repeated when readers indicate that andersonorganization's "wife is an ass" and they hope she "puts on about 60 pounds and loses all her hair." Through such comments, these stories are further related to eBay's regulation of sexuality and women's own frustrated accounts of body size.

eBay's wedding-dress trading card does not mention that Star continues to wear the gown at varied events. Julia Wilkinson reports on Star's eBay Live! appearance in 2004 and that the dress looked "even lovelier on him in person."[107] Star and andersonorganization parodically confess that their wedding dresses made them "feel very pretty."[108] These moments provide some gender confusion at the same time that they distance men from femininity. After all, Star and andersonorganization direct their comments about the dress to the "ladies," promise they have not tainted the gown and are not really in drag because they are "wearing clothes on underneath it," and advise that if it can make "a guy" feel "attractive, it can make" a woman "feel attractive." To "maintain the heterosexual meaning within weddings," as Oswald advises, "participants need to appear heterosexual" and to look "conventionally male and female."[109] Drag listings and the relationship between Star and andersonorganization could trouble traditional gender conventions. However, these male sellers reestablish heterosexuality by incorporating men's clothing, beards, assertions of men's rituals, and overt sexism into listings.

Sellers also deploy stereotypes and dismiss ex-wives when listing other items. For instance, gt2plus2 lists a doll that looks like his "UGLY," promiscuous, and lying "X-WIFE AFTER A PARTY!" when she is "FLAT ON HER BACK."[110] He challenges her femininity and sexuality, particularly the cultural association of good women with cleanliness and purity, when alerting the prospective buyer that "THIS DOLL HAS STAINS ON HER DRESS. (NO PUNS PLEASE) MY X-WIFE HEARD THEM ALL." gt2plus2 justifies the sale by making it into a way of expunging his ex-wife even though the item did not belong to her. solticeman25 also condemns his ex-wife and uses her purportedly bad behavior to explain why he must sell his "entire collection" of sports cards.[111] He has "to pay this Black Widow alimony," even though he "Wasn't even married 8 months" and she "cheats." teaganz_daddy lists a "LOT OF 14 HANDBAGS LEFT BEHIND" by his ex-wife and claims to have been "A SELF-MADE MILLIONAIRE" before he met her and "FOUND OUT ABOUT HER FETISH WITH HANDBAGS."[112] In such accounts, women's "bad" behaviors are used to explain the sale of valuable and thereby good objects.

In a consideration of "eBay's history" and "most memorable" listings, which was sponsored by eBay employees and probably resulted in the company's production of the trading cards, junquegirl urges, "Don't forget that guy who was selling his x-wife's beanies so he could go shopping at Home Depot."[113] There was "a campaign later where you could PayPal him to buy him a beer." A number of the "historical" listings include narratives about heterosexual unions gone bad and reinscriptions of gender norms, such as the seller of Beanie Babies who rids his home of feminine objects, turns feminine collectibles into shopping at Home Depot, and gets rewarded with beer. These narratives are related to the larger eBay ritual of selling the goods of cheating and errant spouses. For instance, Hayley Shaw listed the British disc jockey Tim Shaw's Lotus for fifty pence after he flirted with a model on his radio show and hinted that he was going to leave his wife.[114] 395edmondson offered a pile of her husband's clothing upon discovering he was cheating. According to her, some of the "items might be slightly damp due to them having been chucked out of the bedroom window."[115] She had "since bagged them up and put them in the garage but they may smell a bit damp and mouldy." 395edmondson "sure as hell" was "not washing and ironing his clothes just in case he has to collect them." Because of this, she might "have to remove the listing," but she was sure potential buyers would "understand." Sellers' appeals for understanding are designed to connect buyers and sellers in a supportive community. At the same time, they increase the functionality of social selling and the likelihood sellers will garner better prices.

In listings for women's wedding dresses, items also remain after relationships end and represent the limits of commitment and normativity. estoyblanca is "selling the dress because" she "decided not to marry the Jerk!!!!"[116] kealalaina77 explains, "Due to a RUNAWAY GROOM my wonderful friend got rid of her loser ex-fiance!!! We are trying to get some of her money back on this dress! Thank Goodness for small wonders!"[117] jennyfur1028 "was supposed to wear this for a wedding, however the wedding was cancelled, and now" she is "trying to get rid of the memories" and asks prospective buyers to "Help me out! Please!"[118] In these cases, wedding-dress sellers render buying and selling as part of a community project and a kind of women's empowerment. Sellers configure a feminist community to achieve their economic goals. Nevertheless, the traditional position of the bride and wedding are never completely cast aside in these listings. For instance, 10255blue switches between condemning her former fiancé, advertising the positive attributes of the dress, and reprieving men. In a sort of stream of consciousness, she advises, "Dumped the bastard," "hope you have better Luck," she has "a good one now" because "real men are still out" there "looking for real Women," and the dress has a "Lace top with White liner very nice!!"[119] In these listings, women indicate troubled marriages and their continued investments in heterosexual couplings and marriages.

Women also attempt to purge the past and cannot resist the opportunity to "trash" their former partners in the "divorce" garage sales that Gretchen M. Herrmann discusses.[120] The wedding dresses sold on eBay, including the stories that get connected to them, reflect not only the tastes but also the values of female sellers. Women's narratives about soiled dresses, unruly bodies, unmanageable sexualities, and broken promises do not support eBay's values, production of normative identities (although many sellers certainly work hard to produce normalizing texts), and the idea that people are basically good. Some members perform consumer critiques on varied sites by describing bad eBay participants. Unfortunately, in the case of wedding-dress narratives, the term "bad" is often used to disempower women and resist feminist projects. For instance, the men in wedding dresses dismiss "bad" women who have gained weight, stolen their goods, or chosen a lesbian lifestyle.

Conclusion: Images Do Not Do the Wedding Dress Justice

Fiancés and images of gowns threaten to fail wedding-dress buyers. Many wedding-dress sellers, like the sellers I describe in the introduction, specify that their "pictures do not do it justice."[121] The phrase evokes and threatens to further taint the dress, the role of the justice of the peace, and the process of getting married. On Internet wedding forums, a lot of women express uneasiness about buying dresses through the eBay interface. They worry that they will purchase a wedding dress from an unreliable seller; that the dress will not arrive in time for the wedding; that it will be poorly constructed; and that it will not fit. These concerns are related to cultural beliefs that wedding dresses should be unique and perfect rather than noticeably mass-produced or flawed. Digital images mirror and magnify these troubling aspects of wedding dresses because they are copies, can be exactly duplicated, are cheaply produced, and break down into pixels when enlarged and delivered at low resolutions.

The aspects of digital imaging and category descriptions begin to destabilize the uniqueness, perfection, and quality of wedding dresses. However, sellers try to avoid this by distinguishing between pictures and objects. Readers of these listings, like prospective buyers of many other objects, are informed that the only way to experience dresses is to buy, see, and wear them. zbestreasure's "pictures do not do this gown justice - when you see it - you will agree!!!"[122] Visual inspection is stymied in images because "the wedding was indoors and the lighting was dim."[123] hot12b*'s pictures are also "not a true representation of this dress! It is very white and very beautiful," but this is difficult to convey visually.[124] She "uploaded an actual pic" from the wedding that "only shows the top of the dress," so viewers will "get the idea!" Yet it is not fully clear what individuals are looking at or engaging in when sellers provide partial images and accounts. The images render a different position from that of looking at or wearing items. They also suggest that the wedding day is under threat of a failure in justice, photographic and otherwise, because many women use professional wedding pictures to convey the listed items and buyers are looking for dresses that can be portrayed.

Sellers' narratives about images that do not do items justice underscore some of the failures of the interface and of how eBay treats members. eBay's apocryphal stories about Omidyar's production of the site, Wolfe and Aspling's marriage, and Star's wedding dress do not honor the company's moral code. To represent people who are good, eBay willingly provides bad information. The disenfranchised eBay members I consider in chapter 1 respond to ethical breeches and redeploy site slogans and community promises as critical methods. Sellers' descriptions of imaging failures also offer critical possibilities and highlight instances where the different aspects of the site do not correlate. These wedding-dress sellers do not actively critique eBay's values. However, gay interest and lesbian interest sellers, whose practices I consider in the next two chapters, challenge eBay by writing gay and lesbian interests and attachments into the interface, finding ways to erotically "get it on" the site, interrogating eBay's inequitable listing policies, and reworking the company's organizational logic. They also present radically different readings of weddings and images.

eBay's Visible Masculinities

"GAY" AND "GAY INTEREST" LISTINGS

AND THE POLITICS OF DESCRIBING

Most sellers are encouraged by eBay's traditional representations of engagements, weddings, and other normative roles and provide narratives about gendered behavior and heterosexual relationships. Gay and gay interest sellers present different self-depictions and forms of desire and thereby work to unravel eBay's gendered organizational logic and configuration of normative sexual citizenship. In doing this, they take eBay up on its promise of diverse identities and desires. Gay and gay interest sellers incorporate gay identities, gay communities, and unconventional masculinities into the eBay site when indicating listings are of interest to gay men, the men depicted in listings are gay, images have queer content, and objects and images offer a record of gay history. They perform a consumer critique of the eBay setting and its values while sometimes garnering better prices than related goods. Gay interest sellers thus achieve the blend of personalization and successful marketing eBay promotes but facilitate it through the forms of explicit representations of sexuality eBay has tried to ban.

eBay asserts its role as a selling platform, but gay and gay interest underwear and swimwear listings are a byproduct of men's interests in self-display and communicating with other men. Their sexual representations conflict with eBay's heteronormative focus, and the company often regulates them. In this chapter, I reflect on the political influence gay clothing sellers have when imaging their gym-built bodies, soft flesh, uneven physiques, genital bulges, and flaccid penises. Sellers who list gay interest items in the "Collectibles > Photographic Images > Antique (Pre-1940)" category extend these narratives about masculinity, gay visibility, identities, and desires into historical and imaginative pasts. Through such strategies, sellers' gay and gay interest listings interrogate eBay's conceptions of everyone and undermine its normalizing discourses and traditional ideas about gender, sexuality, and embodiment. They also expand and queer N. Katherine Hayles's association of Internet settings with flickering signifiers, shifting meanings, and impermanence by emphasizing the seen and unseen aspects of gay men's identities and visible penis lines.[1]

I use critical literature on gay consumerism, masculinity, and sexuality to analyze how gay interest listings work with and against eBay's system. For instance, writing by Alexandra Chasin and Katherine Sender that articulates the interdependence of identity, consumerism, and citizenship provides methods for considering how the company and sellers deploy sexuality to constitute the site and individuals.[2] Considerations of masculinity by Susan Bordo, Richard Dyer, Annie Potts, and others help me examine how masculinity is constituted on eBay and the ways these gay self-representations can disturb normative conceptions of binary gender.[3] Sellers' gay and gay interest listings undermine eBay's normalizing discourses and larger conceptions of identity and embodiment because they represent soft male bodies, identify gay identities and desires in objects, and propose that everyone's family history can be read queerly. Through political as well as social selling, gay and gay interest sellers confuse stable categories, desires, and subject positions.

Being Gay and eBay

Sellers intervene in eBay's production of normative identities by deploying the terms "gay" and "gay interest" in listings, encouraging buyers and viewers to find alternative content and making an array of genders and sexualities visible. eBay has regulated these strategies. Firemeg critiques eBay's general policy because the company "has stepped outside the bounds of being a venue and become its own regulatory and enforcement agency for ecommerce."[4] Sellers of gay items regularly wonder about eBay's removal of listings and complain about eBay's inequitable policies. Mark, who describes himself as a "victim of the ebay police," had eBay pull auctions "because they contained the word 'Jock's'" even though "there were over 500 auctions with the word." He identifies this selective cancellation as blatant "discrimination."

Sellers also have auctions removed because images are too "racy."[5] After receiving an email notifying him that artwork showing a flaccid penis had been removed and the listing canceled by eBay, a buyer replied that he "was certainly glad that Michaelangelo wasn't still painting, because the entire Sistine Chapel would violate eBay policy."[6]

romanborn is also "EXTREMELY frustrated by the very ambiguous and sometimes seemingly homophobic guidelines."[7] Sellers can list *Playboy* magazines on the regular site, even though they contain images of nude women; however, when he runs "a similar gay-themed vintage 70s era magazine" called *Gayboy* with "a cropped-at-the-waist image of an adult man," which meets eBay's Adult Only guidelines, he still risks having all of his "auctions yanked, facing selling restrictions and possible suspension." eBay's allowing of the term "boy" in listings for straight magazines but banning of it in listings for gay magazines, romanborn asserts, is contradictory and homophobic. These members are unwilling to accept eBay's position as the arbiter of how things are arranged, what can be viewed, and the appropriate forms of gender and sexuality that can be conveyed through the site. They continue to list items on eBay, find ways around eBay's censoring tendencies, and perform consumer critiques in their listings and forum comments.

Buyers engage with gay and gay interest listings when they look in categories, search for the terms "gay" or "gay interest," and set up favorite searches and receive emailed notification of new listings. Gay listings appear in such varied categories as "Art" (paintings and prints of nearly nude young men), "Photographic Images," "DVDs & Movies," "Books," "Sporting Goods" (mostly socks and briefs), "Men's Clothing" (typically thongs and briefs), "Home & Garden" (bookends depicting attractive men), "Toys & Hobbies" (*Teletubbies*' Tinky Winky and *Star Trek*'s Captain Jean-Luc Picard), "Coins" (medals with images of men), and "eBay Motors" (chaps and other leather items). For example, in the "Photographic Images" category, sellers list studio as well as vernacular images of men together (specifically, sailors, soldiers, sports teams, and fraternity boys); men with their shirts off, from the back, or "from behind"; nudity, genital bulges, and partially or wholly visible penises; images of men touching, almost touching, or even close together; muscled and good-looking men; and men with effeminate gestures or "dapper" dressing.[8] Similar conceptions of gay identities are produced in other site categories.

The commentary in Internet and print sources shows that many people are aware of gay interest practices and share this conceptualization of objects, identity, and desires with others. In the eBay forums, marsha91091 advises putting "'gay interest' in the title" of mal-tbo's listing of a toiletry bag with "40's pinup muscle men."[9] A seller of *Physical Culture* magazine is told how to "find a few more bidders" by adding "gay interest."[10] lillieborghild advises a seller that "auctions with 'gay interest' in the title" are "key to selling that postcard for more bucks!"[11] However, hcquilts challenges the use of the term because the poster owns an image that is similar to the listing. It portrays hcquilts' "great-grandfather."[12] The man's wife and relatives, hcquilts writes, "would be very surprised to find out he was gay." John Ibson, an academic and collector of vintage photography, describes how, on eBay, "'Gay' or 'Gay Interest' is often given to any photograph of two or more men doing no more than standing close to each other."[13] Men's actions, as depicted in vintage photographs, do not always validate the use of the term "gay." Nevertheless, gay interest listings of photographs surprise some viewers and direct them to understand family and history differently. Sellers' practices in listing gay and gay interest underwear and swimwear also disturb eBay's rules by displaying erotic male bodies and personally engaging with men through the setting without focusing on economic transactions. These listings point to important, unintended, and understudied uses of ecommerce settings for social networking.

Sellers' gay listings also produce a written history of gay consumption and collecting that was not previously available.[14] This history is facilitated by gay sellers' descriptions of collecting practices, indications they purchased things from other gay collectors, and addresses to gay buyers. For camp-classics, the term "gay interest" is meant to reach gay collectors, who "are legion," and to "let them know there might be something that will either catch their eye or tickle their fancy."[15] gearsaleaol, who sells vintage briefs, is "culling" his "sportswear collection."[16] He is selling the extra items on eBay so that other men can have a collection. jonmcgarrah knows he does not "have to tell you collectors out there, that Original vintage body builder shots from this period are VERY, very scarce."[17] All listings are removed from the system after a period of time, but a history of such gay interests and desires persists as similar listings are added.

Without the interventions of gay and gay interest buyers, sellers, and viewers, eBay asserts heterosexuality but does not name it. Men are articulated because of their role in heterosexual couples, but their bodies and masculinity ordinarily are not described. This continues traditional conceptions of binary gender, since men are ordinarily associated with the mind rather than the body and are imagined as possessing a body rather than being a body.[18] However, gay listings articulate detailed and complicated versions of men's bodies and desires. Thus, gay listings are one of the sites on eBay where masculinity is overtly articulated. A study of these listings suggests that campy objects; representations of men together; depictions of nude men; items made of leather, rubber, and spandex; and body-revealing clothing are described as "gay" or of "gay interest." Sellers usually use the term "gay" to address men and "lesbian" to address women, but the term "gay" is also sometimes deployed to address all individuals with same-sex desires. Since there is no exact definition of these terms, and the concept of gay interest incorporates gay identities and desires, I will ordinarily use the term "gay interest" throughout this chapter when referring to members' practices.

The gay interest search term requires more consideration in a culture where, as Chasin notes, the "way that gay men and lesbians in the United States come to understand themselves as 'gay,' and as 'American,' has everything to do with understandings of the relationship between citizenship and consumption."[19] The connections between citizenship and consumption are also important to gay identities in other Western countries. The Community link on eBay offers buyers and sellers a message system that is designed to facilitate citizenship, along with better buying and selling strategies. Gay interest items, and the sellers who describe them, visualize bodies and desires left out of the category system while supporting eBay's claims that citizenship and community are achieved by buying and selling. Through their listings and narratives, sellers inform eBay viewers that they are looking at gay products, and that clothes, toys, and other items can make the man gay rather than the more ordinary indication that everyday objects and consumerism support heteronormativity. These sellers thereby complicate the forms of sexual citizenship eBay establishes on the site.

Gay interest sellers overturn part of eBay's heteronormative structure by making gay interest into a kind of category, even though they still work within eBay's category and representational systems. The sorts of collecting and fashion that are constituted in gay and gay interest listings are important. They provide ways to demarcate individuals from mainstream values and desires, to assert identities, and to allow people to be recognized on the site and possibly in physical spaces. Sellers' gay interest listings and eBay's uneasy facilitation connect men and constitute a community through men's mutual admiration of objects, engagements with sellers' erotic self-portrayals, and email and other forms of communication. This community is continued in other Internet forums in which eBay sellers advertise their underwear and swimwear listings, buyers and sellers communicate, readers share their love of underwear and swimwear, and individuals indicate their fan and brand attachment to some sellers. While these individual sites and practices are used for gay social networking and identity production, the connections between them facilitate notably rich engagements.

When Sex Does Not Sell

Gay interest sellers tend to be located in, and such images are ordinarily viewable from, America and Britain, as well as many other parts of Europe. eBay is conceptualized as a global social-selling platform where community practices are connected to economic transactions and produce consumer citizens. However, gay underwear and swimwear sellers' economic transactions are often a byproduct of their interest in self-display and communicating with other men. Sellers assure readers that viewing and communicating are as satisfactory as buying. jocktime/huckleberry informs potential viewers in a forum, "you don't have to bid" but should "just check out" his pictures and let him "know what you think."[20] In his listings, somtom2000 offers a "THANK YOU FOR LOOKING OR BIDDING."[21] These sellers constitute a form of community and ironically fulfill eBay's mandate for collectivity and connections by providing free views. Gay interest sellers thereby achieve a politics that goes beyond acknowledging gay men as consumers, also enabling gay men's position as visible social subjects who engage with other men.

Mainstream advertisers deploy different visual strategies and have different ideological goals from those of gay interest sellers. However, they also provide images of half-naked men when selling underwear, swimwear, and other products. As Deanna A. Rohlinger points out in her study of male eroticism, "Gay male consumers have suspected for years that images of partially-clothed, muscular men with sexually ambiguous appeal were designed to attract their attention."[22] Mainstream publications feature these images because people believe that "sex sells" when the gender of the individual addressed and the sexuality of the depicted men remain unclear. Some advertisers address gay male consumers directly in mainstream venues, but most avoid such strategies because they fear troubling heterosexual consumers' erotic position and angering them. For Sender, the argument that sex sells prevents more detailed interrogations of the sorts of sexuality used in advertisements and the cultural limits placed on this marketing model. Some "manifestations of sex are not commercially viable."[23] Sex is not accepted by heteronormative culture and does not sell products to heterosexual consumers when it is constituted by images of partially clad men who are erotically engaged with other men and when viewers are clearly articulated as gay men.

Mainstream publications, Internet portals, and the eBay company do not accept overtly gay sexual narratives as methods of selling products. Sellers' images of nearly nude and muscled men, which repeat the conventions used in mainstream advertising *and* label things "gay," remind eBay viewers that mainstream media also features and communicates with gay men, and that their consumerist drives have been at least partially activated by erotic images of men. Michael Petit has studied men's sales of used underwear and how eBay's banning of these popular listings in 2000 constituted an instance of sex panic, as Gayle Rubin articulates the term.[24] Sex panics occur, according to Petit, at "particular moments, characterized by conditions of high social, political, cultural, or economic anxieties."[25] During these periods "sex and what constitutes its 'legitimate' parameters are hotly contested and overtly politicized, with those on the sexual margins typically policed and controlled by institutional forces." For instance, eBay explains its ban on all types of used underwear by citing "hygiene" concerns, even though the sale of other used and vintage clothing is allowed.[26] In the wedding-dresses category (see chapter 3), eBay allows listings to remain active even when sellers offer items without cleaning them.

Buyers, sellers, and viewers who look at gay interest listings and read gay-oriented clothing forums are aware of eBay's policies and the risks in selling these items. In Internet forums, sellers note listings with erotic content and ways to avoid eBay's censoring tendencies. They also critique the company's unclear and inequitable policies. Espion warns readers, "Ebay doesn't permit the sale of used underwear, cleaned or otherwise, and if Ebay finds out, you can be temporarily or permanently banned."[27] speedofan9 informs members about "very hot PICS" and that the "ebay police" will "delete auctions for showing" visible "signs of genitalia arousal."[28] His auctions were canceled when he "showed too much excited bulge." jockwolf advises new sellers that "you have to be careful—they will pull auctions if they consider the picture to be too racy," and that some of his auctions were "cancelled, others not, even tho the pose (and level of arousal (NONE))" were "the same in all instances."[29] eBay removed online3's auctions because he "said stuff like 'these make your package look awesome.'"[30]

eBay regulates gay interest underwear and swimwear sellers' visible manifestations of their sexuality. However, sellers still make listings evident by redeploying their eBay images as avatar icons, personal profile depictions, and auction advertisements in such underwear and swimwear settings as Real Jock, Underwear4Men.com, and Underwear Swimwear Guide (USG). In these settings, eBay sellers sometimes group their eBay representations of bulges and visible penis lines with "before" and "after" images where they are revealing their penises, masturbating, and ejaculating. These images become almost indistinguishable from the appropriated pornography that some members claim as their self-depictions and the advertisements for porn that appear on these sites. By deploying gay interest depictions, sellers begin to introduce a wider array of representational strategies and desires into the mainstream eBay setting. eBay responds by removing listings, canceling accounts, and resisting the marketing of gay men's sexuality.

The sale of socks and other unwashed clothing persists on eBay, but most underwear items are new, and swimwear sellers advertise new or cleaned clothing to avoid being regulated. While these items may be "customized" with semen and other bodily traces according to buyers' requests, most sellers do not offer such services in listings. themickster's item "comes in its vintage unused (Brand New and unopened) package. The jock on the model is not for sale but for display purposes only."[31] Other items are "CLEANED AND LAUNDERED TO E BAY STANDARDS."[32] Such comments used to be followed by notices that items were still permeated by traces of the seller, but these practices have been largely evacuated. All of the items mscljocko has "listed on ebay are in full compliance with ebay regulations, all items are cleaned per ebay standards except underwears. All underwear items are in their original condition, new and never been tried on, not even for the picture."[33] While it is sometimes unclear what items sellers are modeling in listings, sellers display erotic representations rather than promise unwashed garments.

Most sellers have changed the ways they describe items and the material conditions of the objects they sell, but the practices of gay interest sellers and of eBay are still not aligned. The company's warnings and tendency to delete auctions continue to make sellers aware that they risk being regulated when they list items with overt sexual narratives and include images of mostly nude male bodies. eBay cautions used underwear sellers that they may experience the following actions: "Listing cancellation," "Limits on account privileges," "Account suspension," "Forfeit of eBay fees on cancelled listings," and "Loss of PowerSeller status."[34] Listings "that contain inappropriate descriptions will be ended." However, eBay does not explain what makes something inappropriate. The numerous viewers of men's underwear and swimwear listings, as indicated by site counters, and the high prices paid for some of the items depicted on sexy men's bodies support the idea that sex attracts eBay viewers and helps sell items. However, the company is not sold on such listings and tends to remove the more explicit listings, even though they encourage personalized selling strategies that engage potential buyers.

eBay continues to change the wording of its documents, but the policies remain. eBay does not allow any "listing that contains images of frontal nudity or of any form of sexual activity, with limited exceptions" on the main site.[35] These exceptions include "part of an artwork that is considered fine art, such as certain paintings" but excludes "Amateur photos." eBay allows "Frontal nudity" in "Art categories when the item is considered fine art," but does not define the category or the parameters of disallowed "explicit sexual content."[36] At eBay Live! conferences and in the forums, employees try to explain such regulation of art and erotica by describing the complaints they receive, including those from parents who are concerned that their children will see drawings of nudes on the site. Of course, similar concerns have been directed at museums and advertisements. It is also the case that eBay can be viewed as an adult portal because individuals are required to be older than eighteen to use it. However, the company is interested in attracting young consumers. It constructs the site as G-rated and is trying to find ways to facilitate shopping for young people who cannot enter into legal contracts in the United States and therefore cannot commit to buying.

Sellers who are confronted by eBay's warnings and regulations are forced to edit their expressions and self-representations or risk being banned. Sellers offer to email images they believe are not allowed or to post them to other sites. gearsale offers images of swimwear "that won't make it past the ebay censors" on a personal site.[37] Tropis says he wants to apologize to forum readers for "'toning down' the photos."[38] eBay canceled one of his listings, but he has "unedited copies of the photos" on another site. Sellers censor their images even when the items are paintings and other artistic works, which eBay's policies allow but the company still sometimes removes. Viewers of dontbesilly's listings for paintings can email "for a larger easier to see uncensored view."[39] One painting shows a reclining male nude with his legs in the air, as if he is asking to be penetrated by the viewer, and an ecstatic look on his face. A sign covering the figure's painted genitalia and buttocks coaxes buyers and viewers to email dontbesilly and to thus situate their body in relationship to the full view, uncover what is not publicly available, and achieve an erotic engagement with the image and seller. john-bishop's "actual drawing is a full nude (below the waist)."[40] According to him, "ebay does not allow an erect penis." To "see the entire artwork," viewers are directed to visit his site. john-bishop and other sellers promise but do not fully deliver erotic content. The images are cropped, and red dots and other obfuscating devices are used to meet eBay's standards.

All of this results in expelling gay sexuality, which, according to Sender, "makes the gay market distinct" and compels individuals to employ other means to distinguish the gay niche.[41] On eBay, performances of regulation and censorship are sometimes used to activate eroticism and articulate the gay niche. For instance, galaxy_shop depicts a well-muscled nude man with a black bar over his groin that advertises the seller's ID.[42] john-bishop's viewers can visit his site to see the full view, but the head of the figure's penis is visible just above the blocked portion of the image in the eBay listing. These sellers deploy an eroticism that flickers between the seen and the unseen, an experience that is also rendered by the technological processes of downloading images and the refresh rate of cathode-ray-tube monitors.[43] Sellers use the proscriptions against more explicit images of men to make their images, listed objects, and bodies more difficult to obtain, and thus—at least, for some buyers and viewers—more desirable.

Constituting the Gay Male Body

Many gay interest underwear and swimwear sellers depict young and toned bodies and focus on muscled chests, nipples, pubic hair, and outlines of genitals. For instance, mscljocko models "JM Contoured Pouch Squarecut 32 gay int. spandex nylon" underwear with his legs spread widely and his groin pushed forward.[44] mscljocko's fisted right hand presses down on his groin, emphasizing the size of his genitals and invoking masturbation. In other underwear listings, he flexes his well-muscled body and tilts his hips out to best display a visible penis line.[45] To some extent, these images work in the same ways that Graham Ward's film research indicates muscular bodies signify, functioning "as one great hard-on."[46] mscljocko's possessing stance and taut body visually evoke an erection and are intended to turn on viewers. Yet his tilted head and ecstatic expression also convey postcoital pleasure and the beginning of flaccidity. These images thereby interlink genital erections and penises listing, falling, and failing. Because of these connections, the masculinities rep-

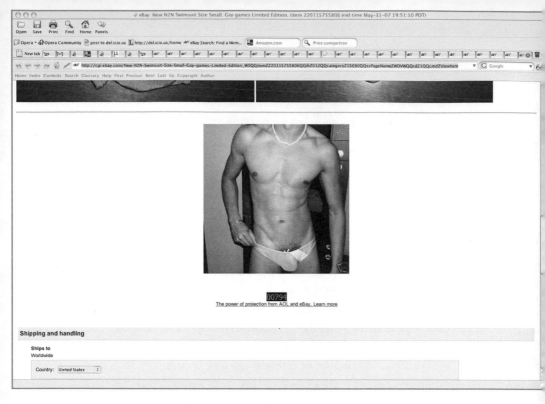

7. usflaboy, "New N2N Swimsuit Size Small. Gay games Limited Edition," eBay, 24 May 2007

resented do not meet the standard Bordo describes in which the male body is expected to be "rock hard" and "without looseness or flaccidity."[47]

Sellers also challenge traditional conceptions of masculinity when they offer their bodies as well as items to viewers. usflaboy's "New N2N Swimsuit Size Small. Gay games Limited Edition" listing, which was viewed an astounding 1,008 times, emphasizes the seller's muscled shoulders, lean torso, genital bulge, and pubic hair (figure 7).[48] usflaboy makes himself available by directing individuals to email "if you have any questions" just above his sinuous torso and visually accessible genitals.[49] gerardo5800 offers even more access to his body: "MY WHOLE PACKAGE IS FOR YOU!!!!. LOOK AT ME" and "MY LITTLE THONG... GET THEM ALL NOW!!!!!!!! VERY GAY."[50] gerardo5800 is selling packages of underwear, offering visual representations of his genitals, and promising more. Individuals are encouraged to imagine that sellers' bodies are available. In an Internet forum, Newbie2it asks, "Does the package inside the 'wrapper' come with the purchase? Cause I will buy them all."[51]

haywardmike advises that the "Current bid on that suit was $94.00. The bidder must think the model comes with it."[52] Gay interest sellers instruct viewers to look at them; they deploy camera viewpoints that move the viewer's gaze from torso toward groin, and they transform images into visceral versions of male bodies.

Sellers create a market for eBay auction images by offering more revealing depictions. One seller identifies as "a bit of an exhibitionist."[53] jockdude90036 lists a "Gray Camo Camouflage Swim Bikini Thong NEW NWOT Gay Int," that has a "rear floss strap."[54] However, the "back side picture" is available only "on request for BIDDERS." These listings allow sellers to offer clothing items for sale, display themselves, and engage with other gay men. Buyers can shop for underwear and swim trunks, look for erotic content, and save favorite images. Sammy writes that he "will start a photo file" on a new seller.[55] Stl_Muscle collects images from eBay auctions and describes a picture that he has "been unable to find . . . since upgrading to a new PC."[56] two-talented-leos offers a collection of digital self-portraits where some "are from previous auctions photos, some are from private shootings" and most "of them are topless, half naked, and or pants down depending on the product."[57] In a similar manner, mscljocko lists "Over 140 pictures of my previous auction pictures" that include "pictures that were used in mature audiences category."[58] These photos, which were once employed to sell underwear but are now more overtly described as images that make sellers visually accessible, indicate the difficulty in differentiating between the images and objects that are for sale. In part, listings are a form of picture exchange that allows individuals to virtually look at sellers.

Buying delivers a material object that has touched the body of the seller in some way and personal contact and email exchanges with that individual. poloboyzz is "the same one behind the auctions" and "in all the pictures."[59] He guarantees that viewing and buying will lead to personal contact and an engagement with his body. rshadz wants the suit of a seller "just to know that butt was in it."[60] If eBay's message boards and other site features produce one kind of arrangement between individuals and traditional forms of identity, then listings for men's undergarments and other erotic clothing produce another community, form of social selling, and way of engaging. In such cases, the normative functions of eBay's auctions and its focus on economic exchanges are replaced by site-facilitated engagements between men. As part of this structure, viewers' enthusiastic comments in forums situate them as fans of specific sellers. Speedoman NYC recommends "a very hot guy . . . on

eBay: NEW MENS N2N SWIMSUIT -NO LINING - GAY INTEREST (item 220114346072 end time May-27-07 18:13:52 PDT)

Description (revised)

Item Specifics - Men's Swimwear
Size: **L**
Style: **Trunks**

Condition: **New: Without Tags**

Very comfortable suit from N2NBodywear.com

There's no lining in it so beware!

The item in the picture is not for sale, the item for sale is identical but the item for sale is NEW.

00245

8. hrdmslguy, "NEW MENS N2N SWIMSUIT -NO LINING - GAY INTEREST," eBay, 20 May 2007

ebay selling suits" and tells readers to "Check him out."[61] Readers respond with the names of other attractive sellers. These gay interest practices produce a brand community that is constituted by the term "gay" rather than "eBay" and includes consciousness of a kind, rituals and traditions, and an ethos. The gay interest brand community is part of the eBay setting, has connections to forums and other Internet sites, uses eBay's systems, and disorders the normative gender and sexuality aspects of its organizational logic. The eBay gay brand community even has a form of eBay-ana, because sellers list mouse pads and T-shirts branded with the word "eGay."[62] In these cases, the term is positively configured.

The eGay mouse pad offers to "let others know the 'real you.'" In a related strategy, sellers' gay underwear and swimwear auctions pose a culture in which buyers, sellers, and viewers are seen. hrdmslguy notifies swimsuit buyers that they will be seen: There is "no lining in it so beware!" (figure 8).[63] Another listed item is "really fun. Nice and respectable and sporty" but "get them wet and they become completely sheer."[64] Mark uses "terms like 'very revealing when wet, clings like a second skin, and not for the shy'" that sound "like a warning."[65] Yet some individuals recognize them as meaning, "Hey guys, this will show your package." Such items also promise gay visibility. Their descriptions evoke the ways the seen and the unseen body are deployed by gay interest sellers and regulated by eBay. Sellers highlight their visibility, the erotic potential of listings, and eBay's regulatory behavior. hrdmslguy would "show you the pics" he "took but people get offended and" he would "be suspended."[66] The buyer, however, will receive "the pics that ebay cancelled" and is thereby awarded an erotic and illicit view. Such arrangements emphasize the erotic promise of listed items, images, and sellers' bodies and withhold some details.

Sellers' descriptions of seen and unseen bodies and penises evoke the staccato and brief, and thus more tantalizing, unveilings that occur in such forms as striptease and personal webcams. By indicating that images and listings are impermanent, sellers connect views of visible penis lines, erotic artwork, and even general listings to a kind of ontology of new technologies, including the unstableness of operating systems and software, the changeability of computer texts, and the disappearance of Internet sites. Since these technologies and their shifts render "flickering signifiers," as Hayles calls them, and make meaning "less stable," they also make the ability to read gender and sexuality less secure.[67] This may be one of the reasons eBay provides all of its regulating and stabilizing rules and texts. Of course, the always present threat that eBay will remove gay interest listings increases the erotic appeal of those listings while making them increasingly unstable. For Roland Barthes, it is the "intermittence of skin flashing between two articles of clothing (trousers and sweater) between two edges (the open-necked shirt, the glove, and the sleeve); it is this flash itself which seduces, or rather: the staging of an appearance-as-disappearance."[68] The gay interest "appearance-as-disappearance" evokes even more sexual frisson and pathos with some men's desires to be out because of eBay's repressive policies, the closeted aspects of a number of gay interest practices, and the catastrophic disappearance of gay communities and individuals due to AIDS. Sellers create a structure in which being seen is desirable and risky. They risk having their gay listings, accounts, and income opportunities canceled by eBay. Most sellers do not provide headshots or full-figure images, but they can still be identified by the detailed self-portraits in listings and personal information individuals automatically receive when they "win" auctions.

Gay interest underwear sellers constitute a community in which men can be seen. However, men traditionally have been depicted as acting rather than appearing and, as Bordo suggests, it is rare to see them engaging in bodily explorations, self-presenting as visual objects, or gazing at their image in mirrors.[69] Heterosexual men are usually believed to be uninterested in how they look and to ignore their position as corporeal and embodied. The gay and gay interest listings on eBay, like many other representations of gay men's sexuality, pose men as the object of the gaze. This position is different from the one occupied by heterosexual women and the men who look at them. All gay men, at least theoretically, are posited as the object of the gaze. Sellers employ mirrors, which have long been used to represent femininity and vanity, and handheld cameras to capture their likenesses and appear framed within these self-reflective and material structures. Their listings act as a composite mirror that allows sellers to see themselves figured in the "public sphere" of the eBay market of objects and the gay cruising "meat market" bazaar. Sellers challenge straight men's sexuality when they propose that eBay is a gay cruising market as well as a bazaar of goods. According to Philip Culbertson, who researches the male body, "It is the imagined effeminacy of homosexual men that makes them objects of heterosexual derision."[70] However, it is "their imagined masculinity (that is, the consciousness of them as active, evaluating sexual subjects, with a defining and 'penetrating' sexual gaze) that makes them the objects of heterosexual fear." Gay listings for underwear, swimwear, and photography pose all male viewers as willing objects of the gaze and active viewers and establish a different formation of everyone from that of eBay.

Shopping on eBay means deploying a consumerist gaze and imagining touching things. poloboyzz describes the erotic delight buyers will have when his clothing items rub against their skin, and ozbestprice advertises underwear that has "soft material" and assures buyers, "You will be attractive!"[71] Within this structure, gay men offer their bodies as one fleshy good in an already complicated market of virtual tactility and sensuality. Straight men are addressed as individuals who desire male bodies and the clothing that will make them more appealing to other men. They are reconfigured as queer individuals who are cruising for consumerist pleasures and as men who are shopping for men. Using the men's clothing category means gazing at images of men who are displaying themselves and, because of gay interest listings, self-identifying as gay. Yet, as Culbertson argues, to "gaze at another man repositions a straight man as a gay man, thereby shattering his fragile masculinity."[72] Men's normative masculinity is challenged, and straight men are re-positioned as gay men by sellers' gay addresses, the tactile engagements that listings promise to deliver, and men's consumer positions, which feminize them.

Masculinities and Femininities

Gay and gay interest sellers have a stake in maintaining empowered forms of masculinity. Their listings include images of the sellers standing rather than languidly reclining. Painters, photographers, and other image producers have depicted women reclining to render them passive and available to the male gaze.[73] Male sellers may stand because it provides for easier display of the genitals. However, standing with legs spread slightly apart and penises jutting forward also imbues them with a more commanding position. Sellers depict themselves in static poses but are also active individuals who orchestrate listings and engage potential buyers. According to Dyer's research on the pin-up, "The male image still promises activity by the way the body is posed," even when it is not depicted as moving or working.[74] The Internet studies researchers Marjorie Kibby and Brigid Costello write that flexed muscles "connote immanent activity."[75] In underwear and swimwear listings, sellers raise their arms to best display limbs and torsos and flex muscles to remind viewers of their past and future actions. Dyer proposes that such figures are "standing taut and ready for action."[76] poloboyzz conveys this readiness for movement and sexual engagement while advertising a shirt that will allow the wearer to "rock the club when you get OFF!"[77] He uses a narrative about after-work partying to equate clothing to erections and ejaculating. Sellers continue these representations of hardness and readiness in their portrayals of semi-erect penises, inclination for exercising, and availability for sexual activity.

Gay clothing listings render erotic bodies that are posed and described for the visual pleasure of viewers. Buyers are encouraged to imagine they will be as erotic and desirable as sellers when they wear the items. The absence of faces in many of the listings make sellers into bodies rather than minds and allow the depictions to stand in for multiple individuals. Images of men modeling underwear, swimwear, and other body-revealing clothing constitute possible selves for buyers and viewers, who are addressed as future owners and the people who wear items. For instance, sexysadiespandex offers a "Men's Hot Pink Leopard Spandex Wrestling Shirt gay sexy" that will enable the buyer to "look your best whether skiing, weightlifting, dancing, wrestling, clubbing, or simply because you look good in spandex!"[78] "Show 'em ALL your muscles!" sexysadiespandex encourages buyers. In a similar manner, poloboyzz presents his toned chest and emphasizes that his items will flatter the "shape of that rocking body you've got!"[79] Sellers' descriptions and images conflate the bodies of buyers and sellers. Through these processes, gay interest sellers also convey social mandates about the importance of being physically attractive and the kind of body gay men are supposed to maintain—hard and muscled.

Sellers market themselves and listings with body-oriented IDs such as progressive-fitness, hrdmslguy, brazenmuscle, and feistymuscle. Such representations are part of the imposition of "hypermasculine and rather rigid appearance standards" that are described in the research of Steven M. Kates and that are emphasized in some gay cultures.[80] Hypermasculinity, according to Mitchell J. Wood's study of the gay male gaze, "dominates gay mass media and gay public life."[81] Consumer culture is "less and less forgiving," writes Rohlinger, "of those who are not sufficiently young, thin, and attractive."[82] Numerous researchers contend that there are many forms of gay masculinity and corporeal desires, but muscularity is still overtly promoted, and this contributes to many gay men's feelings of dissatisfaction with their bodies.[83] The pressures of these social and media messages, and men's affective responses, encourage considerations of alternative proposals for masculinity. eBay sellers' affirmations of unmuscular and male femininities, which appear along with more general clothing auctions, persist in a mainstream setting and make it more complex.

The amateur photographic practices of eBay sellers, which highlight rather than downplay sagging flesh, rounded stomachs, scars, and uneven gym-built bodies, offer a more complicated image of gay bodies and desires. Sellers also tenderly image slender, unexercised, and fleshy bodies and age spots and wrinkles. For instance, feistymuscle's extremely muscled thighs and broad shoulders operate in a different way from his unexercised and slightly potbellied stomach.[84] His long scar, which cuts diagonally from sternum to hip, and tilted pose do not fulfill cultural mandates for bodily symmetry and perfection. The sellers who revel in their fleshy chests and limbs, emphasize their curved bellies and thighs, and highlight how their bodies fold over clothing are more aligned with chubs and chasers, who have or admire men with larger bodies.

Sellers present differently configured bodies by wearing clothing that is too tight for them.[85] kirkieskorner's "sexy-fitting, trim jean" that is "great for

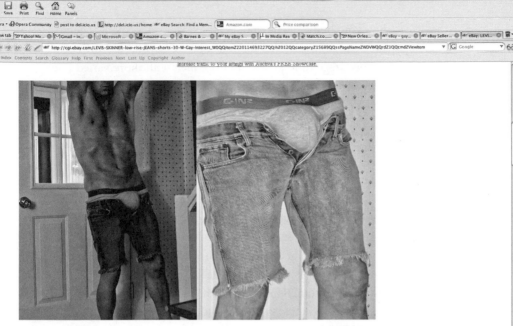

9. kirkieskorner, "LEVIS SKINNER low rise JEANS shorts 30"W Gay Interest," eBay, 21 May 2007

a slim build," and has been "washed enough times so that it FITS very well," distorts the size and shape of his body.[86] In the images, the last two buttons remain undone, and the jeans gape to reveal a large "V" of flesh. With these images, kirkieskorner demonstrates that he has a large body, which is appreciated within conventional gay culture, rather than a "slim build." His tight clothing also functions as a form of erotic bondage. It contains his body and emphasizes the shape and bulk of his penis and testicles. In another image, he wears a pair of jean shorts that are so tight that the fly has to remain undone and the shorts do not fit over his hips (figure 9).[87] His underwear-covered penis and testicles protrude from his clothing and are supported by the fly of the shorts. kirkieskorner's images display his genitals, but they also emphasize the slight softness of his torso and the sag of flesh around his waist and belly.

kirkieskorner's body does not meet cultural ideals, but he still suggests that buyers will find an item appealing if "you are one of those guys like me that like to show your body."[88] His comments and viewers' responses demonstrate how some gay eBay self-presentations operate beyond narrow norms. These listings encourage individuals to desire men with more varied body shapes. One viewer notices kirkieskorner's pleasurable self-display and asks, "Does the model come with/in the thong?" because the "model sizzles!"[89] kirkieskorner thanks the viewer for "the compliment," indicates he is "no small boy"—an embodied position that is emphasized by the too-tight clothing he chooses to model, that shipping himself (the model) would be too expensive, and that the seller should contact him and obtain more personalized items.[90] By encouraging the viewer to "let me know what other items you would like to see me put on auction," kirkieskorner also becomes available. Such listings, kirkieskorner's references to body size and genital bulge, and viewers' reactions are a form of cruising. These instances of gay interest cruising challenge eBay's attempts to configure the site as heterosexual.

Gay interest practices function as a kind of consumer resistance and critique. Sellers' gay underwear and swimwear listings perform a version of what the masculinity scholar R. W. Connell envisions for homosexuality. They rely on and disrupt the "existing gender order in ways that illuminate long-term possibilities of change in the structure of gender relations."[91] These listings contest straight men's claims that they are minds that have bodies, rather than being bodies, and that they do not look at other men. Sellers' practices and listings also disturb gay men's appropriation of and engagement with empowered masculinity. For instance, kirkieskorner's otherwise masculine performance of a large hard body is problematized by the extreme tightness of his clothing, which emphasizes his looser flesh and difficulty fitting into things.

Mark Simpson critiques the aesthetics of gay culture and ironically notes that gay men have "the best underwear shops"; heterosexual men suffer because they cannot "carry off wearing a silver thong"; and Stonewall enabled gay men to stop repressing "their desires or their undergarments."[92] In his book, Simpson calls for a critical consideration of the values, politics, and stereotypes that accompany gay lifestyles. Proposing a similar political inquiry into the marketing strategies that constitute gay identity, Toby Manning studies how gay individuals who do not embody certain codes are at a severe disadvantage.[93] Sellers of gay interest underwear and swimwear constitute rigid versions of gay masculinity and offer other positions. They perform masculinities and femininities. While Simpson interrogates gay men's tendency to focus on their genital performances, galaxy_shop sells a "Translucent BIKINI"

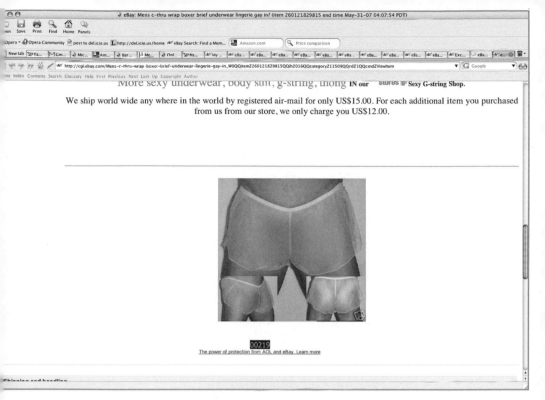

10. thana0, "Mens c-thru wrap boxer brief underwear lingerie gay in?" eBay, 24 May 2007

that does not provide any evidence of the model's genitals, even though he is depicted in a spread-legged pose.[94] thana0 elides rather than performs male genitals (figure 10).[95] He uses a graphics program to technologically remove the penis from images and thereby meet eBay's rules about visible genitals. By employing a "fuzz" technique to delete the penis, using pink fabric, sheathing the testes in shimmering material, and portraying hairless and creamy smooth thighs, thana0 offers a different proposal for gender and gay desire.[96] He feminizes the male body and evokes transgendered positions.

fellowes1964 also displays a less conventional body and gender position. His swimwear and underwear listings, like kirkieskorner's, feature clothing that is too small for him. fellowes1964's upper body curves over his tight trunks, and his stomach protrudes (figure 11).[97] By displaying his body in multiple listings and in varied positions, he makes it clear that all of this is purposeful. He even highlights the difference between his soft flesh and more conventional gym-built bodies by including mass-marketed advertisements of highly muscled men in some listings.[98] In a number of listings, fellowes1964

11. fellowes1964, "MENS TURCO SWIMWEAR SM BLUE / GOLD GAY JOCK LAST CHANCE," eBay, 21 May 2007

crosses his legs and compresses his thighs. fellowes1964's pose and the creases in the suit, which radiate from his crotch, direct viewers to gaze at his groin.[99] The performances of galaxy_shop, thana0, and fellowes1964 depart from the mastering stances in other gay underwear and swimwear listings. Instead, fellowes1964's crossed-leg gesture and tight suit compress his genitals, render his penis small and flaccid, and evoke the penis-tucking techniques that accompany certain forms of forced womanhood and cross-dressing. His choices are also connected to men's pleasurable selection of constricting swimsuits, in which "the package up front" is "squished into oblivion."[100]

The listings by thana0, fellowes1964, and some other sellers reform the investments in large and erect penises that accompany normative forms of straight and gay cultures. Masculinity, as Potts argues, is historically understood as not feminine and as "exteriorized, strong, hard, competitive, controlled, enduring, authoritative, and active."[101] In contrast, the flaccid penis is troubling to binary gender schemes because it is "less active," "has no stamina," and is thus too feminine. The gay interest practices I consider in this section, with their presentations of compressed and elided penises, trouble hegemonic masculinity and dyadic gender. They remind individuals that the limp and even the erect penis cannot sustain the hardness and power that have been associated with masculinity.[102]

Reforming eBay's Logic through Brand Communities and Cultural Genitals

Buyers and viewers chronicle their erotic fascination with gay interest underwear and swimwear listings. bj's friends tease him about the "eBay underwearboy pics" saved on his "hard drive (all the while hogging the chair at the computer - laughing at some, drooling at others)."[103] avi describes the "ebay spandex bulge moment" and enjoys "searching and sharing the spoils" from eBay on his blog.[104] The ebulges site says it has images collected from gay interest listings that "Ya just gotta love."[105] luckybiker07 has collected "thousands of bulges pics" from eBay listings and other sources and wants to "share" his "bulge passion" on his blog.[106] Like eBay Live! attendees, these individuals constitute a brand community and work for members by saving and posting desirable images. They are also eBay collectors. Their practices are related to the larger forms of erotica collecting facilitated by the computer and the Internet.[107]

Buyers' feedback comments highlight the desirability of depicted items and the fan and brand communities that are formed around sellers. fontal430's feedback for hrdmslguy indicates "you soooo sexxxy" while turnage2007 reviews his underwear purchase and rhapsodizes "luv ur stuff Hot pics too."[108] mscljocko is "the hottest thing on EBAY. Excellent EBAYer."[109] These buyers engage with the gay interest brand community when posting advice such as "hot seller. check him out" and "This is the BEST and HOTTEST seller on eBay! YOU WILL ENJOY!!! AAAAA+."[110] In their feedback comments, buyers admire and evaluate sellers' embodied attributes along with their underwear and swimwear products. Through this behavior, the feedback forum, which is a key part of eBay's community and trust-building system—and is sometimes quoted in listings and About Me sites—highlights the ways men gaze at other men. Members' consumer comments thereby reframe eBay's system, gendered organizational logic, and constitution of normative sexual citizenship.

Sellers' gay interest self-presentations are part of eBay's erotic culture. Despite eBay's emphasis on heterosexual couples and families, it has a reputation for being a site where free porn can be accessed. According to Adam Cohen, the listings in the Adult Only category are "filled with photographs of topless women and scantily clad men that were not only being used to sell pornography—they were arguably pornography themselves."[111] Scammers post images of nude women on eBay Motors, then use site redirects and other tactics to get viewers to provide their IDs, passwords, and other personal information without paying too much attention. As I have previously indicated, erotic content from eBay is also posted on other sites. Bloggers such as bj and avi repost gay underwear and swimwear listings with erotic content in their blogs. The producers of ebulges claim that if "there's a bulge at Ebay, you'll probably find it" on their site "sooner or later."[112]

ebulges, which is also called the Visible Penis Line or VPL, presents numerous grids of men's visible penis lines. The site advises viewers, "Ebay seems to be very watchful for these bulges, so if you see one, send it to VPL!"[113] In this way, ebulges manages the seen and unseen ontology of Internet settings, becomes an archive of gay eBay representations, and encourages viewers to work at finding erotic images of men. Its ordered grids demonstrate how another organizational logic and form of immaterial labor is functioning on eBay. ebulges' process of discovering and posting erotic eBay images is related to sellers finding depictions of men with visible bulges in Internet sites and printed sources and selling them on eBay. Although ebulges offers a convenient archive of erotic material, some collectors, such as avi, "enjoy spotting the ebay bulge" in its "natural habitat, the cold cruel world of sex motivated commerce."[114] According to avi, the eBay experience includes discovering listings, personally making the unseen gay aspects of the setting visible, acknowledging the commercial motivations at work, and engaging with sellers. ebulges viewers cannot fully connect with sellers because the site does not provide listing numbers, sellers' IDs, or contact information.

ebulges, in a similar way to avi's blog, mentions the economic aspects of selling gay interest underwear and swimwear: With "the singlet laid on the floor, like some wrinkled rag. Who would buy that? BUT, put a MAN in that singlet, with a nice ebulge" and these items sell for "2 to 5 times more."[115] ebulges also entitles listings "Making More Money With the Male Member."[116] It proposes that good marketing strategies garner higher prices; individuals are buying bulges rather than singlets; and images of gay sex sell. Some gay interest fans suggest similar things in Internet forums. Nevertheless, these propositions diverge from Sender's analysis. Closed auction prices for gay interest underwear and swimwear do not ordinarily support ebulges' claims. For instance, kirkieskorner's "Micro-Bikini" listing, which included a side and rear view of him in the revealing item, generated 903 views but only sold for 7 U.S. dollars.[117] Gay interest underwear and swimwear have a value that is not represented in economic profits.

eBay viewers are invested in bulges and visible penis lines but wonder whether some of the images are falsified. As NYC swimmer asks, "Do you think that's really all him in there?"[118] avi indicates that a depiction is impossible by inquiring, How "is his bulge showing so clearly through both yellow underwear and black shorts?"[119] avi also challenges a representation of a man in patterned shorts. He advises the seller that the "next time you stuff your hideous geometry crotch, try something more realistically penis-and-balls-shaped (like a penis and balls) versus a run over teddy bear or 27 hefty bags or whatever the hell is in there."[120] Thus, avi highlights how representations of penises can be confusing. For example, hrdmslguy's bulge is misshapen, undifferentiated from his stomach, and too large.[121] In one image, hrdmslguy pulls the top of a singlet down so the garment hangs low on his hips, reveals his pubic hair, forms a long vertical panel in front of his crotch, and acts as a stand-in for his penis.[122] As all of this indicates, images cannot be relied on to convey real genitals or material proof. These viewers of visible penis line perform a critique that is similar to intellectual interrogations of the relationship between photography, digital imaging, and specific moments and material objects. Gay interest representations, like the technologies through which they are conveyed, flicker and are unstable.

In addition to simulating genital size in underwear and swimwear listings on eBay, men trouble genital bulk in other situations. The gay interest sellers of support underwear indicate that masculinity needs physical as well as ideological bolstering. hrdmslguy offers "the Nhance feature that pushes you out much like a wonderbra does for women" but "in men it gives you more power in the crotch department."[123] In a similar manner, usflaboy lists underwear with a "built in sling to support your asset. It makes the package look bigger."[124] Sellers chronicle men's production of genital size and the ways these renderings of enhanced masculinity fail. For undermaster87, "No matter how much 'lifting and enhancing' the Wonderjock from AussieBum may provide, there is no way that any man, gay or straight, should ever wear these grotesque undies" because they present men's genitals in an unflattering way.[125] These sellers establish an authentic genital state and show how such positions are mediated by social expectations and underwear technologies.

For men, large penises are "inherent to the macho thing."[126] However, gay interest underwear and swimwear listings challenge men's claims about having large penises and being masculine. Advertisements for pouch technologies that lift and enhance bolster the masculinity of buyers, promise to leave men "feeling amazing," and suggest that men's attributes and masculinity are inadequate without re-engineering.[127] These representations produce cultural genitals, or gender features that are accepted as sex traits, even though such markers as clothing, hair length, posture, and fabric-covered bumps and bulges convey them. Individuals usually believe they see and know the truth about people's material bodies and sex, despite evidence that their knowledge is based on cultural genitals rather than physical examination. Descriptions of constructed bulges and gender markers, which I study in more depth in the next chapter, emphasize how genitals and binary sex are unreliable ways to understand bodies.

Gay interest listings sometimes depict ready penises, but they pose an erotic engagement that is not heterosexually based and that does not correlate men's erections to their penetration of women. Figuring a genital eroticism that is unrelated to penis/vagina penetration challenges heteronormative settings. The "normal erection," as demonstrated by Leonore Tiefer's sexuality research, "is implicitly defined as 'hard enough for penetration'" of the vagina "and lasting 'until ejaculation.'"[128] Since there is no always erect state, the functions of corporeal bodies threaten cultural conceptions of masculinity. The postcoital penis, according to Potts, always shrinks and softens, and the man is disempowered along with "the deflation" of "his (penis-)body."[129] Some gay underwear and swimwear sellers do not even pose a hard penis and body. Representations of erect penises, which indicate that men are always sexually ready and potent, are removed by eBay and thus deflated. However, sellers who present less detailed images of their genitals, while still including faint and partially flaccid genital references, further threaten the relationship between men, masculinity, penises, and the empowered phallus.[130]

Gay Interest Vintage Photography

All gay and gay interest sellers present a position that is different from eBay's standard address. Sellers of gay interest photographs remake and rewrite the past that images are believed to convey, including period-specific masculinities and representations of genitals. Sellers in the "Photographic Images > Antique (Pre-1940)" category use the terms "gay" and "gay interest" to designate a commodity they believe gay individuals will want and thereby acknowledge the diverse sexualities of collectors; suggest that gay, lesbian, bisexual, transgendered, and queer individuals and relationships have been photographically portrayed; describe non-normative masculinities; and queer the past by describing same-sex duos and groups as gay. For example, the listings from pelicancan's "late gay uncle's photo albums" offer a history of gay documenting and recount stories the uncle told the seller.[131] Descriptions of the "Materials from the estate of a Professor of Romance Languages," which were "purchased in 1996 from his gay nephew," render gay families and collecting practices.[132] These "gay photographs" allow sellers such as endymian to highlight a "record of gay culture" that remains "a historic part and contemporary component of gay culture."[133] Through such practices, these sellers encourage members to read eBay for gay content. Their political engagements extend beyond the site when they identify family albums and photography collections as having gay content and depicting gay people.

Sellers of gay interest vintage photography, like underwear and swimwear sellers, address consumers as gay men and express interest in well-endowed men. jonmcgarrah entitles a listing "Vintage Nude Male Bodybuilder handtinted photo Gay Int: Sexy man holding long rod, bulge, Muscle men, Beefcake!"[134] This "almost-naked young man," is "Outstanding in his Field. (GetIt?)." In a similar manner, ziel400 lists an image of men holding sports equipment as "13 beefcake men present their STICKS GAY INT."[135] Sellers use these framing terms and commentary to encourage viewers to look at images differently and to read aspects of images to support their desires. For instance, jonmcgarrah uses the word "rod" as a way to highlight the bodybuilder's penis. These objects enable gay interest sellers to make erotic jokes and find or create gay content. Sellers of gay interest vintage photography offer images of active bodies and describe them as visually accessible, feminine, and alluring. They thereby transform the vigorous male body into "beefcake" and an appealing object.

Sellers mention and elide genital bulges in their gay interest readings of photographs. elephants_collector offers an image of a "man with his p...s being visible through the undies."[136] The seller highlights genitals without fully naming them and makes the term invisible to buyers and the regulating forces that use eBay's search options. In doing this, elephants_collector evokes the ways the seen and unseen body functions on eBay, including how swimwear becomes sheer. In an image of men in bathing suits, 123elroubi finds unrequited gay desire and an erect but not discernible penis. According to the seller, a man "IS COVERING UP SOMETHING" because he was "LOOKING AT NICE BUNS" and now has an erection.[137] Many of the penis lines in gay interest photography listings are visible. However, some sellers deploy alternative reading methods and shift between the seen and unseen. camp-classics offers a photographic detail to make the genital bulge apparent.[138] toomanyretro expends more effort when he finds "a great-looking tall, dark and lean man" in the image.[139] It is not until the viewer has put the image "Under magnification" that "it looks like there's a pack in his pocket." The "Eyes Move Toward The Center" of another image because the groin is positioned there.[140] toomanyretro posits that it is "the photographer's favorite spot." Through these readings, sellers articulate erotic engagements and histories of gay visibility. They pose the penis as a site of desire and a place of heterosexual crisis. Such assertions as crotch grabs and spread-legged seated positions are cultural features, even an operation, of straight men's dominance. However, these listings associate seen and unseen but emphasized bulges and visible penis lines with gay identities and desires.

Gay interest photography sellers also provide narratives about men finding love and being caught. pelicancan describes men realizing they are gay, finding male partners, hiding relationships, and being discovered having sex with other men. The men portrayed in one of his listings "discovered a secret about each other that allowed them to experience the most complete, sensual love imaginable between two gay men."[141] He also tells about sailors who "escaped discovery time and time again as their demands for one another grew increasingly" careless.[142] A gym teacher kisses a student and is found by peers, who "were shocked to see the two men in such a passionate state" but knew what was occurring because a view of their trousers "made it obvious."[143] These historical figures discover gay desires and relationships. In a similar manner, vintage photography viewers find gay content in images because of rods, sticks, and bulges. Nevertheless, the relationship between the image and narrative is conflicted. Although pelicancan and some other sellers provide detailed accounts of gay histories, their images do not usually represent the described encounters. The full narrative and context can be seen only through sellers' descriptions. These listings are grouped with representations that are, as noted by sellers, of erotic gay interest. For instance, pelicancan presents images of "two handsome, young men sitting closely together under a tree" and "pressing their knees together" and "smooth, tanned bodies clad in tight swim trunks."[144] The varied political and marketing strategies of pelicancan and other sellers prevent the formation of a seamless history or homogeneous photographic viewing practice. Sellers' accounts of earlier times and relationships become intermeshed with contemporary queer readings of vintage photography, erotic viewing of underwear and tight swim trunks, and items that are labeled "gay."

Photography sellers echo clothing sellers' narratives about the visibility and invisibility of gay identities and bodies. They disable expectations that photography conveys a fully viewable and material world. In their accounts, photographs must be read, and textual histories and viewing cues may be needed. endymian identifies his practices as a "str8 forward reading of photographic material" by "your egay photo" specialist. According to his comments, photography is presumed to be a direct record of particular times and objects, but readings of it are informed by sexuality positions, require a specialist, and are difficult to understand. Through descriptions of informational breakdown and indications that there is something beyond what was in front of the camera, gay interest vintage photography sellers code photographs in similar ways to the use of the phrase "pictures do not do it justice." They highlight photographic failures, and the norms that usually accompany these forms, so a version of gay can be elucidated from varied hints and sources. In doing this, they perform a kind of consumer critique of straight culture and eBay.

Sellers indicate that images do not do objects justice to direct viewers to engage by buying things. However, gay and gay interest listings are most fully elucidated on the eBay site. This makes what buyers are viewing and purchasing and the characteristics of eBay-facilitated gay and gay interest collections unclear. For instance, gay interest underwear and swimwear, much of which is no more revealing or typecast as gay than other items in the category, does not carry any larger cultural meaning when it is worn. These listings have a presence on the site and create inventive communities, connections, and traces of sellers for the people who wear such items. Sellers assert gay viewing positions and men who admire men's bodies. Female sellers, and women who view these listings, are incorporated into these performances and desires, take up drag positions, and operate in settings where men, rather than women, are looked at. These subject positions are antithetical to eBay's gendered and heterosexual organizational logic and founding narratives.

Conclusion: The Politics of Gay Interest

Sellers' gay and gay interest listings trouble straight men's sexuality and power. It is therefore not surprising that many eBay members are anti-fans and reject the accompanying viewing positions, devalue such images, dismiss the people represented, and resist the ways these materials are described. queen-of-parts promises "not to say 'gay interest'" when listing a photograph.[145] raretomes is opposed to describing postcards as "gay interest" because it "is pure conjecture."[146] Gay interest sellers are sometimes inundated by homophobic comments, such as atukolm, who uses the gay interest and lesbian interest search terms in listings but warns "THOSE OF YOU WHO HAVE SENT VILE EMAILS . . . DO NOT EMAIL ME AGAIN, there are ebay rules against harassment."[147] The "mountain of homophobic emails" camp-classics receives indicates "that some people just don't get" gay interest selling practices."[148] gargantua adds a disclaimer to his listings because of the numerous homophobic emails he receives from irate viewers. He attempts to protect himself and the ways the term "gay interest" reflects on his sexuality by advising that "GAY is a Search Word" and is "Not a LABEL or SOCIAL COMMENTARY about the VIEWER or the SUBJECT of the photo."[149] speakswithmusic is purportedly "not thinking of anything sexual, . . . not referring to the people in the images, but the culture that some of the eBay shoppers identify themselves with."[150] Sellers like speakswithmusic are ambivalent about considering and making fully visible considerations of gay sexualities. They also understandably want to avoid being textually gay-bashed.

Gay interest sellers try to protect their practices and positions, but some viewers send scathing emails because gay interest listings provide social commentary. These viewers convey the ongoing cultural unease with the possibility of gay pasts and presents and how these histories affect cultural and sexual identities. It can be difficult, as Sender argues, to use explicit gay identities and sexualities as typical selling strategies. Fear of alienating mainstream shoppers causes some sellers to perpetuate the advertising strategies described by Danae Clark in her GLBTQ consumer research. They produce "gay window ads" where content is coded so that it is only recognizable to gay consumers.[151] For instance, sellers use the terms "gay" and "lesbian" in listings but make the text the same color as the background. These listings appear in "gay" searches, but the term is not readily visible to viewers. Only scrolling over the words while "cutting and pasting" or searching for the term while viewing listings, which are unlikely practices, reveal the invisible texts. When sellers employ these tactics, even the terms "gay" and "lesbian" are closeted.[152] Gay and lesbian interest buyers may become more knowing consumers who see parts of listings that remain unseen by other viewers, but their reading skills, buying power, and interests are hidden from other groups of buyers and sellers. These marketing behaviors curtail the political possibilities of gay and lesbian interest listings that are otherwise facilitated by sellers' descriptions of gay and lesbian communities and positioning of buyers and viewers.

Some eBay sellers weave current politics into the sale of erotic images and objects. danthemusicman lists "Original Issue Promotional Stickers from 1993 The March On Washington, for Lesbian, Gay & Bi Rights."[153] When endymian offers a nineteenth-century image of a man in drag, he writes that he wants "to say to george bush" that "if your amendment goes through you and dick cheney will never be a legal couple."[154] He calls his eBay store, where other items are available for purchase, "the stonewall endymian gay photo shop" in order "to honor the men whose defiance of new york city police brutality against gay men in 1969 triggered the modern gay liberation movement."[155] He views the "sale of gay merchandise on ebay as a celebration of gay identity and one tied inexorably to the gay liberation movement." Sellers also support gay histories by describing the sexuality of relatives. For example, unclecrickey offers "diaries" and "special memorabilia" from his "Great Uncle Crickey"—a veteran of the Second World War and "an openly gay man in the Navy."[156] The eBay ID unclecrickey allows him to become a version of his gay relative. Through such practices, sellers embrace a variety of sexualities.

Listings accomplish positive political work and articulate essentialist notions of gay identities and desires. A studio photograph of a Tarzan character "is gayer than gay," and a man in another photograph "is gay indeed! He wears a lighter suit but sports polka dot socks!"[157] Clothing sellers also associate tight and revealing underwear and swimwear with gay identities. Some amount of essentialism may be unavoidable, since, as John Elsner and Roger Cardinal outline in their visual culture research, "Collecting is classification lived."[158] Objects become understandable because of the ways they are described and related to other things. Collecting, which includes the desire to acquire and group items, requires articulating a set of essential attributes. Therefore, sellers also render essentialist ideas about sexuality and desire when queering images, undoing the insistent focus on heterosexual identities and desires, and associating being a sailor or dressing in a dapper manner with being gay.

The limiting outcome that queering can have on an array of possible gay identities can at least be partially resolved by employing such tactics as irony and parody when finding gay elements in images. gargantua uses varied images and texts to self-represent as the "500 pound go-rilla." He establishes a difference between himself and viewers by referring to their opposable thumbs, indicating that images will "blow your human mind," creating fanciful tales, and reusing familiar phrases to connect aspects of listings to contemporary gay culture.[159] In depicting an image of shirtless young male rabbit hunters in the 1920s, gargantua evokes some of the stereotyped aspects of gay club cultures by writing, "Kill the wabbit! Kill the wabbit! And you might as well have a few poppers & take your shirts off while you do."[160] He also offers an image of women performing as a heterosexual couple, in which one of them is wearing a suit. gargantua humorously notes, "God help the Mister that comes between Him and her sister."[161] In this text, gargantua uses the pronouns "him" and "her" to describe the person in drag, emphasize the portrayed individuals' unstable gender positions, and highlight the difficulties in reading images for gender and sex attributes. gargantua playfully combines narratives about clubs and gender conventions to encourage viewers to read culture differently. He also uses wordplay, cartoon "self-portraits" of a purple gorilla, and other distinctive visual aspects to emphasize how sellers construct themselves.

Gay and gay interest sellers do not remain conventional bodies or gendered individuals. Some photography sellers complicate their gender positions by using vintage photographic images of individuals to stand in for their businesses and identities. These images rarely correlate to the identities articulated in posted comments and to the full names and email addresses that are provided when buyers "win" auctions. Other sellers tell more fantastic stories about their bodies. For instance, gargantua renders a large male body and genital bulk when self-representing as a naked gorilla. In one listing he notes, "Garg is a bit of a porker."[162] gargantua self-represents in spread-legged gorilla poses, but his genitals never show and his masculinity is thereby challenged. He further complicates his embodied configuration by using "his" gorilla head to hide representations of nude women's breasts and other things eBay might censor. Through these gestures, he renders his practice childish, since he graphically presents on top of women's erotic bodies and gets morphed into and attached to female bodies.

eBay's search engine also destabilizes fixed identity positions and the cultural boundaries between gay and straight. Sellers sometimes use the term "gay" in listings that address heterosexuals as well as gay people. For instance, magnumxl_wholesale offers "100% Legal Synthetic Man Sex Pheromones For Gay Men."[163] His experience with the product "exceeded" expectations; his "wife could not keep her hands off" him, and "a younger female co-worker" suddenly struck up a "flirtatious conversation." magnumxl_wholesale's description may be an attempt to self-present as heterosexual, and thus remain unmarked by gay products, but his use of the term "wife" is queered by his listings. The meaning of gay is also complicated because searching for the term generates objects from the "Gay 1890s," people whose first or last name is "Gay," and companies and products that incorporate the word. For example, sx28 offers a "Pair 6L6 GAY Vacuum tubes."[164] Listings for Mattel's Gay Parisienne Barbie may refer to the company's title for the doll, highlight its queerness, or queer doll collectors. Books and other items with the term "gay" in their titles are also listed seriously and read queerly.

Sellers construct the buyer, collector, and viewer when articulating what gay looks like, the kinds of images and objects that are of "interest" to the gay community, and what may be in the community's best interest. Collections are formed and dispersed on eBay as items from estates and from sellers are offered for sale. For Michael Camille, collecting is a "process" by which objects "are being constantly produced, reconfigured, and redefined."[165] This form of reworking and circulating is different from what eBay's advertisements propose. For instance, eBay associates collecting with normative histories and stable heterosexuality by depicting the reappearance of the engagement ring in the female owner's home. Gay interest readings deform the ways items are normatively conceived at the same time that aspects of gay interest maintain some coherence.

Sellers' gay interest listings and narratives have consequences that exceed the site because, as Elsner and Cardinal argue, collecting is a key part of how people "accommodate," "appropriate," and "extend the taxonomies and systems of knowledge that they have inherited."[166] Gay interest collections help complicate and queer dominant conceptions of society and highlight the value of gay, lesbian, and queer histories because the "categories into which" people and things "are assigned confirm the precious knowledge of culture handed down through the generations." Camille explains how the multiform desires circulating in gay and lesbian interest collecting and the boundlessness of collectors' desires trouble the dyadic logic and heterosexual imaginary of contemporary culture.[167] Sellers of gay listings enact a consumer critique and try to generate a different form of culture and knowledge from the one that eBay management produces. Even as eBay works to assert heteronormativity, these listings articulate the economic and political value of gay interests and sexualities.

Gay interest renderings of masculinity, including flaccid penises and feminine masculinities, cannot fully support men's cultural power and claims about being dominant. Female sellers of gay and gay interest vintage photography, who are occasionally gendered on the site, produce gay listings and desires rather than being rendered as objects of the gaze. The employment of the terms "lesbian" and "lesbian interest," as I analyze it in the next chapter, also destabilizes an empowered male gaze and subject position. Sellers use it to describe a variety of representations and subject positions rather than only articulating erotic images of women engaging with each other, which straight men might enjoy. In gay interest underwear, swimwear, and vintage photography listings, the processes of being looked at and objectified are reserved for men. This breakdown of normative masculinity offers theoretical possibilities for rethinking gender, race, sexuality, and other identity positions in Internet settings and other spheres. Sellers of gay interest underwear and swimwear further trouble the functions and organizational logic of the site because they use listings, and the possibilities of communicating through eBay, to connect figuratively and literally to gay men and "get it on" via the site.

eBay Boys Will Be Lesbians

VIEWING "LESBIAN" AND "LESBIAN INTEREST"

VINTAGE PHOTOGRAPHY LISTINGS

Some eBay vintage photography sellers address heterosexual male buyers but list mass-produced erotic images of women as "lesbian" and "lesbian interest" in the "Collectibles > Photographic Images > Antique (Pre-1940)" and "Collectibles > Postcards > Real Photo" categories. They offer images of women undressing, wearing lingerie, and engaging in erotic play and pictures of "bush sisters" with visible pubic hair. For instance, an image of a seated woman who is nude except for a drape across her groin is titled "1950's NUDE 6" X 8" REAL PHOT0 LESBIAN INTEREST" (figure 12).[1] Sellers of vernacular photography also employ the terms "lesbian" and "lesbian interest" when presenting items to lesbian viewers and consumers. These images, many of which seem more collaboratively produced by the subjects and photographer, are of women standing or sitting close together, acting in lively ways that bring their bodies into contact, being butch, wearing military or sports uniforms, or wearing suits and other forms of masculine drag. photogurl offers a vintage photograph that is dominated by a snowy foreground and a large snow-covered tree. The two women in the image, with their arms loosely around each other, may be a small part of the composition, but photogurl titles the photograph "Women HUGGING in the SNOW Lesbian Int *1930s* Photo" (figure 13).[2]

Sellers use the terms "lesbian" and "lesbian interest" to describe images that are of note to lesbians; photographic documentation of lesbian pasts;

12. lastcall75773, "1950'S NUDE 6" X 8" REAL PHOTO LESBIAN INTEREST- NR," eBay, 27 February 2007

women performing varied kinds of masculinity; queer readings of photographs that confuse stable categories, desires, and subject positions; political positions that enhance lesbian communities; erotic images of women together; and promiscuity—even when only one person is depicted. Through this conflicted usage, sellers make male buyers of images of nude women seem less straight and reconceptualize sexuality and eroticism outside of the straight/gay binary. This also occurs in sellers' gay and gay interest listings for underwear, swimwear, and vintage photography, which trouble the position of heterosexual men. In all of these cases, the political interests of sellers differ from eBay's gendered and heterosexual organizational logic and the normative forms of sexual citizenship eBay promotes. The lesbian interest and gay interest search terms are also economically productive in the photography and real photo categories. They remake generic images of people and families into personal accounts and collectible objects. In these categories, the kinds of identities eBay is promoting achieve the lowest sale prices.

"Straight" men who engage with lesbian and lesbian interest listings by pointing, selecting, pleasurably viewing, and buying indicate they have lesbian interests, become associated with the political aspects of these listings, and are positioned as lesbians. Their gendered identities, which I consider later in the chapter, are sometimes articulated in listings, About Me sites, and member IDs. Individuals who sign in to eBay and use the site's search options to track lesbian listings, or who have included the term "lesbian" as one of their "Favorite Searches," broadcast these interests to people looking at their screens. Searches for the term "lesbian" also deliver lesbian interest

13. photogurl, "Women HUGGING in the SNOW Lesbian Int *1930s* Photo," eBay, 22 February 2007

listings. For individuals searching for mass-produced erotica, the vernacular images of women engaged in varied life activities produce a narrative and visual disturbance in the search results and some men's fantastical construction of what "lesbian" means. These images must be read or skimmed over to find the desired materials. When engaged by this diverse grouping of images and texts, men cannot just pleasurably view the "girl-on-girl" action photographs that were originally directed at them. Men view versions of lesbians that were not coded or designed for them and are situated within and in front of the pictures in subject positions that are different from the ones they anticipated. In doing this, men support the economic and ideological values of gender and sexuality positions that are far from their own. Their unexpected situation encourages a rethinking of the ways binary gender and stable sexualities are articulated by theories of viewing. The construction of men with lesbian interests and portrayal of women performing masculinities promote continued examinations of how gender, sex, and sexuality are identified.

Lesbian interest listings are designed by individual sellers and appear within the photographic images category, as well as in other eBay categories. Hierarchical categories, such as collectibles or photographic images, are produced by eBay, and individuals must accept this system to reach the widest market. Lesbian and gay interest listings are an intervention into the system. They function as consumer critiques of the structuring aspects of the eBay system and the positions produced by the company. Viewers see gay and lesbian listings and read about gay and lesbian interests whenever they look at eBay. Listings for gay interest vintage photographs usually depict men and are directed at gay men, but lesbian interest listings are directed toward divergent audiences. This is different from eBay's standard address. In chapter 3, I interrogated how eBay makes binary gender and heterosexual unions an implicit part of the site through its articulation of gendered consumers, representations of engagements and marriages, and the apocryphal and often repeated origin story about Pierre Omidyar starting the site as a sort of love token so his fiancée, Pam Wesley, could trade Pez dispensers. Sellers of lesbian interest photography challenge eBay's organizational logic and binary gender positions by intervening in the normative reading of images and buyers' and sellers' desires. For example, their images of "mock" weddings disorder the marriage scripts, rituals, and mandates for femininity that are conveyed in eBay's advertisements and sellers' wedding-dress listings. Because of these sellers' practices and the highlighted performances of women in listed images, the photographs no longer seem to deliver unmediated engagements with women.

The work of feminist film theorists, including Laura Mulvey's consideration of gendered forms of viewing, assists me in reflecting on how male buyers are enabled to view erotic images of women.[3] I extend my use of feminist film theory, employed in *The Body and the Screen: Theories of Internet Spectatorship*, to understand how individuals are structured and even produced by Internet settings.[4] It may appear as if applying theories of viewing, which describe how movies and larger cinematic institutions, mechanical projection, the space of the theater, and identification construct spectators, is antithetical to theorizing individuals' "active" Internet use. However, Internet and new media studies is forwarded when there are methods to interrogate the ways traditional subjects are reproduced and developed in Internet settings, as well as how people are provided with options and establish forms of resistance. After all, a great deal of computer use occurs while individuals are fixed in chairs and provided with distinct messages about who they are, how they should look, and the ways they should engage.

Feminist film theories productively critique how women are represented and the kinds of bodies that are expected to engage, but they also describe stable subjects, binary gender, and heterosexual desires. These methods are useful when combined with literature that theorizes how media forms can facilitate shifting subject positions. For instance, Chris Straayer provides tactics for considering the heteronormative positions and queer desires that are rendered by lesbian and lesbian interest listings.[5] Research by Alisa Solomon and Sue-Ellen Case, which describes how butch and camp performances disturb the seemingly natural relationship between masculinity and men, offers ways to think about the position of male lesbian interest viewers who engage with images of butch women and women in men's attire.[6] I will tend to refer to these women as "butches" because it is difficult to fully distinguish people's identities in photographs, and women in men's attire are performing as butches in some way. The complicated combinations of identities, images, and selling strategies included under the lesbian search term also demonstrate the ambiguities of erotica images. According to the pornography research of Avis Lewallen, "Visual images alone—even of naked women in obviously provocative poses—cannot be relied upon" to unambiguously center male viewers and male titillation.[7] Lesbian interest sellers' titles and readings of images highlight how narrative breakdowns occur even when mainstream erotica depicts women together and emphasizes heterosexual male desire. The analysis of images and viewing positions, which I propose in this chapter, may thus be useful in considering Internet-based image archives and porn sites, as well as more general interfaces and practices.

Articulating Lesbians through eBay Photography

Sellers who use the terms "lesbian" and "lesbian interest" in the titles and texts of their listings code images, direct potential buyers to specific aspects of images, obtain better prices (since both mass-produced lesbian erotica and vernacular images of women together tend to garner higher prices than related material), acknowledge lesbian collectors, indicate that lesbian individuals and relationships have been photographically portrayed, and queer the past by describing same-sex duos and groups as lesbians. While the price range for this material is vast, erotic images of women engaged with other women tend to sell for more than 25 U.S. dollars and can garner upward of $100. An immense array of materials is listed under the term "lesbian," but albums with some convincing lesbian content tend to sell for more than $150; individual images, for more than $20. Depending on the content, period, and photographer, they can sell for much more. The prices of photographs of women in drag have been decreasing—a change in the market that occurred before the economic downturn—but these listed items usually sell for more than $9, and it is not unusual for them to sell for more than $40. Images of white heterosexual couples and families, by contrast, tend to sell for only a few dollars.

Sellers use the lesbian interest search term to address divergent consumers, including heterosexual men who are interested in images of women engaging in erotic encounters, women who are searching for documentation of lesbian pasts, and people who read images queerly. Gay interest listings are designed to perform in similar political and economic ways, but sellers tend to address only gay men, despite the likelihood that queer women and men are also interested in these materials. While searching for erotic images of women together, heterosexual men are also directed toward narratives about lesbian community and empowerment. In this way, the organizational logic and search functions of the eBay site fail. In a similar manner, such search engines as Yahoo! and Google offer unexpected combinations of sites and subjects. In the case of eBay and in some other instances, these breakdowns help to unravel traditional viewing structures and stable identity positions. The normative viewer is framed and addressed as someone else. Feminist media studies, including film theory, and conceptions of configuring the user assist in theorizing when the viewer is addressed and produced according to traditional conceptions of bodies and rights and when and how these positions may be transformed or fail.

Vernacular lesbian interest sellers produce conceptions of collecting in listings, About Me sites, and board posts and form an eBay community that can share ancestors, histories, and objects. In this manner, part of the lesbian interest brand community, which is situated on the site and ideologically dismissed by eBay, can imagine a shared past. The histories that are supposedly embedded in vintage photographs, like the memories associated with wedding dresses, circulate on the site and are imagined to be saved rather than lost. However, sellers' gay and lesbian interest listings pose a GLBTQ eBay community and alternative readings of images that are distinctly different from the normative system eBay produces. As traditional images of engagements, weddings, families, and babies circulate on the site and support eBay's rendering of its members, sellers of gay and lesbian interest vintage photography are actively rereading similar images and undermining eBay's family history. Some of the standard images on eBay will be "flipped"—purchased and then sold for more money—by sellers who recognize that images of same-sex groups touching and otherwise engaged can garner higher prices when described as "gay interest" or "lesbian interest" and attached to appealing readings. When sellers flip these images, they point to a certain mutability of erotics and identities. The varied individuals who engage with lesbian interest listings may intensify this fluidity.

The seller auntjennysbox and her lesbian Aunt Jenny propose a history that diverges from photography's ordinary production of the normative family. Photographs, according to Shawn Michelle Smith, are understood as methods of maintaining family histories and recording family genealogies.[8] Yet Jenny constitutes a lesbian-friendly family archive from "everyone she knew."[9] The seller, whose name is a reference to her aunt's boxed collection of photographs, provides a history of lesbians and collecting, emphasizes women's sexuality (since the term "box" is used to describe women's genitals), suggests the queer possibilities of documenting and storing, and may make some viewers humorously ponder the possibilities that the photographs were stored inside Jenny. The seller's aunt loved to "sit down and go through her photos of all the people she met and loved" and "tell about how she met the people, where they were from and a bit about them." While "being gay was greatly frowned upon" during much of Jenny's life, she insisted on being "open and honest with everyone and tried very hard to get others to be proud of who they were." Through these narratives, consumers are offered the chance to audaciously repeat Jenny's processes of collecting and archiving. auntjennysbox thanks them for "purchasing these photos and giving them a good home" and supporting and widening community history. Yet, auntjennysbox and other sellers, such as pelicancan and unclecrickey, all sell single photographs or small lots of photographs rather than maintain the existent archive.

The narratives about visibility and lesbian communities provided by sellers like auntjennysbox are different from the depictions of sexuality that appear in mass-produced lesbian erotica. Producers of mass-market lesbian erotica pose women so viewers can easily look at them. These women are performing and available for the male viewer, even when they are purportedly engaged with each other. For instance in jochen.baeuerle's listing titled "AFFECTION-ATE NUDE GIRLS Vintage 10s RPPC Lesbian Int," an erotically engaged female couple poses so that their bodies and attention are directed toward the viewer (figure 14).[10] jochen.baeuerle describes the image as "Lesbian Int," but the listing includes no text that explains how the mass-produced image is engaged with lesbian interests or community.

The production and location of politically useful images of lesbian sexuality, according to Edith Becker, Michelle Citron, Julia Lesage, and B. Ruby Rich's consideration of filmic portrayals, must be "reconciled with the objectification" of women and how the "continued existence of pornography still clouds the depiction of [lesbian] sexuality."[11] Heterosexual men's interest in women erotically engaging with women is a problem for producers who are trying to render positive images of sexuality for lesbian communities. In these cases, men are alternative viewers who successfully reconfigure images to be useful for their own desires. Some images can engage different subjects. According to Linda Williams, who studies shifting addresses and forms of identification in porn films, it is easy to "identify with diverse subject positions and desire diverse objects" when viewing pornography.[12] Whatever the current gender and desiring position of the viewer, mass-produced and vernacular lesbian interest listings present bodies to the viewer, offer structured images that were produced to be looked at, and address the individual and consumer.

Becker and her colleagues' concerns about the ways pornography appropriates and performs lesbianism may be particularly apt in instances where

14. jochen.baeuerle, "AFFECTIONATE NUDE GIRLS Vintage 10S RPPC Lesbian Int," eBay, 7 April 2006

eBay sellers use the term "lesbian" to describe images of individual nude women. In such cases, the term "lesbian" cannot draw connections between particular aspects of images and a community of women loving women or women engaging in erotic play with other women. Sellers who use the term "lesbian" to indicate erotic depictions of individual women suggest erotic potentials and desires that are not visually conveyed in images but may still be part of viewers' interests and habits. In such cases, images and listings act as a lure for unfulfilled desires that can be imaginatively staged by viewers with the assistance of these representations. Unfortunately, the disparate roles and desires of the portrayed women can be elided through such readings. Since lesbians are still too often marked as having a non-normative or even deviant sexuality, the term "lesbian" is regrettably used to indicate that these women, and perhaps all lesbians, are risqué and sexually available to the gaze and physical encounters.

Sellers of lesbian and lesbian interest photographs do not necessarily imagine listings as part of a lesbian past or continuum in which women had and continue to have erotic relationships with women without needing to address men. fouraker describes a "collection of 1950s era nude images that were found in an elderly lady's attic" and uses the term "lesbian interest," but evacuates lesbian and queer collecting strategies and desires by noting the images "evidently belonged to her late husband."[13] The seller antique_samblue employs the term "lesbian," describes views of the posed woman as "a Busty Blond woman with her pig tails," "a view of her with BIG smile hands on hips nice ass shot," and "a view of her with pouty lips large boobs blanket over privates," and then discusses men's ability to find "risqué" photographs like the ones offered for sale.[14] Lesbian is also associated with depictions of "busty girls wrestling wearing panties" and "busty lesbian girlfriends with a super rear view."[15] In such instances, lesbianism is rendered as a form of eroticism that engages male viewers, configures images, and objectifies women.

Sellers' portrayals of women as a set of erotic and evaluated parts are troubling. Yet sellers also disturb men's heteronormative position when they correlate men's desires to lesbian viewing positions. nobodysa lists an image from a "group of vintage nudes, risque and erotic photographs" that depicts a "Lovely scene between two women in french lingerie" under the lesbian interest search term.[16] By using the term "lesbian interest," nobodysa indicates a women's erotic sphere and that such images can also positively engage women's desires. "Discovering" and being able to voyeuristically watch women renders a different erotic and identity position from being addressed as a lesbian. Of course, lesbians can also occupy delighted positions as invisible viewers. Men's empowered position and ability to immediately access numerous images of women that have been designed for their pleasure are disrupted by the kinds of images eBay sellers include under the lesbian interest search term. For example, pixidiom's vernacular image of a fully dressed playful woman pretending to kick another clothed woman's bottom, which presents a different desiring structure from the mass-produced erotica images, is entitled "1940, GAY VINTAGE LESBIAN, GAL, KICK, SEXY, ASS, REAR-END FUN."[17] The seller uses the title as a lure and thereby disrupts viewers' expectations and desires. The seller promises a depiction of erotic anal play but delivers no such content.

Searching for lesbian and lesbian interest listings on eBay also generates vernacular images of women having fun, being butch, and wearing men's suits. For instance, the seller mr.philipines offers a "Turn of the Century" image of a dressed "Filipina girl" who looks like a lesbian because her hair is "combed upward and cut short" and "her posture is unfeminine."[18] rosie247's vernacular image of women is identified as lesbian interest because of "the boots, or maybe the neck ties."[19] Individual sellers may articulate essentialist notions of who lesbians are, what they look like, and the actions and sexualities that frame their lives in ways that are similar to gay interest listings. However, the disparate images and readings included under lesbian interest make this structure less likely to articulate essentialist ideas than the gay interest search term, where wearing dapper clothing or being in the military is associated with being gay. When using the lesbian interest search term eBay buyers, including men, see images that are of lesbian interest. A relationship is thereby established between their desires and lesbian interests and identities. This occurs when browsing listings using the "risqué" subcategory in "Photographic Images > Antique (Pre-1940)," searching under the term "nude" or "lesbian," or saving the "lesbian" search term and receiving emailed information about auctions. Narratives about lesbian interests reposition male viewers, configuring their use of the site and identity in different ways than male privilege would suggest. Male viewers are presented with a much wider array of lesbian images than many of them probably requested. These sellers thus foil eBay's promise that buyers can easily "get it on eBay."

Viewing Lesbian Interest

Sellers offer diverse images, render varied desires, and list different forms of representations under the lesbian and lesbian interest search terms. For instance, thedragonsmoon lists "VINTAGE RISQUE SEXY FETISH NUDE LESBIAN ART PHOTO" with a depiction of a woman clad in bra, panties, and stockings tying up another woman.[20] thedragonsmoon also presents the similarly entitled "VINTAGE RISQUE 1918 LESBIAN DYKES at COLLEGE PHOTO."[21] However, this image depicts two fully clothed butch women in caps, high-necked shirts, jodhpurs, and sturdy boots. In thedragonsmoon's vernacular college photo, the use of the term "risqué" may indicate the women's unconventional dress and potential erotic engagement. In a similar manner to pixidiom's "REAR-END FUN" listing, the title lures erotica collectors to the listing. However, there is no depicted nudity or show of flesh. The college photo, with its portrayal of two women touching and dressed in similar masculine attire, is visually analogous to listings of vernacular photographs that are described as portraying lesbian pasts. By using similar titles to describe

Vintage Two Nude Women Grooming Photo, Lesbian Interest

Measures 8x10.

*(As always, I have a few more items at auction,
Please click below to view them. Thanks)*

I HAVE A LOT MORE **VINTAGE PHOTOS** UP FOR AUCTION. PLEASE TAKE A LOOK. THANKS

Click Here To See My Other Auctions

15. tomscoolcollectibles, "Vintage Two Nude Women Grooming Photo, Lesbian Interest,"
eBay, 4 April 2006

these disparate images, thedragonsmoon connects diverse forms of image
production, suggests all viewers have lesbian interests, and highlights sensual content.

The "Vintage Two Nude Women Grooming Photo, Lesbian Interest" listing by tomscoolcollectibles addresses male viewers and queers traditional
forms of male desire (figure 15).[22] Without its lesbian interest indication, the
grooming photo articulates fairly traditional forms of looking. The image encourages a male gaze and structures women as the object of this empowered
view—as such arrangements have been described in feminist film theory. For
Mulvey, the women portrayed in traditional film "are simultaneously looked
at and displayed, with their appearance coded for strong visual and erotic impact so that they can be said to connote *to-be-looked-at-ness*."[23] When identification is produced along gender lines, and I consider sexuality and identification later in this chapter, then men are associated with the empowered

protagonist and the camera view. Mulvey has also described how gendered identification and "pleasure in looking" is "split between an active/male and passive/female" and dismissed the possibility that female viewers can identify with the empowered male character. There is no active male character for viewers to identify with in most erotic lesbian interest images. However, the depictions still pose a difference between an active and empowered camera gaze, which is associated in psychoanalytic film theory and popular readings with a male position, and a representational sphere that only women occupy. Women's position as the object of the gaze, or to-be-looked-at-ness, is intensified in images like the grooming photo because no men occupy the representational field, and they therefore cannot be looked at.

The viewer's gaze is encouraged in the grooming photograph by the diagonal that runs across these women's bodies and through the right edge of the shawl. The contrast between the light bodies and dark triangles of background encourages viewers to look at the women's nude forms. It also conceals most of the details of the women's space and continues cultural investments in looking at women as generic types rather than as situated individuals with their own histories and roles. This positioning of women is related to the kinds of images that are displayed in museums and other cultural venues. Representations of women in these settings, states the art historian Carol Duncan, offer little variety. They are "simply female bodies or parts of bodies, with no identity beyond their female anatomy—those ever-present 'Women' or 'Seated Women' or 'Reclining Nudes.'"[24] Some of the vernacular lesbian interest listings include names and detailed information about the women portrayed, which is desirable information that buyers often request when it is not provided, but most of the images of nudes do not provide any information about the identity of the women or the location depicted. On the rare occasions that sellers provide details, they usually give the woman's stage name and thus further situate the depicted woman within an economy of visual availability, although this information may also establish her skill and history.

The grooming photograph emphasizes viewing. The women's interlocked bodies render an angled oval frame, which validates the desire to gaze at them. The "V" of the fringed scarf forms an arrow and points viewers towards the women's nude bodies. These framing elements highlight the tilted back and orgasmic face of the woman in the foreground and emphasize that her body, like those depicted in jochen.baeuerle's listing, is directed at viewers rather than at the other participant. The grooming photograph establishes a series of differences between male and female, active and passive, and subject and object. At the same time, the depiction of a claustrophobic women's boudoir, with varied urns and jugs and compression and entwining of the bodies, correlate women to closeness. Mary Ann Doane has shown in her feminist film theory how intimate, passive, and undesirable viewing positions are all associated with women.[25] In the photograph, the women's intermeshed position, stasis, and relationship to the culturally devalued feminine activities of grooming and beautification are compositionally contrasted with the place viewers occupy. Viewers are at a distance and seemingly able to move through the image if desired. Such an articulation of difference between women—or, at least, these women—and viewers renders onlookers male and heterosexual. If viewing and identification happen along gender lines, and there are other ways viewers become engaged with images, then the photograph situates women close to their bodies and as the static object of the gaze or forces them to reject the depicted feminine interests and choose to establish a distance from women's spaces.

There are many indications that men buy items listed as lesbian and lesbian interest, including images like the grooming photograph. Information about buyers can be obtained by reviewing feedback for such items and was available by examining closed listings before eBay elided the identity of buyers because of problems with fraud. A buyer using the ID douglasclemens, or "Douglas," bought the grooming image.[26] The information on douglasclemens's About Me site includes an image and other information that identifies him as a man.[27] His self-description and list of past purchases also reveal that douglasclemens collects and sells related material, including what he describes as "early erotica." Many of these male buyers, as indicated in feedback profiles, purchase hundreds of mass-produced erotica images. A lot of erotica buyers set up their feedback profiles so they do not provide any information about purchases and, like other sellers, do not give indications about their identity in blogs, About Me, My World, and other parts of the site. However, my study of About Me sites and closed lesbian and lesbian interest listings for mass-produced erotica shows that visible buyers—and therefore, presumably, most buyers—are men.

cash5al, who bought the photograph "HAIR DO, 2 NUDES=LESBIAN? REAL PHOTO 50's NICE NO RESEV," which depicts two women in high heels touching each other, bending over so that their breasts are emphasized, and twisting their hips and knees to enact classic glamour girl poses, identifies as "Alan."[28] He is "a photographer," "collector of vintage photos, postcards," and "cameras" and lives with his "wife and family."[29] Another buyer of items listed as "lesbian" uses the ID herrlast, the first part of which designates a man in German and thereby seems to self-identify as a man.[30] darrins, who offers such items as "Vintage Lesbian Int Photo Pretty Pin Up Girls Outside," provides a depiction of "Darrin Himself in House of Photo Albums."[31] Other buyers and sellers of mass-produced erotica also choose men's names for their user IDs, present images of themselves, and specify their full names on varied parts of the site. In doing this, they connect the term "lesbian" to male viewers.

Men purchase mass-produced lesbian and lesbian interest erotica listings. However, eBay's viewing and listing processes challenge the larger homo-social aspects of men's viewing and buying of erotica. According to Duncan, "The ability of pornography to give its users a feeling of superior male status depends on its being owned or controlled by men and forbidden to, shunned by, or hidden from, women. In other words, in certain situations a female gaze can *pollute* pornography."[32] The "lesbian look," which Karen Hollinger identifies as being shared among women in her analysis of spectatorship, can challenge the "exclusive male prerogative to control the filmic gaze and recon-figures this gaze so that it reflects a new female relation to desire."[33] As sug-gested by these theories, the grooming image cannot remain in a male sphere when it is accompanied by the term "lesbian interest" and when women are gazing at and through the representation. If Duncan's argument is correct, the very visibility of men's viewing and buying may challenge their claim to this erotic terrain and these erotic bodies.

Erotica viewing and collecting may be associated with empowered mas-culinity, but there is also a cultural tendency to relate close viewing and con-sumerism, which are necessary aspects of using eBay, to femininity and fri-volity. The Internet erotica buyer is feminized by the closeness of the screen (although listed erotica photographs may articulate a distant position), overly involved forms of identification that accompany computer and Internet use, indication on Slashdot and other programmer forums that men engage with erotica only when they cannot meet women, enormous number of photo-graphs of naked women that many of these eBay members purchase, and desire to bring objects closer by buying them. As described in the introduc-tion, sellers use varied strategies to make it seem as if the only way to know about an object is by buying it. The multiform desires that accompany collecting, the related feminization of interests in shopping and décor, and the boundlessness of collectors who want to own more, as Camille argues, trouble conceptions of heterosexuality and its dyadic logic.[34]

Women are rendered "the prototypical consumer," but "the same over-presence that ties her to the image" also situates her, according to the media studies scholar Lynn Joyrich, "as both the subject and the object of consumerism."[35] Women are thereby positioned as the exemplary consumer citizen. In lesbian interest listings, women are the subject of listings and addressed as consumers. Men are also positioned as subjects and objects of lesbian interest listings, and their position as distant viewers is further compromised because they are incorporated into narratives. For instance, swampman deploys the shifting pronoun "me" in his listing titled "Duo of busty nude lesbian girls tie me up" and in so doing incorporates the viewer into the narrative.[36] He makes it seem as if the viewer is asking to be tied up and is on display. This production of closeness and a virtual position within the image produces a different engagement from that of the distant male subject, which has been coded as ideal by varied cultural practices and critical theories. For the film theorist Christian Metz, a clear distinction between subject and object and distance are necessary aspects of empowered film spectatorship.[37] Jay David Bolter, a new media studies scholar, identifies intellectual and emotional "distancing" as important aspects of reading and viewing.[38] Nevertheless, with lesbian and lesbian interest listings, men are addressed as lesbians, placed within the depicted scenarios, and ascent to this position by buying. Men's intimate consumer position is intensified by the close-up images in eBay listings.

eBay's lesbian and lesbian interest viewers may note the traditional addresses of images, but they cannot fully occupy the articulated position. Straayer offers methods for considering alternative and shifting subject positions. She considers E. Ann Kaplan's and other feminists' psychoanalytically informed considerations of the male gaze, which describe how the male viewer is acknowledged and his position is privileged.[39] Straayer argues that these theories need "to be combined with the equally pertinent question 'Is the gaze heterosexual?'"[40] The gaze produced by representations cannot remain solely heterosexual when buyers, including male heterosexual buyers, engage with listings such as "Vintage Two Nude Women Grooming Photo, Lesbian Interest" and its search-articulated relationship to myriad lesbian interests, viewing positions, and desires. The heterosexual man with lesbian interests has a less straight and empowered position. His interests place him too close to the screen and these women's bodies, which now represent his body, so he is looked at and offered up to the gaze rather than distantly gazing.

Lesbians may "exercise an active gaze at women in the text," writes Straayer, but lesbians' "experience as women watching women nevertheless may quickly expand to include the feeling of being watched."[41] Straayer challenges assumptions that identification always happens along gender lines while acknowledging the ways women are encouraged to perform as objects. On eBay, the representations of passive women and encouragement for women to self-identify as objects are compromised by eBay's construction of the active gaze and inspecting glance of the consumer. Watching is a key aspect of eBay, and buyers and sellers patrol listings and feedback histories for information about other people's buying habits and reliability. Being watched and surveilled is also a feature of Internet settings with information about such things as individuals' buying habits, posting times, logins, attributes, and preferences available or even streamed to other members.

Lesbian Interests in Butches, Femmes, and Women in Drag

Lesbian art historians at the Barnard Feminist Art and Art History Conference have responded to feminist critiques of how women are objectified in paintings and other visual works. They deploy a spectatorial position that is based on sexual desire as well as gender and describe their delight in depictions of women's breasts. They also recognize the ways such images structure gender positions. Given this active lesbian look, women cannot be scripted solely as the object of the gaze. The photographer Elizabeth Stephens describes her childhood interest in images of pin-up girls as humiliating and exciting. She "wanted them to aim their dewy eyes" at her, rather than only looking at them, and to "be held and caressed like the virgin tools that they lavished their attention on."[42] However, Stephens also expresses some concern about coveting the accompanying "masculine space with its prerogatives and entitlements to look and possess, even if only in fantasy." Stephens adopts the shifting views that such images can facilitate and imagines these representations, and the women who enact these parts, to be looking back at her. These lesbian gazes, and women who pleasurably, performatively, and visibly view representations of women, can prevent men from fully owning erotic images of women and articulating homosocial male spaces.

Like lesbian gazes, which can help to destabilize men's possession of erotic images of women, images of butches and women in masculine drag challenge men's possession of masculinity. Butch masculinity includes bravado postures; the presentation of strength, toughness, and a lack of emotion; wearing men's clothing; conveying men's anatomy; and relationships with feminine women. Due to such features, butch masculinity threatens the correlation between masculine/male and feminine/female that ordinarily articulates the power and rights of heterosexual men. According to Mabel Maney, a writer of lesbian pulp fiction, women "do masculinity so much better than men."[43] Joan Nestle, a writer and co-founder of the Lesbian Herstory Archives, describes butch-femme as a "lesbian-specific way of deconstructing gender."[44] Solomon highlights the political importance of such identity positions. She defines butchness as the "refusal to play a part in the heterosexist binary" and as "the most dangerous queer image."[45]

When images of butches and women in drag are incorporated into wedding representations, they contest eBay's reliance on engagements and weddings as markers of traditional gender and sexuality roles. Weddings are a successful way for eBay to emphasize its community orientation, the array of goods that are consumed at such events, and how things can be purchased on eBay. Drag weddings problematize the consumer aspects of weddings and the relationship between high-end goods and the sanctity of the event.[46] The participants in drag weddings deploy props and unexpected things. On the back of an image, a bride in a drag wedding describes her "Bouquet of soup bunch and shower of string beans" and "Veil and court train of lace curtains."[47] Brides also wear mops and other incongruous fabric to stand in for veils and hair.

The self-presentations in drag images are different from those in traditional bridal photographs and eBay wedding-dress listings, in which women enact and model normative roles. Since slenderness is a central concern for women who are getting married, bridal photographs provide a record of women's weight at the time of the event. These images are then used as the standard by which women's bodies are judged throughout their lives.[48] However, drag weddings propose alternative roles, schemas for body size, and forms of comportment. Butches in mock weddings present in oversize and tight shirts, suit coats, and pants. In a photo postcard titled "RPPC Crossdressing Women Mock Wedding Lesbian Interest," one butch woman shoves her hand in her pants pocket.[49] She thereby emphasizes her bulging stomach and the straining fabric across her midsection. The bride in bb1913's auction is so cocooned in curtain fabric that no assessment of her body is possible.[50] One of the women in dv33's "Vintage 1920's photo / Funny Girlfriends Mock

Wedding" is likewise swathed in tulle.[51] Campy presentations of string-bean bouquets, window-curtain dresses, poorly fitting suits, and prosthetic moustaches challenge the values and rituals of weddings, as well as eBay's deployment of these events. Individuals are incorporated into these critiques when the depicted women look out at the photographer/viewer and smile, laugh, and otherwise communicate their amused relationship to the wedding and the associated gender and sexuality roles.

Butch and Femme Camping

Theorists and GLBTQ scholars have debated whether butches deploy camp.[52] However, the photographic listings on eBay provide visual histories of butch and femme camping. According to Case, camp "both articulates the lives of homosexuals through the obtuse tone of irony and inscribes their oppression with the same device."[53] When camp eradicates the power and authority of heteronormative realism, it can be a particularly productive way to produce and read photographic images. Without such interventions, photography and its representations of gender norms are too often read as unmediated traces of the real. Camp can remind viewers that performances are an aspect of photographic production, and thus these images construct and frame culture. Roland Barthes describes individuals producing an identity and posing when confronted by the structuring processes of the camera.[54] According to David Bergman, camp means to "pose," and "drag performance" is essential to camp.[55] A version of this camping is depicted in pixidiom's "1915, VINTAGE ORIGINAL PHOTO, LESBIAN WEDDING CEREMONY," in which a group of women perform a mock wedding.[56] The rolled eyes and excessive prosthetic moustache of one tuxedo-clad woman highlight the constructed aspects of gender, sexual positions, and family. Equally disruptive to the idea that photography delivers the real is the depicted low ceiling, which underscores the staged aspects of images.

Case employs Joan Riviere's theories about how some powerful women use feminine masquerade to make their position less threatening to men.[57] For Case, "The butch is the lesbian woman who proudly displays the possession of the penis, while the femme takes on the compensatory masquerade of womanliness."[58] The femme is an important part of this performance. She "foregrounds her masquerade by playing to a butch, another woman in a role." Femmes therefore emphasize that femininity is produced rather than natural. The "butch exhibits her penis to a woman who is playing the role of

16. mosonz, "Vintage Photo Women in Drag Pipes, Canes Lesbian Int," eBay, 14 May 2006

compensatory castration. This raises the question of 'penis, penis, who's got the penis,'" because there is no referent. Instead, the fictions of penis and castration are "ironized" and "camped up." Butches and femmes destabilize presumptions about masculine power by enacting camp forms of the male look, gaze, and genitals. Through these strategies, the attributes and related rights of heterosexual men are challenged.

These forms of camping and women's resistance to playing to the penis occur in mosonz's "Vintage Photo Women in Drag Pipes, Canes Lesbian Int" (figure 16).[59] Instead of playing to men, three women in suits pose for the camera and assert their possession of space with a tilt of the head, outspread legs, and thrust of the hips. Their performance references men's similar postures. The butches' pale faces, necks, and hands emphasize the canes that they gesture with in front of and near their crotches. The photographic contrast between extremely light and medium tones emphasizes their possession of phallic canes and the relationship between masculine power and the presumption of the penis/phallus. In a similar manner, one of the butches in "Vintage 1920's photo / Funny Girlfriends Mock Wedding" holds her top hat directly over her crotch so it projects outward like an erection.[60] Butches make these genital gestures but do not maintain a permanent penis/phallus for themselves. Their performances, like other forms of camp that Jack Babuscio theorizes, show how "sex roles" are superficial and a "matter of style" rather than natural qualities.[61] These women use canes and top hats to produce sex roles, genitals, cultural conventions, and fashion statements.

The butches' overt gestures with canes and top hats rather than flesh should remind viewers that presumptions about genitals and other sex traits are better described as cultural genitals, as gender and sexuality studies research by Anne Fausto-Sterling and by Suzanne J. Kessler and Wendy McKenna indicates.[62] Genitals are usually culturally presumed and rendered rather than physically verified. Judith Gerson reviews Kessler and McKenna's work and asserts, "Because we do not routinely see or know each other's genitalia, in practice gender attribution actually depends on cultural genitals—easily observed symbols such as dress, facial structure, voice, and hair that act as surrogates for anatomical genitals."[63] Judith Butler does not use the term "cultural genitals" in her feminist and queer theorizations but describes how the "contours of the body" are rendered as the "ground or surface upon which gender significations are inscribed."[64] The performances of butches and women in men's clothing show how genders, as well as the contours of the body, are produced. These butches construct penises through their spread legs, positioning of canes, and clothing in a much more emphatic way than their social decisions about hair length, which is tucked under hats and more difficult to read, evokes vaginas and labia.

Conclusion: Cultural Performances and Consumer Critiques of Gender

Reminders of the cultural performance of gender appear in houseofmirth's "Lesbian" album page with three photographs (figure 17).[65] The page represents two women wearing suits and ties, with their hair piled high on top of their heads. Cigars wryly project from their mouths. In two of the images, a woman laughs about this drag play, her body and head tipped back in amusement. In the third image, the women's performance of masculinity is accompanied by a white phallic column that punctuates their dark suits and hair and calls further attention to their cigars, which clearly are not just cigars because they help produce other meanings for men and women. These images

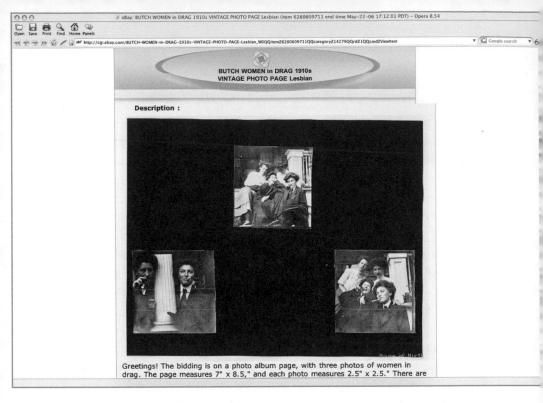

BUTCH WOMEN in DRAG 1910s
VINTAGE PHOTO PAGE Lesbian

Description :

Greetings! The bidding is on a photo album page, with three photos of women in drag. The page measures 7" x 8.5," and each photo measures 2.5" x 2.5." There are

17. houseofmirth, "BUTCH WOMEN in DRAG 1910s VINTAGE PHOTO PAGE Lesbian," eBay, 15 May 2006

function in a manner similar to Judith Halberstam's research on female masculinities and provide "a glimpse of how masculinity is constructed as masculinity."[66] Bravado poses and references to phallic ties, cigars, and columns associate these women with masculinity and foreground the ways masculinity is produced. These women may not have penises, but they provide performances and critiques of the phallus. Their performances of gender and sexuality are different from the representations of erotic availability and sexual engagement discussed earlier in this chapter. Butches and women in masculine drag may always provide a challenge to binary gender and to cultural presumptions that a natural relationship exists between men, masculinity, and power. While focusing on men's performances of women, Butler argues that drag "*reveals the imitative structure of gender*"—that gender is not based on some authentic, natural, and sexed body.[67] In a similar manner, the diverse images grouped under the lesbian interest search term highlight the imitative structure of gender.

Butchness is an even more dangerous queer image when butches are addressed as consumers, who control some production processes and forms of cultural taste, and their images undermine men's expectations about being able to locate and own erotic photographs of naked women.[68] According to research by Case and by Laura Harris and Liz Crocker, femmes are a key part of such destabilizations.[69] Femmes can highlight the performative aspects of femininity, women's engagement with an opposite that is not an opposite, the mythos of natural gender roles, and the ways women's performances of masculinity are more appealing than men's performances. The actions of femmes and butches and their resistance to being fully situated inside binary gender can emphasize an equally disruptive series of excesses and resistances in women's presentations as visually and erotically available. The women posing in erotica images seem bored, their pleasures appear faked, their flesh is oddly arranged, and the spontaneous scenarios look set up. When these problems are foregrounded, it is more difficult for viewers and buyers to believe that they are engaging with ready and available women. In these cases, vintage photographs do not do justice to the genre, normative gender, or sexuality conventions.

Relating masculinity to women encourages viewers to look more carefully at other gender representations. As I have previously suggested, photography is believed to provide an unmediated view of the real, to indicate the truth of situations, and to deliver material bodies, but it often does not convey enough visual information for viewers to classify. When eBay sellers list photographs of butch women and people in drag, buyers are encouraged to attend to the relationship between bits of portrayed face, hair, and body shape and performed and "real" gender. They are taught to apply this examination to other images. After all, these images are more valuable than similar representations of men. Sellers' indications about butch women and drag performances lead to occasional doubts about other identifications. This threatens the structures and organizational logic of how sellers classify images and the ways eBay is organized.

The problems with articulating unique individuals and a set of aspects that distinguish women from men are unintentionally emphasized in the doubling of stance, haircuts, and outfits in darrins's "Vintage Photo Two Girls w/ Butch Haircuts."[70] Some sellers acknowledge such difficulties in reading. surpapier is "not sure if it is a man or a woman. The features are feminine but the subject is wearing men's clothing. Maybe it's an effeminate man or a woman in men's clothing. Perhaps this is a Crossdresser or a Transvestite."[71] Another image, offered by slingwing, is of women "striking a dapper man-type pose" but there are "light pen marks on the photo on the sides of the ladies' heads as if with an after thought they or someone was wanting to show they were really ladies with long hair - not men."[72] In each of these readings, the seller uses hairstyles rather than supposedly stable anatomical attributes to determine individuals' sex. Not surprisingly, such cues also leave sellers confused. There is no stable transhistorical relationship between hair length and gender. Subcultural hairstyles have often been blamed for gender and sex confusion.

Sellers often highlight their difficulties in identifying by using question marks, shifting pronouns, and conflicting terms. klchance offers a "portrait of a boyish girl or a girlish boy, in fur, scarves and lipstick. Definitely ahead of his/her time."[73] hooks_lady lists a "Portrait Great Detail-- Lady or Man?" She "bought this years ago," believing "it to be a man in drag-- something in the look, the stance and the hands/gloves" but "still can't say for sure!"[74] photoguyred's "Lesbian Antique Real Photograph Kissing" includes the proviso, "Lesbian (?) two girls (?) kissing! On a boat with Teens type bathing suits. The more colorfully dressed person on left is of indeterminate gender as far as I can judge. Returnable if you can prove other than my title."[75] These moments of failed identification, with the need for constant contextualizing question and exclamation marks, suggest that clothes make the man and woman, but that the genitals and shapes beneath these clothes can be complicated. Some of eBay's butches may be boys. I use the terms "women" and "men" to describe the people depicted in lesbian and lesbian interest listings, but my identifications are also likely to be incorrect in some instances.

There are economic, political, and erotic reasons to read these images differently. Although darrins offers "Vintage Lesbian Int Photo Woman as Man," aspects of the photograph as it is represented in the listing do not convey that this is a woman self-presenting as a man.[76] Without darrins's title, this depiction of a person wearing such culturally gendered items as a suit and boater would probably be identified as a man. The articulation of gender and sex by darrins encourages the viewer to attend to the details of this figure's masculine performance, which include a crushed suit, a half-tucked-in pocket flap, and a jacket that seems too long. However, these features could also indicate that the suit is a prop or point to the individual's class, ability to obtain a tailored suit, and grooming skills. thewritersden claims to be able to read cultural genitals and binary sex when offering "EDWARDIAN LADIES DRESSED AS MEN LESBIAN INT OLD PHOTO."[77] Some of the faces portrayed in these listings may be round, which sellers often mention when identifying butches and women in drag, but there is not, and cannot be, any reliable evidence of the individuals' binary sex.

Even if "proof" by genital check is possible in some circumstances, such information cannot be gleaned from vintage photographs. Visual examinations can still elide surgical interventions and chromosomal and hormonal characteristics. Feminist science studies scholars have demonstrated how medical and scientific professionals produce sexed attributes, binaries, and other aspects of individuals that are presumed to be natural.[78] In these images, individuals are "dressed as men," and such performances ordinarily produce gender. Nevertheless, cultural genitals are cyclically remade in these listings because sellers' titles and individuals' clothing and performances produce contrary indications about gender and sex. Such formations, reconfigurations, and critiques of cultural genitals suggest that individuals' readings of cultural genitals in Internet avatars and profiles should also be interrogated. These sites flicker between being produced texts, pointing to material bodies, and existing as sexed selves.

Photographs and digital images, whether uploaded to eBay or to Facebook, are supposed to function as proof. However, the readings in this chapter demonstrate how difficult it is to articulate gender presentations, genitals, and sex. Because of the unclear attributions in some lesbian interest listings, viewers and consumers cannot desire a clearly gendered body, expect to control the depicted women, or establish a stable relationship to lesbian and lesbian interest listings, including mass-produced erotica. Lesbian and lesbian interest listings, particularly those that render butch subjects and subjects in drag, highlight the queer political uses for eBay that work along with its construction of a heteronormative world and organizational logic. Lesbian interest listings appear on eBay where numerous people view them next to representations of heterosexual couples, babies, landscapes, and other photographic genres. In situating the images in this terrain, sellers offer a consumer critique of eBay's focus on traditional engagements and marriages and normative gender and sexuality positions. In some cases, sellers' listings implode the very possibility of an organizational logic that is based on dyadic and knowable gender. The conflicted group of photographs that are listed under the lesbian and lesbian interest search terms position viewers and consumers so that the functioning of cultural genitals and the related malfunctioning of eBay's categories and logic are difficult to ignore.

chapter six

Re-collecting Black Americana

"ABSOLUTELY DEROGATORY" OBJECTS

AND NARRATIVES FROM EBAY'S COMMUNITY

Sellers deploy the terms "gay," "gay interest," "lesbian," and "lesbian interest" to make an array of desires visible on eBay and establish oppositional positions. Many of these sellers resist eBay's structures and regulations. However, sellers support eBay's "Black Americana" category and assist in rendering stereotyped black identities and disempowered African Americans. In this category, sellers have not collaboratively developed forms of critical resistance. Instead, sellers attach such insulting terms as "mammy," "sambo," and "nigger" to reprehensible depictions of African Americans performing dim-witted actions, dancing, and serving. For example, writer_art renders African Americans as cheerful, servile, and unable to separate eating from evacuating by offering an "ADORABLE" bank with a "little fella" that "is happily eating a huge slice of juicy, ripe watermelon as he sits on a pottie" and "happily" holds "coins for you."[1] smitherama also conflates caricatures and people, connects disability to African American identities, and dismisses black agency and adulthood with the term "little" by offering "A DELIGHTFUL LITTLE GUY" that "CAN SIT UP BY HIMSELF, BUT NOT STAND BY HIMSELF."[2]

Black Americana items are listed under "Collectibles > Cultures & Ethnicities" and "Collectibles > Postcards > Cultures & Ethnicities."[3] These categories also appear on eBay's Canadian site. eBay's terms and sellers' listings promise to deliver black cultures, collectibles, and history while listing racist representations that empower whites, providing apocryphal narratives that excuse slavery, and constructing an eBay community that appears to be good while reproducing intolerance. The "Cultures & Ethnicities" that are listed under the collectibles category are "African," "Asian," "Australian," "Black Americana," "British," "Canada: First Nations," "Canada: Inuit," "Celtic," "Egyptian," "European," "Ethnic Americana," "European," "Hawaiian," "Latin American," "Middle Eastern," "Native American: US," "Pacific Islands," "Russian," "Western Americana," and "Other." All of the specific identities listed under the postcards' cultures and ethnicities category, which are "Asian," "Black Americana," and "Native Americana," describe people of color.[4] In these instances, eBay uses "Other" to stand for anything not grouped in the specified category but still ideologically connoting difference. eBay makes it seem as if the cultures, products, and even ideas of people of color are collectible and can be owned. This commodification of cultures and identities, which is also produced by museums, the antiques market, and other businesses, needs further critical address because people often conflate cultural objects with individuals. This may be heightened in Internet settings where software programs, technologies, and viruses are identified as animate and avatars and profiles are often understood as people.

eBay's correlation of identity and market is particularly damaging because many of the identities referenced in the cultures and ethnicities categories, including black Americans, have been colonized and inequitably portrayed as less than human. For example, bigbobbie uses the problematic and outmoded term "negro" when listing a "BLACK AMERICANA MINIATURE ORNAMENT" of a "NEGRO GIRL WITH A GREEN SKIRT ON" (figure 18).[5] However, the manufacturer of the figurine also conveys stereotypes by rendering a monkey-like female with a smile stretching from ear to ear, a black knob of hair, oversized eyes, jutting ears, and large feet that look like they can grasp things. The depicted stance, with hips tilted coquettishly to one side and arms placed in a glamour girl pose, emphasizes her uncovered breasts, suggests she is sexually available, and connects her to purportedly primitive and abnormal desires. In such cases, the sexuality of African American women is commodified. Through these listings and category structures, eBay and sellers work together to make it seem as if African Americans can still be bought and sold.

eBay encourages sellers to list different items in the black Americana category. It has subcategories for "Banks," "Books," "Cards," "Dolls & Bears," "Figures & Sculpture," "Housewares & Kitchenwares," "Magazines," "Paper," "Photos," "Prints, Posters, & Paintings," "Signs," "Reproductions," and "Other."[6] eBay does not indicate the features that make a bank or poster black Ameri-

Duration:	7-day listing

payment methods accepted
See details

Description

VINTAGE BLACK AMERICANA MINIATURE ORNAMENT OR FIGURE OF A NEGRO GIRL WITH A GREEN SKIRT ON, LIGHTLY STAMPED ON THE BOTTOM "McFARLIN", THE CLAY USED IS A DUSTY BROWN COLOR, STANDS APPROX. 2 1/2" IN HEIGHT, ONE SMALL FLEABITE SIZED CHIP ON THE HEM OF HER SKIRT AT THE BACK, NICE ADDITION TO ANY BLACK AMERICANA COLLECTION, SEE THE OTHER 3 HAGEN-RENAKER CLOSE RELATIVES TO THIS ONE THAT I HAVE LISTED, BUY MORE THAN ONE AND SAVE ON SHIPPING, CHECK PHOTOS CLOSELY AND PLEASE EMAIL ALL QUESTIONS PRIOR TO BIDDING, SUCCESSFUL BIDDER PAYS SHIPPING AND IS ASKED TO MAKE CONTACT WITH SELLER WITHIN 3 DAYS OF END OF AUCTION TO CONFIRM PURCHASE AND TYPE OF PAYMENT BEING USED, PAYMENT TO BE MADE WITHIN 10 DAYS OF PURCHASE OR SELLER MAY CANCEL SALE, GOOD LUCK!!! CHECK OUT OUR OTHER LISTINGS AT THIS TIME!!!

Select a picture

00035
The power of protection from AOL and eBay. Learn more

18. bigbobbie, "BLACK AMERICANA FIGURE FREEMAN MCFARLIN MINIATURE," eBay, 3 February 2007

cana. Nevertheless, eBay promotes the expansion of this category and the things that sellers include. eBay has added more subcategories since my research began in 2006. Thousands of items are listed under the black Americana category, but sellers rarely define the term "black Americana" or describe the relationship between listed materials and African Americans' histories and cultures. For the seller elegantharlot, black Americana dates "from early American slave-history to the present" and "encompasses the cultural attitudes of Black Americans and America's response to its Black culture."[7] eBay and sellers often claim that black Americana represents African American history, even though many of the depicted objects and descriptions render stereotyped portrayals. For instance, a postcard is supposed to portray "a time gone by" and a factual history, while the back of the postcard provides the unlikely indication that the "happiest person on earth is the negro picking cotton."[8] Most of the materials listed in this category were produced by whites and represent their beliefs about African Americans. These representations justify white culture, which is barely mentioned under the "Cultures & Ethnicities" category, because the eBay site, like America and a great deal of Europe, renders white culture as the norm and presumes that it does not need qualifiers or specific identification.

eBay sellers use the general black Americana category when presenting materials that excuse and romanticize slavery, rendering insulting narratives about blacks, and selling objects that celebrate African American culture. Sellers offer such things as music performed by African Americans, mid-twentieth-century magazines directed at black readers, vernacular photographs of African Americans, images of black historical figures, pottery and other materials depicting black families and relationships, and artwork produced by African Americans. The seller elegantharlot also considers "Black Americana" ceramics that "could be seen in the American homes, kitchens, bathrooms, famous Restaurants and international store chains, ranging from the absolutely derogatory in characterizations to the most beautiful and respectful Black expressions and cultural icons."[9] However, elegantharlot does not interrogate the reasons for combining such materials under the term "Black Americana," what results from this production of black Americana and Americans, and the function of the objects being sold. When sellers use the term "black Americana," they make varied items, including such "derogatory" representations as the green-skirted and animal-like figurine, represent black history and African Americans.

In this chapter, I employ the phrase "black Americana category" to describe eBay's structuring of these materials. This allows me to write about the ways the category functions and how narratives about African Americans, organized through the eBay site, are produced for distinct political functions and support racial oppression. David Pilgrim, a sociologist and curator, describes how the control of black people through social mores and Jim Crow laws was supported by negative portrayals of blacks as ridiculous, subordinate, animal-like, and depraved.[10] These state and local U.S. laws enacted a separate but equal system that provided inferior accommodations for African Americans. Sellers' black Americana narratives tend to continue these earlier negative portrayals and beliefs into the present day. Through the black Americana category, eBay's category system, brand community, and organizational logic support racist conceptions of African Americans. I use the phrase "black Americana produced by whites" when considering materials that were designed by whites in the nineteenth century, twentieth century, and twenty-first century and that represent the values of some Caucasian Americans. I intend it to indicate the ways whiteness, blackness, power, and disenfranchisement are rendered by the objects and listings that are described as "black Americana." It should also convey how the eBay site and members produce black Americana and conceptions of African Americans.

Sellers' listing practices perpetuate the denigrating ideas about African Americans that were originally conveyed by black Americana items produced by whites. Buyers re-collect black Americana items, which have been previously purchased and displayed, and purchase the recollections that come with these items. These highly constructed memories include sellers' nostalgic narratives about slavery. Through such unfortunate eBay practices, the listing and selling of black Americana items works to disenfranchise African Americans and further commodify them. I interrogate the eBay site's and sellers' practices by employing the historical and critical literature on nineteenth-century and twentieth-century representations of African Americans by such authors as Stacey Menzel Baker, Carol M. Motley, and Geraldine R. Henderson; Carolyn Dean; Kenneth W. Goings; Marilyn Kern-Foxworth; and Patricia A. Turner.[11] Combining this literature with texts on identity and the commodification of people of color, including writings by George Pierre Castille, Patricia Hill Collins, Mary Jane Suero Elliott, Herman Gray, Grace Elizabeth Hale, and Kevin Ruggeri, helps me demonstrate how black Americana sellers perpetuate the idea that black peoples and cultures can be owned, marketed, and controlled.[12] I also employ critical literature on cuteness by Anne Allison, Sharon Kinsella, and Sianne Ngai.[13] Their research assists me in considering how sellers displace the racist aspects of black Americana items by using such terms as "cute" and by indicating that objects are appealing rather than offensive. These critical practices are also useful in interrogating how racism and the commodification of blackness circulate in other Internet settings and spheres.

The renderings of black Americana and Americans that are conveyed through the black Americana parts of the eBay site, like lesbian interest listings, incorporate diverse materials and ideologies. As I have already argued, selling mainstream erotic representations of women and vernacular images of women under the lesbian interest search term can destabilize the viewing and desiring position of straight male and lesbian viewers. However, this undermining of standard viewing positions and forms of address does not occur on all aspects of the eBay site. Sellers' black Americana listings tend to emphasize objects and collecting rather than represent an empowered African American viewer or facilitate black empowerment. The race of collectors remains unaddressed in these eBay listings, even though it has been a major concern in other black Americana collecting cultures.[14] Some gay and lesbian interest sellers highlight alternative buyers and resistant collecting practices, but black Americana sellers do not describe African American buyers rereading and reworking the racist past that many of the materials portray. Instead, their listings emphasize nostalgic reenactments of collecting and recollecting. In these instances, racist ideas and objects are kept within the eBay community instead of the child's toy boat or the couple's engagement ring, which eBay depicts as things that the community keeps and cherishes.

My call for critical analysis and tolerance in the marketing of black Americana may seem extreme, since despite their claims the eBay site, sellers, and buyers are focused on profitmaking. Nevertheless, equitable and reflective sales strategies could generate higher prices. Black Americana items have become more valuable since vendors at collectibles shows and other individuals have addressed the politics of black Americana. Thus, the strategies of eBay sellers are founded on racism and, perhaps, a lack of familiarity with the intricacies of the black Americana market, rather than revenue. Sellers could acknowledge the community of African Americans who critically read and collect these materials and thereby engage a broader collector market and facilitate a community that considers histories of racial oppression and does some good.

The Conflicted Position of Black Americana on eBay

Collectors, the authors of books on collectibles, promoters and sellers at collectibles shows, owners of antique shops, and auctioneers have helped to articulate black Americana and make it into a collectible. eBay has increased the presence of black Americana and the reprehensible conceptions of African Americans that items and sellers convey by providing categories for these materials and making black Americana listings a visible part of its site. eBay has encouraged the development of this area by adding subcategories for items in the general black Americana section. This causes some conceptual problems in how eBay renders its corporate and community identity. eBay's production and maintenance of the black Americana category, and buyers and sellers who advance the racist narratives of items, undermine claims that the setting is a caring community, a discourse that I considered in chapters 1 and 2. Such failures of the site's ethos could cause further problems for eBay's brand community. Nevertheless, eBay has not explained the relationship between "bad" objects, including the materials the company removes from the site, and its vision of "good" members who sometimes buy, sell, and are fans of these things.

eBay has an "Offensive Material Policy" and moral stance that should dissuade the company from promoting black Americana materials and prevent individuals from selling these items. As with its policy on nude images, eBay changes the precise wording but retains its regulations. eBay specifies that sellers "may not list items that promote or glorify hatred, violence, racial or religious intolerance, or items that promote organizations with such views."[15] eBay "will generally remove items that bear the marks of such organizations, such as relics from the KKK or certain Nazi memorabilia."[16] eBay emphasizes its values and that "listings that are racially or ethnically offensive are not permitted on eBay. eBay and its community of users will not tolerate such material." Nevertheless, it goes on to note:

> Occasionally, there may be listings of antiques or historical pieces (often referred to as "Black Americana") that, while unacceptable in today's society, are relics of an era where racially inappropriate and insensitive products were widely available. While these items are offensive to eBay and its community, eBay recognizes that such historical items find their way into museums and private collections, and serve as important tools for education about the past.

eBay's decision to remove many items with Nazi and Ku Klux Klan (KKK) markings but actively support the sale of black Americana items is conflicted. While eBay identifies this policy as part of its community values, it seems likely that the policy is based on the anti-hate-group statutes that are enforced in such countries as France and Germany and the lawsuits against Yahoo! for facilitating listings of Nazi items on its now defunct auction site.[17] eBay and Yahoo! prohibited many Nazi items in 2001, after the appearance of legal challenges. Despite its resistance to Nazi and KKK items, eBay justifies black Americana listings because these materials are historically important and can facilitate educational experiences. Of course, Nazi and KKK objects might also be used to critique racism and interrogate the ways hate is deployed. eBay claims that black Americana is part of an educational experience, but its "More Info About Black Americana" section, which is offered at the bottom of the list of category items, does not provide information about these materials or a definition of the term. eBay thereby fails to support its own reasons for including black Americana. Sellers also refer to the historical productivity of black Americana materials without providing examples of how these items might be educationally deployed, offering informational texts about their histories, or indicating the period in which they were produced.

eBay's policy statement distinguishes between "historical pieces" and "reproductions." It bans, "at the request of community members," listings "of racial or ethnically inappropriate reproductions" and sellers' use of "offensive words and phrases." Through these declarations, as in other situations, eBay constitutes good community members to have them conceptually do the work of policing and regulating. eBay provides provisos, but racist terms and reproductions appear in black Americana listings and the related items are bought by community members. eBay actually encourages the production of racism and the breaching of its own policy by including a "Reproduction" subcategory under the general black Americana category. At the same time, sellers of gay and gay interest items, as I suggested in chapter 4, regularly have their listings and accounts canceled by eBay, even though many of their items meet the company's guidelines. Black Americana sellers do not post to the site about the guidelines or indicate that their listings and accounts were canceled. They may not even be aware of the black Americana policy, because it is not mentioned in the category. eBay's policies and better-publicized narratives render a community of care. Nevertheless, its black Americana category supports the reprehensible communities that produce and trade in these items and the existent cohort of sellers who commodify the bodies of African Americans.

eBay sellers produce a more powerful and cohesive rendering of black Americana and Americans than what appears in collectibles shows and other physical venues, because a vast number of listings are always available, items are categorized and can be viewed together, and sellers' written narratives tend to convey similar racist ideas. For instance, sellers' stories about happily working African American women imply the women's willingness to serve; representations of nearly nude black women indicate that they are sexually available; and performances of dialect such as "Chill'en HeresUrMammy!" suggest that African Americans cannot speak properly.[18] Through these devices, eBay's black Americana category and sellers' listings support social and corporate interests in disempowering African Americans and profiting from their devalued labor and bodies. This strategy of disenfranchisement is related to eBay's promise to fulfill all desires, deliver any object, acknowledge a multitude of consumer identities, and empower all people while promoting stereotyped gender positions and white heteronormative relationships.

Commodifying Black Americana and African Americans

The identities of most eBay buyers and sellers remain at least partially obscured, but there is a great deal of evidence that black Americana sellers are white. Sellers note that the people represented in black Americana items are different from them. They also provide visual and textual confirmation of their whiteness. For instance, sellers display numerous items by holding them and thereby display the whiteness of their hands.[19] Sellers also present digital self-portraits that verify they are light-skinned.[20] While race is culturally constructed and a slippery concept, and there are problems with identifying people's race, these sellers produce themselves as Caucasians. Some sellers state that they are white. For instance cajunokie sells "mammy magnets" and "black folk art paintings" and self-identifies as a "57 year old white lady."[21] She differentiates herself from the stereotyped depictions of black people and advises, "Nope This Isn't Me!" near one of her "mammy" figures. For her, "Mammy has become like a real person . . . with a distinct personality." Nevertheless, the producers, designers, and purchasers of black Americana produced by whites use these items to assert their empowered position and the purported differences between African Americans and Caucasian Americans. eBay sellers hold small figural representations of African Americans in their large light-skinned hands. However, I have not found any sellers of reprehensible black Americana who self-identify as African Americans or as people of color.

Some of the literature on consumerism and identity demonstrates how individuals produce their identities in collaboration with groups, consumer processes, and products. Marketers, according to the sociologist Joseph E. Davis, recognize that "an inwardly generated self is a fiction," and we "are selves in dialogue, both internalized and in direct conversation, with others."[22] This "shaping and conditioning of our self-understanding by consumption is one form of the commodification of self." Individuals are valuable commodities. They are produced and addressed by marketers and manufacturers and often willingly align their shopping patterns and identities with brands. This commodification of the self provides such rewards as being recognized and supported by groups, including brand communities. The largest number of representations of African Americans on eBay appears in the black Americana parts of the site. However, the forms of commodification that occur through the black Americana category do not provide any empowering or politically viable identifications for African Americans.

Some people are commodified without their permission, rendered consumable and impotent, and left with little control over how their identities are culturally understood and deployed for profit. Castille considers the commodification of indigenous people: Their "image and identity have simply been extracted from Indian reality as a 'raw material,' to be smelted and forged into new shapes. The processing is managed by wholly owned subsidiaries of the dominant society, entirely free of Indian influence or control."[23] In a similar manner, Caucasian Americans produced black Americana to justify the history of slavery in the United States. They continue to market and control the meanings of black bodies through advertisements and products. By "promoting racist, dehumanizing stereotypes," writes Ruggeri, "black inferiority could essentially be 'sold' to the entire nation."[24] In the black Americana category, African Americans have not visibly engaged in this commodification. Yet the animation of black Americana items and claims that these objects speak make it seem as if African Americans are producing these images and selling themselves.

eBay's black Americana category is worth studying and critically resisting because it promises a community of good people while turning black bodies and identities into marketable products and rendering racism. Collins and Gray consider the problematic marketing of African Americans as dimwitted and dangerous and the ways some black individuals have redeployed these stereotypes and profited from their own commodification. Gray describes how "rappers have used cinema and music video to" appropriate the form "for different ends: namely, to construct or reconstruct the image of black masculinity into one of hyperblackness based on fear and dread" and to gain some power and profit from this process.[25] African Americans recognize that black culture is marketable and marketed and, according to Collins, "put it up for sale, selling an essentialized black culture that white youth could emulate yet never own. Their message was clear—'the world may be against us, but we are here and we intend to get paid.'"[26] These processes continue.

However, eBay produces limiting types of gender, race, and sexuality though an interface that the company claims is new and that nevertheless produces nostalgic representations of racist and slave cultures.

Sellers use racist terms and stereotypes in their listings even though eBay's policy prohibits such behavior. enghousea lists an "Old Milk Bottle. Molded glass w/ baby, negro, mammy face" but the words on the bottle are "liquid... ONE QUART" and "BROOKFIELD BABY TOP."[27] jayhawkks offers the *Antique Trader Black Americana Price Guide* under the title "Black Americana book $2005 Mammy Lawn Jockey Negro MORE."[28] However, the terms do not appear on the cover of the book. Other sellers present a "Delightful Cast Iron Black Americana Pickaninny Mammy" and a "Negro Mammy cast iron Dime Bank."[29] These sellers employ racist narratives about dimwitted and servile African Americans that may appear to be justified by period artifacts. However, their language is rarely supported by the texts that are printed on or otherwise incorporated into objects. Instead, sellers' descriptions further commodify African Americans and produce them as terms and objects.

eBay sellers of black Americana cookie jars, salt and pepper shakers, and other collectibles do not acknowledge contemporary critiques of American slavery. The historian Ira Berlin describes an intense contemporary "engagement over the issue of slavery," including critical considerations of race relations and the relationship between racism and slavery.[30] Sellers sometimes mention slavery in their black Americana listings, but they also use such terms as "mammy"—a black woman who is imagined to be maternal and to happily support white family that is not biologically her own—to soften or elide how African Americans have been treated as property.[31] They offer listings with descriptions such as "THE SWEETEST LITTLE SCENE OF A MAMMY COOKIN' UP DINNER," "BLACK MAMMY nursing a baby, possibly she is a WET NURSE," and "Service with a smile, and faithful too, that's this Black Mammy Cookie Jar!"[32] These sellers justify servitude by describing black women embracing these positions and smiling at oppressors.

Turner uses the phrase "contemptible collectibles" to describe stereotyped representations of African Americans. For her, there are problems with using the terms "black Americana" and "black collectibles" because they consist of "images *of* blacks and images *by* blacks" and do not distinguish "art blacks can be proud of from the mass-produced schlock that distorts and degrades" African Americans.[33] Black Americana sellers use terms like "Negrobilia" and continue to support slurs and perpetuate limited beliefs about people.[34] The use of the term "black" when considering these items makes it seem as if blacks were integrally involved in their production and distribution. However, these images fail to represent the diversity of skin colors, interests, and desires of black people.

The Politics of Black Americana

Caucasians have been evaluating blacks and conveying their beliefs about people from the African diaspora for centuries. The objects offered on eBay tend to repeat the limited and stereotyped conceptions of African Americans that were generated after the U.S. Civil War and abolition of slavery. While slavery existed in the United States, there were economic reasons for individuals, who were offering slaves for sale or trying to recover individuals who had escaped, to provide detailed portrayals that included, as Kern-Foxworth has indicated, African Americans' "virtues as well as their shortcomings."[35] The historian Robert E. Desrochers Jr. studied slave-for-sale listings in a Massachusetts newspaper and discovered that advertisements "included a short description of slaves' physical characteristics" that were often accompanied by an "enthusiastic character assessment. The terminology used to describe slave bodies included 'able,' 'strong,' and 'active.'"[36] Caucasian Americans' reasons for producing these more positive representations of African Americans were far from noble. Their depictions were designed to encourage a better sale price or enable bounty hunters to identify escapees. However, these portrayals still articulated some positive attributes.

With the repeal of slavery, Caucasian Americans were no longer commercially motivated to portray African Americans as skilled. Many whites wanted to explain away the injustices of slavery and their complicity in the institution by indicating they had benevolently taken care of African Americans during the antebellum period. After the Civil War, negative portrayals were popular among Caucasian Americans because they re-established the purported differences between whites and blacks, displaced whites' fears of blacks by making African Americans comic, excused slavery by representing African Americans as embracing servitude, and indicated that blacks were incapable of living as adults without white guidance. These controlling images informed African Americans about the violent punishments for not following prescribed roles and functioned in a similar manner to postcards and other documents of spectacle lynchings.[37] For instance, "funny" items depict black men's legs—and, metaphorically, their genitals—being consumed by alligators. These objects are designed to erase black men's sexuality and remind them of the punishments for having sex with white women. As many African Americans were gaining rights, these derogatory representations worked to control their social position.

Negative portrayals of African Americans that represent them as childish, grotesque, and stupid were produced during Reconstruction and continued along with Jim Crow laws and the expansion of racial segregation. Historians indicate that these items were designed by whites in the North and sold in the South. However, these representations have no regional borders. Blackface minstrelsy shows were popular in the North, and products such as Aunt Jemima pancake mix, which was accompanied by a stereotyped depiction of a mammy, were marketed nationally.[38] Negative representations of African Americans were also produced in Japan and Germany during the first half of the twentieth century. In such cases, Caucasian Americans' narratives about African Americans were transferred to other countries, conflated with larger conceptions of people from the African diaspora, and produced understandings of black people and Americans. Through these processes, African Americans were produced, sold, and commodified worldwide.

Insulting portrayals of black people are still thrown to cheering audiences during Mardi Gras parades in Louisiana; are available in the gift shops attached to former plantations in different parts of Louisiana; are sold in other venues in the U.S. South; and are marketed through numerous ecommerce sites. According to Tara McPherson and her interrogation of racial oppression, tourist sites along Louisiana's River Road and in other parts of the South have displaced the antebellum and postbellum conditions of African Americans by constructing nostalgic descriptions of plantation living, including apocryphal accounts of African Americans who were eager to serve.[39] In such locations, new developments and roads tend to be given names that include the word "plantation" as phantasmatic references to one version of the area's past. For instance, the Internet site for University Club Plantation—a planned community in the Baton Rouge area—invites potential residents to "Come Home to a Louisiana Plantation."[40] University Club Plantation claims that its properties have "all the charm of the old South and all the amenities today's discriminating homeowner wishes for." It is "a lifestyle you can retreat to from the fast-paced life outside." This use of the term "discriminating," in conjunction with descriptions of old Southern living, is disturbing. The word also describes instances in which people are treated differently because of their race, sex, or other perceived characteristics. Disparities between inside and outside are perpetuated as University Club Plantation assures prospective owners, "Behind the monitored entrance a sense of community abounds." Such sites render local communities where people can celebrate the "past" without addressing all of the facets of contemporary society or thinking about racism. eBay presents black Americana as a way for members to address race, presents a community that is opposed to intolerance, *and* uses these structures to forward the ideas and values incorporated into black Americana.

Old narratives about happy plantation communities and new forms of screening and segregating are facilitated in the United States, but many reproductions of black Americana items are made in China and other parts of Asia. For instance, some of Zeus's Mardi Gras throws, which are freely given to people along the parade route in Metairie, Louisiana, represent a black woman with an "O"-shaped mouth, beady eyes, and a slice of watermelon and are marked "Made in China."[41] Such stereotyped images, including those that depict African American women as not understanding things and speaking in incomprehensible dialect, make it seem as if black women are happy to labor and unable to perform more intellectually demanding work. These stereotypical images, as Collins argues, have "been essential to the political economy of domination fostering women's oppressions."[42] At the same time, the women of color laboring to produce black Americana items are dominated by these images and oppressive manufacturing conditions.

David Redmon provocatively argues in his documentary film *Mardi Gras* that this festival is made in China—or, at least, that many of the throws and beads that mark membership in localized American rituals are made in China.[43] The women producing these materials in Chinese factories are poorly paid, work long shifts, face health problems from breathing toxic fumes, and occasionally lose limbs or die because the machines have no safety features. Nevertheless, for many people in New Orleans, the celebratory rituals of Mardi Gras and accompanying swag are believed to unite people into a community along the parade route. This imaginary unification displaces the commodification of African Americans, Chinese people, and other women of color, which is facilitated by racist throws.[44] It also elides the parades that no longer occur because some Caucasian American Mardi Gras krewes refuse to integrate.[45] Such collectibles make Mardi Gras into a brand community with racist underpinnings. Black Americana items sold on eBay, which are incorporated into the site's category system, also undergird the eBay brand community. The exportation of American racism to other countries, where ostracized groups labor to render images from the racist imaginary of Caucasian Americans, suggests the wide reach of black Americana narratives and encourages studies of the complicated ways these materials shape cultures, economies, and brands. On eBay, black Americana items are portrayed as records of the history of slavery in the United States and as educational tools, but many of them are contemporary and made in China and other parts of Asia.

Black Americana has anti-fans as well as links to brand communities. Organized African American boycotts of such reprehensible representations as Aunt Jemima—probably the most recognizable mammy figure—began in the early twentieth century. In the 1960s and 1970s, organizations such as the National Association for the Advancement of Colored People (NAACP) increasingly pressured companies to stop producing stereotyped representations of African Americans. Between the 1950s and the 1970s, a great deal of the promotional material that used stereotyped images of African Americans was removed from sight or destroyed because of pressure from organizations such as the NAACP. Individual African Americans also purchased and then destroyed items to remove them from the consumer chain and popular imagination. The "motivation for these efforts," according to Baker, Motley, and Henderson, "seemed to have been to eradicate items with stereotypical images from the collective memories of Americans."[46] People's re-collecting of objects and employment of them as a way to reminisce were prevented through such practices. For instance, Sharon Jones, who went on to collect black Americana items produced by whites, bought her first Aunt Jemima cookie jar in 1968 "to take it out of circulation" and "make sure it would not get back in the hands of whites."[47] In the 1960s and 1970s, images of the political figures who challenged stereotyped conceptions of race, such as Angela Davis and Malcolm X, began to replace representations of docile black servants. However, in white communities, images of the "threatening street-fighter," as Goings indicates, became the new stereotype and were also used to define African Americans as different and as outsiders.[48]

Representations of African Americans have been incorporated into Caucasian Americans' homes and decorating schemes, particularly in the kitchen, for more than a century. Nevertheless, there was no overt vintage and antique collecting culture for black Americana items produced by whites until the late twentieth century. In the 1980s, the appearance of a number of black Americana shows and coverage of people's collections in the antique-trade and popular press made individuals aware of black Americana items produced by whites; their value increased, and collecting became more common. These items were originally marketed to white consumers, and early collectors were often Caucasian Americans. However, as the collecting trend continued, a growing number of African Americans, including high-profile individuals, began to buy the materials to reconceptualize their historical and cultural position and to recollect differently. Turner traces the interest in black Americana collectibles produced by whites to publicity, including a spot on NBC's *Today Show* that featured Janette Faulkner's vast collection.[49] Faulkner, who was a social worker, believed that teachers could use such items to demonstrate the enormous impact of racism on American culture. Sellers such as 8800anita occasionally argue that an item "is a marvelous educational artwork in the telling of a crucial part and period of Black American History, which has been greatly ignored in the art community."[50] However, there is never any explanation in the eBay market of how these materials will educate people.

Without critical analysis, black Americana items produced by whites displace African Americans' histories and identities. For Elliott, to be "commodified by a colonialist culture" includes an "appropriation of discourse and an oppression of black identity."[51] Hale chronicles the ways black stereotypes, and in some cases body parts that were harvested from lynched African Americans, were used to articulate the identities of Southern whites. There has been a counter-trend in African American communities to collect black Americana produced by whites to document and remember how Caucasian Americans have depicted African Americans. Thus, some African Americans read black Americana as a kind of depiction of Caucasian Americans. In such cases, collecting black Americana includes commodifying the otherwise invisible white identities that are incorporated into these narratives. This enables African Americans to take at least partial control over the marketing of black bodies and cultures.

The reporters Jerry Adler and Frank S. Washington, in a similar manner to Collins and Gray, encourage individuals to read black Americana items as depictions of African American resistance. They advise viewers to look "carefully," because the "'jolly mammy' to whom the white boy and girl turned for cookies is frozen in humiliation; the Coon Jigger is vibrating, not with jazz, but anger. The souls of black people were trapped in these heaps of mass-produced junk. Now at last they are being set free" by critical processes.[52] For Kern-Foxworth, "the negative images promulgated yesterday can be transformed into positive ones today" through cultural recontextualization.[53] The political possibilities of reading black Americana as both representations of Caucasian Americans and whites' attempts to control the meaning of black culture are emphasized in some black Americana collectibles shows and in the ways African Americans collect these materials. For instance, Julian Bond, who was national chairman of the board of the NAACP, offers a critical commentary about these objects in the *Antique Trader Black Americana: Price Guide*.[54] Resistant black Americana collecting practices continue, and some of these collectors use eBay to obtain items, but the eBay market still operates by articulating insulting and derogatory representations of African Americans. If sellers produced political and resistant readings, then they would provide ways to address the functions of these objects, make them into educational tools, raise their market value, and offer a more tolerant and profitable model than eBay's and sellers' current practices. In a similar manner, studies of individuals' resistance to being marketed stereotyped Internet identities in the form of avatars, technology advertisements, and profile configurations can point designers and corporations toward the economic advantages of diversifying avatars and interfaces.

Collecting Black Americana Reproductions

People's interest in collecting black Americana produced by whites has increased the value of these objects and supported a growing reproduction industry. Reproductions highlight the value of these items by indicating they are desirable and a limited resource. At the same time, they contribute to the devaluation of black Americana by making it difficult to determine what is being purchased. Some reproductions are sold as period items. Theorists are excited about the collecting of reproductions because replicas undermine the value of collectibles and the past that the items are supposed to be situated within and to convey. Walter Benjamin and other cultural theorists indicate that copies challenge the authority and history of originals by providing an array of narratives and versions.[55] For Adler and Washington and Kern-Foxworth, collecting black Americana can be the first step in rereading and repurposing items.[56] However, making reproductions, particularly new items that rework reprehensible conventions and narratives, can also validate the stereotypes that earlier works convey. Reproductions perpetuate the nostalgic narratives about plantation pasts and stereotyped portrayals of lazy African Americans into the present.

Some reproductions are dense consolidations of period stereotypes rather than exacting copies. For example, creeksideprimitives makes new game boards with stereotyped images of happy and servile African American men valuable by informing buyers that they are "hand-crafted" and thus one-of-a-kind.[57] However, reproducing "aging" and rendering the "vintage look" is a form of massification. Such reworkings represent a comforting past that continues into the contemporary period in which men "sitting around a pot-bellied stove" facilitate rural community. creeksideprimitives advertises its operation as a "woodworking and crafting business," location "on the family homestead for about 16 years," and ancestry from "pioneer stock" that "settled" in the mountains of Virginia "over 230 years ago!"[58] With such stories, sellers displace the technological aspects of selling on eBay, the processes of manufacturing reproductions, and the locations and conditions under which many of these items are made with proclaimed connections to the American land and preindustrial place. Sellers' descriptions of authentic forms of crafting and lifestyles also elide the deeply constructed aspects of black Americana items produced by whites and make them appear to be more real. Black Americana thereby depicts a cohesive community that continues eBay's narratives about members being family and doing good work, even though items support racist stereotypes. Members are tied into these positive community narratives when they buy.

Reproductions repeat the past. They also make it difficult to determine the details of the period because they reference multiple times. On eBay, reproductions of cast-iron banks and other items are often sold as nineteenth-century artifacts or as records of the antebellum period. This has created problems for individuals who sell and collect period artifacts. The provenance of items and their material details are difficult to determine on eBay because buyers cannot look at all aspects of an object and cannot observe markings, paint quality, and materials firsthand. These issues are referenced in sellers' indications that "photographs don't do it justice," but in these cases, items may be less desirable than their representations. It is likely that duplicitous marketing motivates eBay's banning of reprehensible reproductions. eBay cannot claim to be doing good work by enabling the sale of items with historical and educational value if it unreservedly allows reproductions. Nevertheless, these sales offer some critical possibilities. Individuals' difficulties identifying the period in which items were produced can remind them that most listed objects were manufactured after the antebellum period.

Buyers of black Americana items produced by whites are often concerned about condition as well as attribution. Items are usually less valuable when they have damage such as cracks, creases, fade marks, mildew, lost parts, scrapes, stains, and worn paint. However, flaws also indicate that an object is old. The yellowing of paper or wear to the handle of a wooden tool conveys its long history of use. According to nowarkedd, it "is wise to remember that most used and antique collectibles will have nicks, cracks, scratches and dings consistent with age" and that such wear is a form of "'patina'—proof of their pedigree."[59] Nevertheless, nowarkedd's item is "brand new! It looks 1890s, but no, it's a reproduction!" Through patina-suffused reproductions, sellers contradictorily assure buyers about the objects' pedigree and worth. Reproductions are more reasonable than period items; they have a poor resale value; and their history can be physically cleaned up and conceptually rewritten. By actively ignoring eBay's rules about reprehensible reproductions, sellers also problematize eBay's model of trust. These contradictions may offer productive methods from which to launch critical resistance, since eBay's general policy changes have already caused disenfranchisement among members.

Wear is sometimes faked, but eBay sellers still demonstrate that items are old and original by listing flaws such as worn glazes from repeated handling. For instance, wham2001 lists "A GREAT OLD SET OF BLACK MEMORABILIA SALT AND PEPPER SHAKERS" that are obviously old because of "THE RUBBED OFF PAINT."[60] This history of wear, which is visibly documented in many of the listings, is a disturbing aspect of black Americana items produced by whites. Weathering may be produced at the back of a disreputable antique shop, but wear appears to—and often does—convey the long periods of everyday engagement people had with these denigrating representations. According to Goings, individuals "consciously and unconsciously accepted the stereotypes" by using these materials every day and in a "familiar manner."[61] Worn paint and chipped ceramics indicate that people were comfortable incorporating racist beliefs about African Americans into their homes and lives and that these pieces helped generate cultural beliefs for decades or even more than a century.

Sellers' descriptions of wear, which imagine the pleasant homes within which black Americana items produced by whites were situated and the delights in using them, help further the racist intents of these objects. For instance, newsquarepa offers a children's book with a stereotyped depiction of a large African American woman doing laundry that "appears to have been enjoyed, because it does show wear."[62] Of course, the literature on doll play shows how wear can be a mark of cultural resistance and a record of burning, burying, or otherwise destroying toys that assert undesired norms.[63] African Americans have been taking these objects out of the consumer stream for decades to supplant the racist beliefs conveyed by these representations. However, eBay ordinarily displaces these forms of cultural resistance and instead renders a never-ending cycle of consuming, collecting, relinquishing, and encouraging new owners to experience racist narratives through objects. eBay facilitates a vast virtual array of black Americana items, which includes individual depictions, iterations, and objects within each type. eBay's representation of this large and insistent text and sellers' nostalgic chronicles of wear continue nineteenth-century and twentieth-century racist narratives into the present day. Buyers and sellers of gay interest underwear and swimwear describe eBay's censorship and make it clear that individuals cannot get everything on eBay. However, eBay's own policy indicates that there are black Americana listings that should be canceled or sold differently.

The Problem of Reading Black Americana as Black Americans

Representations of African American women, including portrayals of smiling "mammies," are the most common form of black Americana sold on eBay. Mammies, according to Hale, are key components of Southern cultural production in both literary and visual forms.[64] In his study of Aunt Jemima, M. M. Manring identifies depictions of mammies as some of the most persistent media representations of black people.[65] Representations of happy mammies are similar to the claims of proslavery propagandists such as George Fitzhugh and beliefs that slaves were as "happy as a human can be."[66] On eBay, mammies smile while acting as note holders that are always there to remind; are eviscerated so twine can be dispensed through their bodies; are formed into banks that store and save; and serve as hard laborers who have places for utensils grafted onto their backs. They are represented cooking, scrubbing, sweeping, performing child care, and doing other kinds of labor. The mammy is thereby a controlling image and, according to Collins, justifies "the economic exploitation of house slaves" in the antebellum period, explains black "women's long-standing restriction to domestic service," and directs African American women to labor.[67] In the last few chapters, I have demonstrated how eBay's representations and narratives about work, engagements, and weddings configure users. In a related and destructive manner, the large number of black Americana items on eBay configures conceptions of African Americans and the kinds of work they can perform.

Black women seem to acquiesce to even the most intolerable conditions when their bodies are re-crafted into a variety of implements and a smile

Description

Vintage 1940s or 50s figural beer stein or mug. Body of mug is a palm tree with palm fronds and coconuts. Handle is a googly-eyed bare-breasted black female with blue eyes, a short afro hairdo, hoop earrings, and blue bikini bottoms. 5-3/8" tall. No chips or cracks. Overall crazing, some dust/dirt on inside. Bottom of mug stamped Japan in black under the glaze. Great addition to black americana or beer mug collection!

Please email with all ?s BEFORE bidding--Returns are NOT ACCEPTED. No guarantees, expressed or implied. Shipping based on weight/destination, ship via USPS priority mail, optional insurance. PAYMENT TERMS: CHECKS ARE NOT ACCEPTED--PAYMENT VIA PAYPAL, USPS POSTAL MONEY ORDER, OR BANK CASHIER'S CHECK ONLY--ABSOLUTELY NO PERSONAL OR BUSINESS CHECKS. NO EXCEPTIONS!!!!! Winning bidder must contact me within 3 days, payment must be received within 7 days of auction close. Thanx for lookin'!

Select a picture

00071
Get more protection online with eBay and AOL. Learn more

Shipping, payment details and return policy

Domestic Handling Time
Will usually ship within 3 business days of receiving cleared payment.

Services Available   **Available to**
US Postal Service Priority Mail®   United States only

Will ship to United States.

Save on shipping - buy additional items now from this seller's other listings!

Calculate shipping
Enter your US   70118
ZIP Code:
Calculate
Learn more about how
calculated shipping works

19. mollyester, "Vintage Palm Tree Black Demi Nude Handle Beer Mug Stein," eBay, 28 July 2006

accompanies these shapes and roles. Feminist film scholars have critiqued the ways white women are objectified through such cinematic processes as cropping and framing.[68] However, designers of collectibles who depict parts of black bodies protruding from ceramics do even more metaphorical violence to women's bodies. eBay sellers perpetuate these derogatory connections. For instance, mollyester offers a mug whose handle has been sculpted into a "googly-eyed bare-breasted black female" with protruding buttocks (figure 19).[69] Black women's supposedly abnormal buttocks, which the mug's pose emphasizes, have been associated with an unruly sexuality and primitive characteristics.[70] According to the gender and race scholar bell hooks, black women's sexual colonization under slavery and presumptions about their promiscuity continue to inform cultural conceptions of African American women's sexuality.[71] The transformation of the mug's handle into a woman's body that can be erotically grasped and held makes it seem as if

African American women also live to be grasped, touched, and owned. The mug producer's depiction and mollyester's description of "googly" eyes and an uncomprehending mind continue cultural conceptions that black woman do not understand gender and sexuality standards.

Black Americana items produced by whites, according to Goings, function as "surrogate African-Americans in people's minds."[72] For instance, oddpilott animates a black Americana set of salt and pepper shakers: "Peppy is in mint condition but Salty has had a fall and his head had to be glued back on."[73] With this description of Salty's "fall," the shaker becomes a named person with a history. ruthlesspromotions describes the height and condition of a set of "Mammy dolls from New Orleans" but also articulates them as people with gestures and personalities.[74] One "rings a bell," and "the other two just stand there and boss you around." ruthlesspromotions does not "know if you need three more women in your house but" is willing to "part with these to the lucky winner." brewersgeneralstor offers a "BAKERY CHEF HOLDING FRESHLY BAKED BREAD (THAT YOU CAN ALMOST SMELL)."[75] With such descriptions, black Americana items become part of a living, tactile, and multisensory world. Sellers also animate objects in other categories and thereby support an array of cultural stereotypes.

A ceramic depiction of a young black child on a chamber pot suggests black people debase themselves (figure 20).[76] In the depiction, the child's head is tipped too far back, and his mouth stretched open in a grimace. The open mouth, which the seller identifies as either a bank or an ash collector, conveys the child's willingness to be violated. In simultaneously gulping something and evacuating into the chamber pot, the child combines processes that, according to social norms, are supposed to remain separate and ostensibly demonstrates his lack of knowledge about hygiene and humanness. This combination of eating and evacuating is also featured in numerous representations of black children consuming watermelon while sitting on chamber pots. In the nineteenth century and early twentieth century, many Caucasian Americans wanted African Americans not only to be second-class citizens, as Goings states, but also "to actively acknowledge their subordinate position by smiling, by showing deference, and, most importantly, by appearing to be happy even as they were treated horribly."[77] The representation of the gulping child justifies abuse of African Americans because the individual seems to sit and wait to be debased by ash or dirty coins. This excuse is continued in a variety of black Americana items.

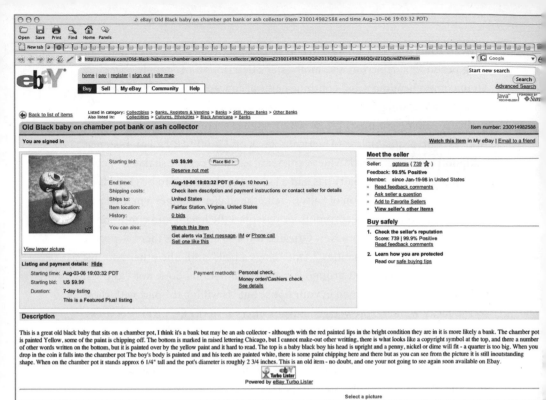

Displacing Racism

Sellers have found ways to incorporate the most reprehensible black Americana narratives into the everyday lives of buyers and sellers. mr.haneys
.truck evokes a racist continuum when listing a chalkware representation of black children with bulging eyes, gigantic mouths, and an enormous slice of watermelon as being "RIGHT OFF GRANDMAS WALL."[78] A cast-iron bell of a mammy figure, which depicts a large and lumpy body, is described by oldwest as "a very nice item for your Front door! It would look great on the door to a FARM HOUSE In the COUNTRY!!"[79] countrygal70 auctions a "Wonderful old souvenir doll from New Orleans" that "would look really cute in a country home."[80] Sellers use terms such as "nice" and "great" to describe the quality of the material object and thus avoid addressing the racist renderings of African Americans. Sellers envision these items, and the African American workers that many of these objects portray, as complementing certain kinds of interiors, homes, and lifestyles. The race of buyers is not mentioned in

these descriptions. However, the places that these representations are imagined to decorate, including farmhouses, suggest that black Americana items produced by whites can persist in agrarian communities that purportedly facilitate more relaxed and traditional ways of life.

In the nineteenth century and early twentieth century, many Caucasian Americans identified representations of African Americans as humorous and lighthearted. Depictions of African American children with "enlarged crania, rounded features and wide eyes charmed the average viewer," according to Dean, and were identified as "appealing, if not adorable" because "the embedded bias operates subtly."[81] Writing about the same time period, Goings suggests that many white people found these representations to be "very endearing."[82] eBay sellers continue to read and describe these representations as cute and charming. For instance, ratsden43 offers a "really cute Mammy doll."[83] surfbunnyanne presents a vintage pair of "caricature" ashtrays, where the figures' widespread mouths are the ash collectors.[84] According to the seller, they are "cute cartoon faces with earrings and bones in hair." Such sellers do not address the ways their objects render African Americans as primitive and ready to be defiled.

By using the term "cute," sellers describe items without addressing—or, perhaps, even acknowledging—the offensive stereotypes that are operating. Cute objects, as well as the people they portray, appear to pose no physical or conceptual threat because, according to Ngai, they "have no edge."[85] Objects that are called "cute" are likely to be soft and round. They are associated with the infantile and feminine through age and gender stereotyping. For instance, eBay sellers also employ the term "cute" when they list toys and young girls' clothing since those items reference children and are soft and frilly. It may be difficult to see how "cute" black Americana objects denigrate African Americans because, on a certain level, they portray charming and endearing beings. They also represent African Americans as childish. In her work on "minstrelized girls," Kinsella connects Japanese representations of cute, erotic, and idiotic girls who have oversize features and "chubby feet" to nineteenth-century blackface performances of infantile African Americans. Minstrel shows included racist blackface portrayals of African Americans with oversize lips, noses, collars, and shoes.[86] eBay sellers describe these same characteristics, including oversize painted mouths, as cute.

Kinsella's and Allison's studies of cuteness, while focusing on contemporary Japan, hint at what these black Americana narratives about cuteness displace. According to Kinsella, a cute cartoon character is "small, soft, infantile, mammalian, round, without bodily appendages (e.g. arms), without bodily orifices (e.g. mouths), non-sexual, mute, insecure, helpless or bewildered."[87] In Japan, as Allison states, cuteness is associated with "sweetness, dependence, and gentleness."[88] eBay sellers of black Americana articulate a similar set of attributes. shopperoasis offers "a cute hinged tin advertising Uncle Leroy's Licorice Drops" that depicts an African American man with a round, bald, and bulbous head and facial features.[89] Whether it is the depiction of the bulbous and not fully formed shape of Uncle Leroy's head or Hello Kitty's flat face and not fully detailed features, cute is often associated with visually simplified things. For Ngai, this makes cuteness "a sort of primitivism."[90] In black Americana items produced by whites, this primitivism and simplification of elements is associated with simple individuals. For instance, abstracting the person's mouth as an "O" associates the individual with incomprehension, the inability to speak clearly, and the inability to determine morals and values.

shopperoasis also describes a "Black Americana Hit Me Hard Carnival Toss Target Game" as "cute" (figure 21).[91] In the depiction, the man's large head, small body, and chubbiness fulfill some of the characteristics of cuteness. Nevertheless, whether it is understood as a game or as a larger cultural mandate, it is hard to engage with this item as if it is cute. The game depicts a seated black man who is flanked by the phrase "Hit me hard." The man seems to be happily requesting abuse because he is grasping his stomach in laughter and widely grinning to welcome tossed balls. The "Hit me hard" request makes it seem as if black people invite physical punishment. The game, like other black Americana items produced by whites, associates African Americans with infantilism, primitivism, and incomprehension. After all, cultural ideas about identity suggest that physically aware and sensible adults do not invite such pain and punishment. Instead, games and challenges to "hit me hard" are associated with child's play. The game, like other depictions of passive and vulnerable cute beings, excites "a consumer's sadistic desires for mastery and control."[92] Associating African Americans with cuteness thus connects them to powerlessness.

eBay sellers describe black Americana items that contrast large and small features as cute and adorable, particularly when these objects render mobility limits. These items include depictions of African Americans handling objects that are too large for them and representations of individuals who have a combination of large and small appendages that prevent them from moving easily and render a form of disability. thesecondchef markets an African

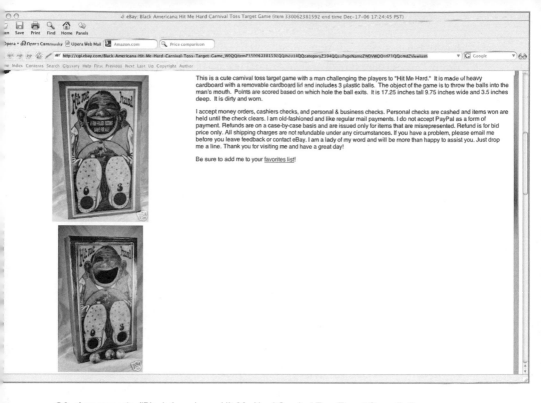

21. shopperoasis, "Black Americana Hit Me Hard Carnival Toss Target Game," eBay, 12 December 2006

American "little boy's" face that is overwhelmed by gigantic features by describing it as a "cartoon character" with "sweet and innocent features."[93] This African American may be described as "adorable" because he has no body and no mobility; his head is directly perched on tiny and dysfunctional feet. Cute things also tend to emulate weak members of society and, as Kinsella states, "can't walk, can't talk, can't in fact do anything at all for themselves because they are physically handicapped."[94] Black Americana items produced by whites associate incapacity and disability with African Americans, who are presumed to need help from Caucasian Americans. Through this process, black Americana items produced by whites associate disabled individuals with disempowerment rather than acknowledge the varied ways people engage and navigate the world.

A buyer of Coon Chicken Inn dishware describes it as "cute" and "fun to have" despite the grotesque representation.[95] This china depicts an excessively wrinkled black man with one eye screwed closed, a widely stretched mouth that still seems too small for his numerous teeth, and a madly perched porter hat. In black Americana items produced by whites, such gigantic mouths and fleshy bodies suggest that African Americans are unable to control their appetites. Representations of African Americans swallowing ash and balls make them seems animalistic and unable to judge what is edible. African Americans are also represented as semi-mute despite oversize mouths. They try to communicate with almost incomprehensible dialect. These denigrating depictions of African Americans, like sellers' narratives about smallness and cuteness, articulate a Caucasian American culture that is big, virile, and powerful. The tendency to use the term "cute" when describing technologies designed for women also controls and configures women's relationship to knowledge and skill.

Some eBay sellers magnify the racist aspects of black Americana items by employing derogatory phrases. Using offensive terms and highlighting the most negative aspects of depictions is profitable because extremely derogatory objects sell for more money.[96] aaahmazing offers "Amazing Banned & Censored Crazy Cartoon Classics" and lists a variety of stereotypes.[97] aaahmazing references the "historical significance" of these racist animations, but neither a government nor eBay has banned them. Several of dwells00collectibles' "postcards are racially insensitive, to say the least."[98] millerzt offers "an interesting pair of racist salt and pepper shakers."[99] However, millerzt does not provide an indication of what is interesting, so it seems as if the items are fascinating because they deploy offensive stereotypes. Sellers may indicate that items provide a racist view, which also suggests an item's greater value, but they do not provide considerations of how the racism operates or the problems in showing and selling this material. Instead, they mime cultural sensitivity and regulation to highlight the value of their items. Without deleting images or texts, these sellers evoke censorship in a manner that is related to gay interest sellers' performances of the seen and unseen. However, gay interest sellers must deal with eBay's removals of listings and resistance to their sexual expressions. Black Americana sellers do not self-identify with African American positions and do not deal with the consequences of their breaches of eBay policy or marketing of intolerance.

The Auction and Slavery

The ability to buy and sell black Americana representations supports the continued commodification of African Americans by Caucasian Americans. According to Turner, representations of "thick-lipped faces on cereal boxes" and "sloppily dressed figures on sheet music" allowed American consumers to buy and sell "the souls of black folk" even after slavery was over.[100] It also affects African Americans, as Elliott states, because they struggle to develop an "empowered, agentive sense of self" while being articulated as commodified beings.[101] It is more difficult to articulate empowered forms of self when confronted with eBay listings for black dolls that are twisted into different configurations and described as people. During slave auctions, according to the observer C. R. Weld, bodies were examined carefully, and marks "were criticized with the knowing air assumed by horse-dealers."[102] Max Berger's research on slave auctions describes how women were "examined on the hands, arms, legs, bust, and teeth. If they claimed to have had no children, their bosoms were carefully fondled to check on this."[103] In listings for black Americana dolls, images seem to enable viewers to perform similar inspections. Condition is chronicled as if the dolls were people. For example, auctionittodayby recontextualizes damage as a form of surgery when noting that a listed doll "may have had a tummy tuck at one point, as it looks as if her stomach has been repaired."[104]

Sellers offer images of dolls in different positions. These representations are supposed to allow buyers to judge the condition of dolls, but sellers often repeat views. The depictions make it seem as if dolls—and, possibly, the evoked black bodies—have been and can be violated. Some listings include portrayals of female dolls' crotches and buttocks. kentuckybluebird markets a doll by providing images of the head, back, and lower half of the doll. In one image, the skirt is pulled up so the viewer can inspect the doll's muslin groin and legs.[105] themeyermansion depicts a doll with her dress covering her face and pantaloons pulled down to reveal her torso.[106] annie*boomer includes an image of a rag doll in which the back of the skirt is flipped up, the fabric forms a circle around her buttocks, and the image is cropped to center the doll's ass in the frame (figure 22).[107]

These images of dolls are related to "up-skirt" photographs, which depict women from below, reveal what women's clothing would ordinarily hide, and provide a voyeuristic view. The eroticism of this genre is based on the premise that these views, and the accompanying "penetration" into the interior of women's clothing, are outside of the depicted person's control. Sellers' images of dolls' underwear and the underside of skirts are also invasive. Sellers literally turn dolls inside out. There are numerous images of the ragged seams and awkward stumps that define the end of dolls' torsos (figure 23).[108] Depictions of ovoid holes and the fabric gathered around stumps, which are

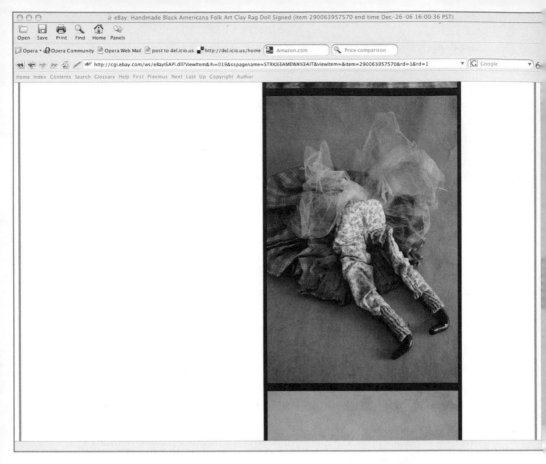

22. annie*boomer, "Handmade Black Americana Folk Art Clay Rag Doll Signed," eBay, 19 December 2006

created by the dolls' construction, evoke genitalia. These images perpetuate cultural ideas about owning, sexually possessing, and taking pleasure in African American women. For hooks, representations of black women's bodies are of "the body taken over, stripped of its own agency and made to serve the will, desire, and needs of others."[109] Yet sellers repress the multiple levels of commodification and racism that they are facilitating by using such terms as "adorable" and "cute" to describe the dolls.

Sellers' doll listings also conflate objects and people. In these accounts, dolls cannot take care of themselves and need to be adopted and owned. For instance, kentuckybluebird's doll is "looking for a really good home for the holidays."[110] poobelle offers a "BLACK AMERICANA RAG DOLL" and asks, "Would you like to adopt her???"[111] A doll beseeches, "PLEASE TAKE

ME HOME AND LOVE ME."[112] These narratives envision the site, buyers, and sellers as a concerned community that takes care of dolls and African Americans who purportedly cannot support themselves. Nevertheless, listings for dolls, like the marketing of African American texts that Eric Gardner studies, equate the sale of black Americana to the auctioning of black bodies.[113] dolls*from*happier*times offers "a 5" Black Americana Pony tail Doll."[114] The seller "will be moving from the south to the north in a few months so most of" her "babies will not" be coming with her. "These girls are being sold as is and as stated." Dolls are commodities, but describing them as black babies and offering to sell them evokes a reprehensible history of selling and

23. attic_wench, "Vintage 40's? Black Folk Art Mammy Toaster Cover Doll," eBay, 18 December 2006

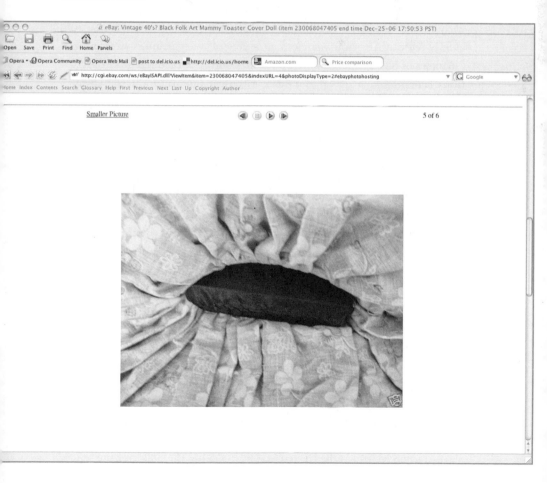

enslaving people. Whether dolls*from*happier*times' member ID is referring
to the time that the dolls were produced or the history of African Americans,
it is not clear what makes these earlier times happier.

Envisioning New Orleans and American Culture

People's understanding of American culture has been shaped by stereotyped
renderings of African Americans.[115] eBay unfortunately supports the circulation of these materials and the further incorporation of these notions of African Americans into American society and global settings. Sellers in the black
Americana category use IDs such as sellinghistory to emphasize the value of
their products and the historical importance of the past.[116] Sellers also make
it seem as if their black Americana items are truthful representations. Postcards of a "MAMMY and TAP DANCING" feature "life for the black race in
early 1900's Florida."[117] A fold-out booklet that portrays an unthreatening
elderly African American man and an image of watermelon is advertised as
"16 views of Black American life in the old south."[118] Through these descriptions, sellers make it appear as if black Americana items produced by whites
convey the details and geographies of particular times and places. eBay sus-
tains these claims by describing black Americana as historically important.

Black Americana items produced by whites frame and produce America,
including the city of New Orleans. Many items are stamped with the city's
name. For instance, numerous "mammy" dolls with red-and-white turbans
and polkadot dresses have aprons with "New Orleans" imprinted on them.[119]
Potholders, salt and pepper shakers, spoons, dish towels, boxes of cotton,
match holders, and other items portray stereotyped images of African Americans and are labeled as being from New Orleans. jayhawkme offers a "Vintage 'Souvenir of New Orleans cotton picker' Black American plastic doll"
that is holding a cotton bale with "Souvenir of New Orleans" imprinted on
it.[120] Sellers list recently produced versions of these items and make it seem
as if visitors and buyers can still access the depicted services and obtain such
bodies. Imprinting these objects with the name of the city also associates
them with a particular place and depicts a specific cultural past and possible
present.

These items seem to provide detailed information about New Orleans because they are marked with the name of the city. However, there is no consideration of the history of New Orleans as the largest and one of the oldest
slave-trading centers in the United States.[121] Neither the dolls nor the sellers'

descriptions articulate aspects of New Orleans. Even the printed claim that these items are from the area and presumably produced in New Orleans should be interrogated. These objects may be marked "New Orleans," but many of them, like other black Americana items, are produced in Asia and encourage the reproduction of America's racist past and present in other countries. For instance, sarcole offers a "SET OF VINTAGE 1977 AUNT JAMIMA SALT & PEPPER SHAKERS."[122] The woman may be "HOLDING A POT OF GUMBO" that "READS 'NEW ORLEANS, LA'" but "THE STICKER READS 'MADE IN TAIWAN.'" ceegeel auctions a set of salt and pepper shakers. The items are stamped "'New Orleans' and 'Louisiana'" on "the front" but they are "marked inside the base with the words 'Hong Kong.'"[123] Sellers can try to prevent people from conflating black Americana items and African Americans by indicating these assorted heritages and attributions. The labels on black Americana items highlight their diverse production histories, which includes people of color laboring in varied parts of the world to reproduce these stereotyped items.

Conclusion: Resisting Black Americana

Some eBay engagements provide ways of resisting the overt racism of black Americana items and sellers' stereotyped narratives. As I have noted, the visible wear that appears on black Americana items produced by whites can indicate pleasurable engagements with stereotyped representations or resistant use. On rare occasions, condition indicates attempts to destroy black Americana items and the accompanying stereotypes. For instance, naillnh55 lists a defaced racist postcard of an African American man with an oversize head and tiny eyes who is dressed in a tuxedo and top hat, sitting on a chamber pot, and revealing his buttocks (figure 24). The postcard's text reads, "I'm all set for the big blowout! Expect to have a good time here!"[124] The caricatured aspects of the man's physiognomy and his social transgressions, which combine high-class entertainment with flatulence and evacuating, repeat many stereotyped black Americana narratives and render the man as less than human. Nevertheless, the seller describes the item as "adorable" and advises, "SOMEONE SCRIBBLED ON IT. BUT THE PICTURE AND WORDING ON IT IS STILL LEDGIBLE." In spite of the seller's promises, a previous owner appears to have intentionally drawn over the stereotyped face and body, marred the postcard, and intervened in its racist narratives and its value as "humorous" and a collectible. Even the postcard's plastic sleeve elides the affront-

Happy Bidding &

Have a Great Day

Eric

LIKE WHAT YOU SEE? OR LOOKING FOR SOMETHING ELSE? CHECK OUT MY STORE FOR MANY NON AUCTION ITEMS, AND OTHER AUCTION ITEMS. THANK YOU

00021

The power of protection from AOL and eBay. Learn more

Shipping, payment details and return policy

24. nail1nh55, "Vintage Black Americana Post Card Adorable Collectible," eBay, 19 December 2006

ing image. Such documented effacements offer an intervention into eBay's black Americana representations. Unfortunately, such resistant tactics are not prevalent enough to permanently disrupt the narratives that accompany eBay's black Americana category or the ways sellers render New Orleans.

The artists Mendi + Keith Obadike sabotage the black Americana category through different means. In 2001, they interrogated the commodification of blackness in contemporary society by offering Keith Obadike's "Blackness" for auction under the black Americana category.[125] They warned possible purchasers that they did not recommend that "this Blackness be used while" performing such actions as "seeking employment," "making or selling 'serious' art," "shopping or writing a personal check," "making intellectual claims," or "voting in the United States or Florida."[126] Through humor, they critique social perceptions that being black provides a new form of privilege. Mendi + Keith also evoke a past where black bodies were sold without consideration. For the artist and theorist Coco Fusco, the listing is full of "references to the history of objectifying black bodies in the slave trade and the contemporary commodifying of black culture."[127] When black Americana is viewed as people, it constitutes a black community of commodified bodies, smiling mammies, happy watermelon consumers, and goodwill. The black Americana category and its fantastical people thereby becomes part of eBay's moral community. Mendi + Keith challenge people's ideas about owning and controlling black bodies, including the ability to experience a version of identity tourism in which white people can temporarily and safely perform as African Americans. As artists they supplant eBay's equitable community and critique the troubling sexualities, power structures, and forms of community that underlie eBay's and sellers' commodification of blackness.

eBay's cancellation of Mendi + Keith's auction four days after its posting demonstrates the static and rigid aspects of the category structure and the risks and promises in incorporating critical commentary into the site. According to Mendi + Keith, "eBay closed the auction due to the 'inappropriateness' of the item."[128] Yet Mendi + Keith were deploying the auction as a critical and educational tool. The company's cancellation of the auction raises serious questions about eBay's claims that it retains black Americana on the site because of its educational functions. Mendi + Keith have highlighted the cancellation by posting information about it on their site. In a similar manner to gay interest sellers, they emphasize eBay's duplicitous promises about providing a setting where all objects can be bought and sold and identities and desires can be facilitated. Mendi + Keith were "a little shocked that a company like ebay that sells ceramic coons and mammies, African exotica and Nazi paraphernalia would shy away from" their project.[129] eBay may have canceled the auction because Mendi + Keith deploy the kinds of critical commodifications of blackness envisioned by Collins and Gray. They reappropriate and profit from their own position as product and temporarily rupture eBay's categories and community. The artists write into the site instead of allowing black Americana produced by whites to speak for them.

Mendi + Keith perform a consumer critique and challenge ideas about what is being bought and sold on eBay, the ways eBay produces categories and conceptions of things, and its rendering of identity and desiring positions. They point to strategies for resistance by inserting their assessment into the system and maintaining it on another site. Otherwise, eBay erases records of resistance, difference, and the limits of its organizational logic when it deletes listings. Consumer critics can also use the language and ethos of corporations to question companies' values and structures; deploy brand logos and communities for personal messages; highlight conflicts within and beyond Internet settings; exemplify the essence of products better than companies; reinvent the services and features that attracted them; assert their role and value as consumer citizens; and use their knowledge and methods to assess other sites, products, and companies. Consumer critics can bring to light the dangerous power of corporations. However, they might also use such methods to examine culture more broadly; assess the relationship between corporations and state structures; and imagine other possibilities for consumers, products, producers, and citizenship. In the afterword, I consider the similar workings of craigslist's organizational logic and brand community features and demonstrate how eBay's troubling promises and functions are part of the larger workings of Internet settings.

Everything in Moderation

THE REGULATING ASPECTS OF CRAIGSLIST AND

THE MORAL ASSERTIONS OF "COMMUNITY FLAGGING"

The similarities between eBay and craigslist point to some larger tendencies in Internet settings and important research questions. craigslist's "factsheet" describes the site in this way: "Local classifieds and forums - community moderated" through flagging "and largely free."[1] The parallels between this description and eBay's narratives encourage further considerations of the meaning of "community" and "local" in Internet settings, the functions of community moderation, the relationship between the sites' values and members' identities and desires, the significance of "largely free" for consumers and citizens, and the responsibilities of individuals who are conceptualized as a community. eBay and craigslist also make related claims about sexual freedom and institute community morals and rules. Craig Newmark, the site's developer, heard about a woman arranging sexual encounters through craigslist and argued that the setting reflects "basic American values, and freedom of choice couldn't be any more basic."[2] craigslist promises women a tolerant and erotically liberating experience, gains their trust in local sites and community moderation, and then regulates their gendered roles and sexuality. For instance, craigslist facilitates the "flagging" and removal of women's dating advertisements. My studies throughout this book and research by Nelly Oudshoorn, Els Rommes, and Marcelle Stienstra indicate how Internet sites promise universal access while configuring—and, in some cases, effacing—members' identities and behavior.[3] By critically addressing these issues through the literature on brand community, configuring the user, organizational logic, and sexual citizenship, I provide theoretical models for thinking about Internet settings and new media studies.

Community is a key structuring device in Internet settings and other spheres because it seems to embrace everyone while using the problems arising from inclusiveness to justify rules and values. For instance, some individuals request and enforce delimiting structures when confronted by the profusion of Internet settings and the lack of clearly organized arrangements. Listserv and forum participants often regulate the topics that are "appropriate" and even the ways posts are titled. A willing group of craigslist readers flags and removes postings that do not fit into the selected category. With eBay, such wonderfully unruly forms of sexual citizenship as gay men's representations of their nearly naked bodies are removed and thereby articulate the company's rules and norms. In a related manner, reality television programs such as *A Shot at Love with Tila Tequila*, *The Real Housewives of Orange County* (and *Atlanta*, *Beverly Hills*, *DC*, *New Jersey*, and *New York City*), *Rock of Love with Bret Michaels*, and *Rock of Love Bus with Bret Michaels* depict women's bodies as visually accessible and out of control. Viewers of the programs are thereby justified in watching, schooling, and bringing women into cultural conformity for what is purportedly their own good.

Television programs like *Rock of Love: Charm School* claim to re-educate the hypersexual women who have failed to win Michaels's permanent affection in *Rock of Love*. Such texts validate the regulation of women by having female participants reflect on their comportment and ask to be normed. Women also seem to ask for schooling, and are scripted as initiates who need training in the rules of the community and technology, when their dating posts on craigslist are flagged and removed and they request assistance in the flag help forum. This regulation is produced at an organizational level because aspects of the site, including the option to flag, the email directing people with flagged posts to consult the forum, and the wide-scale flagging of women's personal ads, create a culture in which women need support and need to be socially reformed to remain members of the craigslist system. The number of flags required to remove posts is extremely low in the "women seeking men" (w4m) part of the site, ostensibly so members can flag spam and fake ads.[4] Nevertheless, the site's structure and flagging processes enable members to remove what they identify as not fitting or conforming.

The craigslist Company and Community

Newmark started craigslist as an email list in 1995 to tell people from San Francisco about events and "help out, in a very small way."[5] Company and media narratives about Newmark beginning craigslist to support the needs of others are similar to accounts about Pierre Omidyar starting eBay, also in 1995, to help out Pam Wesley. Newmark identifies as "just" a customer-service representative and politically deploys humility even though he controls a significant portion of craigslist's stock.[6] craigslist has eschewed being bought out by larger companies, raising revenue through banner ads, and charging higher fees for services. Newmark argues, "Who needs the money? We don't really care."[7] Newmark and the company align themselves with the brand community, which is invested in the craigslist culture. Of course, craigslist's purportedly distinctive ethos and Newmark's service to members also generate consumer loyalty and profits. In 2010, craigslist's revenue was estimated at about 122 million U.S. dollars, with a 22 percent increase from the previous year.[8]

Newmark, in similar ways to Whitman, has been involved in recent U.S. politics. Newmark identifies as a "community organizer" and presents himself as an activist and local political figure.[9] During Barack Obama's run for the 2008 presidency, Newmark campaigned for him, acted as his "official technology surrogate," and blogged and spoke about Obama's technology platform.[10] Newmark also contributed funds to the U.S. Democratic National Committee and to Obama's campaign. Obama planned and has now set up what he describes as a "craigslist for service" to increase volunteer work.[11] The site makes a call to community, collective, and the "Power of We."[12] Obama's proposal has been lauded in the media, particularly among technology pundits and programmers. However, craigslist's organizational logic, with its underlying assertions of gender and sexuality norms, makes such connections troubling.

eBay has an economic stake in craigslist because of its purchase of about 25 percent of the company in 2004 from a former employee, Phillip Knowlton.[13] eBay had a member on the craigslist board and pledged not to interfere with the running of the company. However, lawsuits were initiated in 2008 after eBay introduced its own classified site into the American market and craigslist reorganized its stock allocations to remove eBay from its board.[14] After the legal filing, Kim Rubey, an eBay spokesperson, articulated the companies' similar brand ethos: eBay "believes in Craigslist, shares its values and acts with openness, honesty and integrity in its dealings with Craigslist's board and the online community."[15] Newmark and Jim Buckmaster, CEO of craigslist, were initially comfortable with the stock sale because of comparable brand community identities. During the stock transfer, Newmark noted that both companies emphasize "trustworthiness and reputation," are "about building community," and are focused on "humanizing and democratizing the 'net."[16] eBay's and craigslist's related narratives about trust and co-production highlight how such tendencies structure Internet operations.

craigslist constitutes community by making assertions about localness and affinity. For instance, craigslist uses the San Francisco Bay Area as the default site to connect the company to the city where the site was started.[17] Each regional craigslist includes a section entitled "community" with such place-specific categories as "lost+found," "local news," and "rideshare." According to the frequently asked questions (FAQ), individuals should ordinarily post to "the site closest to where you are located. If your ad is equally relevant to all locations, your ad does not belong on local craigslist."[18] The company has also stopped third-party developers from offering search engines that provide results from across the sites because they go "against the basic intent of Craigslist to be a local tool."[19] craigslist is related to early versions of Facebook, which situated members within an academic setting and allowed them to access full information only about people in their network, even though individuals from different locations used the site. All of this makes people feel that only individuals like them, who are in their area and cohort, are engaging. These features support trust and consciousness of a kind and help foster brand community formation.

craigslist is supposed to reflect members' desires. People "would suggest things," Newmark would figure out what "people were asking for," and then he would "do it."[20] Even with the astronomic expansion of craigslist, the site design is imagined to be "almost 100 percent based on what people ask" for. craigslist does not charge people for posting except for "jobs" and "housing" advertisements in a few cities and "therapeutic services." However, in return for craigslist's features, members are expected to do other sorts of labor, including reviewing the site for illegal activities and acting as a form of customer-service representative in the help forums. According to the author Jessica Livingston, Newmark has built a "community on the Internet," kept "craigslist as free as possible," and is "able to operate cheaply" by letting "users do much of the work."[21] This model allows the company to pay only about thirty employees.[22] Yet the reporter Adam Lashinsky argues that the company is not community-centered because the "content comes from the site's devoted users, who provide the listings that are its lifeblood, for free" and that craigslist "is indifferent to money" but "gushes profits."[23] In addition, self-identified advisers in the flag help forum instruct people in appropriate positions and roles rather than facilitate what individuals want. Since "helping" encourages a combination of assistance and schooling, this raises questions about how Internet and computer help systems support people, configure members, and produce knowledge.

eBay references an array of objects and desires while associating the company and good members with heterosexuality. In a similar manner, media accounts about craigslist mention the diverse sexual subjects who use the site and the ways it is "empowering a new generation of swingers" while equating the relationship between Buckmaster and Susan MacTavish Best, the craigslist publicist, to the company and its ethos.[24] In these reports, Best's job as "spokeswoman" is connected to her position as Buckmaster's "girlfriend."[25] Newmark's partner, Eileen Whelpley, insists that her correct name be used in news reports, but both women are often referred to as the "girlfriend."[26] In a related way, Wesley is frequently identified as Omidyar's "wife." eBay, craigslist, and other interfaces employ narratives about wives and girlfriends to prop up the status of their male inventors. In Internet forums such as Digg and Slashdot and media texts such as *Dark Angel*, *Hackers*, *Fringe*, and *NUMB3RS*, technologies are associated with skill, power, and poorly socialized men who cannot engage with women. Technologies thereby threaten to feminize men if they are not managed. Accounts about inventors' girlfriends differentiate between empowered male producers and women who act as inspiration and users. These narratives incorporate heterosexual identity positions and the standards of sexual citizenship into the founding and continuance of these settings.

craigslist, in a similar manner to eBay, claims to facilitate sexual freedom. For instance, Newmark argues that legal "adult ads," including people seeking casual sex, fit with the "moral compasses" of participants.[27] Nevertheless, legal representatives from several U.S. states and other countries have challenged craigslist about the appearance of sex workers' advertisements in the "adult services" category, and the company began removing this part of the site in 2010. craigslist referred to these legal and cultural pressures as censorship and performed a kind of consumer and brand community critique of governmentality.[28] After removing the adult services category, craigslist replaced the link on the opening part of the site with "a black bar reading 'censored.'"[29] However, some female posters also refer to their flagged and removed ads as "censorship" and perform a consumer critique of craigslist's claims about freedom.[30] The opportunity to flag and the ways women are advised in the flag help forum reassert normative sexuality.

Community Flagging

Community flagging is supposed to keep the site safe and people honest and, as on eBay, facilitate transactions. If enough people flag an ad—and this number is determined by the company, is not shared with readers, and varies based on city and type of listing—then the advertisement is removed, and the person who posted the ad receives a notification. When people's ads are flagged and removed, they are marked as bad, denied the ability to express themselves, and prevented from engaging with craigslist. They can repost advertisements, although reposted ads are even more likely to be flagged, and members are prevented from posting after too many listings have been deleted. craigslist only makes personal ad readers "agree to flag as 'prohibited' anything illegal or in violation of the craigslist terms of use" and constitutes intimate relationships between people as initially and inherently regulatory and under the watchful gaze of the community.[31] craigslist also makes it seem as if it can be libratory only by getting members to be regulators and that identity, membership, and citizenship must always have limits and limiters. As Diane Richardson argues, sexual minorities are allowed to become full citizens only when their claims of normalcy and good citizenship are accepted.[32] Some craigslist posters, as I suggest in more detail later, are flagged as undesirable by their "community," prevented from having full rights, instructed to be better citizens by flagging and doing other sorts of labor, and chided or even humiliated in the flag help forum.

There are "issues" with craigslist, notes Newmark, "but we do trust people. That's why we have a flagging mechanism, which is how people who use the community can deal with bad stuff."[33] Newmark's narratives about "shared values" and trust are related to Omidyar's claims that people are basically good. The unofficial FAQ, which is mentioned in the craigslist help document and referenced by self-appointed advisers, argues that members need to create the sort of setting they want. It encourages members to flag: "You are the 'community' part of 'Community moderation.'"[34] Members' work is constituted as positive, but the rights of craigslist participants are less clearly articulated. When confronted by such conceptions of community, it makes sense to consider the cost to the individuals doing the work and the toll on people who are controlled and constituted by their labor.

craigslist claims to facilitate open dialogue and connections between people. "The Internet is about inclusion," proposes Newmark. "On the Net, no one should be left out."[35] However, readers of craigslist's FAQ are advised, "If you feel the need to give your opinion, please respond to the poster directly via email, rather than posting a reply. Discussion postings belong ONLY in" the "discussion forums."[36] The unofficial FAQ also indicates that "discussions in the classified categories are unwieldy and unpopular with most users."[37] Of course, craigslist never addresses how a community might be constituted, or its positions might be negotiated, when members cannot communicate in the setting where the practices are occurring. craigslist articulates collaborative dialogue, consensus, and the development of group values at the same time that it prevents these arrangements from being formed among participants. In a similar manner, eBay promises community but does not guarantee communication unless individuals are engaged in an economic transaction.

craigslist's rule about not replying to advertisements prevents discussions about issues, including considerations of the process of flagging and removing posts, where most people would see them. Personal posters who ask individuals not to flag them are particularly likely to be flagged and removed. When individuals try to have a discussion about flagging or community in the flag help forum, where replies purportedly are allowed, they are informed by advisers that they should not interfere in other members' problems. People who are critical of craigslist's policies, or who want to comment on its systems, are prevented from finding each other, intervening in most aspects of the setting, collaboratively considering things, and forming community. In the advertising sections, craigslist does not have linked and traceable posts, a design feature that enables engagement in many Internet settings. Each craigslist ad is an isolated text rather than part of a connected and developing culture. The dearth of stable IDs because most ads are anonymized, the lack of threaded posts, and the rules against commenting on listings stymie individuals who want to engage, provide warnings, or locate members who are acting duplicitously. Enabling these features would start to make craigslist into a setting where dialogue is facilitated rather than just promised.

craigslist states that "Millions of postings" are "removed through community flagging each month," "98–99% are in violation of the craigslist terms of use or other posted guidelines," and "craigslist would quickly become unusable" without flagging.[38] Members' investments in posts and concerns about the politics of flagging are discouraged. According to the unofficial FAQ, it is not appropriate to be angry over the removal of a free ad: "If you are getting a big emotional reaction over it stop reading right about now. You have emotional issues. You need a therapist, not a FAQ."[39] In a similar manner, a respondent in the flag help forum advises, "If having your free personal ad flagged down is making you angry, you need to run, not walk, to a mental health care professional."[40] Advisers never consider that members' work establishes a social contract, and individuals have thereby earned the right for posts to remain. By framing responses to flagging as unwarranted and unhealthy, the site and many of its members discourage considerations of the ideological influences of such behavior and community formations. They also downplay the processes of flagging and removal in forming the craigslist interface. The organization of craigslist, particularly its rules about posting in the right category and not replying to other people's posts, results in most people not being aware of the regulatory experiences individuals have with the setting.

Moderation of posts is supposed to be based in local communities and their values, but some participants use craigslist forums to facilitate massive site-wide flagging of advertisements. Listings for women seeking men and for pets are most often flagged and removed. Pet-sale listings are flagged because this is not allowed on the site. Pet-adoption listings are supported by the terms of use but are constantly flagged because many readers suspect they are from dog breeders who are widely vilified, think that the allowable rehoming fee is too high, believe that all pets should be spayed or neutered before being put up for adoption, and disapprove of people giving their pets away. Widescale flagging has caused a lot of people to give up on listing their animals and resulted in the abandonment and death of pets that otherwise might have been adopted. The intensity of such actions has led members who are involved in this category to write letters to Newmark and the company. They want Newmark to "show you care about your users" by stopping the "control-freaks who apparently enjoy harassing craigslist users"; "have hijacked your list"; "form 'flagging groups'"; "conspire with one another to 'gang flag' posts"; and flag "posts that don't in any way, shape or form violate craigslist rules."[41] These members seek Newmark's care and expressions of community support, which he identifies as key aspects of craigslist. However, he has not helped them.

Advertisements from women seeking men are frequently flagged and removed on the craigslist site, even though community flagging is supposed to support different moral codes. According to the help section for flagging, the "system allows craigslist users to mark inappropriate postings for speedy removal, while preserving everyone's ability to express themselves freely."[42] Yet women—and particularly women who are older, larger, differently classed, and deemed less physically perfect than social norms and who try to assert some form of power and politics—come under extreme forms of scrutiny and dismissal. Understanding how instruction, regulation, and the constitution of normalized subjects occur in these settings is imperative because academic and popular discourses tend to depict craigslist and more recent social networking sites as deeply liberating. With craigslist, an overt sexual outpouring, even a subcultural expression of less conventional forms of sex and desire, is coupled to the limiting of women's roles and the unlikelihood of these women living culturally acceptable lives.

The flagging and removal of women-seeking-men ads are acknowledged and widely accepted by the people offering assistance in the flag help forum. A forum adviser asks, "Why does the W4M section get so many more flags than the M4W section?"[43] Another adviser responds, "Men flag more. Men get more scams. Men are fed up."[44] Ninety percent of the "flagged off personal ads that come in here for help are posted by women," writes lovesleo, and "rather than a double standard, women simply need to flag more."[45] Yet such arguments direct women toward a form of agency that is not available. Women's deployment of flagging would not change the status of their ads, and there is no way to locate individuals who are flagging and regulate them. Instead of women flagging more, craigslist might require people to sign in before they can flag, reduce the number of flags individuals can assign, require more information about why an ad has been flagged, and increase the number of flags needed to remove women's advertisements.

Self-appointed advisers in the flag help forum often argue that it is the poster's geographic community rather than anyone in the forum or company that flags posts and repeat craigslist's notion of local community. Advisers such as FunkyshoeZ "don't flag ads here," "just look at ads and give suggestions on how they can stay up," and "don't control the community."[46] Other advisers, such as no_spammers, tell posters what "YOUR COMMUNITY did not like about your post."[47] Nevertheless, advisers tend to constitute community desires, include personal values in their comments, and direct women to do gender more conventionally. The processes of doing gender, according to the sociologists Candace West and Don H. Zimmerman, involve "a complex of socially guided perceptual, interactional, and micropolitical activities that cast particular pursuits as expressions of masculine and feminine 'natures.'"[48] Advisers and flaggers assert community and gender norms and the organizational aspects of the site. Yet many individuals do not notice craigslist's regulating aspects and traditional values.

People who have their advertisements flagged and removed often express extreme surprise. Posts to the flag help forum are typically entitled "Why??" and "why is this being flagged?"[49] karakicks would "be amazed if" the advisers found "something offensive" or "miscatergorized" with her advertisement.[50] When imakittykitty learns that readers can flag for any reason, she asks, "So people are flagging my ad because they simply don't like it?? I've done nothing to violate ANY terms of service and it seems so ignorant for people to just flag me for no reason other than they don't like the way I set it up."[51] Posters tend to list the reasons craigslist provides for flagging (miscategorized, prohibited, and spam/overpost) because they cannot understand how these violations relate to what the "community" does not like in their ads.[52] Nevertheless, active cohorts who flag are the community and de facto law. If craigslist required these individuals to log in and provide reasons for flagging ads, this information could be forwarded to flagged members, used to evaluate the system and flaggers' behavior, and reviewed by employees to reinstitute ads. This would also make the labor of flagging and its social functions more apparent.

Women are ideologically and sexually controlled and directed to do gender and sexuality more conventionally when their ads are flagged and removed and they are advised in the forum. For instance, women who appear to be looking for extramarital relationships are likely to have their posts removed. Advisers then tend to inform women that their "community has_some_shred of decency and is trying to tell you just how much they hate cheaters."[53] Gail54321 was removed in the strictly platonic section for asking, "Are you wicked smart? Wanna chat with someone else who is too?" and for indicating she was "married but not happily" and was "NOT looking for someone to rescue" her "or listen to" her "whine."[54] "If you post as married unhappily," paul_baumer advises, even "if you say you don't want him to listen to you complain about it, it's assumed you want to cheat on your hubby."[55] He also argues that "it's fine for people to flag if they think Gail was cheating! That's what community moderation means."[56] Gail54321 is rightfully shocked that she "can't request platonic friends" and is thereby required to filter her life through that of her husband, even when they are not getting along.[57] Women like Gail54321 question the processes of flagging but help forum advisers tend to suggest that flaggers' actions constitute site policy. According to an adviser, cheating is "seen as immoral by almost everyone and in some states such as the one i reside in it's also illegal. I would flag every cheater ad and prostitute ad and any other ad that encourages others to engage in amoral and or illegal activities. Flagging is community moderation and that's not the kind of thing I want going on in my community."[58] In such instances, advisers reveal that they are deeply identified with flaggers and resist everything but the most conventional forms of gender and sexuality.

Advisers also use sex workers' advertisements to render all women as sexually suspect. For example, a woman who is looking "to hook up for some NSA fun," a "no strings attached" sexual encounter, is told that "95% of w4m ads are either spam or hookers" and "your ad sounded just like them."[59] Women who appear to be looking for any kind of support from men are identified as whores, golddiggers, and prostitutes and summarily dismissed. These terms are used to shame women. For instance, curves82_la, who is advertising for "a mentor, benefactor, friend anything rather than 'sugar daddy,'" is told to "peddle your gold diggin' whore ass -elsewhere- you ain't wanted on CL."[60] tigerli555 is labeled a "whore"; advised, "Your ad is prohibited, penis breath"; and told "to lose the 'friend$$'" phrasing "because that tips people off that you're a prostitute."[61] pythagorus is informed, "PROSTITUTION IS NOT WANTED HERE. Go elswhere to advertise you desease ridden wares."[62]

Advisers imagine that women's bodies are rotten, repulsive, and abject when they extend beyond advice givers' acceptable limits for women's roles. According to Julia Kristeva's psychoanalytic theory, people experience abjection when something "disturbs identity, system, order" and "does not respect borders, positions," and "rules" and try to expel this experience or thing.[63] Sex workers actively profit from their bodies and sexuality and thereby threaten the terms of traditional gender relationships. Openly sexual women who are not looking for a single male partner also threaten cultural understandings of dyadic gender relationships. Male flaggers and advisers therefore try to excise them from the system. Advisers also work to remove these posters from the discussion forum because they are imagined to be beyond instruction. This exclusion succeeds with AppleCure. She finds the advisers' comments "brutal" and the respondents to be "bullies on the playground."[64] AppleCure tells them that she is sorry she "came here asking for help. Don't worry, it won't happen again." In such instances, advisers constitute women as undesirable sexual citizens, inform them that they have no place in the setting or claim to community membership, and insult them until they stop posting.

A cohort of readers also vilifies large women because they do not embody femininity as it is normatively conceived and because they have not met the desires and instructions of most men. In being, but not corporeally assenting to the ways many men want women to appear, these women represent a site of resistance to men's values and are removed from the system. Women are advised, "BBW is a trigger phrase that draws flags" and that "some men will flag ANY woman who uses" big beautiful woman (BBW) in her ad.[65] hazelcat, who was flagged and advised not to use the term BBW, wonders why a poster should "have to hide who she is?"[66] She asserts that women are being "discriminated against by the small minded, negative, low, loathsome, pigs of the world who think they're better than a big woman. What gives them the right to decide who posts an ad?" Jane1010 writes that flagging for the use of the term BBW is "just plain discriminatory--on their part and on the part of anyone who permits it."[67] These consumer critiques have little influence because they appear in the flag help forum, where few people read them. Jane1010 is told "complain all you want, but that's not going to change," "Craigslist allows anyone to flag anything they want," and "obviously a lot of guys hate the phrase BBW (can't say I blame them)."[68] Advisers' comments reduce the value of critiques and further the patriarchal control of women. However, women's irritated observations are important. They highlight the failures of the interface and its broken promises of equity. Newmark is believed to have designed craigslist to fulfill members' desires, and he is supposed to be responsive to their requests. Nevertheless, women's commentary and the low number of flags required to remove their ads present a different account of the site. Their critiques also point to problems with other flagging and rating systems, including Digg and Slashdot.

Advisers school women to do gender, be more affable, provide physiognomic details, and make themselves into objects. Posters are instructed to "leave out the bitching," tone "down the 'tude," and "Be nicer."[69] Advisers' indications that women should be pleasant and attractive could be appended with the phrase "for men." These mandates extend beyond dating advertisements and suggest that women should create themselves according to the terms of men's desires in other settings. Instruction is something that is done to women in these settings but is not a process that is available to them as posters or help seekers. Instead, women are chided for "doling out instructions in their dating ads."[70] Women are expected to avoid negativity and the kinds of deep and personal thinking that might cause them to resist the social constraints of sexual citizenship. Directives for women to be empathetic may always be at the cost of their own psychic lives. Nevertheless, many individuals consent to this configuration. For instance, SexySingleSweetie is looking to "post without getting flagged and be educated about the errors so" she does not "repeat them."[71]

The site advisers and the interface reference community while discouraging women from collaboratively engaging. When karakicks describes how "people are abusing their powers" in flagging, other removed members respond.[72] myadbeingflagged adds that she "had the same thing happen" and is "so upset about it."[73] However, Snappy_Comeback dismisses this commentary and indicates that karakicks "got threadjacked by yet another person complaining, but TOTALLY IGNORING the directions."[74] Loku_v7 provides viable suggestions about how advisers can convey site policies without supporting intolerant flagging but is told to stop posting in "other people's threads spouting your personal opinions."[75] Help seekers are advised to "please ignore Loku_v7. Just a silly troll bent on" giving "bad advice and causing ill feelings here in this forum."[76] Loku_v7's posts were given negative numbers, which discourages people from reading them. Through such actions, the advisers support their power, defend the instructional aspects of the forum, resist the constitution of alternative communities, and stymie a larger interrogation of the ideology behind flagging women.

Posters perform a kind of critique when they relate their advertisements to other listings. For example, karakicks argues that her self-portrayals are "not suggestive," while men are "posting pictures of" their "dicks in MEN SEEKING WOMAN."[77] When jpoqalot is informed, "Negativity draws flags," she points to the need to flag "the enormous amount of guys posting pics of their dicks" because "that makes more sense."[78] Rather than addressing the possibility that women are flagged in particularly egregious ways, yasuragi replies, "Do YOU flag the cock shots? If you don't flag them, they won't go away."[79] Women's critiques of morals and behavior are directed back at them and used to mandate their work. Women who advocate change are told to adopt the current system and follow its codes and are thereby incorporated into the brand community.

Conclusion: The Politics of Community

Members of eBay, craigslist, and many other Internet settings are expected to give to the interface but only the most normalized and involved individuals can expect empathy or response in kind, even though care and goodness are scripted as key aspects of these settings. In a similar manner, women seeking men are instructed on craigslist not to anticipate and not to ask for anything. Feminists who expect equity, women who identify their desires, and women who are looking for support from men are all dismissed as controlling and repulsive. Women's irritated responses to flagging do not change the craigslist interface, but they do offer a model for critically engaging. Newmark proposes that "using any kind of public forum for support means that a company will be faced with disgruntled customers. But much of the time, disgruntled customers are right -- and they're giving you valuable feedback."[80] This idea is important even though Newmark does not use it to consider craigslist's flagging mechanism. Internet and new media scholars should look to disgruntled customers and their critiques as ways to understand the problematic aspects of Internet settings. The interactions in help forums, posted conflicts between brand community members, angry video responses, mass circulation of dialogues between consumers and customer-service representatives, and sites about how companies and settings "suck" provide researchers with valuable information and feedback, but they have been understudied.

Studying the controlling aspects of eBay and craigslist points to how promises of tolerance and freedom act as a screen. Disparities between the assurances and functions of Internet settings should encourage consumer critiques when using, reading, and writing about these sites. Researchers are also adopters of software and settings, which makes it imperative to analyze the ways academic language and use can repeat the extremely positive sentiments of producers and traditional structures of commercial enterprises. Internet studies scholars might therefore pose methods of irritated and critical use in addition to exhibiting enthusiasm and fandom. Such methods can allow researchers to acknowledge the ways settings positively engage members, configure individuals, and create an alienated other. For instance, a closer attention to the academic and popular use of the term "community" in Internet settings and other spheres is advisable. Newmark's identification as a "community organizer" encourages an address to how people are formed into societies, as well as the functions of already constituted communities.[81] After all, the term "organized" also means that something is controlled.

Internet studies is the examination of governmentality, social regulation, and resistance. The designers and corporate employees of eBay, craigslist, and other Internet settings may be the new political and ruling class, even though they ignore many constituencies. *BusinessWeek* magazine identifies Newmark as one of the twenty-five most influential people on the web.[82] In a related manner, craigslist is described as "a profoundly collaborative venture, with political potential."[83] Governments and political figures use social networking models and become more intermeshed with sites and designers. For instance, Obama is working to "harness new technologies to put information" about the operations and decisions of executive departments and agencies "online" and to make this information "readily available to the public."[84] News reviews of these plans identify social networking technologies as "the clearest path to an open government" and assume that these technologies address and are available to everyone.[85] Problems with craigslist's flagging demonstrate that technologies are not inherently free of bias or transparent, but these issues remain largely unnoted. Yet some of these issues are foregrounded by the Obama campaign's practices. His campaign deployed change.org to take questions from the public but then deleted inquiries about whether Governor Rod Blagojevich of Illinois had tried to sell Obama's Senate seat. When Obama's weekly address was first included on YouTube, viewers were not provided with the option to post comments.

Newmark is often consulted about plans for Internet-facilitated citizenship. However, there is never any recognition that craigslist has deleted and alienated a large cohort of women. When the craigslist model is applied at the government level, members' concerns that flagging curtails freedom of speech are even more worrisome. eBay's and craigslist's intermeshed promises of inclusion and rendering of traditional identities and social control are too likely to work with state models of norming and regulation. Whether referenced by the U.S. government or presented as models for new forms of generosity, including the microfinancing site Kiva's mention of craigslist, these settings are helping to produce our embodied limits and worldview. The bodies and regulatory strategies that are produced in these settings are therefore likely to constitute our lives and rights. Researchers can interrogate these settings by attending to the ideologies that accompany promises of empowerment and participants' angry evaluations. It is not easy to note the kinds of individuals who are removed from systems or invisible to most members, but such tactics are vital for developing critical forms of Internet and new media studies and more functional interfaces and settings.

NOTES

Preface and Acknowledgments

1. untitledprojects, "Staten Island Ferry Statue Liberty 1980'scolor postcard: an UNTITLED PROJECT: eBay/POSTCARDS/INDIANA," eBay, 1 March 2005 ⟨http://cgi.ebay.com/ws/eBayISAPI.dll?ViewItem&category=127&item=61583 75861&rd=1⟩; Conrad Bakker, "0002 : 03:01 Staten Island Ferry Statue Liberty 1980'scolor postcard," Untitled Projects, 2005, 10 July 2011 ⟨http://www .untitledprojects.com/index3.php⟩.
2. This series was simultaneously exhibited at the 2005 DePauw Biennial: Contemporary Art in the Midwest and auctioned on eBay.
3. White, "My Queer eBay."
4. White, "Listing eBay Masculinity."
5. White, "Engaged with eBay."
6. White, "What a Mess."
7. White, "Babies Who Touch You."

Introduction

1. twingles33, "Twingles Collectibles eBay Store About My Store," eBay, 26 July 2011 ⟨http://members.ebay.com/ws/eBayISAPI.dll?ViewUserPage&userid=twin gles33⟩. In the citations in this book, detailed information about website references is included. The constant reconfiguration of Internet representations and changes in Internet service providers make it difficult to find previously quoted material and important to chronicle the kinds of depictions that happen in Internet settings. Many Internet texts include typographical errors and unconventional forms of spelling, uppercase and lowercase typefaces, punctuation, and spacing. I have retained these formatting features in quotations and

Internet references, with the exception of citations for news and journal sites. Some of the sites listed in these citations are no longer available. Others have changed and do not offer the text or images that I describe. In the references, the date listed before the URL is the "publication" date or the last time the site was viewed in the indicated format. When two dates are included, the first date points to when the current configuration of the site was initially available and the second date is the latest access date. Some versions of referenced sites can be viewed by using the Internet Archive's Wayback Machine (Internet Archive, "Internet Archive: Wayback Machine," 4 January 2011 ⟨http://www.archive.org/web/web.php⟩).

2. WorldofGood.com, "Welcome to WorldofGood.com," 25 June 2011 ⟨http://worldofgood.ebay.com/ns/AboutUs.html⟩.

3. Of course, some boys (and men) have a long history of playing with such toys as baby dolls and "Barbies" and their "safe" incarnation as action figures.

4. eBay, "Community Values," 4 January 2011 ⟨http://pages.ebay.com/community/people/values.html?ssPageName=CMDV:CC040615⟩. eBay began using the "Whatever it is, you can get it on eBay" slogan throughout the site and in advertisements in 2005.

5. Etsy identifies the site as "more than a marketplace: we're a community of artists, creators, collectors, thinkers and doers." Etsy, "Etsy – Community," 14 July 2011 ⟨http://www.etsy.com/community?ref=so_com⟩. See also craigslist, "new orleans all community classifieds – craigslist," 26 July 2011 ⟨http://neworleans.craigslist.org/ccc/⟩.

6. Griffith, *The Official eBay Bible*, 6.

7. eBay, "Community Overview," 24 December 2010 ⟨http://hub.ebay.com/community⟩.

8. eBay, "About Us | eBay Main Street," 4 January 2011 ⟨http://www.ebaymainstreet.com/about⟩.

9. Cova and Pace, "Brand Community of Convenience Products." According to Adam Arvidsson, who works on the history of marketing, brands are not primarily products. Brands represent particular ways to use objects, "a propertied form of life" with economic and identificatory features that are "realized in consumption." Arvidsson, "Brands," 244.

10. Muñiz and O'Guinn, "Brand Community," 412.

11. Sicilia and Palazón, "Brand Communities on the Internet," 256.

12. Prahalad and Ramaswamy, "Co-creation Experiences," 6.

13. Cook, "The Contribution Revolution," 62.

14. Zwick et al., "Putting Consumers to Work," 186.

15. Hollenbeck and Zinkhan, "Consumer Activism on the Internet"; Holt, "Why Do Brands Cause Trouble?"; Muñiz and Schau, "Religiosity in the Abandoned Apple Newton Brand Community"; Muñiz and Schau, "Vigilante Marketing

and Consumer-Created Communications"; Ozanne and Murray, "Uniting Critical Theory and Public Policy to Create the Reflexively Defiant Consumer."

16. Cova and Dalli, "Working Consumers."

17. Cohen, *The Perfect Store*, 29; eBay, "History – eBay Inc.," 25 June 2011 〈http://www.ebayinc.com/list/milestones〉.

18. Chris Taylor, "Meg Whitman: Host of eBay's Passionate Party," *Time*, 26 April 2004, 27 June 2011 〈http://www.time.com/time/magazine/article/0,9171,9939 94,00.html〉.

19. Cohen, *The Perfect Store*, 29; eBay, "History – eBay Inc.," 28 June 2011 〈http://www.ebayinc.com/list/milestones〉.

20. Associated Press, "EBay to Cut 1,600 Jobs, Buy Bill Me Later," MSNBC, 6 October 2008, 4 January 2011 〈http://www.msnbc.msn.com/id/27046287/〉; eBay, "eBay Inc. Buys Leading Payments and Classifieds Businesses, Streamlines Existing Organization To Improve Growth," 6 October 2008 〈http://news.ebay.com/releasedetail.cfm?ReleaseID=338505〉; Stephen Gandel, "eBay's Biggest Bargain: The Company's Shares," *Fortune*, 11 December 2008, 4 January 2011 〈http://money.cnn.com/2008/12/11/technology/gandel_ebay.fortune/index.htm?postversion=2008121110〉.

21. For a discussion of how values are modeled in other settings, see Andersen, "Relationship Marketing and Brand Involvement of Professionals through Web-Enhanced Brand Communities"; Cova et al., "Global Brand Communities across Borders"; and Jang et al., "The Influence of On-Line Brand Community Characteristics on Community Commitment and Brand Loyalty."

22. eBay, "eBay Media Center: Our History," 15 March 2008 〈http://news.ebay.com/history.cfm〉.

23. eBay, "Community Values," 3 July 2011 〈http://pages.ebay.com/community/people/values.html?ssPageName=CMDV:CC040615〉.

24. Woolgar, "Configuring the User." Some scholars have interrogated these arguments. Anne Sofie Lægran and James Stewart, who study new media settings, describe Woolgar's theory as a mechanistic view of the user that privileges the designers' viewpoint. For Lægran and Stewart, configuration is a more flexible and interactive process in which users contribute. In his research on geographic information systems (GIS), Nicholas Chrisman also identifies a design process in which "software shapes social relationships and is shaped by them." People co-produce technologies when articulating the needs of cohorts, maintaining technologies after designers and producers have abandoned them, and supporting brands and devices by buying. Lægran and Stewart, "Nerdy, Trendy or Healthy?" 360. See also Chrisman, "Full Circle," 30; Lindsay, "From the Shadows"; Parthasarathy, *Building Genetic Medicine*; and Schot and de la Bruheze, "The Mediated Design of Products, Consumption, and Consumers in the Twentieth Century."

25. Woolgar et al., "Abilities and Competencies Required, Particularly by Small Firms, to Identify and Acquire New Technology," 579.

26. eBay, "Community Values," 3 July 2011 ⟨http://pages.ebay.com/community/people/values.html?ssPageName=CMDV:CC040615⟩.

27. Thrift, "Closer to the Machine?"

28. Cowan, "The Consumption Junction."

29. Stuart Elliott, "The Billion Designers of Windows 7," *New York Times*, 21 October 2009, 9 February 2011 ⟨http://www.nytimes.com/2009/10/22/business/media/22adco.html⟩.

30. eBay, "eBay: IT Finder," 3 December 2006 ⟨http://pages.ebay.com/itfinder/⟩.

31. eBay, "eBay: IT Finder," Wayback Machine, 10 December 2006, 11 March 2008 ⟨http://web.archive.org/web/20061210060418/http://pages.ebay.com/itfinder/⟩.

32. TheFind, "TheFind.com – Shopping Search Reinvented – What can we find for you?" 20 June 2007 ⟨http://www.thefind.com/⟩.

33. eBay, "eBay – New Used Baby Items, Baby Strollers and Baby Car Seats items on eBay.com. Find IT on eBay," 11 January 2009 ⟨http://baby.ebay.com/_W0QQfromZR12⟩.

34. eBay, "eBay – New Used Baby Items, Baby Strollers and Baby Car Seats items on eBay.com. Find IT on eBay," 11 January 2009 ⟨http://baby.listings.ebay.com/_W0QQfromZR4QQsacatZ2984QqsocmdZListingItemList⟩.

35. Acker, "Hierarchies, Jobs, Bodies," 147.

36. Britton, "Gendered Organizational Logic"; Swanberg, "Illuminating Gendered Assumptions."

37. Steve Gilman, "More Unusual Ways to Make Money," Unusual Ways to Make Money, 14 January 2011, ⟨http://www.unusualwaystomakemoney.com/uncountablewaystomakemoney.html⟩.

38. Ingraham, "The Heterosexual Imaginary."

39. eBay, "Hot holiday gifts for 2010 at The Gift Spot on eBay!" 24 December 2010 ⟨http://gifts.ebay.com/gifts#⟩.

40. Kofman, "Citizenship for Some but Not for Others," 122.

41. Richardson, "Locating Sexualities," 392.

42. Bell, "Pleasure and Danger"; Bell and Binnie, *The Sexual Citizen*; Binnie and Skeggs, "Cosmopolitan Knowledge and the Production and Consumption of Sexualized Space"; Evans, *Sexual Citizenship*. All of this creates an organizational (and governmental) logic in which cultural and legal conceptions of citizens are posed as neutral terms and correlated with gender and sexuality positions. Within this structure, citizens' rights depend on proof of a common good rather than being guaranteed, and individuals are expected to be responsible for reflecting and maintaining what is morally just. For instance, in the eBay setting, the company and many members code traditional mothers as good because they are imagined to be self-disciplining and selfless, concepts that are useful to the site and its ethos.

43. In 1995, Omidyar was also supporting a biotechnology startup, a college alumni group, and a tribute to the Ebola virus on the ebay.com domain. eBay thus started as a kind of "Whatever it is"—a site with multiple and conflicting collections and positions. Cohen, *The Perfect Store*, 22; eBay, "Founder's Note," 4 January 2011 ⟨http://pages.ebay.com/services/forum/feedback-foundersnote .html⟩.

44. Cohen, *The Perfect Store*, 11, 83.

45. Mary Lou Song, as quoted in David Rowan, "The Times: How eBay Invented Its Creation Myth," 19 July 2002, 4 January 2011 ⟨http://www.davidrowan.com/ 2002/07/times-how-ebay-invented-its-creation.html⟩.

46. Kevin Pursglove, as quoted in Matthew Beale, "E-Commerce Success Story: eBay, Exclusive Interview with Kevin Pursglove," *E-Commerce Times*, 4 January 2000, 4 January 2011 ⟨http://www.ecommercetimes.com/story/2127.html⟩.

47. Jackson, "Gender, Sexuality, and Heterosexuality."

48. Bradley and Porter, "eBay Inc.," 84.

49. Walton, *Forgery, Lies, and eBay*.

50. eBay, "lesbian | eBay," 10 July 2011 ⟨http://shop.ebay.com/i.html?_nkw=lesbian &_sacat=0&_odkw=gay&_osacat=0&_trksid=p3286.c0.m270.l1313⟩.

51. Livingstone and Lunt, "Representing Citizens and Consumers in Media and Communications Regulation"; Scammell, "The Internet and Civic Engagement"; Schild, "Empowering 'Consumer-Citizens' or Governing Poor Female Subjects?"; Schudson, "Citizens, Consumers, and the Good Society."

52. Breen, *The Marketplace of Revolution*; Shah et al., "Political Consumerism"; Stolle et al., "Politics in the Supermarket."

53. Buycotts are political actions in which consumers actively support or oppose something through purchasing decisions. Studies of consumer citizenship and of how consumer objects and practices shape identities include Canclini, *Consumers and Citizens*; Daunton and Hilton, *The Politics of Consumption*; and Scammell, "The Internet and Civic Engagement." While some literature on consumer citizenship identifies how individuals critically resist aspects of the market, media studies scholars also chronicle the ways media facilitate citizenship and empowerment. Henry Jenkins describes people enthusiastically engaging and recrafting media products so they address personal interests. Thus, it is no longer apt, according to him, to understand media's and individuals' interests as oppositional and viewers as co-opted. In a related manner, Sarah Banet-Weiser argues that women's empowerment can be part of commercial culture. The Nickelodeon television channel exploits the commercial market of girl power *and* produces girl power culture. Toby Miller acknowledges the agentive aspects of consumerism but interrogates the idea that consumers are at the center of politics. Authors such as Caren Kaplan and Inderpal Grewal further address how identities, including gender, ethnicity, and consumer positions, become intertwined with national and transnational formations. See Banet-Weiser,

Kids Rule!; Grewal, *Transnational America*; Jenkins, "Interactive Audiences?";
Kaplan, "A World without Boundaries"; and Miller, *Cultural Citizenship.*

54. WorldofGood.com, "WorldofGood.com by eBay: Shop for People and Eco Positive Products," eBay, 4 January 2011 ⟨http://worldofgood.ebay.com/⟩.

55. Blais et al., "Where Does Turnout Decline Come from?"; Dalton et al., "Advanced Democracies and the New Politics"; Putnam, *Democracies in Flux*; Shah et al., "Political Consumerism."

56. Scammell, "The Internet and Civic Engagement," 354.

57. Lesley Stahl, "Meg Whitman on What's Next After eBay," wowOwow, 18 March 2008, 29 June 2011 ⟨http://www.wowowow.com/point-of-view/meg-whitman-on-whats-next-after-ebay/⟩; Meg Whitman, "Remarks as Prepared for Delivery: Meg Whitman," 2008 Republican National Convention, 3 September 2008, 3 January 2009 ⟨http://portal.gopconvention2008.com/speech/details.aspx?id=45⟩.

58. In 2007, the White House and the U.S. Department of Commerce honored eBay with the National Medal of Technology and Innovation. White House, "President Bush Presents 2007 National Medals of Science and Technology and Innovation," 29 September 2008, 4 January 2011 ⟨http://georgewbush-whitehouse.archives.gov/news/releases/2008/09/20080929-4.html⟩; eBay, "eBay Inc. Reports Third Quarter 2008 Results," 15 October 2008, 13 January 2009 ⟨http://news.ebay.com/releases.cfm⟩.

59. George W. Bush, as quoted in White House, "President Bush Presents 2007 National Medals of Science and Technology and Innovation," 29 September 2008, 4 January 2011 ⟨http://georgewbush-whitehouse.archives.gov/news/releases/2008/09/20080929-4.html⟩.

60. John McCain, as quoted in Daniel Gross, "My eBay Job: Do 1.3 Million People Really Earn Their Living from the Auction Site?" *Slate*, 21 May 2008, 4 January 2011 ⟨http://www.slate.com/id/2191907/⟩.

61. Doug Holtz-Eakin, as quoted in Hans Nichols, "McCain's EBay Model for Jobs Finds Few Buyers among Economists," Bloomberg.com, 24 June 2008, 4 January 2011 ⟨http://www.bloomberg.com/apps/news?pid=20601103&sid=aJXBcBPLYnWY⟩.

62. See the discussion in chapter 1 about the varied ways eBay prompts members to labor for free.

63. Nichols, "McCain's EBay Model for Jobs Finds Few Buyers among Economists."

64. Gross, "My eBay Job."

65. Katharine Zaleski, "McCain Claims Surrogate Meg Whitman 'Founded' eBay; Actual Founder Is Obama Supporter Pierre Omidyar," *Huffington Post*, 27 November 2008 ⟨http://www.huffingtonpost.com/2008/10/27/mccain-claims-surrogate-m_n_138123.html⟩.

66. Anne E. Kornblut and Lexie Verdon, "Plane Not Sold on eBay," *Washington*

Algesheimer et al., "The Social Influence of Brand Community"; Andrejevic, "Watching Television without Pity"; Bielby et al., "Whose Stories Are They?"; Jenkins, "Interactive Audiences?"; Muñiz and O'Guinn, "Brand Community"; Sartelle, "As If We Were a Community"; and Slater, "Collecting The Real Thing."

93. Research on weddings includes Currie, "Here Comes the Bride"; Ingraham, *White Weddings*; Oswald, "A Member of the Wedding?"; and Otnes and Pleck, *Cinderella Dreams*. I employ critical literature on dirt by Belk et al., "Dirty Little Secret"; Douglas, *Implicit Meanings*; and Kristeva, *Powers of Horror*. I engage with collecting through writings by Belk, *Collecting in a Consumer Society*; and Stewart, *On Longing*.

94. Bordo, *The Male Body*; Chasin, *Selling Out*; Clark, "Commodity Lesbianism"; Dyer, "Don't Look Now"; Sender, "Sex Sells."

95. Case, "Toward a Butch-Femme Aesthetic"; Fausto-Sterling, *Sexing the Body*; Kessler and McKenna, *Gender*; Solomon, "Not Just a Passing Fantasy."

96. I use histories and critiques of nineteenth-century and twentieth-century representations of African Americans by Baker et al., "From Despicable to Collectible"; Dean, "Boys and Girls and 'Boys'"; Goings, *Mammy and Uncle Mose*; Kern-Foxworth, *Aunt Jemima, Uncle Ben, and Rastus*; and Turner, *Ceramic Uncles and Celluloid Mammies*. The literature on the commodification of African American identity includes Collins, *Black Feminist Thought*; Gray, "Black Masculinity and Visual Culture"; and Hale, *Making Whiteness*.

97. Kathy Sierra, as quoted in Dan Fost, "The Tech Chronicles: The Attack on Kathy Sierra," *San Francisco Chronicle*, 27 March 2007, 4 January 2011 〈http://sfgate .com/cgi-bin/blogs/sfgate/detail?blogid=19&entry_id=14783〉.

98. Dan Fost, "Bad Behavior in the Blogosphere: Vitriolic Comments Aimed at Tech Writer Make Some Worry about Downside of Anonymity," *San Francisco Chronicle*, 29 March 2007, 4 January 2011 〈http://sfgate.com/cgi-bin/article .cgi?f=/c/a/2007/03/29/MNGT3OTVAO1.DTL&hw=kathy+sierra&sn=001& sc=1000〉.

99. Tim O'Reilly, "Call for a Blogger's Code of Conduct," O'Reilly Radar, 31 March 2007, 4 January 2011 〈http://radar.oreilly.com/archives/2007/03/call-for-a-blog-1.html〉.

100. "Spam" is usually removed through programming or individual authors' actions. This may also delete critical commentary about identity positions because some of the key terms used in Internet porn advertisements, Viagra offers, medical and activist writings about sexuality, and theorizations of the body are the same.

101. 440674102, "DICTIONARY FOR DECODING WOMEN'S PERSONAL ADS:" craigslist, 5 October 2007, 4 January 2011 〈http://www.craigslist.org/about/best/lvg/ 440674102.html〉.

102. Joan Walsh, "Men Who Hate Women on the Web, and the Women (Like Me)

Who Try to Ignore Them. Or at Least I Did—until the Kathy Sierra Affair," *Salon*, 31 March 2007, 4 January 2011 ⟨http://www.salon.com/opinion/feature/ 2007/03/31/sierra/print.html⟩.

103. Vanessa Gisquet and Lacey Rose, "Top Characters Gross $25B," *Forbes*, 19 October 2004, 2 July 2011 ⟨http://www.forbes.com/lists/2004/10/20/cz_vq_ lr_1020fictionalintro.html⟩.

104. Walsh, "Men Who Hate Women on the Web, and the Women (Like Me) Who Try to Ignore Them."

105. Herring et al., "Women and Children Last."

1. Between Security and Distrust

1. eBay, "Group gifts," 30 November 2010 ⟨http://groupgifts.ebay.com/?_trksid =p2041592.m548⟩.

2. Nino, "Finding Connections – How Lasting Friendships Form on eBay," *Chatter* 4, no. 5, March 2005, 16 January 2011 ⟨http://pages.ebay.com/community/ chatter/2005march/connections.html⟩.

3. Scammell, "The Internet and Civic Engagement," 354.

4. John C. Abell, "'Buy It Now' FAIL: Former eBay CEO Whitman Is the Biggest Loser," *Wired*, 3 November 2010, 9 December 2011 ⟨http://www.wired.com/ epicenter/2010/11/the-biggest-loser/comment-page-1/⟩.

5. leapord420, "I Want to get MARRIED at EBAY LIVE THIS YEAR !!!" eBay, 24 January 2008, 12 January 2011 ⟨http://forums.ebay.com/db1/topic/Ebay-Live-Community/I-Want-To/1000632509⟩.

6. Jarrett, "The Perfect Community," 107.

7. Griffith, *The Official eBay Bible*, 6.

8. Ibid., xvi.

9. Lillie, "Immaterial Labor in the eBay Community," 91.

10. Pierre Omidyar, "Regarding the Feedback Forum," Wayback Machine, 9 June 1998, 9 December 2011 ⟨http://web.archive.org/web/19991012230459/pages .ebay.com/community/news/letter-060998-feedback.html⟩; Pierre Omidyar, "Regarding SafeHarbor 2.0," Wayback Machine, 7 October 1999, 3 February 2011 ⟨http://web.archive.org/web/*/http://pages.ebay.com/community/news/ letter-011599-safeharbor.html⟩; Meg Whitman, "eBay Community: Overview," Wayback Machine, 30 December 1999, 9 December 2011 ⟨http://web.archive .org/web/20000229141028/http://pages.ebay.com/community/letter.html⟩.

11. eBay, "eBay Media Center: About eBay," 13 March 2008 ⟨http://news.ebay.com/ about.cfm⟩.

12. Nino, "Finding Connections – How Lasting Friendships Form on eBay," *Chatter* 4, no. 5, March 2005, 16 January 2011⟨http://pages.ebay.com/community/ chatter/archive/⟩.

13. Cohen, *The Perfect Store*, 29.

14. Lindsay, "From the Shadows"; Muñiz and Schau, "Vigilante Marketing and Consumer-Created Communications."

15. Cohen, *The Perfect Store*, 53.

16. Curien et al., "Online Consumer Communities."

17. Jay Marathe, "Creating Community Online," Jay Marathe's Website, 5 November 1999, 7 January 2011 ⟨http://jay.marathe.net/profile/articles/1999-11community.htm⟩.

18. eBay, "eBay:: The Power of All of Us," 12 September 2007 ⟨http://www.thepowerofallofus.com/flash.html⟩.

19. eBay, "Community: Discussion Boards," 5 September 2007 ⟨http://pages.ebay.com/community/boards/⟩.

20. Putnam, *Bowling Alone*.

21. Etzioni, "Is Bowling Together Sociologically Lite?"; Wellman, "From Little Boxes to Loosely Bound Networks."

22. For a discussion of how the *Toy Boat* ad makes it seem as if nothing is ever lost from the eBay community, see Hillis, "A Space for the Trace."

23. Trodd, "Reading eBay."

24. Lingis, *The Community of Those Who Have Nothing in Common*, 4.

25. Secomb, "Fractured Community," 133.

26. Anderson, *Imagined Communities*; Blanchot, *The Unavowable Community*; Lingis, *The Community of Those Who Have Nothing in Common*; Lyotard, *Postmodern Fables*; Miami Theory Collective, *Community at Loose Ends*; Nancy, *The Inoperative Community*.

27. Anderson, *Imagined Communities*; Nancy, *The Inoperative Community*.

28. Cova and Pace, "Brand Community of Convenience Products," 1089.

29. Hickman and Ward, "The Dark Side of Brand Community," 315.

30. Rheingold, *The Virtual Community*, 5.

31. Ibid., 2.

32. Hauben and Hauben, *Netizens*, x.

33. Hagel and Armstrong, *Net Gain*, 2.

34. Murphy, *Web Rules*, 1.

35. Bennett, "Communicating Global Activism"; Kahn and Kellner, "New Media and Internet Activism"; Micheletti and Stolle, "Fashioning Social Justice through Political Consumerism."

36. Lingis, *The Community of Those Who Have Nothing in Common*, 5.

37. Ibid.

38. Cova and Pace, "Brand Community of Convenience Products," 1101.

39. Cook, "The Contribution Revolution"; Prahalad and Ramaswamy, "Co-creation Experiences."

40. Pierre Omidyar, "Regarding SafeHarbor 2.0," Wayback Machine, 15 January 1999, 7 January 2011 ⟨http://web.archive.org/web/19991012215529/pages.ebay.com/community/news/letter-011599-safeharbor.html⟩.

41. janica-online, "Don't be Confused When you see PROTESTORS at your happy Ebay LIVE," eBay, 19 June 2004, 7 January 2011 ⟨http://forums.ebay.com/db1/thread.jspa?threadID=410178111&tstart=1880&mod=1088376980057⟩.

42. Gary Rivlin, "Ebay's Joy Ride: Going Once . . . ," *New York Times*, 6 March 2005, 7 January 2011 ⟨http://www.nytimes.com/2005/03/06/business/yourmoney/06 ebay.html?ex=1267851600&en=dbe7293580e4f364&ei=5089&partner=rssyahoo⟩.

43. Steven Phillips, as quoted in Cohen, *The Perfect Store*, 52.

44. Ina Steiner, "eBay Auction Fraud Spawns Vigilantism Trend," *AuctionBytes* 411, 12 October 2002, 7 January 2011 ⟨http://www.auctionbytes.com/cab/abn/y02/m10/i12/s01⟩.

45. Karen Christian, as quoted in Steiner, "eBay Auction Fraud Spawns Vigilantism Trend."

46. Gordon, *Buying and Selling Jewelry on eBay*, 85.

47. Lillie, "Immaterial Labor in the eBay Community," 91.

48. Hardt and Negri, *Multitude*, 65.

49. Lazzarato, "Towards an Inquiry into Immaterial Labour."

50. Berlant, "Nearly Utopian, Nearly Normal."

51. Caffentzis, "Crystals and Analytic Engines," 43.

52. Ibid.

53. Coté and Pybus, "Learning to Immaterial Labour 2.0"; Suhr, "Underpinning the Paradoxes in the Artistic Fields of MySpace."

54. Terranova, "Free Labor," 49; Terranova, *Network Culture*.

55. Terranova, "Free Labor," 49.

56. Kücklich, "Precarious Playbour."

57. Postigo, "From Pong to Planet Quake," 597.

58. Hardt and Negri, *Multitude*, 66.

59. Cooley, "It's All About the Fit."

60. Terranova, "Free Labor," 48.

61. elf, "eBay View About Me for elf@ebay.com," eBay, 7 January 2011 ⟨http://cgi3 .ebay.com/ws/eBayISAPI.dll?ViewUserPage&userid=elf%40ebay.com⟩.

62. Ina Steiner, "eBay Live Exposition Hall Showcases Products & Services for eBay Users," *AuctionBytes* 343, 22 June 2002, 7 January 2011 ⟨http://www.auction bytes.com/cab/abn/y02/m06/i24/s03⟩.

63. eBay, "Community: Discussion Boards," 5 September 2007 ⟨http://pages.ebay .com/community/boards/⟩.

64. Bloch and Bruce, "Product Involvement as Leisure Behavior," 197.

65. Ford et al., "Questions and Answers about Fun at Work," 24; Perrin, "A Serious Business."

66. Gamers, as quoted in Yee, "The Labor of Fun," 69, 70.

67. Muñiz and O'Guinn, "Brand Community," 413; Cova et al., "Global Brand Communities across Borders," 314.

68. Cohen, *The Perfect Store*, 8.

69. eBay, "Community Values," 7 January 2011 ⟨http://pages.ebay.com/community/people/values.html?ssPageName=CMDV:CC040615⟩.

70. MAC Cosmetics Online, "VIVA GLAM LIP BAG: 'Tis Noble to Give for World AIDS Day." 1 December 2010 ⟨macnews@e.maccosmetics.com⟩.

71. de Chernatony, "Brand Management through Narrowing the Gap between Brand Identity and Brand Reputation."

72. eBay, "WorldofGood.com by eBay: Shop for People and EcoPositive Products," WorldofGood.com, 13 January 2011 ⟨http://worldofgood.ebay.com/⟩.

73. Carducci, "Culture Jamming"; Obst et al., "Sense of Community in Science Fiction Fandom, Part 1."

74. Pigg, "Applications of Community Informatics for Building Community and Enhancing Civic Society," 513.

75. O'Neill, introduction to *The Sources of Normativity*, xi.

76. Korsgaard, "The Authority of Reflection," 94; Korsgaard, "The Normative Question," 44.

77. Herrmann, "Gift or Commodity," 910.

78. Nelson et al., "Freecycle Community Downshifting Consumer = Upshifting Citizen?"

79. Freecycle, "The Freecycle Network," 10 December 2011 ⟨http://www.freecycle.org/⟩.

80. eBay, "eBay Green Team," 5 March 2009 ⟨http://www.ebaygreenteam.com/⟩; Stephanie Clifford, "As Earth Day Nears, eBay Shows Its Green Side," *New York Times*, 3 March 2009, 7 January 2011 ⟨http://www.nytimes.com/2009/03/04/business/media/04adco.html⟩.

81. eBay, "eBay Green Team," 28 March 2010 ⟨http://www.ebaygreenteam.com/⟩.

82. Bob Kagle, "Coffee Talk," eBay Developers Conference, 13 June 2007 ⟨http://pages.ebay.com/devcon/tracks.html⟩.

83. msklusa, "988 ANTIQUE LONG ART GLASS LAPIS BEAD DETAILED NECKLACE," eBay, 2 March 2009 ⟨http://cgi.ebay.com/988-ANTIQUE-LONG-ART-GLASS-LAPIS-BEAD-DETAILED-NECKLACE_W0QQitemZ220370858191QQcmdZViewItemQQptZVintage_Costume_Jewelry?hash=item220370858191&_trksid=p3911.c0.m14&_trkparms=66%3A2%7C65%3A1%7C39%3A1%7C240%3A131⟩.

84. eBay, "Update: The eBay Box," 1 September 2010, 7 January 2011 ⟨http://www.ebaygreenteam.com/projects/the-ebay-box⟩.

85. Crocker and Linden, *Ethics of Consumption*, 3.

86. Bloch and Bruce, "Product Involvement as Leisure Behavior," 197.

87. tankdriver7753, "Brand New U.S.M.C. MOLLE II Rifleman Back Set: Brand New! In The Original Box! Look at the Pictures!!!" eBay, 28 August 2007 ⟨http://cgi.ebay.com/ws/eBayISAPI.dll?ViewItem&item=270160085420&ssPageName=ADME:B:SS:US:1⟩; eBay, "Firearms, Weapons and Knives," 7 January 2011 ⟨http://pages.ebay.com/help/policies/firearms-weapons-knives.html⟩.

88. tamotol, "Aristocrats Wool," eBay, 22 August 2007 ⟨http://cgi.ebay.com/ws/

eBayISAPI.dll?ViewItem&item=280145965065&ssPageName=ADME:B:SS:US:1〉. eBay's policy was that "Used underwear including, but not limited to, boxer shorts, panties, briefs, athletic supporters and cloth diapers (including diaper covers) are not permitted." eBay, "Used Clothing," 31 January 2008 〈http:// pages.ebay.com/help/policies/used-clothing.html〉. eBay now allows the sale of diapers and related items.

89. tamoto1, "Aristocrats Wool," eBay, 22 August 2007, 〈http://cgi.ebay.com/ws/ eBayISAPI.dll?ViewItem&item=280145965065&ssPageName=ADME:B:SS: US:1〉.

90. A variety of sellers use the term "eGay" to critique the site and thereby convey homophobic sentiments. erickc complains about eBay banning listings and notes that it is "Ultra-Gay of ebay." jrl0nisangel uses the term "eGay" to suggest that eBay makes errors, fails to provide sellers with explanations for canceled auctions, and is ill informed. jrl0nisangel listed a car on "Egay but the morons who run it cancelled the auction for some reason known only to them." erickc, "VooDoo Coconut ONE OF A KIND! RE-List see desc." eBay, 24 May 2007 〈http://cgi.ebay.com/VooDoo-Coconut-ONE-OF-A-KIND-RE-List-see-desc_ W0QQitemZ230134345949QQihZ013QQcategoryZ1469QQssPageNameZWDV WQQrdZ1QQcmdZViewItem〉; jrl0nisangel, "1992 BMW : 5-Series 525i," eBay, 16 June 2007 〈http://cgi.ebay.com/ebaymotors/ws/eBayISAPI.dll?ViewItem&ss pagename=ADME%3AB%3ASS%3AUS%3A1&viewitem=&item=320128048385〉; jrl0nisangel, "1987 Suzuki : Samurai," eBay, 20 June 2007 〈http://cgi.ebay.com/ ebaymotors/ws/eBayISAPI.dll?ViewItem&sspagename=ADME%3AB%3ASS%3 AUS%3A1&viewitem=&item=270135409205〉.

91. Katie Vail, "To Allow Sales of All Cloth Diapers, Both Used and New, On Ebay," PetitionOnline, 12 September 2007 〈http://www.petitiononline.com/mod_perl/ signed.cgi?clothdpr&5951〉; Krista Barosh, "To Allow Sales of All Cloth Diapers, Both Used and New, On Ebay," PetitionOnline, 12 September 2007 〈http://www .petitiononline.com/mod_perl/signed.cgi?clothdpr&5951〉. For a critical analysis of online petitions, see Earl and Schussman, "Contesting Cultural Control."

92. Louise Pendry, "To Allow Sales of All Cloth Diapers, Both Used and New, On Ebay," PetitionOnline, 12 September 2007 〈http://www.petitiononline.com/ mod_perl/signed.cgi?clothdpr&5951〉.

93. Seidman, "From Identity to Queer Politics."

94. Ihator, "Communication Style in the Information Age," 202.

95. Lingis, "New Walls in the Information Age," 274.

96. Jowett, "Origins, Occupation, and the Proximity of the Neighbour," 19.

97. eBay, "Used clothing policy," 7 January 2011 〈http://pages.ebay.com/help/ policies/used-clothing.html〉. Diaper covers are now "allowed." "Used cloth diapers can be sold, as long as the listing states clearly that the item has been cleaned per manufacturer standards."

98. auntava, "Listing used cloth diapers...did you know?" eBay, 30 September

2009, 9 December 2011 ⟨http://forums.ebay.com/db2/topic/Childrens-Clothing-Boutique/Listing-Used-Cloth/520157485&#msg523054526⟩.

99. Cohen, *The Perfect Store*, 27.

100. Pierre Omidyar, "Founder's Note," eBay, 26 February 1996, 7 January 2011 ⟨http://pages.ebay.com/services/forum/feedback-foundersnote.html⟩.

101. Dellarocas, "The Digitization of Word of Mouth," 1408.

102. Pierre Omidyar, "Founder's Note," eBay, 26 February 1996, 7 January 2011 ⟨http://pages.ebay.com/services/forum/feedback-foundersnote.html⟩.

103. In 2003, eBay added mutual feedback withdrawal. With this option, each member's feedback score is adjusted, but the initial comments remain on the site. eBay introduced other changes to the feedback system in 2006. eBay now neutralizes feedback if members do not participate in issue-resolution processes, removes feedback given by individuals who are "indefinitely suspended within 90 days of registration" because eBay believes that they "were never truly members of the Community," and requires "new members to complete a tutorial before leaving neutral or negative feedback" because research shows that they leave a "disproportionate amount of the total negative feedback." In 2007, eBay added the DSR feedback options that allow individuals to score sellers on a five-point scale. Buyers can rate "Item as described," "Communication," "Shipping time," and "Shipping and handling charges." Nino, "eBay in Person: Brian Burke," *Chatter*, May 2006, 2 June 2010 ⟨http://pages.ebay.com/community/chatter/2006May/InPerson.html⟩.

104. eBay, "Feedback," 21 August 2007 ⟨http://pages.ebay.com/services/forum/feedback.html⟩.

105. Lingis, "New Walls in the Information Age," 273.

106. Lewis, *Twenty Questions to Ask before Buying on eBay*, 65.

107. Ina Steiner, "ebaylivelog," *AuctionBytes*, 25 June 2003, 7 January 2011 ⟨http://www.auctionbytes.com/cab/ebaylive2003/ebaylivelog⟩.

108. Brown and Morgan, "Reputation in Online Auctions," 66. For research on how sellers' reputations affect price and sales, see Bajari and Hortacsu, "Winner's Curse, Reserve Prices, and Endogenous Entry"; Livingston, "How Valuable Is a Good Reputation?"; McDonald and Slawson, "Reputation in an Internet Auction Market"; and Melnik and Alm, "Does a Seller's Reputation Matter?"

109. baseballsteve123, "2006 TOPPS STERLING MANTLE/BERRA BASE CARD #34-117/#250," eBay, 23 August 2007 ⟨http://cgi.ebay.com/2006-TOPPS-STERLING-MANTLE-BERRA-BASE-CARD-34-117-250_W0QQitemZ280146390371QQihZ018QQcategoryZ20876QQssPageNameZWDVWQQrdZ1QQcmdZViewItem⟩.

110. coilovers, "10 BLANK SKATEBOARD 7.75 SKATEBOARDS DECK + Grip Tape," eBay, 23 August 2007 ⟨http://cgi.ebay.com/10-BLANK-SKATEBOARD-7 75-SKATEBOARDS-DECK-Grip-Tape_W0QQitemZ140151158841QQihZ004QQcategoryZ58124QQssPageNameZWDVWQQrdZ1QQcmdZViewItem⟩.

111. itrimming, "Home Wall Charger For Apple iPod Mini Nano Video Photo," eBay,

26 August 2007 ⟨http://cgi.ebay.com/Home-Wall-Charger-For-Apple-iPod-Mini-Nano-Video-Photo_W0QQitemZ160151579001QQihZ006QQcategoryZ48680QQssPageNameZWDVWQQrdZ1QQcmdZViewItem⟩.

112. jayandmarie, "JayAndMarie eBay Store About My Store," eBay, 11 August 2007 ⟨http://members.ebay.com/ws/eBayISAPI.dll?ViewUserPage&userid=jayandmarie⟩.

113. Lissa McGrath, "Thriller: eBay Sends 18,000 to Great America Amusement Park," *AuctionBytes* 1048, 25 June 2005, 7 January 2011 ⟨http://www.auctionbytes.com/cab/abn/y05/m06/i25/s02⟩; jayandmarie, "Feedback Profile for jayandmarie," eBay, 11 August 2007 ⟨http://feedback.ebay.com/ws/eBayISAPI.dll?ViewFeedback2&userid=jayandmarie&ftab=AllFeedback&myworld=true&seeallfeedback=See%20All%20Feedback⟩.

114. Brown and Morgan, "Reputation in Online Auctions."

115. Alan Williamson, "The Great EBAY Feedback scam - buyer beware," 22 March 2007, 7 January 2011 ⟨http://alan.blog-city.com/ebay_feedback.htm⟩.

116. minorprofits59, "100 Ebay Positive Feedback FAST ebook 4 cents RESELL 01," eBay, 28 August 2007 ⟨http://cgi.ebay.com/100-Ebay-Positive-Feedback-FAST-ebook-4-cents-RESELL-01_W0QQitemZ300145879247QQihZ020QQcategoryZ47103QQssPageNameZWDVWQQrdZ1QQcmdZViewItem⟩.

117. ebaysellers, "ebay account for sale!" PayPalSucks, 18 June 2008, 7 January 2011 ⟨http://www.paypalsucks.com/forums/showthread.php?fid=16&tid=26178&old_block=0⟩.

118. zarkid, "Obtain Feedback for 99 cents," eBay, 2 September 2007 ⟨http://cgi.ebay.com/Obtain-Feedback-for-99-cents_W0QQitemZ280149453707QQihZ018QQcategoryZ88433QQssPageNameZWDVWQQrdZ1QQcmdZViewItem⟩.

119. Brown and Morgan, "Reputation in Online Auctions," 65.

120. Cova and Dalli, "Working Consumers."

121. Cohen, *The Perfect Store*, 259.

122. Doc, "Welcome to Doc's eBayMotorsSucks.com Website," 18 June 2007 ⟨http://www.ebaymotorssucks.com/index1.htm⟩.

123. Ed "DOC" Koon, "It's Time For An eBay Management Change," PetitionOnline, 18 June 2007 ⟨http://www.petitiononline.com/time4chg/petition.html⟩.

124. Mark Baldin, "It's Time For An eBay Management Change," PetitionOnline, 2 September 2007 ⟨http://www.petitiononline.com/mod_perl/signed.cgi?time4chg&51⟩; E. Kloubkova, "It's Time For An eBay Management Change," PetitionOnline, 2 September 2007 ⟨http://www.petitiononline.com/mod_perl/signed.cgi?time4chg&51⟩; L. Olson, "It's Time For An eBay Management Change," PetitionOnline, 2 September 2007 ⟨http://www.petitiononline.com/mod_perl/signed.cgi?time4chg&1⟩.

125. Firemeg, "FireMeg.com: THE anti-eBay management website!" FireMeg.com, 8 January 2011 ⟨http://www.firemeg.com/⟩.

126. Firemeg, "July 9th the Genocide Begins? How eBay Inc. Plans on Stealing Con-

tent and Getting Rid of Undesirables," FireMeg.com, 21 May 2007 ⟨http://www
.firemeg.com/2007/05/july-9th-genocide-begins-how-eay-inc.html⟩.

127. eBay, "Your User Agreement," 9 January 2010 ⟨http://pages.ebay.com/help/
policies/user-agreement.html⟩.

128. nonnie*mouse*posting*id, "eBay Forums," eBay, 21 May 2007 ⟨http://forums
.ebay.com/db2/thread.jspa?threadID=1000498148&tstart=0&mod=117976593
1630⟩.

129. Firemeg, "FireMeg.com: THE anti-eBay management website!" FireMeg.com,
8 January 2011 ⟨http://www.firemeg.com/⟩.

130. Secomb argues that the "creation of a totalizing unity is the movement of totali-
tarianism and unfreedom," while disagreement "holds a space open for diversity and for freedom." Secomb, "Fractured Community," 134.

131. Rick Aristotle Munarriz, "Give eBay a Kick in the Pants," Motley Fool, 18 February 2009, 7 January 2011 ⟨http://www.fool.com/investing/general/2009/02/18/
give-ebay-a-kick-in-the-pants.aspx⟩.

132. Alexander Wolfe, "EBay Feedback Cutoff Kicking In, Sellers Angry," InformationWeek, 16 May 2008, 7 January 2011 ⟨http://www.informationweek.com/
blog/main/archives/2008/05/ebay_feedback_c.html;jsessionid=GG3MWTKSSJ
4ACQSNDLRSKHSCJUNN2JVN⟩.

133. Linda Carey, "EBay Rivals Circle Vulnerable Auctions Kingpin," CNNMoney,
28 February 2008, 7 January 2011 ⟨http://fsbfeatures.blogs.fsb.cnn.com/2008/
02/06/ebay-rivals-circle-vulnerable-auctions-kingpin/⟩.

134. Chris Johnston, "EBay Rivals Circle Vulnerable Auctions Kingpin," CNN-
Money, 28 February 2008, 7 January 2011 ⟨http://fsbfeatures.blogs.fsb.cnn
.com/2008/02/06/ebay-rivals-circle-vulnerable-auctions-kingpin/⟩.

135. Secomb, "Fractured Community," 134.

136. Karen E. Klein, "The Growing Frustration of eBay Sellers," BusinessWeek, 28
October 2008, 7 January 2011 ⟨http://app.businessweek.com/UserComments/
combo_review;jsessionid=593AD319FA5ED4829A41094A7E5E0620?action=all&
style=wide&productId=36977&pageIndex=2⟩.

137. Meg Whitman, as quoted in Chris Taylor, "Meg Whitman," Time, 26 April 2004,
7 January 2011 ⟨http://www.time.com/time/magazine/article/0,9171,993994,00
.html⟩.

138. Brian D., "EBay Rivals Circle Vulnerable Auctions Kingpin," CNNMoney,
3 March 2008, 7 January 2011 ⟨http://fsbfeatures.blogs.fsb.cnn.com/2008/02/06/
ebay-rivals-circle-vulnerable-auctions-kingpin/⟩.

139. Justice For All, "PayPal & Ebay to Rule the World: Part Four: Trust & Safety No
Longer Exists," Blogger News Network, 7 November 2008, 7 January 2011 ⟨http://
www.bloggernews.net/118523⟩.

140. One of many, "Re: EBay Feedback Cutoff Kicking In, Sellers Angry," InformationWeek, 17 May 2008, 9 November 2008 ⟨http://login.cmp.com/btgcommu
nity/thread.jspa?threadID=25592⟩.

141. chatanooga, "Sales Up, eBay CEO Backs Changes," CNNMoney, 18 October 2008, 7 January 2011 ⟨http://fsbfeatures.blogs.fsb.cnn.com/2008/04/16/sales-up-ebay-ceo-backs-changes/⟩.

142. KD, "Re: EBay Feedback Cutoff Kicking In, Sellers Angry," *InformationWeek*, 16 May 2008, 9 November 2008 ⟨http://login.cmp.com/btgcommunity/thread.jspa?threadID=25592⟩.

143. lessthenavrgjoe, "eBay (EBAY) shares hit a seven-year low," *BloggingStocks*, 27 February 2009, 7 January 2011 ⟨http://www.bloggingstocks.com/2009/02/27/ebay-ebay-shares-hit-a-seven-year-low/⟩.

144. Slater, "Collecting The Real Thing."

145. Cova and Dalli, "Working Consumers."

146. Karen, "EBay Rivals Circle Vulnerable Auctions Kingpin," CNNMoney, 3 March 2008, 7 January 2011 ⟨http://fsbfeatures.blogs.fsb.cnn.com/2008/02/06/ebay-rivals-circle-vulnerable-auctions-kingpin/⟩.

147. cabanalolita, "The Growing Frustration of eBay Sellers," *BusinessWeek*, 24 October 2008 ⟨http://app.businessweek.com/UserComments/combo_review?action=all&style=wide&productId=36977&productCode=spec⟩.

148. Bonanzle, "Bonanzle :: Buy and sell unique items with the friendliest community online," 4 January 2009 ⟨http://bonanzle.com/⟩.

149. Hickman and Ward, "The Dark Side of Brand Community."

2. Pins, Cards, and Griffith's Jacket

1. mattie-lily-rose, "I'm excited, really excited, no really really really excited," eBay, 9 June 2008, 9 January 2011 ⟨http://forums.ebay.com/db1/topic/Ebay-Live-Community/Im-Excited-Really/2000584120&#msg2010764163⟩.

2. surfsilicon1, "15 Days and Counting for the Big Event- - I AM EXCITED!!!!!!!!!!!!" eBay, 6 June 2005, 9 January 2011 ⟨http://forums.ebay.com/db1/topic/Ebay-Live-Community/15-Days-And/410550392&#msg201863711⟩.

3. Nino, "Finding Connections – How Lasting Friendships Form on eBay," *Chatter* 4, no. 5, March 2005, 16 January 2011 ⟨http://pages.ebay.com/community/chatter/2005march/connections.html⟩.

4. eBay has held On Location conferences in Atlanta, Dallas, Chicago, and San Jose, California.

5. raglebagle, as quoted in Nino, "Finding Connections – How Lasting Friendships Form on eBay," *Chatter* 4, no. 5, March 2005, 16 January 2011 ⟨http://pages.ebay.com/community/chatter/2005march/connections.html⟩.

6. eBay Shop, eBay Live! 2007, Boston; Susanna Millman, "Photos From eBay Live! 2008 So Far," *Chatter*, 20 June 2008, 15 July 2011 ⟨http://www.ebaychatter.com/the_chatter/2008/06/photos-from-eba.html⟩.

7. Jenkins, "Categorization," 8.

8. Panek, "Who Are Wii?"

9. Blackwell and Stephan, *Brands That Rock*, 4.

10. Bielby et al., "Whose Stories Are They?" 35–36.

11. Bacon-Smith, *Science Fiction Culture*; Fiske, "The Cultural Economy of Fandom"; Jenkins, "Interactive Audiences?"

12. Gray et al., introduction to *Fandom*, 2.

13. Jenkins, "Interactive Audiences?" 158.

14. Fiske, "The Cultural Economy of Fandom."

15. Jenkins, *Fans, Bloggers, and Gamers*, 1.

16. Kjus, "Idolizing and Monetizing the Public," 277.

17. Örnebring, "Alternate Reality Gaming and Convergence Culture," 448.

18. Cohen, *The Perfect Store*, 36.

19. Herring, "Critical Analysis of Language Use in Computer-Mediated Contexts."

20. Stacey King Gordon describes eBay's forums as "active, vocal, and surprisingly supportive." Gordon, *Buying and Selling Jewelry on eBay*, 26.

21. Fayard and DeSanctis, "Evolution of an Online Forum for Knowledge Management Professionals."

22. Muñiz and O'Guinn, "Brand Community," 413.

23. Steven P. Westly, as quoted in Bradley and Porter, "eBay Inc.," 88.

24. Cohen, *The Perfect Store*, 50.

25. Baym, *Tune In, Log On*, 4–5.

26. eBay, "eBay Live! Community Conference," 4 September 2007 ⟨http://forums.ebay.com/db1/forum.jspa?forumID=112⟩.

27. Driskell and Lyon, "Are Virtual Communities True Communities?" 381.

28. chasnjohn, "Anyone from Oklahoma going to ebay live?" eBay, 25 May 2005, 9 January 2011 ⟨http://forums.ebay.com/db1/topic/Ebay-Live-Community/Anyone-From-Oklahoma/410543845?&tstart=1520&mod=1119308290525⟩; foxcreekwares, "Any Canadians Going?" eBay, 20 June 2005, 9 January 2011 ⟨http://forums.ebay.com/db1/topic/Ebay-Live-Community/Any-Canadians-Going/200115490?&tstart=1520&mod=1119362224574⟩; paulationstore, "Owner or interested in an Ebay CONSIGNMENT BIZ? LET'S MEET at Ebay Live!!!!" eBay, 8 June 2005, 9 January 2011 ⟨http://forums.ebay.com/db1/topic/Ebay-Live-Community/Owner-Or-Interested/200107991?&tstart=1480&mod=1119380359840⟩; anytimecampus_com, "Any Asian wanna hang out together?" eBay, 21 June 2005, 9 January 2011 ⟨http://forums.ebay.com/db1/topic/Ebay-Live-Community/Any-Asian-Wanna/410559153?&tstart=1480&mod=1119395791669⟩.

29. scooch@ebay.com, "***eBay Live 2003***," eBay, 31 July 2002, 10 December 2011 ⟨http://forums.ebay.com/db1/topic/Ebay-Live-Community/Ebay-Live-2003/42595?&tstart=2920&mod=1044253828671⟩.

30. Muñiz and O'Guinn, "Brand Community," 423.

31. artful.seller, "Ebay & Ebay Staff – YOU ROCK!" eBay, 30 June 2003, 9 January 2011 ⟨http://forums.ebay.com/db1/topic/Ebay-Live-Community/Ebay-38-Ebay/2230726?&tstart=2440&mod=1057027499116⟩.

32. danse, "What did you learn at ebay live?" eBay, 2 July 2005, 9 January 2011 ⟨http://forums.ebay.com/db1/topic/Ebay-Live-Community/What-Did-You/100 0003596?&tstart=1360&mod=1122957940489⟩.

33. misswigglesemporium, "Ebay & Ebay Staff – YOU ROCK!" eBay, 30 June 2003, 9 January 2011 ⟨http://forums.ebay.com/db1/topic/Ebay-Live-Community/ Ebay-38-Ebay/2230726?&tstart=2440&mod=1057027499116⟩.

34. beachbadge uses the guide for a slightly unconventional purpose. According to the eBay site, guides are designed to allow individuals to "Research products and learn about all kinds of topics." eBay encourages readers to use them to get "the information you need—including shopping advice from eBay." By using the guide format, beachbadge's chronicle becomes information that the eBayer needs. eBay, "eBay Reviews & Guides," 9 January 2011 ⟨http://reviews.ebay .com/⟩.

35. beachbadge, "My Rumballs are now a part of eBay History! Ebayana," eBay, 14 October 2006, 9 January 2011 ⟨http://reviews.ebay.com/My-Rumballs-are-now-a-part-of-eBay-History-Ebayana_W0QQugidZ10000000002131848?ssPage Name=BUYGD:CAT:-1:SEARCH:4⟩.

36. Ruth H. Landman identifies the yard sales she studies as "predominantly a world of women." Landman, "Washington's Yard Sales," 158. Gretchen Herrmann argues that garage sales are a "woman-dominated institution." Herrmann, "Women's Exchange in the U.S. Garage Sale," 708.

37. kathryn, "Does eBay really NEED to go to an expensive tourist city for eBay Live?" eBay, 14 January 2004, 9 January 2011 ⟨http://forums.ebay.com/db1/ topic/Ebay-Live-Community/Does-Ebay-Really/400099215?&tstart=2320& mod=1076531862911⟩.

38. gianni@ebay.com, "Newbie at eBay Live!" eBay, 27 February 2007, 9 January 2011 ⟨http://forums.ebay.com/db1/topic/Ebay-Live-Community/Newbie-At-Ebay/1000446928?messageID=2005644810&forumID=112&x#2005644810⟩.

39. tradrmom, "Why would Anyone go to Ebay LIVE leaving their business?????" eBay, 30 April 2003, 9 January 2011 ⟨http://forums.ebay.com/db1/topic/Ebay-Live-Community/Why-Would-Anyone/164474?&tstart=2640&mod=1055528 568012⟩.

40. tradertif, "eBay live dress code?!?!?!?" eBay, 15 January 2004, 9 January 2011 ⟨http://forums.ebay.com/db1/topic/Ebay-Live-Community/Ebay-Live-Dress/ 400094920?&tstart=2280&mod=1078189023082⟩.

41. tradrmom, "Why would Anyone go to Ebay LIVE leaving their business?????" eBay, 30 April 2003, 9 January 2011 ⟨http://forums.ebay.com/db1/topic/Ebay-Live-Community/Why-Would-Anyone/164474?&tstart=2640&mod=105552856 8012⟩.

42. axzar3000, "Any other younger single people to attend?" eBay, 24 March 2004, 9 January 2011 ⟨http://forums.ebay.com/db1/topic/Ebay-Live-Community/Any-Other-Younger/410065807?&tstart=2080&mod=1085770204219⟩.

43. www-internetishop-com, "Any other younger single people to attend?" eBay, 30 March 2004, 9 January 2011 〈http://forums.ebay.com/db1/topic/Ebay-Live-Community/Any-Other-Younger/410065807?&tstart=2080&mod=108577020 4219〉.

44. myfavorites4u, "Any older folks who don't party going?" eBay, 8 May 2006, 9 January 2011 〈http://forums.ebay.com/db1/topic/Ebay-Live-Community/Any-Older-Folks/2000137678?&tstart=960&mod=1148828986466〉; surplusbox, "Any party people going who are younger than 30?" eBay, 11 March 2006, 9 January 2011 〈http://forums.ebay.com/db1/topic/Ebay-Live-Community/Any-Party-People/1000280491?messageID=2002338499&forumID=112&x#2002338499〉; reliasite, "ebay live- What's your age?" eBay, 24 April 2006, 9 January 2011 〈http://forums.ebay.com/db1/topic/Ebay-Live-Community/Ebay-Live-Whats/1000269874?&tstart=720&mod=1150167853418〉.

45. Nelson, "Ageism," 208.

46. acmeusa, "Any other younger single people to attend?" eBay, 22 April 2004, 9 January 2011 〈http://forums.ebay.com/db1/topic/Ebay-Live-Community/Any-Other-Younger/410065807&start=15〉.

47. Minichiello et al., "Perceptions and Consequences of Ageism," 260.

48. craftypetstuff, "Any older folks who don't party going?" eBay, 13 May 2006, 9 January 2011 〈http://forums.ebay.com/db1/topic/Ebay-Live-Community/Any-Older-Folks/2000137678&start=15〉.

49. susiecraft, "ebay live- What's your age?" eBay, 5 June 2006, 9 January 2011 〈http://forums.ebay.com/db1/topic/Ebay-Live-Community/Ebay-Live-Whats/1000269874&start=60〉.

50. deco2mod4u, "ebay live- What's your age?" eBay, 7 June 2006, 3 February 2011 〈http://forums.ebay.com/db1/topic/Ebay-Live-Community/Ebay-Live-Whats/1000269874&start=60〉.

51. theimpus, "ebay live- What's your age?" eBay, 11 June 2006, 9 January 2011 〈http://forums.ebay.com/db1/topic/Ebay-Live-Community/Ebay-Live-Whats/1000269874&start=60〉.

52. Jackson, "Gender, Sexuality and Heterosexuality," 105.

53. fiberwireguy, "Any one from Houston TX going to Ebay Live 2005?" eBay, 18 February 2005, 9 January 2011 〈http://forums.ebay.com/db1/topic/Ebay-Live-Community/Any-One-From/200020065?&tstart=1760&mod=11096 24197586〉.

54. queen-ebabe, "Any one from Houston TX going to Ebay Live 2005?" eBay, 18 February 2005, 9 January 2011 〈http://forums.ebay.com/db1/topic/Ebay-Live-Community/Any-One-From/200020065?&tstart=1760&mod=1109624197586〉.

55. fiberwireguy, "Any one from Houston TX going to Ebay Live 2005?" eBay, 22 February 2005, 9 January 2011 〈http://forums.ebay.com/db1/topic/Ebay-Live-Community/Any-One-From/200020065?&tstart=1760&mod=1109624197586〉.

56. unique_finds93, "Any one from Houston TX going to Ebay Live 2005?" eBay,

18 February 2005, 9 January 2011 ⟨http://forums.ebay.com/db1/topic/Ebay-Live-Community/Any-One-From/200020065?&tstart=1760&mod=11096 24197586⟩.

57. fiberwireguy, "Any one from Houston TX going to Ebay Live 2005?" eBay, 22 February 2005, 9 January 2011 ⟨http://forums.ebay.com/db1/topic/Ebay-Live-Community/Any-One-From/200020065?&tstart=1760&mod=1109624197586⟩.

58. fiberwireguy, "What to wear, what to wear?" eBay, 10 March 2005, 9 January 2011 ⟨http://forums.ebay.com/db1/topic/Ebay-Live-Community/What-To-Wear/410261719?start=75&#msg200793768⟩.

59. one-gr8-deal, "Tents and Portable Bathrooms for eBay Live 2005," eBay, 27 January 2005, 9 January 2011 ⟨http://forums.ebay.com/db1/topic/Ebay-Live-Community/Tents-And-Portable/200008981?&start=40⟩.

60. fiberwireguy, "Tents and Portable Bathrooms for eBay Live 2005," eBay, 28 January 2005, 9 January 2011 ⟨http://forums.ebay.com/db1/topic/Ebay-Live-Community/Tents-And-Portable/200008981?&start=40⟩.

61. unique_finds93, "Tents and Portable Bathrooms for eBay Live 2005," eBay, 30 January 2005, 9 January 2011 ⟨http://forums.ebay.com/db1/topic/Ebay-Live-Community/Tents-And-Portable/200008981?&start=40⟩.

62. fiberwireguy, "Tents and Portable Bathrooms for eBay Live 2005," eBay, 30 January 2005, 9 January 2011 ⟨http://forums.ebay.com/db1/topic/Ebay-Live-Community/Tents-And-Portable/200008981&start=45⟩.

63. Baym, *Tune In, Log On*, 174.

64. Ibid., 202.

65. extraordinary-ellie, "What to wear, what to wear?" eBay, 9 March 2005, 9 January 2011 ⟨http://forums.ebay.com/db1/topic/Ebay-Live-Community/What-To-Wear/410261719&start=75⟩.

66. curiously-strong-ellie-mint, "eBay Live board vs grouch board," eBay, 20 July 2005, 9 January 2011 ⟨http://forums.ebay.com/db1/topic/Ebay-Live-Community/Ebay-Live-Board/1000020845&start=0⟩.

67. *queen*cheese*, "_____GIANNI_____:)," eBay, 31 July 2002, 9 January 2011 ⟨http://forums.ebay.com/db1/topic/Ebay-Live-Community/Gianni/42590?&start=120⟩.

68. been_there*done_that, "_____GIANNI_____:)," eBay, 4 November 2002, 9 January 2011 ⟨http://forums.ebay.com/db1/topic/Ebay-Live-Community/Gianni/42590&start=225⟩.

69. claire@ebay.com, "_____GIANNI_____:)," eBay, 2 August 2002, 9 January 2011 ⟨http://forums.ebay.com/db1/topic/Ebay-Live-Community/Gianni/42590&start=135⟩.

70. scooch@ebay.com, "Is everyone getting excited?" eBay, 3 June 2003, 9 January 2011 ⟨http://forums.ebay.com/db1/topic/Ebay-Live-Community/Is-Everyone-Getting/203378?&tstart=2520&mod=1056395897541⟩.

71. **christymj**, "Is everyone getting excited?" eBay, 3 June 2003, 9 January 2011

⟨http://forums.ebay.com/db1/thread.jspa?threadID=203378&tstart=2520& mod=105639589754⟩.

72. suebeany, "Is everyone getting excited?" eBay, 3 June 2003, 9 January 2011 ⟨http://forums.ebay.com/db1/topic/Ebay-Live-Community/Is-Everyone-Getting/203378?&tstart=2520&mod=1056395897541⟩.

73. abovethemall, "Is everyone getting excited?" eBay, 4 June 2003, 9 January 2011 ⟨http://forums.ebay.com/db1/topic/Ebay-Live-Community/Is-Everyone-Getting/203378?&tstart=2520&mod=1056395897541⟩.

74. Fayard and DeSanctis, "Evolution of an Online Forum for Knowledge Management Professionals."

75. bobals_wife, "Pinks – how's recovery going?" eBay, 25 June 2002, 9 January 2011 ⟨http://forums.ebay.com/db1/topic/Ebay-Live-Community/Pinks-Hows-Recovery/42547&start=30⟩.

76. valentinemcgee, "Pins, Cards, Get a Life People....," eBay, 1 July 2003, 9 January 2011 ⟨http://forums.ebay.com/db1/topic/Ebay-Live-Community/Pins-Cards-Get/2230971&start=15⟩.

77. funfindsfromsuz, "What's you're favorite Annual Meet & Greet Memory?" eBay, 5 June 2006, 9 January 2011 ⟨http://forums.ebay.com/db1/topic/Ebay-Live-Community/Whats-Youre-Favorite/2000153820?&tstart=720&mod=11501 71486523⟩.

78. Milo, "Milo: Local Shopping," 25 December 2010 ⟨http://milo.com/⟩.

79. Casey, "'Come, Join Our Family,'" 161.

80. cuties4u, "What exactly happens at eBay Live Conference???" eBay, 15 March 2004, 9 January 2011 ⟨http://forums.ebay.com/db1/topic/Ebay-Live-Community/What-Exactly-Happens/400084809?&tstart=2240&mod=1079392424545⟩.

81. ion_treasures, "so, what exactly happens at EBay live?" eBay, 20 May 2004, 12 February 2011 ⟨http://forums.ebay.com/db1/topic/Ebay-Live-Community/So-What-Exactly/410142506?&tstart=2080&mod=1085157982073⟩.

82. Sartelle, "As If We Were a Community."

83. Anderson, *Imagined Communities*; Nancy, *The Inoperative Community*.

84. dawn_luvz_matt, "Harleyglasses eBay Live Vegas 2006 Thread..," eBay, 1 April 2006, 9 January 2011 ⟨http://forums.ebay.com/thread.jspa?start=45&threadID =2000099877&rw=true&anticache=1294617243828⟩.

85. Susanna Millman, "Photos From eBay Live! 2008 So Far," *Chatter*, 20 June 2008, 15 July 2011 ⟨http://www.ebaychatter.com/the_chatter/2008/06/photos-from-eba.html⟩.

86. sanda-girls_closet, "On my way!!!!" eBay, 22 June 2005, 9 January 2011 ⟨http:// forums.ebay.com/db1/topic/Ebay-Live-Community/On-My-Way/410559449?&t start=1480&mod=1119462716489⟩.

87. frednmag, "HOW WILL I RECOGNIZE YOU AT EBAY LIVE? EVERYONE LOOK," eBay, 2 March 2006, 9 January 2011 ⟨http://forums.ebay.com/db1/topic/Ebay-Live-Community/How-Will-I/1000235264?&tstart=1240&mod=1142077690432⟩.

88. katy@ebay.com, "The Official eBay Live 2003 Picture Thread!!!!" eBay, 25 June 2003, 9 January 2011 ⟨http://forums.ebay.com/db1/topic/Ebay-Live-Community/The-Official-Ebay/2226920?&start=0⟩.

89. rizal@ebay.com, "Share your photos from eBay Live! 2005!" eBay, 6 May 2005, 9 January 2011 ⟨http://forums.ebay.com/db1/topic/Ebay-Live-Community/Share-Your-Photos/410531609?&start=0⟩.

90. beadhappys, "Share your photos from eBay Live! 2005!" eBay, 25 June 2005, 9 January 2011 ⟨http://forums.ebay.com/db1/topic/Ebay-Live-Community/Share-Your-Photos/410531609&start=30⟩.

91. wigglzzzz, "Thank you TIEDYEJOHN!!!!" eBay, 29 June 2003, 9 January 2011 ⟨http://forums.ebay.com/db1/topic/Ebay-Live-Community/Thank-You-Tiedyejohn/2230401?messageID=25801834&forumID=112&x#25801834⟩.

92. beachbadge, "Thank you TIEDYEJOHN!!!!" eBay, 2 July 2003, 12 February 2011 ⟨http://forums.ebay.com/db1/topic/Ebay-Live-Community/Thank-You-Tiedyejohn/2230401?messageID=25801834&forumID=112&x#25801834=112&x#25801834⟩.

93. Ibid.

94. Cohen, *The Perfect Store*, 51.

95. Laura, "A Tribute to Bobal – By Giraffer and Shipscript," *Chatter*, 28 October 2008, 9 January 2011 ⟨http://www.ebaychatter.com/the_chatter/2008/10/a-tribute-to-bo.html⟩.

96. Jeff, "Legendary eBay Member Bobal Says Hello (Sideways)," *Chatter*, 14 June 2007, 9 January 2011 ⟨http://www.ebaychatter.com/the_chatter/2007/06/legendary_ebay_.html⟩.

97. Oppermann and Chon, "Convention Participation Decision-Making Process."

98. auctiontrain, "2006 eBay Live Board Party," eBay, 15 June 2006, 9 January 2011 ⟨http://forums.ebay.com/db1/topic/Ebay-Live-Community/2006-Ebay-Live/1000301029&start=15⟩.

99. consignmentpal, "Atlanta Ebay on Location report. SAVE THE Tas," eBay, 24 March 2010, 9 January 2011 ⟨http://forums.ebay.com/db1/topic/Trading-Assistant/Atlanta-Ebay-On/510205643&start=0⟩.

100. sanda-girls_closet, "****Heartbroken over Boston****," eBay, 14 June 2007, 9 January 2011 ⟨http://forums.ebay.com/db1/topic/Ebay-Live-Community/Heartbroken-Over-Boston/2000384955?&tstart=0&mod=1182523929187⟩.

101. beachbadge, "OK, Who has pins to trade?" eBay, 21 June 2007, 9 January 2011 ⟨http://forums.ebay.com/db1/topic/Ebay-Live-Community/Ok-Who-Has/2000387712&start=60⟩.

102. bamaj1, "Will Somebody There Ask About Skippy Bucks?" eBay, 6 June 2003, 9 January 2011 ⟨http://forums.ebay.com/db1/topic/Ebay-Live-Community/Will-Somebody-There/207054?&tstart=2640&mod=1055043463850⟩.

103. bobal, "Will Somebody There Ask About Skippy Bucks?" eBay, 6 June 2003,

9 January 2011 ⟨http://forums.ebay.com/db1/topic/Ebay-Live-Community/Will-Somebody-There/207054?&tstart=2640&mod=1055043463850⟩.

104. cherbear, "Will Somebody There Ask About Skippy Bucks?" eBay, 6 June 2003, 9 January 2011 ⟨http://forums.ebay.com/db1/topic/Ebay-Live-Community/Will-Somebody-There/207054?&tstart=2640&mod=1055043463850⟩.

105. bamajl, "Will Somebody There Ask About Skippy Bucks?" eBay, 6 June 2003, 9 January 2011 ⟨http://forums.ebay.com/db1/topic/Ebay-Live-Community/Will-Somebody-There/207054?&tstart=2640&mod=1055043463850⟩.

106. Muñiz and O'Guinn, "Brand Community," 425.

107. Algesheimer et al., "The Social Influence of Brand Community," 19.

108. Havens, "Exhibiting Global Television," 21; Kerin and Cron, "Assessing Trade Show Functions and Performance," 88; Rice, "Using the Interaction Approach to Understand Trade Shows," 35.

109. Ina Steiner, "'eBay Live' Conference Sold Out, Registration Closes," *Auction-Bytes* 1293, 2 June 2006, 9 January 2011 ⟨http://auctionbytes.com/cab/abn/y06/m06/i02/s02⟩.

110. eBay, "eBay Live! 2004," 2004, 28 June 2007 ⟨http://pages.ebay.com/ebaylive/highlights2004.html⟩.

111. Smith, "Buttons, T-Shirts, and Bumperstickers," 144.

112. Ninad, "eBay Live! -- The Gory Details," *Chatter*, 27 June 2007, 9 January 2011 ⟨http://www.ebaychatter.com/the_chatter/2007/06/ebay-live----th.html⟩.

113. Eric S. Raymond, ed., "Welcome to the Jargon File," Jargon File 4.4.8, 1 October 2004, 21 November 2011 ⟨http://catb.org/jargon/html/online-preface.html⟩; Eric S. Raymond, ed., "suit," Jargon File 4.4.8, 1 October 2004, 21 November 2011 ⟨http://catb.org/jargon/html/S/suit.html⟩.

114. Eric S. Raymond, ed., "Dress," Jargon File 4.4.8, 1 October 2004, 21 November 2011 ⟨http://catb.org/jargon/html/dress.html⟩.

115. Micah Alpern, "My first day at eBay," 20 July 2003, 9 January 2011 ⟨http://www.alpern.org/weblog/stories/2003/07/07/myFirstDayAtEbay.html⟩.

116. Sartelle, "As If We Were a Community."

117. Jones and Slater, *What's in a Name?* 215.

118. Wikipedia, "Disney pin trading," 9 January 2011 ⟨http://en.wikipedia.org/wiki/Disney_pin_trading⟩.

119. Disney, "Official Disney Pin Trading – Get Started," 9 January 2011 ⟨http://eventservices.disney.go.com/pintrading/page?id=getStarted#start⟩.

120. eBay, *2002 Community Conference*, eBay Live! Anaheim, Calif., 21–23 June 2002, 4.

121. Micah Alpern, "My first day at eBay," 20 July 2003, 9 January 2011 ⟨http://www.alpern.org/weblog/stories/2003/07/07/myFirstDayAtEbay.html⟩.

122. eBay, *Funtastic 2007 Conference Guide*, eBay Live! Boston, 14–16 June 2007, 37.

123. ah6tyfour, "EBay Live Pins?.......explain this to a newbie please," eBay, 23 June

2005, 9 January 2011 ⟨http://forums.ebay.com/db1/topic/Ebay-Live-Commu
nity/Ebay-Live-Pinsexplain/410558903?&tstart=1480&mod=1119740768646⟩.

124. toys2keep, "WOW eBay did it up right! See you at 2004 New Orleans," eBay,
29 June 2003, 9 January 2011 ⟨http://forums.ebay.com/db1/topic/Ebay-Live-
Community/Wow-Ebay-Did/2230283?&tstart=2440&mod=1057002912543⟩.

125. Belk, *Collecting in a Consumer Society*, 74.

126. Burton, "Collectible Aesthetics."

127. Ninad, "eBay Live! -- The Gory Details," *Chatter*, 27 June 2007, 9 January 2011
⟨http://www.ebaychatter.com/the_chatter/2007/06/ebay-live----th.html⟩.

128. stmmcmanus, "Pins, Cards, Get a Life People....," eBay, 30 June 2003, 9 January
2011 ⟨http://forums.ebay.com/db1/topic/Ebay-Live-Community/Pins-Cards-
Get/2230971?&tstart=2400&mod=1057419394977⟩.

129. Danet and Katriel, "No Two Alike," 260.

130. Kool & the Gang, "Celebration," *Celebrate!* (Mercury Records, 1980).

131. Julia Wilkinson, "Images from eBay Live 2007: Friday Madness," bidbits, 15 June
2007, 9 January 2011 ⟨http://juliawww.typepad.com/bidbits/2007/06/images_
from_eba.html⟩.

132. For considerations of how collecting is rendered as obsessive, see Belk, *Collecting in a Consumer Society*; and McIntosh and Schmeichel, "Collectors and Collecting."

133. andyl@ebay.com, "Help! Lost TV-star 'IT' at eBay Live! Reward for clues...,"
eBay, 29 June 2006, 9 January 2011 ⟨http://forums.ebay.com/db1/topic/Ebay-
Live-Community/Help-Lost-Tv/1000310599?&start=0⟩.

134. bcousins53, "Bad experience at eBay Live," eBay, 28 June 2003, 9 January 2011
⟨http://forums.ebay.com/db1/topic/Ebay-Live-Community/Bad-Experience-
At/2229975?&tstart=2360&mod=1058909213132⟩.

135. johnjohn@ebay.com, "Hmm?? Where did it all go?" eBay, 22 July 2005, 9 January 2011 ⟨http://forums.ebay.com/db1/topic/Ebay-Live-Community/Hmm-
Where-Did/1000000948?&tstart=1360&mod=1122396466279⟩.

136. chix_nuggets, "Hmm?? Where did it all go?" eBay, 28 June 2005, 9 January 2011
⟨http://forums.ebay.com/db1/topic/Ebay-Live-Community/Hmm-Where-Did/
1000000948?&tstart=1360&mod=1122396466279⟩.

137. giraffer, "Hmm?? Where did it all go?" eBay, 29 June 2005, 9 January 2011
⟨http://forums.ebay.com/db1/topic/Ebay-Live-Community/Hmm-Where-Did/
1000000948?&tstart=1360&mod=1122396466279⟩.

138. Slater, "Collecting The Real Thing."

139. coniemiller, "I NEED HELP LOCATING 2 REALLY NICE PEOPLE!!" eBay, 29 June
2003, 9 January 2011 ⟨http://forums.ebay.com/db1/topic/Ebay-Live-Commu
nity/I-Need-Help/2230905?&tstart=2440&mod=1056979889158⟩.

140. phreaky2, "Pins, Cards, Get a Life People....," eBay, 29 June 2003, 9 January 2011
⟨http://forums.ebay.com/db1/topic/Ebay-Live-Community/Pins-Cards-Get/223
0971?&tstart=2400&mod=1057419394977⟩.

141. Wikipedia, "William Shatner," 9 January 2011 ⟨http://en.wikipedia.org/wiki/William_Shatner⟩.

142. skip555, "Pins, Cards, Get a Life People....," eBay, 30 June 2003, 9 January 2011 ⟨http://forums.ebay.com/db1/topic/Ebay-Live-Community/Pins-Cards-Get/2230971?&tstart=2400&mod=1057419394977⟩.

143. uswapl, "eBay Live Adoption," eBay, 11 April 2005, 9 January 2011 ⟨http://forums.ebay.com/db1/topic/Ebay-Live-Community/Ebay-Live-2005/200068236?&tstart=1720&mod=1113942800789⟩. chainmaillady also mentions the eBay-ana category: "Last year was our first year at ebay live. We quickly learned that when they were handing out stuff, stick your hand out. Never turn down anything someone is willing to give you. We got tons of cool stuff. Check out the ebayana category for examples." chainmaillady, "freebies and pins....," eBay, 26 April 2006, 9 January 2011 ⟨http://forums.ebay.com/db1/topic/Ebay-Live-Community/Freebies-And-Pins/1000270702?&tstart=760&mod=1149997683698⟩.

144. Barbara Shaugnessy, "eBay Live Wrap-up: AuctionBytes Reports on Second eBay Convention," *AuctionBytes* 98, 13 July 2003, 9 January 2011 ⟨http://www.auctionbytes.com/cab/abu/y203/m07/abu0098/s03⟩.

145. Belk, *Collecting in a Consumer Society*, 67.

146. johnjohn@ebay.com, "Recordings Available of Each Session at eBay Live?" eBay, 14 June 2005, 9 January 2011 ⟨http://forums.ebay.com/db1/topic/Ebay-Live-Community/Recordings-Available-Of/410554089?&tstart=1560&mod=1118896772795⟩.

147. denverain, "Lightning Johnny limited ed. eBay Car Collectible Toy," eBay, 1 July 2007 ⟨http://cgi.ebay.com/Lightning-Johnny-limited-ed-eBay-Car-Collectible-Toy_W0QQitemZ150138095212QQihZ005QQcategoryZ18789QQrdZ1QQcmdZViewItem⟩.

148. arubadubis, "eBay Employee Pink Fuzzy IT No Reserve," eBay, 23 June 2006 ⟨http://cgi.ebay.com/eBay-Employee-Pink-Fuzzy-IT-No-Reserve_W0QQitemZ200001095655QQihZ010QQcategoryZ18789QQrdZ1QqcmdZViewItem⟩.

149. dottie, "Ebay Live 2003 Pin for Feedback Over 1000?" eBay, 8 July 2003, 9 January 2011 ⟨http://forums.ebay.com/db1/topic/Ebay-Live-Community/Ebay-Live-2003/2238434?&tstart=2400&mod=1057794480906⟩.

150. lll080551g4rwb, "Hard Rock Cafe EBay Live Boston Complete Set Of Pins ++," eBay, 30 June 2007 ⟨http://cgi.ebay.com/Hard-Rock-Cafe-Ebay-Live-Boston-Complete-Set-Of-Pins_W0QQitemZ320133065827QQihZ011QQcategoryZ18789QQrdZ1QQcmdZViewItem⟩.

151. aleegold, "ebaY live 2007 Boston Pins Lanyard buttons 100% charity: FREEDOMFUNDS care packages 4 deployed soldiers in Iraq," eBay, 16 June 2007 ⟨http://cgi.ebay.com/ebaY-live-2007-Boston-Pins-Lanyard-buttons-100-charity_W0QQitemZ130125651523QQihZ003QQcategoryZ18789QQrdZ1QQcmdZViewItem⟩.

152. Stewart, *On Longing*, 166.

153. Slater, "Collecting The Real Thing," 205.

154. gailcatl, "Ebay Live 2007 Deluxe Collectors Set Coins Pins Mug 40+," eBay, 2 July 2007 ⟨http://cgi.ebay.com/Ebay-Live-2007-Deluxe-Collectors-Set-Coins-Pins-Mug-40_W0QQitemZ200125091215QQihZ010QQcategoryZ18789QQrdZ 1QQcmdZViewItem⟩.

155. Lasusa, "Eiffel Tower Key Chains and Other Pieces of Reality," 279.

156. possessions_recycled, "Ebay Live Boston 07 Backpack Pins Cards Pens LOTS MORE," eBay, 19 June 2007 ⟨http://cgi.ebay.com/Ebay-Live-Boston-07-Back pack-Pins-Cards-Pens-LOTS-MORE_W0QQitemZ130126674757QQihZ003QQ categoryZ18789QQrdZ1QQcmdZViewItem⟩.

157. A number of companies offer three-dimensional "prints." See, e.g., Figure-Prints, "FigurePrints – World of Warcraft," 9 January 2011 ⟨http://www.figure prints.com/⟩.

158. Stephen M. Silverman, "Britney's Used Chewing Gum Sold on eBay," *People*, 3 September 2004, 9 January 2011 ⟨http://www.people.com/people/article/ 0,,692094,00.html⟩.

159. uncle_griff, "Griff's Cool Mylar Blazer from eBay Live 2007 Keynote: 100% of proceeds to benefit the DOUA," eBay, 22 June 2007 ⟨http://cgi.ebay.com/Griffs-Cool-Mylar-Blazer-From-eBay-Live-2007-Keynote_W0QQitemZ140131872446 QQihZ004QQcategoryZ18789QQrdZ1QQcmdZViewItem⟩.

160. baANHZA, "eBay Live - Boston Part 2," YouTube, 20 June 2007, 12 February 2011 ⟨http://www.youtube.com/watch?v=bLyqrZewbak&feature=channel⟩; rrrandyyy, "my eBay Live experience," YouTube, 26 February 2008, 12 February 2011 ⟨http://www.youtube.com/watch?v=ThfWsH7ctL8&feature=related⟩.

161. Barbara Shaugnessy, "eBay Live Wrap-up: AuctionBytes Reports on Second eBay Convention," *AuctionBytes* 98, 13 July 2003, 9 January 2011 ⟨http://www .auctionbytes.com/cab/abu/y203/m07/abu0098/s03⟩.

162. jenuinelyjill, "AUTOGRAPHED MEG WHITMAN COLLECTOR CARD EBAY LIVE 2004," eBay, 1 July 2007 ⟨http://cgi.ebay.com/AUTOGRAPHED-MEG-WHIT MAN-COLLECTOR-CARD-EBAY-LIVE-2004_W0QQitemZ110145078546QQ ihZ001QQcategoryZ18789QQrdZ1QQcmdZViewItem⟩.

163. toys2keep, "Would love to see 'Real Pictures,'" eBay, 29 June 2003, 9 January 2011 ⟨http://forums.ebay.com/db1/topic/Ebay-Live-Community/Would-Love-To/2230863&#msg25780686⟩.

164. postalrainey3, "EBAY LIVE! BOSTON ENTREPRENEUR'S CHATTER LOBSTER PIN," eBay, 28 June 2007 ⟨http://cgi.ebay.com/EBAY-LIVE-BOSTON-ENTRE PRENEURS-CHATTER-LOBSTER-PIN_W0QQitemZ330141216038QQihZ014 QQcategoryZ18789QQrdZ1QQcmdZViewItem⟩.

165. ion_treasures, "young seller in nola," eBay, 6 April 2004, 9 January 2011 ⟨http:// forums.ebay.com/db1/topic/Ebay-Live-Community/Young-Seller-In/41009066 4?&tstart=2200&mod=1081302068122⟩.

166. biggbill, "EBAY LIVE POWERSELLER PERKS? WHAT ARE THEY?" eBay, 25 June 2003, 9 January 2011 ⟨http://forums.ebay.com/db1/topic/Ebay-Live-Commu nity/Ebay-Live-Powerseller/217535?&tstart=2440&mod=1056896640726⟩.

167. wmack2, "EBAY O'RAMA STUFF I'D LIKE TO SEE AT EBAY LIVE 2004!" eBay, 9 July 2003, 9 January 2011 ⟨http://forums.ebay.com/db1/topic/Ebay-Live-Community/Ebay-Orama-Stuff/2233680&start=15⟩.

168. interiorartl, "eBay Live 2007 TRADING CARD signed P Omidyar RARE new," eBay, 8 August 2007 ⟨http://cgi.ebay.com/ws/eBayISAPI.dll?ViewItem&rd=1& item=260147574263&ssPageName=STRK:MEWA:IT&ih=016⟩.

169. Hollenbeck and Zinkhan, "Consumer Activism on the Internet," 479.

170. Gray, "Antifandom and the Moral Text," 840.

171. Johnson, "Fan-tagonism," 293.

172. Ina Steiner, "eBay Live Conference: A Made for TV Event," *AuctionBytes* 73, 30 June 2002, 9 January 2011 ⟨http://www.auctionbytes.com/cab/abu/y202/ m06/abu0073/s03⟩.

173. howtooster, "You'll have to see me there," eBay, 12 May 2006, 9 January 2011 ⟨http://forums.ebay.com/db1/topic/Ebay-Live-Community/Youll-Have-To/ 1000280935?&tstart=1080&mod=1147479777891⟩.

174. fiberwireguy, "You'll have to see me there," eBay, 12 May 2006, 9 January 2011 ⟨http://forums.ebay.com/db1/topic/Ebay-Live-Community/Youll-Have-To/ 1000280935?&tstart=1080&mod=1147479777891⟩.

175. creations1106, "Exhibitor wants to share a booth with you. Let's save money," eBay, 13 May 2006, 9 January 2011 ⟨http://forums.ebay.com/db1/topic/Ebay-Live-Community/Exhibitor-Wants-To/1000281278?mod=1148315744454&&tstart =1000&anticache=1276362385419⟩.

176. Ibid.

177. dennis2kang, "Exhibitor wants to share a booth with you. Let's save money," eBay, 16 May 2006, 9 January 2011 ⟨http://forums.ebay.com/db1/topic/Ebay-Live-Community/Exhibitor-Wants-To/1000281278?&tstart=1000&mod=1148 315744454⟩.

178. wjkski, "I will not attend ebay live 2006," eBay, 26 March 2006, 9 January 2011 ⟨http://forums.ebay.com/db1/topic/Ebay-Live-Community/I-Will-Not/100025 1921?&tstart=1120&mod=1146464090299⟩; dogcatrescue, "I will not attend ebay live 2006," eBay, 27 March 2006, 9 January 2011 ⟨http://forums.ebay.com/db1/ topic/Ebay-Live-Community/I-Will-Not/1000251921?&tstart=1120&mod=1146 464090299⟩.

179. chainmaillady, "I will not attend ebay live 2006," eBay, 12 April 2006, 9 January 2011 ⟨http://forums.ebay.com/db1/topic/Ebay-Live-Community/I-Will-Not/100 0251921&start=30⟩.

180. howtooster, "I will not attend ebay live 2006," eBay, 12 April 2006, 9 January 2011 ⟨http://forums.ebay.com/db1/topic/Ebay-Live-Community/I-Will-Not/ 1000251921&start=30⟩.

181. Algesheimer et al., "The Social Influence of Brand Community," 22.

182. Hills, "Patterns of Surprise."

183. Geoffrey A. Fowler, "EBay Live Is Going, Going, Gone," *Wall Street Journal*, 14 July 2009, 9 January 2011 ⟨http://blogs.wsj.com/digits/2009/07/14/ebay-live-is-going-going-gone/⟩; Chris Dawson, "eBay Live! is dead and buried," tamebay, 13 July 2009, 9 January 2011 ⟨http://tamebay.com/2009/07/ebay-live-is-dead-and-buried.html⟩.

184. funboy1227, "Re: EBAY Live in Orlando cancelled," eBay, 14 July 2009, 9 January 2011 ⟨http://forums.ebay.com/db1/topic/Halfcom/Ebay-Live-In/510116029&#msg512515418⟩.

185. Kozinets, "E-Tribalized Marketing?" 258.

186. Andrejevic, "Watching Television without Pity," 25.

3. You Can "Get It On" eBay

1. Ingraham, "The Heterosexual Imaginary."

2. Acker, "Hierarchies, Jobs, Bodies"; Britton, "Gendered Organizational Logic"; Swanberg, "Illuminating Gendered Assumptions."

3. Woolgar, "Configuring the User," 59.

4. van Oost, "Materialized Gender."

5. Sender, "Selling Sexual Subjectivities," 172.

6. Ingraham, "The Heterosexual Imaginary"; Jackson, "Gender, Sexuality and Heterosexuality," 111.

7. Oswald, "A Member of the Wedding?" 108.

8. Jackson, "Gender, Sexuality and Heterosexuality."

9. Literature on wedding cultures includes Currie, "'Here Comes the Bride'"; Ingraham, *White Weddings*; Oswald, "A Member of the Wedding?"; and Otnes and Pleck, *Cinderella Dreams*.

10. eBay, "eBay Gift Finder," 29 March 2009 ⟨http://giftfinder.ebay.com/⟩.

11. Meg Whitman, "Remarks as Prepared for Delivery: Meg Whitman," 2008 Republican National Convention, 3 September 2008, 3 January 2009 ⟨http://portal.gopconvention2008.com/speech/details.aspx?id=45⟩.

12. Meg Whitman, as quoted in Eric Kleefeld, "Meg Whitman: I Didn't Vote Because I Was Focused on My Family," Talking Points Memo, 30 September 2009, 10 January 2011 ⟨http://tpmdc.talkingpointsmemo.com/2009/09/meg-whitman-i-didnt-vote-because-i-was-focused-on-my-family.php⟩.

13. Meg Whitman, as quoted in Lesley Stahl, "Meg Whitman on What's Next after eBay," wowOwow, 18 March 2008, 10 January 2011 ⟨http://www.wowowow.com/point-of-view/meg-whitman-on-whats-next-after-ebay/⟩.

14. Rheingold, *The Virtual Community*.

15. NetLingo, "NetLingo.com Dictionary of Internet Terms: Online Definitions & Text Messaging," 10 January 2011 ⟨http://www.netlingo.com/lookup.cfm?term

=eBay⟩. The same set of numbers is mentioned in Miguel Helft, "What Makes eBay Unstoppable," *Industry Standard*, 6 August 2001, 10 January 2011 ⟨http://www.findarticles.com/p/articles/mi_m0HWW/is_30_4/ai_77826049⟩.

16. Griffith, *The Official eBay Bible*, 7.

17. eBay, "Diamond Ring Designer – Build Your Bling – eBay," 25 February 2010 ⟨http://diamonds.ebay.com/BuildYourBling⟩.

18. eBay, "eBay – New & used electronics, cars, apparel, collectibles, sporting goods & more at low prices," 23 June 2006 ⟨http://www.ebay.com/⟩.

19. Mike, "eBay: Engagement & Wedding Jewelry," eBay, 23 June 2006 ⟨http://pages.ebay.com/bridal/Testimonials.html⟩.

20. eBay, "eBay – Costume, Antique, Vintage Jewelry," 24 October 2004 ⟨http://jewelry.listings.ebay.com:80/Vintage-Antique_Costume_W0QQfromZR4QQ sacategoryZ500QQsocmdZListingItemListQQsocolumnlayoutZ3QQsocom parecolumnlayoutZ1QQsorecordsperpageZ100QQsosortorderZ1QQsosort propertyZ1QQsotimeZ1QQsotrZ1⟩.

21. Theresa Howard, "Ads Pump Up eBay Community with Good Feelings," *USA Today*, 18 October 2004, 10 January 2011 ⟨http://www.usatoday.com/tech/web guide/internetlife/2004-10-17-ebay-community-ads_x.htm⟩.

22. Ina Steiner, "Couple Exchange Vows at eBay's Annual User Conference," *AuctionBytes* 792, 28 June 2004, 10 January 2011 ⟨http://www.auctionbytes.com/ cab/abn/y04/m06/i28/s02⟩.

23. rizal, "***Reminder: Save up to $20 on eBay Live! 2004 registration if you sign up before April 16***," eBay, 1 March 2004, 10 January 2011 ⟨http://forums.ebay .com/db1/topic/Ebay-Live-Community/Reminder-Save-Up/410044084?mod=1 080843846288&&tstart=3240&anticache=1294697816768⟩.

24. eBay, "eBay Live! 2004," 2004, 28 June 2007 ⟨http://pages.ebay.com/ebaylive/ highlights2004.html⟩.

25. Brad Aspling, as quoted in Betty Nguyen, "Transcripts," CNN, 26 June 2004, 10 January 2011 ⟨http://transcripts.cnn.com/TRANSCRIPTS/0406/26/smn.03 .html⟩.

26. the*sniping*family, "Hey sniping*family! eBay Groups," eBay, 9 September 2003, 10 August 2007 ⟨http://groups.ebay.com/thread.jspa?threadID=69248⟩.

27. eBay, "eBay – Come To Think Of It," 12 March 2010 ⟨http://70.32.107. /⟩.

28. Camille, "Editor's Introduction," 163.

29. eBay, "eBay," 11 August 2007 ⟨http://whatisit.com/⟩. See also MrSmith356, "eBay-Ring," YouTube, 10 January 2011 ⟨http://www.youtube.com/watch?v=z BmNwp8IUuU⟩.

30. eBay, "eBay :: The Power of All of Us," 16 November 2008 ⟨http://thepowerof allofus.com/flash.html⟩.

31. Nino, "The Power of All of Us – The Making of an Ad Campaign," *Chatter* 4, no. 2, December 2004, 10 January 2011 ⟨http://pages.ebay.com/community/ chatter/2004december/poaou.html⟩.

32. eBay, "Move In," The Power of All of Us, 16 March 2008 ⟨http://thepowerof allofus.com/flash.html⟩.

33. eBay, "Clocks," The Power of All of Us, 16 March 2008 ⟨http://thepowerofall ofus.com/flash.html⟩.

34. eBay, "Maze," The Power of All of Us, 16 March 2008 ⟨http://thepowerofallofus .com/flash.html⟩.

35. David Steiner, "Survey: How Do Users Feel about eBay's Feedback System?" *AuctionBytes* 87, 19 January 2003, 10 January 2011 ⟨http://www.auctionbytes .com/cab/abu/y203/m01/abu0087/s02⟩.

36. Richardson, "Locating Sexualities."

37. Shea, *Netiquette.*

38. Eric S. Raymond, ed., "Gender and Ethnicity," Jargon File 4.4.8, 1 October 2004, 21 November 2011 ⟨http://www.catb.org/~esr/jargon/html/demographics.html⟩.

39. Benkler, *The Wealth of Networks.*

40. Sender, "Selling Sexual Subjectivities," 172.

41. Adesso, "Adesso --⟩ Home," 29 March 2009 ⟨http://adesso.com/⟩.

42. Logitech, "Logitech ⟩ Home ⟩ Notebook Essentials," 15 September 2008 ⟨http:// www.logitech.com/index.cfm/initiatives/notebook_essentials/&cl=us,en?src =logi_home&lnk=initiatives_notebook_essentials&WT.ac=ib|notebook_essen tials||hp⟩.

43. Geni, "Genealogy - Free Family Tree - Geni," 22 November 2008 ⟨http://www .geni.com/⟩.

44. Flickr, "About Flickr," 10 April 2008 ⟨http://www.flickr.com/about/⟩.

45. Smith, "'Baby's Picture Is Always Treasured,'" 200.

46. Phanfare, "phanfare – Photo sharing and video sharing network for families," 12 April 2008 ⟨http://www.phanfare.com/learnmore.aspx⟩.

47. Schuster, "Here Comes the Bride," 279–80.

48. Currie, "'Here Comes the Bride,'" 416.

49. Otnes and Lowrey, "'Til Debt Do Us Part," 32; Otnes and Pleck, *Cinderella Dreams*, 8.

50. Cohen, *The Perfect Store*, 8.

51. Ingraham, "The Heterosexual Imaginary," 203–4.

52. Best, "The Production of Heterosexuality at the High School Prom," 195.

53. eBay, "eBay – clothing, shoes, accessories items at low prices. Find IT on eBay," 3 June 2010 ⟨http://clothing.shop.ebay.com/?_from=R40&_trksid=p3872.m570 .11313&_nkw=wedding&_sacat=11450⟩.

54. eBay, "wedding dresses, designer wedding dresses and wedding veils items on eBay.com. Find IT on eBay," 16 December 2008 ⟨http://clothing.listings.ebay .com:80/Wedding-Apparel_Wedding-Dresses_W0QQfclZ3QQfromZR11QQ sacatZ63851QqsocmdZListingItemList⟩.

55. racefanou812, "Your perfect wedding dress,Yes you,size 10-12," eBay, 28 July 2007 ⟨http://cgi.ebay.com/Your-perfect-wedding-dress-Yes-you-size-10-12_

WoQQitemZ190136152809QQihZ009QQcategoryZ63851QQssPageNameZW
DVWQQrdZ1QQcmdZViewItem); kennedyjrl, "Alfred Angelo Collection
Wedding - W/Scalloped Train," eBay, 31 July 2007 〈http://cgi.ebay.com/Alfred-
Angelo-Collection-Wedding-W-Scalloped-Train_WoQQitemZ170135993911
QQihZ007QQcategoryZ63851QQssPageNameZWDVWQQrdZ1QQcmdZView
Item); jordi723, "Vera Wang Wedding Dress," eBay, 30 July 2007 〈http://cgi
.ebay.com/Vera-Wang-Wedding-Dress_WoQQitemZ260144949977QQihZ016
QQcategoryZ63851QQssPageNameZWDVWQQrdZ1QQcmdZViewItem);
khartbridal, "BNWT $995 MAGNIFICENT Bridal Gown Wedding Dress HALTER:
MOONLIGHT MADNESS SALE In Stock for Immediate Shipment," eBay, 28 Sep-
tember 2007 〈http://cgi.ebay.com/BNWT-995-MAGNIFICENT-Bridal-Gown-
Wedding-Dress-HALTER_WoQQitemZ120166014709QQihZ002QQcategoryZ
63851QQssPageNameZWDVWQQrdZ1QQcmdZViewItem).

56. Schuster, "Here Comes the Bride," 281.

57. carolineprezzano, "Caroline Herrera Ivory Wedding Gown with Champagne
Sash," eBay, 14 August 2007 〈http://cgi.ebay.com/Carolina-Herrera-Ivory-
Wedding-Gown-with-Champagne-Sash_WoQQitemZ200142088548QQihZ
010QQcategoryZ63851QQssPageNameZWDVWQQrdZ1QQcmdZViewItem).

58. emelias2242, "Monique Lhuillier Alcenon Lace Wedding Gown," eBay, 12 No-
vember 2007 〈http://cgi.ebay.com/Monique-Lhuillier-Alcenon-Lace-Wedding-
Gown_WoQQitemZ220171424214QQihZ012QQcategoryZ63851QQssPageName
ZWDVWQQrdZ1QQcmdZViewItem).

59. Sobal et al., "Weight and Weddings," 113.

60. Ibid., 131.

61. Lewis, "Working the Ritual."

62. xylleth, "Stunning IVORY Wedding Gown NWT," eBay, 27 September 2007
〈http://cgi.ebay.com/Stunning-IVORY-Wedding-Gown-NWT_WoQQitemZ
220154913119QQihZ012QQcategoryZ63880QQssPageNameZWDVWQQrdZ1
QQcmdZViewItem); rosedragon75, "WHITE CHIFFON WEDDING DESTINATION
DRESS," eBay, 14 November 2007 〈http://cgi.ebay.com/WHITE-CHIFFON-
WEDDING-DESTINATION-DRESS_WoQQitemZ140179626552QQihZ004
QQcategoryZ63851QQssPageNameZWDVWQQrdZ1QQcmdZViewItem).

63. cowboyssting, "Pronovias Designer Wedding Dress Gown 'Helena' Size 22,"
eBay, 29 July 2007 〈http://cgi.ebay.com/Pronovias-Designer-Wedding-Dress-
Gown-Helena-Size-22_WoQQitemZ200136085432QQihZ010QQcategoryZ
63851QQssPageNameZWDVWQQrdZ1QQcmdZViewItem).

64. Sobal et al., "Weight and Weddings," 119.

65. twopickerz, "ROMANTIC!JESSICA MCCLINTOCK Gunne Sax Wedding Dress
NR!" eBay, 15 November 2007 〈http://cgi.ebay.com/ROMANTIC-JESSICA-
McCLINTOCK-Gunne-Sax-Wedding-Dress-NR_WoQQitemZ130174558847
QQihZ003QQcategoryZ63851QQssPageNameZWDVWQQrdZ1QQcmdZ
ViewItem).

66. mariannejanet, "Michaelangelo strapless A-line beaded corset type gown," eBay, 2 October 2007 ⟨http://cgi.ebay.com/Michaelangelo-strapless-A-line-beaded-corset-type-gown_W0QQitemZ300157367497QQihZ020QQcategoryZ63851QQssPageNameZWDVWQQrdZ1QQcmdZViewItem⟩.

67. Colls, "Outsize/Outside," 531.

68. Patterson, "Why Are All the Fat Brides Smiling?" 244.

69. Corrado, "Teaching Wedding Rules," 60–61.

70. princesa052607, "Eve of Milady Famous E10," eBay, 29 July 2007 ⟨http://cgi.ebay.com/Eve-of-Milady-Famous-E10_W0QQitemZ230157529210QQihZ013QQcategoryZ63851QQssPageNameZWDVWQQrdZ1QQcmdZViewItem⟩.

71   autumn_gunnels, "wedding dress," eBay, 9 November 2007 ⟨http://cgi.ebay.com/wedding-dress_W0QQitemZ170167766345QQihZ007QQcategoryZ63851QQssPageNameZWDVWQQrdZ1QQcmdZViewItem⟩.

72. jimenez68, "NEW Designer Wedding Gown –GORGEOUS!!!" eBay, 30 July 2007 ⟨http://cgi.ebay.com/NEW-Designer-Wedding-Gown-GORGEOUS_W0QQitemZ330151988871QQihZ014QQcategoryZ63851QQssPageNameZWDVWQQrdZ1QQcmdZViewItem⟩; ariesangel4400, "Mon Cheri Wedding Gown Dress NEW size 6 BEAUTIFUL IVORY," eBay, 15 August 2007 ⟨http://cgi.ebay.com/Mon-Cheri-Wedding-Gown-Dress-NEW-size-6-BEAUTIFUL-IVORY_W0QQitemZ180149308656QQihZ008QQcategoryZ63851QQssPageNameZWDVWQQrdZ1QQcmdZViewItem⟩.

73. eBay, "Wedding Dresses, cheap wedding dresses and discount wedding dresses items on eBay.com. Find IT on eBay," 1 June 2009 ⟨http://clothing.listings.ebay.com/Wedding-Apparel_Wedding-Dresses_W0QQdfspZ1QQfromZR4QQsacatZ63851QQsocmdZListingItemList⟩.

74. corrieandmike, "Mori Lee wedding dress - brand new," eBay, 5 November 2007 ⟨http://cgi.ebay.com/Mori-Lee-wedding-dress-brand-new_W0QQitemZ120180303279QQihZ002QQcategoryZ63851QQssPageNameZWDVWQQrdZ1QQcmdZViewItem⟩.

75. maileib, "RENA KOH COUTURE Beach Wedding Bridal Dress Gown 6/8: BNWT - MUST SEE! Amsale Vera Wang Melissa Sweet Style," eBay, 12 November 2007 ⟨http://cgi.ebay.com/RENA-KOH-COUTURE-Beach-Wedding-Bridal-Dress-Gown-6-8_W0QQitemZ160179915286QQihZ006QQcategoryZ63851QQssPageNameZWDVWQQrdZ1QQcmdZViewItem⟩.

76. julieann4him, "Jasmine Haute Couture Wedding Dress $825 Size 10 Ivory," eBay, 8 November 2007 ⟨http://cgi.ebay.com/Jasmine-Haute-Couture-Wedding-Dress-825-Size-10-Ivory_W0QQitemZ120181660742QQihZ002QQcategoryZ63851QQssPageNameZWDVWQQrdZ1QQcmdZViewItem⟩.

77. julieann4him, "Pronovias $2200 Belize Wedding Dress Size 14," eBay, 8 November 2007 ⟨http://cgi.ebay.com/Pronovias-2200-Belize-Wedding-Dress-Size-14_W0QQitemZ120181737977QQihZ002QQcategoryZ63851QQssPageNameZWDVWQQrdZ1QQcmdZViewItem⟩.

78. Belk, *Collecting in a Consumer Society*, 67.

79. Stewart, *On Longing*, 166.

80. Otnes and Lowrey, "'Til Debt Do Us Part," 326.

81. Friese, "The Wedding Dress," 53.

82. 25chanelgirl, "$1000 wedding dress by julius bridal," eBay, 5 August 2008 ⟨http://cgi.ebay.com/1000-wedding-dress-by-julius-bridal_WoQQitemZ120291 217100QQcmdZViewItem?hash=item120291217100&_trkparms=72%3A1015%7C 39%3A1%7C66%3A3%7C65%3A12&_trksid=p3286.co.m14.l1318⟩.

83. Nissanoff, *FutureShop*.

84. Paysha Stockton Rhone, "Here Comes the Slob," *Boston Globe*, 13 June 2008, 10 January 2011 ⟨http://www.boston.com/lifestyle/weddings/articles/2008/06/ 13/here_comes_the_slob/⟩.

85. Ingraham, *White Weddings*, 34.

86. jackool78, "BONNY AN ELEGANT WEDDING DRESS," eBay, 30 July 2007 ⟨http:// cgi.ebay.com/Bonny-An-Elegant-White-Wedding-Dress_WoQQitemZ200135 996638QQihZ010QQcategoryZ63851QQssPageNameZWDVWQQrdZ1QQcmd ZViewItem⟩.

87. sport222, "Beautiful Empire-Waist Wedding Gown--Size 6," eBay, 19 December 2009 ⟨http://cgi.ebay.com/Beautiful-Empire-Waist-Wedding-Gown-Size-6_ WoQQitemZ270491226352QQcmdZViewItemQQptZWedding_Dresses?hash =item3efa8890fo⟩.

88. pinkpinkiesmom, "WEDDING GOWN SEQUINED/Beaded Size 8/10 Waist 24"," eBay, 25 December 2009 ⟨http://cgi.ebay.com/WEDDING-GOWN-SEQUIN ED-Beaded-Size-8-10-Waist-24_WoQQitemZ110383850684QQcmdZViewItem QQptZWedding_Dresses?hash=item19b363e4bc⟩.

89. Lori Adalsteinsson, as quoted in Donna Tam, "Wedding Attire Subjected to Un-conventional Treatment," *SpokesmanReview*, 16 August 2007, 10 January 2011 ⟨http://donnatam.wordpress.com/2007/08/16/trash-the-dress-photo-shoot-targets-keepsake/⟩.

90. Grosz, *Volatile Bodies*, 192.

91. Kristeva, *Powers of Horror*, 98.

92. Douglas, *Implicit Meanings*, 109.

93. aquarius12960, "GORGEOUS WEDDING GOWN DRESS SIZE 12, NEW NEVER WORN," eBay, 10 November 2007 ⟨http://cgi.ebay.com/GORGEOUS-WEDDI NG-GOWN-DRESS-SIZE-12-NEW-NEVER-WORN_WoQQitemZ19017252 2623QQihZ009QQcategoryZ63851QQssPageNameZWDVWQQrdZ1QQcmdZ ViewItem⟩.

94. racefanou812, "Your perfect wedding dress,Yes you,size 10-12," eBay, 28 July 2007 ⟨http://cgi.ebay.com/Your-perfect-wedding-dress-Yes-you-size-10-12_ WoQQitemZ190136152809QQihZ009QQcategoryZ63851QQssPageNameZW DVWQQrdZ1QQcmdZViewItem⟩.

95. roslynn, "DESIGNER ORIGINAL PRINCESS WEDDING DRESS - SIZE 20- NWT,"

eBay, 13 March 2008 〈http://cgi.ebay.com/DESIGNER-ORIGINAL-PRINCESS-WEDDING-DRESS-SIZE-20-NWT_W0QQitemZ350036309763QQihZ022QQcategoryZ63851QQssPageNameZWDVWQQrdZ1QQcmdZViewItem〉.

96. Belk et al., "Dirty Little Secret," 134.

97. Young, *On Female Body Experience.*

98. Gregson et al., "Narratives of Consumption and the Body in the Space of the Charity/Shop."

99. rhonda5707, "Wedding Dress used once," eBay, 28 July 2007 〈http://cgi.ebay.com/Wedding-Dress-used-once_W0QQitemZ140142853828QQihZ004QQcategoryZ63851QQssPageNameZWDVWQQrdZ1QQcmdZViewItem〉.

100. pipoca13, "Used Bridal OriginalWedding Dress," eBay, 15 August 2007 〈http://cgi.ebay.com/Used-Bridal-Original-Wedding-Dress_W0QQitemZ110159925260QQihZ001QQcategoryZ63851QQssPageNameZWDVWQQrdZ1QQcmdZViewItem〉.

101. nuttytoys, "Wedding Dress size 14 Beaded by Venus w/ VAIL USED N/R," eBay, 3 October 2007 〈http://cgi.ebay.com/Wedding-Dress-size-14-Beaded-by-Venus-w-VAIL-USED-N-R_W0QQitemZ220156849585QQihZ012QQcategoryZ63851QQssPageNameZWDVWQQrdZ1QQcmdZViewItem〉.

102. Larry Star, "eBay's Wedding Dress Guy: Bitter, Party of One… Your Table is Ready (Book)," 10 January 2011 〈http://www.weddingdressguy.net/〉.

103. eBay, "Size 12 Wedding Dress/Gown: Pop Culture Classic Listing," Trading Card, 2005.

104. Nicole Brodeur, "Fact Is, Wedding-Dress Guy's eBay Pitch Includes Some Fiction," *Seattle Times*, 3 May 2004, 10 January 2011 〈http://seattletimes.nwsource.com/html/localnews/2001915316_brodeur29m.html〉; Barbara "smash hit" Mikkelson, "Wedding Dress Guy," Snopes, 3 July 2007, 10 January 2011 〈http://www.snopes.com/love/revenge/weddress.asp〉.

105. ajp1999, "VINTAGE USED WEDDING DRESS!!!! LQQK !!! NR !!!!!!!!!!" eBay, 30 September 2007 〈http://cgi.ebay.com/VINTAGE-USED-WEDDING-DRESS-LQQK-NR_W0QQitemZ130158998830QQihZ003QQcategoryZ63851QQssPageNameZWDVWQQrdZ1QQcmdZViewItem〉.

106. andersonorganization, "Ex-wife's Wedding Dress," eBay, 15 November 2007 〈http://cgi.ebay.com/Ex-wifes-Wedding-Dress_W0QQitemZ280174206800QQihZ018QQcategoryZ63851QQssPageNameZWDVWQQrdZ1QQcmdZViewItem〉.

107. Julia Wilkinson, "Bizarre eBay Stories: eBay Live Session," *AuctionBytes* 791, 26 June 2004, 10 January 2011 〈http://www.auctionbytes.com/cab/abn/y04/m06/i26/s04〉.

108. andersonorganization, "Ex-wife's Wedding Dress," eBay, 15 November 2007 〈http://cgi.ebay.com/Ex-wifes-Wedding-Dress_W0QQitemZ280174206800QQihZ018QQcategoryZ63851QQssPageNameZWDVWQQrdZ1QQcmdZViewItem〉; Larry Star, "eBay Item 4146756343 (Ends Apr-28-04 15:37:01 PDT) – SIZE

12 WEDDING DRESS/GOWN NO RESERVE," 28 April 2004, 11 June 2010 〈http://
weddingdressguy.com/original_ebay_ad/ebaylisting.html〉.

109. Oswald, "A Member of the Wedding?" 117.

110. gt2plus2, "*UGLY like my X-WIFE *CHUCKY'S GIRLFRIEND Ugly DOLL!" eBay,
12 November 2008 〈http://cgi.ebay.com/UGLY-like-my-X-WIFE-CHUCKYS-
GIRLFRIEND-Ugly-DOLL_W0QQitemZ220311508322QQcmdZViewItemQQpt
ZDolls?hash=item220311508322&_trksid=p3286.co.m14&_trkparms=66%3A2%7
C65%3A1%7C39%3A1%7C240%3A1318〉.

111. solticeman25, "ALIMONY SALE 〉Ex Girlfriends/Wife sport card collection:
Complete dispersal of my entire collection!" eBay, 9 November 2008 〈http://
cgi.ebay.com/ALIMONY-SALE-Ex-Girlfriends-Wife-sport-card-collection_
W0QQitemZ200273747528QQcmdZViewItemQQptZUS_SM_Sports_Cards
?hash=item200273747528&_trksid=p3286.co.m14&_trkparms=66%3A2%7C65%
3A1%7C39%3A1%7C240%3A1308〉.

112. teaganz_daddy, "LOT OF 14 HANDBAGS LEFT BEHIND BY EX WIFE: KATE
SPADE,GUCCI,DONNEY,BEIJO,COACH,TOMMY HILFIGER," eBay, 14 February
2009 〈http://cgi.ebay.com/LOT-OF-14-HANDBAGS-LEFT-BEHIND-BY-EX-
WIFE_W0QQitemZ170302897863QQcmdZViewItemQQptZLH_Default
Domain_0?hash=item170302897863&_trksid=p3286.co.m14&_trkparms=66%
3A2%7C65%3A1%7C39%3A1%7C240%3A1318〉.

113. rizal@ebay.com, "Questions about eBay history," eBay, 3 March 2005, 10 January 2011 〈http://forums.ebay.com/db1/topic/Ebay-Live-Community/Questions-
About-Ebay/200040826?&tstart=1640&mod=1118121098434〉; junquegirl, "Questions about eBay history," eBay, 20 March 2005, 10 January 2011 〈http://forums
.ebay.com/db1/topic/Ebay-Live-Community/Questions-About-Ebay/20004082
6&start=15〉.

114. Jonathan Brown, "Wife Sells DJ's Lotus on eBay in Revenge for His On-Air
Flirting," *Independent*, 22 June 2005, 10 January 2011 〈http://www.independent
.co.uk/news/uk/this-britain/wife-sells-djs-lotus-on-ebay-in-revenge-for-his-
onair-flirting-496138.html〉.

115. 395edmondson, as quoted in Ian Sparks, "Fuming Wife Puts Cheating Husband's Possessions up for Sale on eBay," *MailOnline*, 18 October 2006, 10 January 2011 〈http://www.dailymail.co.uk/news/article-411242/Fuming-wife-puts-
cheating-husbands-possessions-sale-eBay.html〉.

116. estoyblanca, "WEDDING GOWN with ALL the fixings: DRESS, SHOES,VEIL
PETTICOAT, BRA," eBay, 8 November 2007 〈http://cgi.ebay.com/WEDDING-
GOWN-with-ALL-the-fixings_W0QQitemZ300170086076QQihZ020QQcate
goryZ63851QQssPageNameZWDVWQQrdZ1QQcmdZViewItem〉.

117. kealalaina77, "MICHAELANGELO Ivory wedding dress size 16 NWT NEW: RUN-
AWAY GROOM Off Shoulder Empire Waist beaded corset," 15 November 2007
〈http://cgi.ebay.com/MICHAELANGELO-Ivory-wedding-dress-size-16-NWT-

NEW_W0QQitemZ260139672352QQihZ016QQcategoryZ63851QQrdZ1QQss
PageNameZWD1VQQcmdZViewItem⟩.

118. jennyfur1028, "David's Bridal Wedding Dress NWT," eBay, 18 November 2007
⟨http://cgi.ebay.com/Davids-Bridal-Wedding-Dress-NWT_W0QQitemZ25018
9718676QQihZ015QQcategoryZ63851QQssPageNameZWDVWQQrdZ1QQcmd
ZViewItem⟩.

119. 10255blue, "Wedding Dress from the Dress Barn," eBay, 7 November 2008
⟨http://cgi.ebay.com/Wedding-Dress-from-the-Dress-Barn_W0QQitemZ30027
1884483QQcmdZViewItemQQptZWedding_Dresses?hash=item300271884483&_
trksid=p3286.co.m14&_trkparms=66%3A2%7C65%3A1%7C39%3A1%7C240%
3A1318⟩.

120. Herrmann, "Women's Exchange in the U.S. Garage Sale," 718.

121. edmkreed, "Beautiful Kleinerts Ivory Wedding Gown Size 3 Used Once," eBay,
11 December 2011 ⟨http://www.ebay.com/itm/Beautiful-Kleinerts-Ivory-Wed
ding-Gown-Size-3-Used-Once-/220392708169?pt=Wedding_Dresses&hash
=item33506dd849⟩. fatesmessenger2009 also writes, "Pictures do not do it
justice." fatesmessenger2009, "Mori Lee Wedding Dress- Brand New~by
Madeline Gardner," eBay, 11 December 2011 ⟨http://www.ebay.com/itm/Mori-
Lee-Wedding-Dress-Brand-New-by-Madeline-Gardner-/140659054686?pt
=Wedding_Dresses&hash=item20bfeed85e⟩.

122. zbestreasure, "Alfred Angelo Wedding Dress, Train, Lace & Sequins SZ 4," eBay,
21 August 2009 ⟨http://cgi.ebay.com/Alfred-Angelo-Wedding-Dress-Train-
Lace-Sequins-SZ-4_W0QQitemZ230292128329QQcmdZViewItemQQptZWed
ding_Dresses?hash=item359e7b0249&_trksid=p3286.co.m14⟩.

123. oldude2, "Large size wedding dress, plus sized wedding dress,: Large sized,
size 22,Pre owned,Slightly Used,plus sized," eBay, 13 Nov. 2007 ⟨http://cgi.ebay
.com/Large-size-wedding-dress-plus-sized-wedding-dress_W0QQitemZ2801
73466165QQihZ018QQcategoryZ63851QQssPageNameZWDVWQQrdZ1QQ
cmdZViewItem⟩.

124. hot12b*, "Beautiful White Beaded Wedding Dress Sz 14," eBay, 25 June 2008
⟨http://cgi.ebay.com/Beautiful-White-Beaded-Wedding-Dress-Sz-14_W0QQ
itemZ320267645241QQihZ011QQcategoryZ63851QQssPageNameZWDVWQQ
rdZ1QQcmdZViewItem⟩.

4. eBay's Visible Masculinities

1. Hayles, *How We Became Posthuman*.

2. Chasin, *Selling Out*; Sender, "Sex Sells."

3. Bordo, *The Male Body*; Dyer, "Don't Look Now"; Potts, "The Essence of the
Hard On."

4. Firemeg, "eBay Bans Ivory Sales, But Allows It........ What It Means for the

Future," FireMeg.com, 6 June 2007 ⟨http://www.firemeg.com/2007/06/ebay-bans-ivory-sales-but-allows-itwhat.html⟩.

5. Mark, "Re: eBay speedos," Gay Speedos Fantasy Board, 26 August 2002, 16 July 2008 ⟨http://speedoarchive.ctecomputer.com/2002/august/000021ed.htm⟩; Tropis, "Tropis Swimwear eBay Auction Photos," Gay Speedos Fantasy Board, 10 August 2005, 12 January 2011 ⟨http://speedoarchive.ctecomputer.com/2005/August/00000108.htm⟩.

6. Buyer, as quoted in magmozine, "gBay . Justdecadent's Artwork," 16 August 2006, 12 January 2011 ⟨http://www.magmozine.com/gbay/⟩.

7. romanborn, "FRUSTRATED MA CATEGORY POWERSELLER REQUESTING HELP/ADVICE," eBay, 18 May 2007 ⟨http://forums.ebay.com/db2/thread.jspa?threadID=1000496786&tstart=0&mod=1179613683342⟩.

8. kingoflithia, "Sexy Guy Swimsuit From Behind Gay Int. !" eBay, 18 March 2004 ⟨http://cgi.ebay.com/ws/eBayISAPI.dll?ViewItem&item=3282137332&category=48⟩; pixidiom, "1940 UNUSUAL GAY INTEREST-MAN FROM BEHIND," eBay, 30 September 2004 ⟨http://cgi.ebay.com/ws/eBayISAPI.dll?ViewItem&category=14279&item=6119833757⟩.

9. marsha91091, "Where to List?!!!" eBay, 6 June 2008 ⟨http://forums.ebay.com/db2/thread.jspa?messageID=2010668897&forumID=7&x#2010668897⟩; maltbo, "Where to List?!!!" eBay, 6 June 2008 ⟨http://forums.ebay.com/db2/thread.jspa?messageID=2010668897&forumID=7&x#2010668897⟩.

10. femmefan1946, "Physical Culture magazines(1913-1915)any help with estimating their value in Category-Specific Boards in eBay Forums," eBay, 7 June 2008, 12 January 2011 ⟨http://forums.ebay.com/db2/topic/Vintage/Physical-Culture-Magazines1913/2000573843&#msg2010679893⟩.

11. lillieborghild, "1911 Written Morse code help in Category-Specific Boards in eBay Forums," eBay, 21 April 2004, 12 January 2011 ⟨http://forums.ebay.com/db1/topic/Historical-Memorabilia/1911-Written-Morse/410108753&#msg412749062⟩.

12. hcquilts, "1911 Written Morse code help in Category-Specific Boards in eBay Forums," 22 April 2004, 12 January 2011 ⟨http://forums.ebay.com/db1/topic/Historical-Memorabilia/1911-Written-Morse/410108753&#msg412749062⟩.

13. Ibson, *Picturing Men*, 154.

14. Kates, "The Protean Quality of Subcultural Consumption," 383.

15. camp-classics, "CAMP CLASSICS eBay Store About My Store," eBay, 6 July 2007 ⟨http://members.ebay.com/ws/eBayISAPI.dll?ViewUserPage&userid=camp-classics⟩.

16. gearsaleaol, "Men's Vintage Swim Briefs 100% Nylon Swimwear Black 36," eBay, 7 April 2007 ⟨http://cgi.ebay.com/ws/eBayISAPI.dll?ViewItem&ih−011&sspagename=STRK:MESE:IT&viewitem=&item=320101293560&rd=1&rd=1⟩.

17. jonmcgarrah, "Vintage Nude Male Bodybuilder hand-tinted photo Gay Int:

Sexy man holding long rod, bulge, Muscle men, Beefcake!" eBay, 17 May 2007 ⟨http://cgi.ebay.com/Vintage-Nude-Male-Bodybuilder-hand-tinted-photo-Gay-Int_W0QQitemZ120121372473QQihZ002QQcategoryZ66465QQrdZ1QQ cmdZViewItem⟩.

18. For a discussion of how men are associated with the mind, see Hayles, *How We Became Posthuman*.

19. Chasin, *Selling Out*, 36.

20. jocktime/huckleberry, "Swapping suits," Gay Speedos Fantasy Board, 14 March 2003, 12 January 2011 ⟨http://speedoarchive.ctecomputer.com/2003/ March/000043cf.htm⟩.

21. somtom2000, "USED MAN HUNT SINGLET MEDIUM AS NEW GAY INTERESTED," eBay, 17 July 2008 ⟨http://cgi.ebay.com/USED-MAN-HUNT-SINGLET-MEDIUM-AS-NEW-GAY-INTERESTED_W0QQitemZ160262710389QQcmdZ ViewItem?hash=item160262710389⟩.

22. Rohlinger, "Eroticizing Men," 65.

23. Sender, "Sex Sells," 331.

24. Rubin, "Thinking Sex."

25. Petit, "'Cleaned to eBay Standards,'" 267.

26. eBay, "Used Clothing," 23 March 2009 ⟨http://pages.ebay.com/help/policies/ used-clothing.html⟩.

27. Espion, "Which category on ebay do you put used underwear under?" Under wear4Men.com, 17 May 2006, 12 January 2011 ⟨http://www.underwear4men .com/under/viewtopic.php?t=8931&highlight=ebay⟩.

28. speedofan9, "Re: eBay lycra auction (HOT pix!)," Gay Lycra Fantasy Board, 25 January 2005, 16 July 2008 ⟨http://lycraarchive.ctecomputer.com/2005/ January/000010a4.htm⟩.

29. jockwolf, "Re: want to seel speedos on ebay," Gay Speedos Fantasy Board, 21 February 2005, 12 January 2011 ⟨http://speedoarchive.ctecomputer.com/2005/ February/0000b8f0.htm⟩.

30. online3, "eBay speedos," Gay Speedos Fantasy Board, 26 August 2002, 13 February 2011 ⟨http://speedoarchive.ctecomputer.com/2002/august/000021e5.htm⟩.

31. themickster, "Vintage 1980 Red Lion Dunlop Jockstrap Jock Strap Cup S," eBay, 6 June 2007 ⟨http://cgi.ebay.com/Vintage-1980-Red-Lion-Dunlop-Jockstrap-Jock-Strap-Cup-S_W0QQitemZ110136129748QQihZ001QQcategoryZ11506 QQssPageNameZWDVWQQrdZ1QQcmdZViewItem⟩.

32. mynameisditao, "RED SPEEDO's swim Briefs trunks Gay int? 44"waist xxl," eBay, 26 May 2007 ⟨http://cgi.ebay.com/RED-SPEEDOS-swim-Briefs-trunks-Gay-int-44-waist-xxl_W0QQitemZ230135370452QQihZ013QQcategoryZ15690 QQssPageNameZWDVWQQrdZ1QQcmdZViewItem⟩.

33. mscljocko, "New Seamfree Spandex Nylon blend Bikini SMALL Navy," eBay, 3 July 2007 ⟨http://cgi.ebay.com/New-Seamfree-Spandex-Nylon-blend-Bikini-

SMALL-Navy_W0QQitemZ130131164273QQihZ003QQcategoryZ11509QQrdZ
1QQcmdZViewItem⟩.

34. eBay, "Used Clothing," 23 March 2009 ⟨http://pages.ebay.com/help/policies/
used-clothing.html⟩; eBay, "Mature Audiences," 8 June 2007 ⟨http://pages.ebay
.com/help/policies/mature-audiences.html⟩.

35. eBay, "Mature Audiences," 8 June 2007 ⟨http://pages.ebay.com/help/policies/
mature-audiences.html⟩.

36. eBay, "Adult Only category policy," 1 March 2010 ⟨http://pages.ebay.com/help/
policies/adult-only.html⟩.

37. gearsale, "Pics You Won't See on Ebay," Gay Speedos Fantasy Board, 26 March
2003, 12 January 2011 ⟨http://speedoarchive.ctecomputer.com/2003/March/
000045be.htm⟩.

38. Tropis, "Tropis Swimwear eBay Auction Photos," Gay Speedos Fantasy Board,
10 August 2005, 12 January 2011 ⟨http://speedoarchive.ctecomputer.com/2005/
August/00000108.htm⟩.

39. dontbesilly, "NUDE GAY MALE-HANDSOME YOUNG MAN-Orig Oil Painting,"
eBay, 17 May 2007 ⟨http://cgi.ebay.com/NUDE-GAY-MALE-HANDSOME-
YOUNG-MAN-Orig-Oil-Painting_W0QQitemZ320115353761QQihZ011QQ
categoryZ20158QQrdZ1QQcmdZViewItem⟩.

40. john-bishop, "Original Charcoal Male Nude Drawing Gay Interest Art," eBay,
24 May 2007 ⟨http://cgi.ebay.com/Original-Charcoal-Male-Nude-Drawing-
Gay-Interest-Art_W0QQitemZ130117731361QQihZ003QQcategoryZ552QQ
rdZ1QQcmdZViewItem⟩.

41. Sender, "Sex Sells," 360.

42. galaxy_shop, "* Diesel Men underwear SEXY JOCK STRAP White L Gay int,"
eBay, 1 July 2007 ⟨http://cgi.ebay.com/Diesel-Men-underwear-SEXY-JOCK-
STRAP-White-L-Gay-int_W0QQitemZ120137741799QQihZ002QQcategoryZ
11509QQrdZ1QQcmdZViewItem⟩.

43. However, not all monitors support this technologically rendered erotic. The
refreshing of the screen occurs with cathode-ray-tube monitors but not with
liquid-crystal-display flat screens. Montfort, "Continuous Paper."

44. mscljocko, "JM Contoured Pouch Squarecut 32 gay int. spandex nylon," eBay,
2 July 2007 ⟨http://cgi.ebay.com/JM-Contoured-Pouch-Squarecut-32-gay-int-
spandex-nylon_W0QQitemZ130130643048QQihZ003QQcategoryZ15690QQ
rdZ1QQcmdZViewItem⟩.

45. mscljocko, "AntiBacterial Brief Watson's tight whities Medium," eBay, 25 June
2007 ⟨http://cgi.ebay.com/ws/eBayISAPI.dll?ViewItem&item=130128600588⟩;
mscljocko, "New Seamfree Spandex Nylon blend Bikini SMALL Navy," eBay,
26 June 2007 ⟨http://cgi.ebay.com/New-Seamfree-Spandex-Nylon-blend-Bikini-
SMALL-Navy_W0QQitemZ130128878068QQihZ003QQcategoryZ11509QQss
PageNameZWDVWQQrdZ1QQcmdZViewItem⟩.

46. Ward, "Hung Like a Horse."

47. Bordo, "Reading the Male Body," 55.

48. usflaboy, "New N2N Swimsuit Size Small. Gay games Limited Edition," eBay, 24 May 2007 ⟨http://cgi.ebay.com/New-N2N-Swimsuit-Size-Small-Gay-games-Limited-Edition_W0QQitemZ220115755806QQihZ012QQcategoryZ15690QQssPageNameZWDVWQQrdZ1QQcmdZViewItem⟩.

49. usflaboy, "New In Box C-In2 Jockstrap Size Medium," eBay, 18 June 2007 ⟨http://cgi.ebay.com/New-In-Box-C-In2-Jockstrap-Size-Medium_W0QQitemZ220123349681QQihZ012QQcategoryZ11509QQssPageNameZWDVWQQrdZ1QQcmdZViewItem⟩.

50. gerardo5800, "MY WHOLE PACKAGE IS FOR YOU!!!!. LOOK AT ME..GET THE 6." eBay, 2 June 2007 ⟨http://cgi.ebay.com/MY-WHOLE-PACKAGE-IS-FOR-YOU-LOOK-AT-ME-GET-THE-6_W0QQitemZ290124860112QQihZ019QQcategoryZ11509QQrdZ1QQcmdZViewItem#ShippingPayment⟩; gerardo5800, "MY LITTLE THONG... GET THEM ALL NOW!!!!!!!! VERY GAY." eBay, 2 June 2007 ⟨http://cgi.ebay.com/ MY-LITTLE-THONG-GET-THEM-ALL-NOW-VERY-GAY W0QQitemZ290124854988QqihZ11509QQrdZ1QQcmdZViewItem⟩.

51. Newbie2it, "shorts pic," USG forums, 29 April 2006, 12 January 2011 ⟨http://usg-online.com/forums/showthread.php?t=4254&highlight=ebay⟩.

52. haywardmike, "Re: Nolan West on ebay," Gay Speedos Fantasy Board, 28 February 2003, 12 January 2011 ⟨http://speedoarchive.ctecomputer.com/2003/February/000040f2.htm⟩.

53. "Re: eBay speedos," Gay Speedos Fantasy Board, 27 August 2002, 12 January 2011 ⟨http://speedoarchive.ctecomputer.com/2002/august/0000220d.htm⟩.

54. jockdude90036, "Gray Camo Camouflage Swim Bikini Thong NEW NWOT Gay Int," eBay, 19 May 2007 ⟨http://cgi.ebay.com/Gray-Camo-Camouflage-Swim-Bikini-Thong-NEW-NWOT-Gay-Int_W0QQitemZ160118990575QQihZ006QQcategoryZ15690QQrdZ1QQcmdZViewItem⟩.

55. Sammy, "Ebay Butt," Gay Speedos Fantasy Board, 6 December 2003, 16 July 2008 ⟨http://speedoarchive.ctecomputer.com/2004/January/00006fea.htm⟩.

56. Stl_Muscle, "Re: Ebay Butt," Gay Speedos Fantasy Board, 6 December 2003, 12 January 2011 ⟨http://speedoarchive.ctecomputer.com/2004/January/00006ff7.htm⟩.

57. two-talented-leos, "My HOT College Jock Boy Men Modeling Photos GAY Int NEW," eBay, 24 May 2007 ⟨http://cgi.ebay.com/My-HOT-College-Jock-Boy-Men-Modeling-Photos-GAY-Int-NEW_W0QQitemZ330124761626QQihZ014QQcategoryZ313QQrdZ1QQcmdZViewItem⟩.

58. mscljocko, "Mscljocko's Previous Auction Pictures Vol 1 and Vol 2," eBay, 26 June 2007 ⟨http://cgi.ebay.com/Mscljockos-Previous-Auction-Pictures-Vol-1-and-Vol-2_W0QQitemZ130128877875QQihZ003QQcategoryZ4794QQssPageNameZWDVWQQrdZ1QQcmdZViewItem⟩.

59. poloboyzz, "eBay View About Me for poloboyzz," eBay, 24 May 2007 〈http://members.ebay.com/ws/cBayISAPI.dll?ViewUserPage&userid=poloboyzz〉.

60. rshadz, "Re: Ebay Butt," Gay Speedos Fantasy Board, 3 December 2003, 12 January 2011 〈http://speedoarchive.ctecomputer.com/2004/January/00006fbb.htm〉.

61. Speedoman NYC, "Hot Guy on Ebay," Gay Speedos Fantasy Board, 20 June 2005, 12 January 2011 〈http://speedoarchive.ctecomputer.com/2005/June/0000cd79.htm〉.

62. jamaculate, "EGAY funny parody logo gay pride mousepad mouse pads," eBay, 20 February 2009 〈http://cgi.ebay.com/ws/eBayISAPI.dll?ViewItem&ssPageName=STRK:MEWAX:IT&item=330309288062〉.

63. hrdmslguy, "NEW MENS N2N SWIMSUIT -NO LINING - GAY INTEREST," eBay, 20 May 2007 〈http://cgi.ebay.com/NEW-MENS-N2N-SWIMSUIT-NO-LINING-GAY-INTEREST_W0QQitemZ220114346072QQihZ012QQcategoryZ15690QQssPageNameZWDVWQQrdZ1QQcmdZViewItem〉.

64. hrdmslguy, "NEW MENS N2N SWIM ALMOST SHEER NO LINING - GAY INTEREST," eBay, 17 May 2007 〈http://cgi.ebay.com/ws/eBayISAPI.dll?ViewItem&item=220103785509〉.

65. Mark, "Re: eBay speedos," Gay Speedos Fantasy Board, 26 August 2002, 12 January 2011 〈http://speedoarchive.ctecomputer.com/2002/august/000021ed.htm〉.

66. hrdmslguy, "NEW MENS N2N SWIM ALMOST SHEER NO LINING - GAY INTEREST," eBay, 17 May 2007 〈http://cgi.ebay.com/ws/eBayISAPI.dll?ViewItem&item=220103785509〉.

67. Hayles, *How We Became Posthuman*, 30.

68. Barthes, *The Pleasure of the Text*, 10.

69. Bordo, "Gay Men's Revenge," 21.

70. Culbertson, "Designing Men."

71. poloboyzz, "KENNETH COLE stud dress shirt/jock/gay/sz 16 32-33," eBay, 20 May 2007 〈http://cgi.ebay.com/KENNETH-COLE-stud-dress-shirt-jock-gay-sz-16-32-33_W0QQitemZ140120305821QQihZ004QQcategoryZ57991QQrdZ1QQcmdZViewItem〉; ozbestprice, "MEN KINKY SEXY BLACK MESH BRIEF BODYSUIT gay Free Size," eBay, 9 July 2007 〈http://cgi.ebay.com/MEN-KINKY-SEXY-BLACK-MESH-BRIEF-BODYSUIT-gay-Free-Size_W0QQitemZ230150634353QQihZ013QQcategoryZ70697QQrdZ1QQcmdZViewItem〉.

72. Culbertson, "Designing Men."

73. Duncan, "The MoMA's Hot Mamas."

74. Dyer, "Don't Look Now," 67.

75. Kibby and Costello, "Displaying the Phallus," 352.

76. Dyer, "Don't Look Now," 67.

77. poloboyzz, "KENNETH COLE stud dress shirt/jock/gay/sz 16 32-33," eBay, 20 May 2007 〈http://cgi.ebay.com/KENNETH-COLE-stud-dress-shirt-jock-gay-

sz-16-32-33_WoQQitemZ140120305821QQihZ004QQcategoryZ57991QQrdZ
1QQcmdZViewItem⟩.

78. sexysadiespandex, "Men's Hot Pink Leopard Spandex Wrestling Shirt gay sexy,"
eBay, 24 May 2007 ⟨http://cgi.ebay.com/Mens-Hot-Pink-Leopard-Spandex-
Wrestling-Shirt-gay-sexy_WoQQitemZ270123973690QQihZ017QQcategoryZ
57990QQrdZ1QQcmdZViewItem⟩.

79. poloboyzz, "2 HOT shirts BANANA REPUBLIC spandex & IZOD/ jock/gay/M,"
eBay, 18 May 2007 ⟨http://cgi.ebay.com/2-HOT-shirts-BANANA-REPUBLIC-
spandex-IZOD-jock-gay-M_WoQQitemZ140119805516QQihZ004QQcategoryZ
57990QQrdZ1QQcmdZViewItem⟩.

80. Kates, "The Protean Quality of Subcultural Consumption," 386.

81. Wood, "The Gay Male Gaze," 59.

82. Rohlinger, "Eroticizing Men," 70.

83. Drummond, "Men's Bodies"; Gill et al., "Body Projects and the Regulation of
Normative Masculinity."

84. feistymuscle, "MEN'S BODYBUILDING MUSCLE POSING SUIT GAY INTEREST:
MEN'S HOT PINK BODYBUILDER MUSCLE POSING SUIT-MEDIUM," eBay, 26
June 2007 ⟨http://cgi.ebay.com/MENS-BODYBUILDING-MUSCLE-POSING-
SUIT-GAY-INTEREST_WoQQitemZ280128928799QQihZ018QQcategoryZ
137084QQssPageNameZWDVWQQrdZ1QQcmdZViewItem⟩.

85. fellowes1964, "MENS TURCO SWIMWEAR SM BLUE / GOLD GAY JOCK LAST
CHANCE," eBay, 21 May 2007 ⟨http://cgi.ebay.com/MENS-TURCO-SWIM
WEAR-SM-BLUE-GOLD-GAY-JOCK-LAST-CHANCE_WoQQitemZ280
117431717QQihZ018QQcategoryZ15690QQssPageNameZWDVWQQrdZ1QQ
cmdZViewItem⟩; feistymuscle, "MEN'S SPANDEX MUSCLE SHORTS GAY INTER-
EST: Black Coated Spandex Muscle Shorts -Men's Med/Lg," eBay, 31 May 2007
⟨http://cgi.ebay.com/MENS-SPANDEX-MUSCLE-SHORTS-GAY-INTEREST_
WoQQitemZ280120785303QQihZ018QQcategoryZ137084QQrdZ1QQcmdZ
ViewItem⟩.

86. kirkieskorner, "29X32 LEVI'S 501 student JEANS USED GAY INTEREST jock,"
eBay, 22 May 2007 ⟨http://cgi.ebay.com/29X32-LEVIS-501-student-JEANS-
USED-GAY-INTEREST-jock_WoQQitemZ220114954367QQihZ012QQcategory
Z11483QQrdZ1QQcmdZViewItem⟩.

87. kirkieskorner, "LEVIS SKINNER low rise JEANS shorts 30"W Gay Interest," eBay,
21 May 2007 ⟨http://cgi.ebay.com/LEVIS-SKINNER-low-rise-JEANS-shorts-30-
W-Gay-Interest_WoQQitemZ220114693227QQihZ012QQcategoryZ15689QQ
ssPageNameZWDVWQQrdZ1QQcmdZViewItem⟩.

88. kirkieskorner, "'Orgasm DONOR' stretch T-shirt men's M/L Gay interest," eBay,
6 May 2007 ⟨http://cgi.ebay.com/ws/eBayISAPI.dll?ViewItem&item=22010965
6300⟩.

89. Viewer, as quoted in kirkieskorner, "Questions from other members : Patriotic
THONG Custom Made M Nylon/Lycra Gay Interest," eBay, 16 May 2007 ⟨http://

contact.ebay.com/ws/eBayISAPI.dll?ShowAllQuestions&requested=kirkieskorn
er&iid=220111521245&frm=284&redirect=0&ShowASQAlways=1&SSPageName
=PageAskSellerQuestion_VI⟩.

90. kirkieskorner, "Questions from other members : Patriotic THONG Custom Made
M Nylon/Lycra Gay Interest," eBay, 16 May 2007 ⟨http://contact.ebay.com/ws/
eBayISAPI.dll?ShowAllQuestions&requested=kirkieskorner&iid=220111521245&
frm=284&redirect=0&ShowASQAlways=1&SSPageName=PageAskSellerQuesti
on_VI⟩.

91. Connell, "A Very Straight Gay," 735.

92. Simpson, "Gay Dream Believer," 1, 2, 3.

93. Manning, "Gay Culture."

94. galaxy_shop, "SkinXWear Men Underwear Silky Translucent BIKINI Size L,"
eBay, 2 July 2007 ⟨http://cgi.ebay.com/SkinXWear-Men-Underwear-Silky-Trans
lucent-BIKINI-Size-L_W0QQitemZ120103237560QQihZ002QQcategoryZ313
QQrdZ1QQcmdZViewItem⟩.

95. thana0, "Mens c-thru wrap boxer brief underwear lingerie gay in?" eBay, 24 May
2007 ⟨http://cgi.ebay.com/Mens-c-thru-wrap-boxer-brief-underwear-lingerie-
gay-in_W0QQitemZ260121829815QQihZ016QQcategoryZ11509QQrdZ1QQcmd
ZViewItem⟩.

96. thana0, "male g-string c-thru jockstrap underwear thong gay int?" eBay, 8 June
2007 ⟨http://cgi.ebay.com/male-g-string-c-thru-jockstrap-underwear-thong-
gay-int_W0QQitemZ260108841655QQihZ016QQcategoryZ11509QQrdZ1QQ
cmdZViewItem#⟩.

97. fellowes1964, "MENS TURCO SWIMWEAR SM BLUE / GOLD GAY JOCK LAST
CHANCE," eBay, 21 May 2007 ⟨http://cgi.ebay.com/MENS-TURCO-SWIM
WEAR-SM-BLUE-GOLD-GAY-JOCK-LAST-CHANCE_W0QQitemZ280117
431717QQihZ018QQcategoryZ15690QQssPageNameZWDVWQQrdZ1QQcmd
ZViewItem⟩.

98. fellowes1964, "MENS TULIO SWIMWEAR # 3 SM-MD BLUE GAY JOCK LAST
CHANCE," eBay, 21 May 2007 ⟨http://cgi.ebay.com/MENS-TULIO-SWIM
WEAR-3-SM-MD-BLUE-GAY-JOCK-LAST-CHANCE_W0QQitemZ280117
432612QQihZ018QQcategoryZ15690QQssPageNameZWDVWQQrdZ1QQcmd
ZViewItem⟩.

99. fellowes1964, "MENS TURCO SWIMWEAR SM BLUE / GOLD GAY JOCK LAST
CHANCE," eBay, 21 May 2007 ⟨http://cgi.ebay.com/MENS-TURCO-SWIM
WEAR-SM-BLUE-GOLD-GAY-JOCK-LAST-CHANCE_W0QQitemZ280117
431717QQihZ018QQcategoryZ15690QQssPageNameZWDVWQQrdZ1QQcmd
ZViewItem⟩.

100. JpnSpeedoFan, "Re: Japanese Speedo SIZE MATTERS," Gay Speedos Fantasy
Board, 6 April 2006, 12 January 2011 ⟨http://speedoarchive.ctecomputer.com/
2006/April/00000406.htm⟩.

101. Potts, "The Essence of the Hard On," 94.

102. For a discussion of how flaccid and erect penises are associated with masculinity, see Dyer, "Don't Look Now," 72.

103. bj, "bj's gay porno-crazed ramblings," 10 December 2004, 22 November 2011 ⟨http://bjland.ws/weblog/2004_12_01_archive.html⟩.

104. avi, "ebay spandex bulge moment," ultranow, 14 December 2005, 12 January 2011 ⟨http://ultranow.typepad.com/ultranow/2005/12/ebay_spandex_bu.html #more⟩; avi, "do it yourself pornography," ultranow, 18 October 2005, 12 January 2011 ⟨http://ultranow.typepad.com/ultranow/2005/10/do_it_yourself_.html⟩.

105. ebulges, "Hot August 2007 Ebay Bulges," 1 August 2007, 12 January 2011 ⟨http://ebulges.com/2007summer1.htm⟩.

106. luckybiker07, "Some interesting information about male bulges," TheBulge Worshipper, 17 March 2007, 23 October 2008 ⟨http://thebulgeworshipper.blogspot.com/2007/03/some-interesting-information-about-male.html⟩.

107. For discussions of porn trading and the Internet, see, e.g., Lehman, "You and Voyeurweb"; and Slater, "Trading Sexpics on IRC."

108. fontal430, "eBay Feedback Profile for hrdmslguy," eBay, 23 March 2008 ⟨http://feedback.ebay.com/ws/eBayISAPI.dll?ViewFeedback2&userid=hrdmslguy&&ftab=FeedbackAsSeller&sspagename=VIP:feedback:3:us⟩; turnage2007, "eBay Feedback Profile for hrdmslguy," eBay, 24 May 2007 ⟨http://feedback.ebay.com/ws/eBayISAPI.dll?ViewFeedback2&ftab=FeedbackAsSeller&userid=hrdmslguy&iid=-1&de=off&items=25&page=2⟩.

109. bone735, "eBay Feedback Profile for mscljocko," eBay, 1 July 2007, 12 January 2011 ⟨http://feedback.ebay.com/ws/eBayISAPI.dll?ViewFeedback2&ftab=AllFeedback&userid=mscljocko&iid=-1&de=off&items=200&interval=0&mPg=8&page=4⟩.

110. i_gant_man, "eBay Feedback Profile for mscljocko," eBay, 31 May 2007, 12 January 2011 ⟨http://feedback.ebay.com/ws/eBayISAPI.dll?ViewFeedback2&ftab=AllFeedback&userid=mscljocko&iid=-1&de=off&items=200&interval=0&mPg=8&page=4⟩; dpjd7, "eBay Feedback Profile for mscljocko," eBay, 11 May 2007, 12 January 2011 ⟨http://feedback.ebay.com/ws/eBayISAPI.dll?ViewFeedback2&ftab=AllFeedback&userid=mscljocko&iid=-1&de=off&items=200&interval=0&mPg=8&page=5⟩.

111. Cohen, The Perfect Store, 276.

112. ebulges, "The Home of Big Ebulges," 12 January 2011 ⟨http://www.ebulges.com/⟩.

113. ebulges, "Ebulges from Ebay," 4 February 2007, 12 January 2011 ⟨http://www.vpl.bz/ebaybulges.htm⟩.

114. avi, "do it yourself pornography," ultranow, 18 October 2005, 12 January 2011 ⟨http://ultranow.typepad.com/ultranow/2005/10/do_it_yourself_.html⟩.

115. ebulges, "Jan 04 at Ebay," January 2004, 12 January 2011 ⟨http://www.ebulges.com/galleries/040130.htm⟩.

116. ebulges, "March 04 at Ebay," March 2004, 12 January 2011 ⟨http://www.ebulges
.com/galleries/040328a.htm⟩.

117. kirkieskorner, "Men's Micro-Bikini swimsuit custom made Gay Interest," eBay,
6 May 2007 ⟨http://cgi.ebay.com/ws/eBayISAPI.dll?ViewItem&item=22010966
6728⟩.

118. NYC swimmer, "Re: 1500 people enjoying this guy he must feel good," Gay
Speedos Fantasy Board, 14 April 2005, 12 January 2011 ⟨http://speedoarchive
.ctecomputer.com/2005/April/0000c260.htm⟩.

119. avi, "ultranow: law of physics defy ebay scowler," ultranow, 23 May 2006, 12
January 2011 ⟨http://ultranow.typepad.com/ultranow/2006/05/law_of_physics
_.html⟩.

120. avi, "ultranow: ebay seriously bitchy ebay critique," ultranow, 2 December 2005,
12 January 2011 ⟨http://ultranow.typepad.com/ultranow/2005/12/_seriously_
bitc.html⟩.

121. hrdmslguy, "MENS N2N 'SLINKY' WRESTLING SINGLET - GAY INTEREST," eBay,
22 April 2007 ⟨http://cgi.ebay.com/ws/eBayISAPI.dll?ViewItem&item=22010548
2976⟩; hrdmslguy, "MENS N2N SPANDEX WRESTLING SINGLET - GAY INTER-
EST," eBay, 17 May 2007 ⟨http://cgi.ebay.com/MENS-N2N-SPANDEX-WREST
LING-SINGLET-GAY-INTEREST_W0QQitemZ220113557625QQihZ012QQcate
goryZ79797QQssPageNameZWDVWQQrdZ1QQcmdZViewItem⟩.

122. hrdmslguy, "MENS N2N 'SLINKY' WRESTLING SINGLET - GAY INTEREST," eBay,
22 April 2007 ⟨http://cgi.ebay.com/ws/eBayISAPI.dll?ViewItem&item=22010548
2976⟩.

123. hrdmslguy, "NEW MENS BIKINI BRIEF WITH ENHANCE - GAY INTEREST,"
eBay, 24 May 2007 ⟨http://cgi.ebay.com/NEW-MENS-BIKINI-BRIEF-WITH-
ENHANCE-GAY-INTEREST_W0QQitemZ220115401428QQihZ012QQcategory
Z11509QQssPageNameZWDVWQQrdZ1QQcmdZViewItem⟩.

124. usflaboy, "New Size L C-In2 BoxerBriefs Underwear w Sling Support," eBay,
29 May 2007 ⟨http://cgi.ebay.com/New-Size-L-C-In2-BoxerBriefs-Underwear-
w-Sling-Support_W0QQitemZ220117143129QQihZ012QQcategoryZ11509QQ
ssPageNameZWDVWQQrdZ1QQcmdZViewItem⟩.

125. undermaster87, "Aussiebum Wonderjock Hip Brief Underwear (USA)," eBay,
2 July 2007 ⟨http://cgi.ebay.com/Aussiebum-Wonderjock-Hip-Brief-Under
wear-USA_W0QQItemZ190128330334QQihZ009QQcategoryZ11509QQssPage
NameZWDVWQQrdZ1QQcmdZViewItem⟩.

126. Byron, as quoted in Loe, "Fixing Broken Masculinity," 109.

127. undermaster87, "Aussiebum Wonderjock Hip Brief Underwear (USA)," eBay,
2 July 2007 ⟨http://cgi.ebay.com/Aussiebum-Wonderjock-Hip-Brief-Under
wear-USA_W0QQItemZ190128330334QQihZ009QQcategoryZ11509QQssPage
NameZWDVWQQrdZ1QQcmdZViewItem⟩.

128. Tiefer, "The Medicalization of Impotence," 372.

129. Potts, "The Essence of the Hard On," 91.

130. Miller, "A Short History of the Penis."

131. pelicancan, "Vintage Photo 2 Affectionate HANDSOME SCOUTS 1914 Gay I," eBay, 24 February 2005 ⟨http://cgi.ebay.com/ws/eBayISAPI.dll?ViewItem&cate gory=14279&item=6157723162&rd=1&ssPageName=WDVW⟩.

132. pisto4, "Karoll of Havana Cuba 1940s Gay Male Nude," eBay, 25 April 2004 ⟨http://cgi.ebay.com/ws/eBayISAPI.dll?ViewItem&category=1507&item=328932 0493&rd=1⟩.

133. endymian, "unique vtg photo male modeling gay int c.1960," eBay, 2 May 2004 ⟨http://cgi.ebay.com/ws/eBayISAPI.dll?ViewItem&category=128&item=3272885 976&tc=photo#ebayphotohosting⟩.

134. jonmcgarrah, "Vintage Nude Male Bodybuilder hand-tinted photo Gay Int: Sexy man holding long rod, bulge, Muscle men, Beefcake!" eBay, 17 May 2007 ⟨http://cgi.ebay.com/Vintage-Nude-Male-Bodybuilder-hand-tinted-photo- Gay-Int_W0QQitemZ120121372473QQihZ002QQcategoryZ66465QQrdZ1QQ cmdZViewItem⟩.

135. ziel400, "13 beefcake men present their STICKS GAY INT. 20s photo," eBay, 5 July 2007 ⟨http://cgi.ebay.com/13-beefcake-men-present-their-STICKS-GAY- INT-20s-photo_W0QQitemZ280131417392QQihZ018QQcategoryZ14279QQrd Z1QQcmdZViewItem⟩.

136. elephants_collector, "1940s near NUDE affectionate man 'big' pants PHOTO Gay," eBay, 30 June 2007 ⟨http://cgi.ebay.com/1940s-near-NUDE-affectionate- man-big-pants-PHOTO-Gay_W0QQitemZ280130043484QQihZ018QQcate goryZ1507QQrdZ1QQcmdZViewItem⟩.

137. 123elroubi, "SEXY BOYS ON THE BEACH ;)= 1935=VINTAGE GAY int," eBay, 1 July 2007 ⟨http://cgi.ebay.com/SEXY-BOYS-ON-THE-BEACH-1935-VINTA GE-GAY-int_W0QQitemZ320133112194QQihZ011QQcategoryZ14279QQrdZ1 QQcmdZViewItem⟩.

138. camp-classics, "Vintage Photo HANDSOME Football Player BULGE Gay Int," eBay, 1 July 2007 ⟨http://cgi.ebay.com/Vintage-Photo-HANDSOME-Football- Player-BULGE-Gay-Int_W0QQitemZ150138127970QQihZ005QQcategoryZ48 QQssPageNameZWDVWQQrdZ1QQcmdZViewItem⟩.

139. toomanyretro, "Psycho Woman & FiSh~Hot Man's BuLge/50's Photo Gay Int?" eBay, 4 July 2007 ⟨http://cgi.ebay.com/Psycho-Woman-FiSh-Hot-Mans-BuLge- 50s-Photo-Gay-Int_W0QQitemZ160134694587QQihZ006QQcategoryZ48QQ rdZ1QQcmdZViewItem⟩.

140. toomanyretro, "Hot MAN MOUSTACHE buLgE/cRotCh ShOT~Cabinet Photo\ gAy," eBay, 3 July 2007 ⟨http://cgi.ebay.com/Hot-MAN-MOUSTACHE-buLgE- cRotCh-ShOT-Cabinet-Photo-gAy_W0QQitemZ160134386959QQihZ006QQ categoryZ13705QQssPageNameZWDVWQQrdZ1QQcmdZViewItem⟩.

141. pelicancan, "VINTAGE PHOTO AFFECTIONATE MEN FIND LOVE IN 1913 GAY IN," eBay, 16 June 2007 ⟨http://cgi.ebay.com/ws/eBayISAPI.dll?ViewItem&item =180131261005⟩.

142. pelicancan, "VINTAGE PHOTO SEXY NEAR NUDE SAILORS FEEL CROTCHES GAY," eBay, 16 June 2007 ⟨http://cgi.ebay.com/ws/eBayISAPI.dll?ViewItem& item=180131261420⟩.

143. pelicancan, "VINTAGE PHOTO SEXY GAY GYM TEACHER HIDES SECRET 1914," eBay, 6 June 2007 ⟨http://cgi.ebay.com/ws/eBayISAPI.dll?ViewItem&item=1801 28154582⟩.

144. pelicancan, "Vintage Photo 2 Men Sitting Under Tree 1890 Gay Interes," eBay, 24 November 2004 ⟨http://cgi.ebay.com/ws/eBayISAPI.dll?ViewItem&item= 6134046298&fromMakeTrack=true⟩; pelicancan, "Vintage PHoto Near Nude Sailors Flex Butts On Beach Gay," eBay, 24 November 2004 ⟨http://cgi.ebay .com/ws/eBayISAPI.dll?ViewItem&category=48&item=6134046634&rd=1#ebay photohosting⟩.

145. queen-of-parts, "Help with Dating Football Player Photo Please in Category-Specific Boards in eBay Forums," eBay, 19 July 2006, 12 January 2011 ⟨http:// forums.ebay.com/db1/topic/Historical-Memorabilia/Help-With-Dating/100032 1336&#msg1005796075⟩.

146. raretomes, "Recent finds!....... Post yours here. in Category-Specific Boards in eBay Forums," eBay, 13 July 2008, 12 January 2011 ⟨http://forums.ebay.com/db2/ topic/Antiques/Recent-Finds-Post/1000707751?start=510&#msg1013775248⟩.

147. atukolm, "VIN PHOTO-ID'D -LIFTING SKIRTS at HOME...LESBIAN INT, lovers from Westbrook, Maine d. 1915," eBay, 13 February 2006 ⟨http://cgi.ebay.com/ VIN-PHOTO-IDD-LIFTING-SKIRTS-at-HOME-LESBIAN-INT_W0QQitemZ 6253802605QQcategoryZ14279QQrdZ1QQcmdZViewItem⟩.

148. camp-classics, "CAMP CLASSICS eBay Store About My Store," eBay, 6 July 2007 ⟨http://members.ebay.com/ws/eBayISAPI.dll?ViewUserPage&userid=camp-classics⟩.

149. gargantua, "1910s PHOTO! SeXY COWBOY COSTUME MAN CIGARETTE GUN! gay," eBay, 30 May 2004 ⟨http://cgi.ebay.com/ws/eBayISAPI.dll?ViewItem&cate gory=29484&item=3294961113&rd=1⟩.

150. speakswithmusic, "eBay View About Me for speakswithmusic," eBay, 12 January 2011 ⟨http://members.ebay.com/ws2/eBayISAPI.dll?ViewUserPage&userid= speakswithmusic⟩.

151. Clark, "Commodity Lesbianism," 187.

152. This closeting occurs in kashmier, "Old Photograph Semi Profile WOMAN in WHITE HAT Scarf," eBay, 11 February 2006 ⟨http://cgi.ebay.com/Old-Photo graph-Semi-Profile-WOMAN-in-WHITE-HAT-Scarf_W0QQitemZ625330 6264QQcategoryZ48QQrdZ1QQcmdZViewItem⟩.

153. danthemusicman, "10 Stickers Gay Lesbian Pride 1993 March on Washington," eBay, 2 July 2007 ⟨http://cgi.ebay.com/10-Stickers-Gay-Lesbian-Pride-1993-March-On-Washington_W0QQitemZ170127687560QQihZ007QQcategoryZ 14892QQrdZ1QQcmdZViewItem⟩.

154. endymian, "GAY INT CABINET CARD GREAT DRAG X DRESS GUY," eBay,

27 April 2004 ⟨http://cgi.ebay.com/ws/eBayISAPI.dll?ViewItem&category=1370
5&item=3289666107&rd=1⟩.

155. endymian, "eBay Store – stonewall endymian gay photo shop," eBay, 2 May
2004 ⟨http://stores.ebay.com/stonewallendymiangayphotoshop/pages/store-
policies⟩.

156. unclecrickey, "VINTAGE PHOTO GAY AMETEUR SEXY MAN IN WOODS COACH
SHORT," eBay, 8 July 2007 ⟨http://cgi.ebay.com/VINTAGE-PHOTO-GAY-
AMETEUR-SEXY-MAN-IN-WOODS-COACH-SHORT_W0QQitemZ1201
39988598QQihZ002QQcategoryZ14279QQrdZ1QQcmdZViewItem⟩.

157. rancherhamp, "2 8x10 studio PHOTOS of Tarzan Denny Miller GAY INT!!!!"
eBay, 12 May 2004 ⟨http://cgi.ebay.com/ws/eBayISAPI.dll?ViewItem&category
=48&item=3292317572⟩; bizzilizzit, "Cabinet Card of two gay and dandy men
weird props," eBay, 16 October 2004 ⟨http://cgi.ebay.com/ws/eBayISAPI.dll?
ViewItem&category=13705&item=6125129476&rd=1⟩.

158. Elsner and Cardinal, introduction to *The Cultures of Collecting*, 2.

159. gargantua, "eBay About Me View for gargantua," eBay, 14 July 2007 ⟨http://
members.ebay.com/ws/eBayISAPI.dll?ViewUserPage&userid=gargantua⟩. A
more detailed account of gargantua's representation as a gorilla appears at gargantua, "GargantuaPhotos.com – Vintage Photographs and Snapshots," 14 July
2007 ⟨http://www.gargantuaphotos.com/whatisthisplace.html⟩.

160. gargantua, "20s PHOTO! SHIRTS OFF & SEXY HUNTING MEN & RABBIT! Gay,"
eBay, 21 November 2004 ⟨http://cgi.ebay.com/ws/eBayISAPI.dll?ViewItem&cate
gory=14279&item=6133409494&rd=1⟩.

161. gargantua, "20s PHOTO! DRAG GANGSTER WOMEN LOVING LESBIAN MO-
MENT," eBay, 25 February 2007 ⟨http://cgi.ebay.com/ws/eBayISAPI.dll?View
Item&item=120091505851&fromMakeTrack=true⟩.

162. gargantua, "40s PHOTO! GARGANTUAN WOMAN TESTS WEIGHT LIMIT of
DOCK!" eBay, 8 July 2007 ⟨http://cgi.ebay.com/40s-PHOTO-GARGANTUAN-
WOMAN-TESTS-WEIGHT-LIMIT-of-DOCK_W0QQitemZ120140197680QQ
ihZ002QQcategoryZ14279QQrdZ1QQcmdZViewItem⟩.

163. magnumxl_wholesale, "100% Legal Synthetic Man Sex Pheromones For Gay
Men 25X: Free Shipping - Money Back Promise - See Our Comparison," eBay,
15 May 2007 ⟨http://cgi.ebay.com/100-Legal-Synthetic-Man-Sex-Pheromones-
For-Gay-Men-25X_W0QQitemZ110127666255QQihZ001QQcategoryZ36383
QQrdZ1QQcmdZViewItem⟩.

164. sx28, "Pair 6L6 GAY Vacuum tubes," eBay, 9 May 2007 ⟨http://cgi.ebay.com/
Pair-6L6-GAY-Vacuum-tubes_W0QQitemZ110125506589QQihZ001QQcate
goryZ58174QQrdZ1QQcmdZViewItem⟩.

165. Camille, "Editor's Introduction," 163.

166. Elsner and Cardinal, introduction to *The Cultures of Collecting*, 2.

167. Camille, "Editor's Introduction," 164.

5. eBay Boys Will Be Lesbians

1. lastcall75773, "1950's NUDE 6" X 8" REAL PHOT0 LESBIAN INTEREST- NR," eBay, 27 February 2007 ⟨http://cgi.ebay.com/1950s-NUDE-6-X-8-REAL-PHOT0-LESBIAN-INTEREST-NR_W0QQitemZ250089209293QQihZ015 QQcategoryZ1507QQrdZ1QQcmdZViewItem⟩.

2. photogurl, "Women HUGGING in the SNOW Lesbian Int *1930s* Photo," eBay, 22 February 2007 ⟨http://cgi.ebay.com/Women-HUGGING-in-the-SNOW-Lesbian-Int-1930s-Photo_W0QQitemZ150095115144QQihZ005QQcategoryZ 14279QQrdZ1QQcmdZViewItem⟩.

3. Mulvey, *Visual and Other Pleasures*.

4. White, *The Body and the Screen*.

5. Straayer, *Deviant Eyes, Deviant Bodies*.

6. Case, "Toward a Butch-Femme Aesthetic"; Solomon, "Not Just a Passing Fantasy."

7. Lewallen, "Lace," 99.

8. Smith, "'Baby's Picture Is Always Treasured,'" 198.

9. auntjennysbox, "eBay View About Me for auntjennysbox," eBay, 15 January 2011 ⟨http://members.ebay.com/ws/eBayISAPI.dll?ViewUserPage&userid=aunt jennysbox⟩.

10. jochen.baeuerle, "AFFECTIONATE NUDE GIRLS Vintage 10s RPPC Lesbian Int," eBay, 7 April 2006 ⟨http://cgi.ebay.com/AFFECTIONATE-NUDE-GIRLS-Vintage-10s-RPPC-Lesbian-Int _W0QqitemZ6270033445QQcategoryZ1507QQ rdZ1QQcmdZViewItem⟩. To some extent, this address to the photographer and viewer is an aspect of all photographs of people.

11. Becker et al., "Lesbians and Film," 37.

12. Williams, "Second Thoughts on *Hard Core*," 56.

13. fouraker, "Five Nude Girlfriends in the Backyard," eBay, 31 May 2004 ⟨http:// cgi.ebay.com/ws/eBayISAPI.dll?ViewItem&category=1507&item=3293441631& rd=1⟩.

14. antique_samblue, "9 NUDE Blonde Woman Lady Risque Photograph Photo c1940s," eBay, 23 March 2006 ⟨http://cgi.ebay.com/9-NUDE-Blonde-Woman-Lady-Risque-Photograph-Photo-c1940s_W0QQitemZ6265978690QQcategoryZ 1507QQrdZ1QQcmdZViewItem⟩.

15. elephants_collector, "1930s Stereoview Photo 4 NUDE Lesbian girls P-358 RARE!" eBay, 13 November 2005 ⟨http://cgi.ebay.com/1930s-Stereoview-Photo-4-NUDE-Lesbian-girls-P-358-RARE_W0QQitemZ6226566058QQcategoryZ 14279QQrdZ1QqcmdZViewItem⟩; swampman, "DUO OF LESBIAN GIRLS BUSTY SUPER REAR VIEW," eBay, 2 November 2005 ⟨http://collectibles.search-desc.ebay.com/lesbian_Photographic-Images_W0QQa43ZQ2d24QQa44ZQ 2d24QQa47ZQ2d24QQalistZa44Q2ca52Q2ca43Q2ca47Q2ca3801QQbsZSearch QQcatrefZC6QQcoactionZcompareQQcoentrypageZsearchQQcopagenum Z1QQfclZ3QQfgtpZQQfposZ95060QQfromZR2QQfsooZ1QQfsopZ1QQftrtZ

1QQftrvZ1QQftsZ2QQgcsZ16QQlopgZQQpf_queryZlesbianQQpfidZ17QQ
pfmodeZ1QQreqtypeZ2QQsacatZ14277QQsadisZ200QQsaprchiZQQsaprclo
ZQQsargnZQ2d1QQsaslcZ2QQsbrftogZ1QqsofocusZbs⟩.

16. nobodysa, "LOVELY RISQUE - BIEDERER 1930's - Lesbian interest," eBay, 28
    May 2006 ⟨http://cgi.ebay.com/ws/eBayISAPI.dll?ViewItem&item=6282992257
    &rd=1&sspagename=STRK%3AMEWA%3AIT&rd=1⟩.

17. pixidiom, "1940, GAY VINTAGE LESBIAN, GAL, KICK, SEXY, ASS, REAR-END
    FUN," eBay, 10 June 2006 ⟨http://cgi.ebay.com/1940-GAY-VINTAGE-LESBIAN-
    GAL-KICK-SEXY-ASS-REAR-END-FUN_W0QQitemZ6288086466QQihZ
    010QQcategoryZ14279QQssPageNameZWDVWQQrdZ1QQcmdZViewItem⟩.

18. mr.philipines, "1890 Philippine CDV Unusual Lesbian Girl MIGUEL REYES,"
    eBay, 6 November 2005 ⟨http://cgi.ebay.com/1890-Philippine-CDV-Unusual-
    Lesbian-Girl-MIGUEL-REYES_W0QQitemZ6224257584QQcategoryZ409QQ
    rdZ1QQcmdZViewItem#ebayphotohosting⟩.

19. rosie247, "Manitou Falls Old Photos Of Women Lesbian Interest," eBay, 14
    November 2005 ⟨http://cgi.ebay.com/Manitou-Falls-Old-Photos-Of-Women-
    Lesbian-Interest_W0QQitemZ6226857829QQcategoryZ14279QQrdZ1QqcmdZ
    ViewItem⟩.

20. thedragonsmoon, "VINTAGE RISQUE SEXY FETISH NUDE LESBIAN ART
    PHOTO," eBay, 30 May 2006 ⟨http://cgi.ebay.com/VINTAGE-RISQUE-SEXY-
    FETISH-NUDE-LESBIAN-ART-PHOTO_W0QQitemZ6284945433QQihZ010
    QQcategoryZ1507QQrdZ1QQcmdZViewItem⟩.

21. thedragonsmoon, "VINTAGE RISQUE 1918 LESBIAN DYKES at COLLEGE
    PHOTO," eBay, 25 May 2006 ⟨http://cgi.ebay.com/ws/eBayISAPI.dll?ViewItem
    &item=6283510900&rd=1&sspagename=STRK%3AMEWA%3AIT&rd=1⟩.

22. tomscoolcollectibles, "Vintage Two Nude Women Grooming Photo, Lesbian
    Interest," eBay, 4 April 2006 ⟨http://cgi.ebay.com/Vintage-Two-Nude-Women-
    Grooming-Photo-Lesbian-Interest_W0QQitemZ6269338167QQcategoryZ
    48QQrdZ1QQcmdZViewItem⟩.

23. Mulvey, *Visual and Other Pleasures*, 19.

24. Duncan, "The MoMA's Hot Mamas," 349.

25. Doane, *The Desire to Desire*, 2.

26. tomscoolcollectibles, "Vintage Two Nude Women Grooming Photo, Lesbian
    Interest," eBay, 4 April 2006 ⟨http://cgi.ebay.com/Vintage-Two-Nude-Women-
    Grooming-Photo-Lesbian-Interest_W0QQitemZ6269338167QQcategoryZ48
    QQrdZ1QQcmdZViewItem⟩.

27. douglasclemens, "eBay View About Me for douglasclemens," eBay, 27 November
    2011 ⟨http://members.ebay.com/ws/eBayISAPI.dll?ViewUserPage&userid=doug
    lasclemens⟩. For instance, he bought the following vintage erotic ephemera:
    revelation4, "RARE NUDE BOOK - NYMPH & NAIAD-EVERARD," eBay, 22 April
    2006 ⟨http://cgi.ebay.com/ws/eBayISAPI.dll?ViewItem&category=616&item
    =7025439164⟩.

28. pannan1120, "HAIR DO, 2 NUDES=LESBIAN? REAL PHOTO 50'S NICE NO RESEV," eBay, 18 December 2007 ⟨http://cgi.ebay.com/ws/eBayISAPI.dll?View Item&item=250199014597⟩.

29. cash5al, "cash5al vintage postcard and photo eBay Store About My Store," eBay, 15 January 2011 ⟨http://members.ebay.com/ws/eBayISAPI.dll?ViewUserPage& userid=cash5al⟩.

30. herrlast, "eBay View About Me for herrlast," eBay, 15 January 2011 ⟨http://mem bers.ebay.com/ws/eBayISAPI.dll?ViewUserPage&userid=herrlast⟩.

31. darrins, "Vintage Lesbian Int Photo Pretty Pin Up Girls Outside," eBay, 25 October 2007 ⟨http://cgi.ebay.com/Vintage-Lesbian-Int-Photo-Pretty-Pin-Up-Girls-Outside_W0QQitemZ140172458965QQihZ004QQcategoryZ48QQssPageName ZWDVWQQrdZ1QQcmdZViewItem⟩; darrins, "Darrins Photoclique eBay Store About My Store," eBay, 10 August 2007 ⟨http://members.ebay.com/ws/ eBayISAPI.dll?ViewUserPage&userid=darrins⟩.

32. Duncan, "The MoMA's Hot Mamas," 355.

33. Hollinger, "Theorizing Mainstream Female Spectatorship," 12.

34. Camille, "Editor's Introduction," 164.

35. Joyrich, Re-viewing Reception, 63.

36. swampman, "DUO OF BUSTY NUDE LESBIAN GIRLS TIE ME UP," eBay, 5 November 2005 ⟨http://cgi.ebay.com/DUO-OF-BUSTY-NUDE-LESBIAN-GIRLS-TIE-ME-UP_W0QQitemZ6223792766QQcategoryZ1507QQrdZ1QqcmdZView Item⟩.

37. Metz, The Imaginary Signifier.

38. Bolter, Writing Space, 227.

39. Kaplan, "Is the Gaze Male?"

40. Straayer, Deviant Eyes, Deviant Bodies, 3.

41. Ibid.

42. Stephens, "Looking-Class Heroes," 278.

43. Mabel Maney, as quoted in Harris and Crocker, "Mysteries, Mothers, and Cops," 78.

44. Nestle, "Flamboyance and Fortitude," 14.

45. Solomon, "Not Just a Passing Fantasy," 264, 273.

46. Currie, "'Here Comes the Bride'"; Otnes and Pleck, Cinderella Dreams.

47. **jlp**, "Cross-Dressing Women Hold MOCK WEDDING c. 1935 PHOTO," eBay, 22 December 2008 ⟨http://cgi.ebay.com/ws/eBayISAPI.dll?ViewItem&item =130277331578⟩.

48. Sobal et al., "Weight and Weddings," 113.

49. joycemorish, "RPPC Crossdressing Women Mock Wedding Lesbian Interest," eBay, 23 February 2009 ⟨http://cgi.ebay.com/RPPC-Crossdressing-Women-Mock-Wedding-Lesbian-Interest_W0QQitemZ270169485310QQihZ017QQ categoryZ29484QQssPageNameZWDVWQQrdZ1QQcmdZViewItem⟩.

50. bb1913, "!938 PHOTO ALL WOMEN MOCK WEDDING PRENTICE CHICAGO,"

eBay, 23 February 2009 ⟨http://cgi.ebay.com/938-Photo-All-Women-Mock-Wedding-Prentice-Chicago_WoQQitemZ370134261035QQihZ024QQcategoryZ29483QQssPageNameZWD1VQQrdZ1QQcmdZViewItemQQ_trksidZp1638Q2em118Q2el1247⟩.

51. dv33, "Vintage 1920's photo / Funny Girlfriends Mock Wedding," eBay, 30 January 2009 ⟨http://cgi.ebay.in/ws/eBayISAPI.dll?ViewItem&item=290292827079⟩.

52. Elizabeth Lapovsky Kennedy and Madeline Davis, who provide an important history of butch and femme identities in the 1940s and 1950s, have disagreed with Case's theory of butch camp and argued that "the lesbian community had no parallel to the camp culture that developed around queens in male homosexual communities, despite the fact that butch identity was constructed around being masculine but not male, and was therefore based in artifice. Although all butches can be said to be in drag, few butches performed as male impersonators. . . . No cultural aesthetic seems to have developed around male impersonation. Furthermore, camp humor and camp performers were not central to the lesbian community of this period." Nevertheless, Lisa E. Davis describes butch drag and camp as part of the lesbian community and indicates how these performances were incorporated into clubs in New York City during the same period. Davis, "The Butch as Drag Artiste"; Kennedy and Davis, *Boots of Leather, Slippers of Gold*; Kennedy and Davis, "'They Was No One to Mess With,'" 75.

53. Case, "Toward a Butch-Femme Aesthetic," 298.

54. Barthes, *Camera Lucida*, 12.

55. Bergman, introduction to *Camp Grounds*, 6.

56. pixidiom, "1915, VINTAGE ORIGINAL PHOTO, LESBIAN WEDDING CEREMONY," eBay, 9 May 2006 ⟨http://cgi.ebay.com/ws/eBayISAPI.dll?ViewItem&item=6278982256&fromMakeTrack=true⟩.

57. Riviere, "Womanliness as Masquerade."

58. Case, "Toward a Butch-Femme Aesthetic," 300. There have also been critical debates about whether butch and femme are performances, masquerades, roles, or identities. For Nestle, a friend's "butch self was not a masquerade of a gender cliché, but her final and fullest expression of herself." These debates engage larger disagreements over whether people exist as stable identities or, as suggested by some contemporary forms of feminism, postmodernism, and my arguments in this chapter, identity is always culturally constructed and regulated. Nestle, "Flamboyance and Fortitude," 20.

59. mosonz, "Vintage Photo Women in Drag Pipes, Canes Lesbian Int," eBay, 14 May 2006 ⟨http://cgi.ebay.com/Vintage-Photo-Women-in-Drag-Pipes-Canes-Lesbian-Int_WQQitemZ6278716747QQcategoryZ14279QQcmdZViewItem⟩.

60. dv33, "Vintage 1920's photo / Funny Girlfriends Mock Wedding," eBay, 30 January 2009 ⟨http://cgi.ebay.in/ws/eBayISAPI.dll?ViewItem&item=290292827079⟩.

61. Babuscio, "Camp and Gay Sensibility," 24.

62. Fausto-Sterling, *Sexing the Body*; Kessler and McKenna, *Gender.*

63. Gerson, "'There Is No Sex without Gender,'" 180.

64. Butler, *Gender Trouble*, 129.

65. houseofmirth, "BUTCH WOMEN in DRAG 1910s VINTAGE PHOTO PAGE Lesbian," eBay, 15 May 2006 〈http://cgi.ebay.com/ws/eBayISAPI.dll?ViewItem& item=6280609711&rd=1&sspagename=STRK%3AMEWA%3AIT&rd=1〉.

66. Halberstam, *Female Masculinity*, 1.

67. Butler, *Gender Trouble*, 137.

68. Solomon, "Not Just a Passing Fantasy," 264, 273.

69. Case, "Toward a Butch-Femme Aesthetic"; Harris and Crocker, "An Introduction to Sustaining Femme Gender."

70. darrins, "Vintage Photo Two Girls w/ Butch Haircuts 075553," eBay, 13 May 2006 〈http://cgi.ebay.com/Vintage-Photo-Two-Girls-w-Butch-Haircuts-075553_WoQQitemZ6191886595QQcategoryZ14279QQrdZ1QQcmdZViewItem〉.

71. surpapier, "MAN/WOMAN CROSSDRESSER GAY INTEREST! MANCHESTER ENGLAND," eBay, 23 February 2007 〈http://cgi.ebay.com/ws/eBayISAPI.dll?ViewItem&item=260086713601&ssPageName=MERCOSI_VI_ROSI_PR4_PCN_BIX_Stores&refitem=110080532074&itemcount=4&refwidgetloc=closed_view_item&refwidgettype=osi_widget〉.

72. slingwing, "RPPC- Cross Dressing Women Looking Like Men, c1910," eBay, 9 March 2007 〈http://cgi.ebay.com/ws/eBayISAPI.dll?ViewItem&item=120096094169&fromMakeTrack=true〉.

73. klchance, "Vintage Photo / Gender Bender / Lesbian & Gay Interest," eBay, 19 February 2008 〈http://cgi.ebay.com/ws/eBayISAPI.dll?ViewItem&rd=1&item=280202315906&ssPageName=STRK:MEWA:IT&ih=018〉.

74. hooks_lady, "Interesting TT Portrait Great Detail-- Lady or Man?" eBay, 23 February 2008 〈http://cgi.ebay.com/ws/eBayISAPI.dll?ViewItem&rd=1&item=200202533538&ssPageName=STRK:MEWA:IT&ih=010〉.

75. photoguyred, "Lesbian Antique Real Photograph Kissing," eBay, 19 March 2006 〈http://cgi.ebay.com/Lesbian-Antique-Real-Photograph-Kissing_WoQQitemZ6264607552QQcategoryZ14279QQrdZ1QQcmdZViewItem〉.

76. darrins, "Vintage Lesbian Int Photo Woman as Man 088374," eBay, 23 March 2007 〈http://cgi.ebay.com/Vintage-Lesbian-Int-Photo-Woman-as-Man-088374_WoQQitemZ6215299387QQcategoryZ14279QQrdZ1QQcmdZViewItem〉.

77. thewritersden, "EDWARDIAN LADIES DRESSED AS MEN LESBIAN INT OLD PHOTO," eBay, 23 March 2007 〈http://cgi.ebay.com/EDWARDIAN-LADIES-DRESSED-AS-MEN-LESBIAN-INT-OLD-PHOTO_WoQQitemZ230097992366QQcategoryZ14279QQrdZ1QQcmdZViewItem〉.

78. Fausto-Sterling, *Sexing the Body*; Martin, *The Woman in the Body.*

6. Re-collecting Black Americana

1. writer_art, "ADORABLE CAST IRON BLACK AMERICANA BANK," eBay, 15 November 2007 ⟨http://cgi.ebay.com/ADORABLE-CAST-IRON-BLACK-AMERICANA-BANK_W0QQitemZ180180902929QQihZ008QQcategoryZ 35795QQssPageNameZWDVWQQrdZ1QQcmdZViewItem⟩.

2. smitherama, "VERY RARE LITTLE BLACK BABY." eBay, 13 November 2007 ⟨http://cgi.ebay.com/VERY-RARE-LITTLE-BLACK-BABY_W0QQitemZ 260182398218QQihZ016QQcategoryZ29458QQssPageNameZWDVWQQ rdZ1QQcmdZViewItem⟩.

3. eBay, "eBay – Collectibles, Decorative Collectibles and Militaria items on eBay .com," 20 January 2011 ⟨http://collectibles.shop.ebay.com/⟩.

4. eBay, "indian painting items – Get great deals on Indian bust, Ethnic items on eBay.com," 20 January 2011 ⟨http://collectibles.shop.ebay.com/Cultures-Ethnicities-/36079/i.html?_catref=1&_trksid=p3910.co.m449⟩.

5. bigbobbie, "BLACK AMERICANA FIGURE FREEMAN MCFARLIN MINIATURE," eBay, 3 February 2007 ⟨http://cgi.ebay.com/BLACK-AMERICANA-FIGURE-FREEMAN-MCFARLIN-MINIATURE_W0QQitemZ190078880059QQihZ 009QQcategoryZ29458QQrdZ1QQcmdZViewItem⟩.

6. eBay, "collectible black Americana items – Get great deals on black collectible, black memorabilia items on eBay.com!" 20 January 2011 ⟨http://collectibles .shop.ebay.com/Black-Americana-/29457/i.html?_catref=1&_trksid=p3910 .co.m449⟩.

7. elegantharlot, "eBay Guides – HAND-PAINTING BLACK AND AFRICAN AMERI-CAN CERAMICS," eBay, 23 October 2010, 20 January 2011 ⟨http://reviews.ebay .com/HAND-PAINTING-BLACK-AND-AFRICAN-AMERICAN-CERAMICS_ W0QQugidZ10000000000021904?ssPageName=BUYGD:CAT:-1:LISTINGS:33⟩.

8. sandik, "Picking Cotton Near Vicksburg MS Mississippi PC," eBay, 1 August 2006 ⟨http://cgi.ebay.com/Picking-Cotton-Near-Vicksburg-MS-Mississippi-PC_W0QQitemZ120015812864QQihZ002QQcategoryZ36081QQrdZ1QQcmdZ ViewItem⟩.

9. elegantharlot, "eBay Guides – HAND-PAINTING BLACK AND AFRICAN AMERI-CAN CERAMICS," eBay, 23 October 2010, 20 January 2011 ⟨http://reviews.ebay .com/HAND-PAINTING-BLACK-AND-AFRICAN-AMERICAN-CERAMICS_ W0QQugidZ10000000000021904?ssPageName=BUYGD:CAT:-1:LISTINGS:33⟩.

10. Pilgrim, "The Garbage Man."

11. Baker et al., "From Despicable to Collectible"; Dean, "Boys and Girls and 'Boys'"; Goings, *Mammy and Uncle Mose*; Kern-Foxworth, *Aunt Jemima, Uncle Ben, and Rastus*; Turner, *Ceramic Uncles and Celluloid Mammies*.

12. Castille, "The Commodification of Indian Identity"; Collins, *Black Feminist Thought*; Elliott, "Postcolonial Experience in a Domestic Context"; Gray, "Black

Masculinity and Visual Culture"; Hale, *Making Whiteness*; Ruggeri, "Not for Sale."

13. Allison, "Portable Monsters and Commodity Cuteness"; Kinsella, "Cuties in Japan"; Ngai, "The Cuteness of the Avant-garde."

14. For African American collectors of black Americana, buying these items can provide ways to document the past, own and rework denigrating representations, and keep such items out of the hands of white collectors who may view them quite differently. White collectors are sometimes discouraged from buying objects at black Americana shows and other events. For a discussion of the different racial engagements in collecting and readings of these objects, see Motley et al., "Exploring Collective Memories Associated with African-American Advertising Memorabilia."

15. eBay, "Offensive Material Policy," 27 February 2009 ⟨http://pages.ebay.com/help/policies/offensive.html⟩.

16. Ibid. eBay does allow "German coins and postage stamps (canceled or otherwise) from the WWII era regardless of markings."

17. Keith Regan, "Yahoo Wins New Hearing in Nazi Memorabilia Case," *E-Commerce Times*, 11 February 2005, 20 January 2011 ⟨http://www.ecommercetimes.com/story/40555.html?wlc=1295585216⟩; Reuters, "Court Rules against Yahoo in Nazi Speech Case," *Computerworld*, 12 January 2006, 20 January 2011 ⟨http://www.computerworld.com/s/article/107690/Court_rules_against_Yahoo_in_Nazi_speech_case?taxonomyId=071⟩; Tom Tugend, "'Nazi' Auctions Banned," *Jewish Chronicle*, 11 May 2001, 20 January 2011 ⟨http://www.fpp.co.uk/online/01/05/JChron180501b.html⟩.

18. fayes_southern_memories, "Chill'en HeresUrMammy! Black Americana Mammy Headvase," eBay, 5 February 2007 ⟨http://cgi.ebay.com/Chillen-HeresUrMammy-Black-Americana-Mammy-Headvase_W0QQitemZ140083013352QQihZ004QQcategoryZ394QQrdZ1QQcmdZViewItem⟩.

19. Images of white hands appear in deborah-rich, "Vintage BLACKAMOOR Belt/DressMetal SEW Vintage Clothing," eBay, 19 November 2007 ⟨http://cgi.ebay.com/Vintage-BLACKAMOOR-Belt-DressMetal-SEW-Vintage-Clothing_W0QQitemZ290183747370QQihZ019QQcategoryZ29458QQssPageNameZWDVWQQrdZ1QQcmdZViewItem⟩; forchicky, "Black Americana Chicken Inn Large Cup & Saucer," eBay, 23 December 2007 ⟨http://cgi.ebay.com/Black-Americana-Chicken-Inn-Large-Cup-Saucer_W0QQitemZ370008386614QQihZ024QQcategoryZ394QQssPageNameZWDVWQQrdZ1QQcmdZViewItem⟩; oldwest, "Iron Negro Black Face Man Red Bowtie Bottle Opener CUTE," eBay, 17 November 2007 ⟨http://cgi.ebay.com/Iron-Negro-Black-Face-Man-Red-Bowtie-Bottle-Opener-CUTE_W0QQitemZ140180443917QQihZ004QQcategoryZ394QQssPageNameZWDVWQQrdZ1QQcmdZViewItem⟩.

20. Sellers who deploy self-portraits include dandgtins! "eBay View About Me for

dandgtins!" eBay, 21 November 2007 ⟨http://members.ebay.com/ws/eBayISAPI
.dll?ViewUserPage&userid=dandgtins%21⟩; debraleesales, "eBay Store About
My Store for debraleesales," eBay, 8 December 2011 ⟨http://members.ebay.com/
ws/eBayISAPI.dll?ViewUserPage&userid=debraleesales⟩; equineapha, "eBay
View About Me for equineapha," eBay, 8 December 2011 ⟨http://members.ebay
.com/ws/eBayISAPI.dll?ViewUserPage&userid=equineapha⟩; lilbit25, "eBay
View About Me for lilbit25," eBay, 8 December 2011 ⟨http://members.ebay.com/
ws/eBayISAPI.dll?ViewUserPage&userid=lilbit25⟩.

21. cajunokie, "MAMMY MAGNETS and MORE eBay Store About My Store," eBay,
    20 January 2011 ⟨http://members.ebay.com/ws/eBayISAPI.dll?ViewUserPage&
    userid=cajunokie⟩.

22. Davis, "The Commodification of Self," 46.

23. Castille, "The Commodification of Indian Identity," 743.

24. Ruggeri, "Not for Sale."

25. Gray, "Black Masculinity and Visual Culture," 403.

26. Collins, "New Commodities, New Consumers," 298.

27. enghousea, "Old Milk Bottle. Molded glass w/ baby,negro, mammy face," eBay,
    4 February 2007 ⟨http://cgi.ebay.com/Old-Milk-Bottle-Molded-glass-w-baby-
    negro-mammy-face_W0QQitemZ160081989308QQihZ006QQcategoryZ35664
    QQrdZ1QQcmdZViewItem⟩.

28. jayhawkks, "Black Americana book $2005 Mammy Lawn Jockey Negro MORE,"
    eBay, 4 July 2006 ⟨http://cgi.ebay.com/Black-Americana-book-2005-Mammy-
    Lawn-Jockey-Negro-MORE_W0QQitemZ330004371834QQihZ014QQcategoryZ
    394QQrdZ1QQcmdZViewItem⟩.

29. tntiquer, "Cast Iron Pickaninny Mammy Potholder Hanger," eBay, 6 February
    2007 ⟨http://cgi.ebay.com/Cast-Iron-Pickaninny-Mammy-Potholder-Hanger_
    W0QQitemZ300078857046QQihZ020QQcategoryZ29459QQrdZ1QQcmdZ
    ViewItem⟩; cecil53, "NEGRO MAMMY COOK CHECKED APRON BANK CAST
    IRON," eBay, 4 February 2007 ⟨http://cgi.ebay.com/NEGRO-MAMMY-COOK-
    CHECKED-APRON-BANK-CAST-IRON_W0QQitemZ280078917220QQihZ
    018QQcategoryZ394QQrdZ1QQcmdZViewItem⟩.

30. Berlin, "American Slavery in History and Memory and the Search for Social Jus-
    tice," 1251.

31. For critical discussions of the concept of the mammy, see Bogle, *Toms, Coons,
    Mulattoes, Mammies, and Bucks*; Morgan, "Mammy the Huckster"; and St. John,
    "'It Ain't Fittin'.'"

32. zannejoshua, "MAMMY'S IN THE KITCHEN TEA TOWEL," eBay, 2 January 2007
    ⟨http://cgi.ebay.com/MAMMYS-IN-THE-KITCHEN-TEA-TOWEL_W0QQ
    itemZ190079164794QQihZ009QQcategoryZ29459QQrdZ1QQcmdZViewItem⟩;
    oldwest, "Old Black MAMMY Nursing Baby Wet Nurse Crystal Ashtray," eBay,
    3 February 2007 ⟨http://cgi.ebay.com/Old-Black-MAMMY-Nursing-Baby-Wet-
    Nurse-Crystal-Ashtray_W0QQitemZ140082224247QQihZ004QQcategoryZ394

QQrdZ1QQcmdZViewItem⟩; suanreed, "Aunt Jemima Black Americana
Mammy Cookie Bisquit Jar," eBay, 4 February 2007 ⟨http://cgi.ebay.com/Aunt-
Jemima-Black-Americana-Mammy-Cookie-Bisquit-Jar_W0QQitemZ2000762
40133QQihZ010QQcategoryZ29459QQrdZ1QQcmdZViewItem⟩.

33. Turner, *Ceramic Uncles and Celluloid Mammies*, 10.
34. kimberlypink60, "Vintage menu Black Americana Negrobilia Colorado," eBay,
16 December 2006 ⟨http://cgi.ebay.com/Vintage-menu-Black-Americana-
Negrobilia-Colorado_W0QQitemZ190063702655QQihZ009QQcategoryZ
394QQrdZ1QQcmdZViewItem⟩.
35. Kern-Foxworth, *Aunt Jemima, Uncle Ben, and Rastus*, 3.
36. Desrochers, "Slave-for-Sale Advertisements and Slavery in Massachusetts."
37. During spectacle lynchings, trains were scheduled to bring viewers to advertised
events, and large numbers of people attended. For a discussion of these events,
see Hale, *Making Whiteness*.
38. Eric Lott, in *Love and Theft*, describes the important ways minstrelsy shows
were deployed to consider class issues in the Northern parts of the United
States.
39. McPherson, *Reconstructing Dixie*.
40. Stirling Properties, "University Club Plantation – Welcome," 20 January 2011
⟨http://universityclub.stirlingprop.com/home_new.html⟩.
41. I thank Allison Truitt for providing this throw of a seated African American
woman, Zeus Mardi Gras Parade, Metairie, La., 6 January 2007.
42. Collins, *Black Feminist Thought*, 67.
43. David Redmon, *Mardi Gras: Made in China*, documentary (Calley Media,
Brooklyn, N.Y., 2005).
44. For critical considerations of Mardi Gras, see Gotham, "Marketing Mardi Gras";
Lipsitz, "Mardi Gras Indians"; and Venman, "Boundary Face-Off."
45. Roach, "Carnival and the Law in New Orleans"; Venman, "Boundary Face-Off."
46. Baker et al., "From Despicable to Collectible," 40.
47. Jerry Adler and Frank S. Washington, "Cookie Jars of Oppression: Shades of Jim
Crow Make It Big as Collectibles," *Newsweek*, 16 May 1988, 75.
48. Goings, *Mammy and Uncle Mose*, 89.
49. Turner, *Ceramic Uncles and Celluloid Mammies*, 5.
50. 8800anita, "Black Americana Mose's Bank, Early 20th Century,Perfect," eBay,
17 December 2006 ⟨http://cgi.ebay.com/Black-Americana-Moses-Bank-Early-
20th-Century-Perfect_W0QQitemZ130060527924QQihZ003QQcategoryZ
35795QQrdZ1QQcmdZViewItem⟩.
51. Elliott, "Postcolonial Experience in a Domestic Context," 190.
52. Adler and Washington, "Cookie Jars of Oppression," 75.
53. Kern-Foxworth, *Aunt Jemima, Uncle Ben, and Rastus*, xii.
54. Bond, introduction to *Black Americana Price Guide*.
55. Benjamin, "The Work of Art in the Age of Mechanical Reproduction."

56. Adler and Washington, "Cookie Jars of Oppression"; Kern-Foxworth, *Aunt Jemima, Uncle Ben, and Rastus.*

57. creeksideprimitives, "Primitive Vintage-Style ~BLACK AMERICANA~ GAME-BOARD: Uniquely Designed FULL-SIZED GAMEBOARD, from CREEKSIDE!" eBay, 29 July 2006 ⟨http://cgi.ebay.com/Primitive-Vintage-Style-BLACK-AMERICANA-GAMEBOARD_W0QQitemZ140013349907QQihZ004QQcate goryZ35800QQrdZ1QQcmdZViewItem⟩.

58. creeksideprimitives, "eBay View About Me for creeksideprimitives," eBay, 5 August 2006 ⟨http://members.ebay.com/ws/eBayISAPI.dll?ViewUserPage&userid =creeksideprimitives⟩.

59. nowarkedd, "Nostalgic cast-iron bottle-opener of Black minstrel," eBay, 2 July 2006 ⟨http://cgi.ebay.com/Nostalgic-cast-iron-bottle-opener-of-Black-min strel_W0QQitemZ270004116473QQihZ017QQcategoryZ29459QQrdZ1QQ cmdZViewItem⟩.

60. wham2001, "~OLD BLACK MEMORABILIA SALT AND PEPPER SHAKER SET ~OLD!~" eBay, 28 August 2006 ⟨http://cgi.ebay.com/OLD-BLACK-MEMORA BILIA-SALT-AND-PEPPER-SHAKER-SET-OLD_W0QQitemZ160024370287 QQihZ006QQcategoryZ29459QQrdZ1QQcmdZViewItem⟩.

61. Goings, *Mammy and Uncle Mose,* xiii.

62. newsquarepa, "Book Corky's Pet Parade 1946 By Maggi Fiedler," eBay, 1 September 2006 ⟨http://cgi.ebay.com/Book-Corkys-Pet-Parade-1946-By-Maggi-Fiedler_W0QQitemZ290025351402QQihZ019QQcategoryZ279QQrdZ1QQ cmdZViewItem⟩.

63. Formanek-Brunell, *Made to Play House*; Jenkins, *The Children's Culture Reader.*

64. Hale, *Making Whiteness.*

65. Manring, *Slave in a Box.*

66. George Fitzhugh, as quoted in Yetman, "The Background of the Slave Narrative Collection," 536.

67. Collins, *Black Feminist Thought.*

68. Doane, *The Desire to Desire*; Mulvey, *Visual and Other Pleasures.*

69. mollyester, "Vintage Palm Tree Black Demi Nude Handle Beer Mug Stein," eBay, 28 July 2006 ⟨http://cgi.ebay.com/Vintage-Palm-Tree-Black-Demi-Nude-Handle-Beer-Mug-Stein_W0QQitemZ320011722548QQihZ011QQcategoryZ 29459QQrdZ1QQcmdZViewItem⟩.

70. For a discussion of how black women's bodies are objectified, see Gilman, "Black Bodies, White Bodies."

71. hooks, *Ain't I a Woman.*

72. Goings, *Mammy and Uncle Mose,* xxi.

73. oddpilott, "LARGE SALTY & PEPPY SHAKERS," eBay, 1 September 2006 ⟨http:// cgi.ebay.com/LARGE-SALTY-PEPPY-SHAKERS_W0QQitemZ190026982770 QQihZ009QQcategoryZ29459QQrdZ1QQcmdZViewItem⟩.

74. ruthlesspromotions, "Vintage Collectible Black American Mammy Dolls Set

of 3," eBay, 15 December 2006 ⟨http://cgi.ebay.com/Vintage-Collectible-Black-American-Mammy-Dolls-Set-of-3_WoQQitemZ260065831168QQihZ016QQ categoryZ29459QQssPageNameZWDVWQQrdZ1QQcmdZViewItem⟩.

75. brewersgeneralstor, "BLACK BAKERY CHEF COOKIE JAR BLACK AMERICANA ADORABLE," eBay, 3 September 2006 ⟨http://cgi.ebay.com/BLACK-BAKERY-CHEF-COOKIE-JAR-BLACK-AMERICANA-ADORABLE_WoQQitemZ 130023582375QQihZ003QQcategoryZ29459QQrdZ1QQcmdZViewItem⟩.

76. ggterps, "Old Black baby on chamber pot bank or ash collector," eBay, 3 August 2006 ⟨http://cgi.ebay.com/Old-Black-baby-on-chamber-pot-bank-or-ash-collector_WoQQitemZ230014982588QQihZ013QQcategoryZ886QQrdZ1QQ cmdZViewItem⟩.

77. Goings, *Mammy and Uncle Mose*, 14.

78. mr.haneys.truck, "CHALKWARE POT HOLDER,,W/ VINTAGE HOLDERS, GREAT!!!" eBay, 15 November 2007 ⟨http://cgi.ebay.com/CHALKWARE-POT-HOLDER-W-VINTAGE-HOLDERS-GREAT_WoQQitemZ220172766266QQ ihZ012QQcategoryZ394QQssPageNameZWDVWQQrdZ1QQcmdZViewItem⟩.

79. oldwest, "CAST IRON Black MAMMY Bell Aunt Jemima VERY LOUD," eBay, 15 June 2006 ⟨http://cgi.ebay.com/CAST-IRON-Black-MAMMY-Bell-Aunt-Jemima-VERY-LOUD_WoQQitemZ7775351331QQihZ018QQcategoryZ394 QQrdZ1QQcmdZViewItem⟩.

80. countrygal70, "Very Old New Orleans Black Souvenir Doll MUST SEE," eBay, 17 December 2006 ⟨http://cgi.ebay.com/Very-Old-New-Orleans-Black-Souvenir-Doll-MUST-SEE_WoQQitemZ170062243330QQihZ007QQcategoryZ35797QQ ssPageNameZWDVWQQrdZ1QQcmdZViewItem⟩.

81. Dean, "Boys and Girls and 'Boys,'" 18.

82. Goings, *Mammy and Uncle Mose*, 13.

83. ratsden43, "VINTAGE BLACK AMERICANA MAMMY CLOTH DOLL," eBay, 15 June 2006 ⟨http://cgi.ebay.com/VINTAGE-BLACK-AMERICANA-MAMMY-CLOTH-DOLL_WoQQitemZ7775493868QQihZ018QQcategoryZ35797QQrd Z1QQcmdZViewItem⟩.

84. surfbunnyanne, "Vintage 50s Black Americana African Native Ashtrays," eBay, 3 September 2006 ⟨http://cgi.ebay.com/Vintage-50s-Black-Americana-African-Native-Ashtrays_WoQQitemZ290025974098QQihZ019QQcategoryZ29459QQ rdZ1QQcmdZViewItem⟩.

85. Ngai, "The Cuteness of the Avant-garde," 814.

86. Kinsella, "Minstrelized Girls," 70.

87. Kinsella, "Cuties in Japan," 226.

88. Allison, "Portable Monsters and Commodity Cuteness," 387.

89. shopperoasis, "Black Americana Uncle Leroy Licorice Drops Medicine Tin," eBay, 2 September 2006 ⟨http://cgi.ebay.com/Black-Americana-Uncle-Leroy-Licorice-Drops-Medicine-Tin_WoQQitemZ330024463854QQihZ014QQcate goryZ29459QQrdZ1QQcmdZViewItem⟩.

90. Ngai, "The Cuteness of the Avant-garde," 815.

91. shopperoasis, "Black Americana Hit Me Hard Carnival Toss Target Game," eBay, 12 December 2006 ⟨http://cgi.ebay.com/Black-Americana-Hit-Me-Hard-Carnival-Toss-Target-Game_W0QQitemZ330062381592QQihZ014QQcategoryZ 394QQssPageNameZWDVWQQrdZ1QQcmdZViewItem⟩.

92. Ngai, "The Cuteness of the Avant-garde," 816.

93. thesecondchef, "black americana CAST IRON BANK smiley face bank CUTE," eBay, 16 July 2006 ⟨http://cgi.ebay.com/black-americana-CAST-IRON-BANK-smiley-face-bank-CUTE_W0QQitemZ260009148773QQihZ016QQcategoryZ 394QQrdZ1QQcmdZViewItem⟩.

94. Kinsella, "Cuties in Japan," 236.

95. aaune, "Negative/Neutral Feedback received by whiterabbitonmain," Toolhaus .org, 6 April 2006, 20 January 2011 ⟨http://www.toolhaus.org/cgi-bin/negs?User =whiterabbitonmain&Dirn=Received+by⟩. African Americans were equated with raccoons, or coons, because the same hunting dogs were used to track raccoons and runaway slaves during the antebellum period.

96. Pilgrim, "The Garbage Man."

97. aaahmazing, "Black Sambo Disney Daffy BANNED CENSORED CRAZY CAR-TOONS," eBay, 30 June 2006 ⟨http://cgi.ebay.com/Black-Sambo-Disney-Daffy-BANNED-CENSORED-CRAZY-CARTOONS_W0QQitemZ160004899908QQ ihZ006QQcategoryZ617QQssPageNameZWDVWQQrdZ1QQcmdZViewItem⟩.

98. dwells00collectibles, "7 Jim Crow Dixie African American Postcards 1920s-40s," eBay, 1 August 2006 ⟨http://cgi.ebay.com/7-Jim-Crow-Dixie-African-American-Postcards-1920s-40s_W0QQitemZ230014086013QQihZ013QQcategoryZ36081 QQrdZ1QQcmdZViewItem⟩.

99. millerzt, "Racist Pottery Salt & Pepper Shakers 1930-40s," eBay, 28 July 2006 ⟨http://cgi.ebay.com/Racist-Pottery-Salt-Pepper-Shakers-1930-40s_W0QQ itemZ320011705553QQihZ011QQcategoryZ13928QQrdZ1QQcmdZViewItem⟩.

100. Turner, *Ceramic Uncles and Celluloid Mammies*, 11.

101. Elliott, "Postcolonial Experience in a Domestic Context," 181.

102. C. R. Weld, as quoted in Berger, "American Slavery as Seen by British Visitors," 187.

103. Berger, "American Slavery as Seen by British Visitors," 187–88.

104. auctionittodayby, "Vintage Black Doll 21" Dancer Blue Eyes Yarn Hair," eBay, 19 December 2006 ⟨http://cgi.ebay.com/Vintage-Black-Doll-21-Dancer-Blue-Eyes-Yarn-Hair_W0QQitemZ180066039415QQihZ008QQcategoryZ35797QQ ssPageNameZWDVWQQrdZ1QQcmdZViewItem⟩.

105. kentuckybluebird, "HOMEMADE BLACK DOLL CLOTH 24" LONG ADORABLE," eBay, 18 December 2006 ⟨http://cgi.ebay.com/HOMEMADE-BLACK-DOLL-CLOTH-24-LONG-ADORABLE_W0QQitemZ180065700145QQihZ008QQ categoryZ35797QQrdZ1QQcmdZViewItem⟩.

106. themeyermansion, "Vintage Black Rag Doll Handmade & Hand Embroidered," eBay, 3 July 2006 ⟨http://cgi.ebay.com/Vintage-Black-Rag-Doll-Handmade-Hand-Embroidered_W0QQitemZ250004434665QQihZ015QQcategoryZ35797QQrdZ1QQcmdZViewItem⟩.

107. annie*boomer, "Handmade Black Americana Folk Art Clay Rag Doll Signed," eBay, 19 December 2006 ⟨http://cgi.ebay.com/ws/eBayISAPI.dll?ViewItem&ih=019&sspagename=STRK%3AMEWA%3AIT&viewitem=&item=290063957570&rd=1&rd=1⟩.

108. Depictions of dolls' seams and stumps include attic_wench, "Vintage 40's? Black Folk Art Mammy Toaster Cover Doll," eBay, 18 December 2006 ⟨http://cgi.ebay.com/ws/eBayISAPI.dll?ViewItem&item=230068047405&indexURL=4&photoDisplayType=2#ebayphotohosting⟩.

109. hooks, "Naked without Shame," 67.

110. kentuckybluebird, "HOMEMADE BLACK DOLL CLOTH 24" LONG ADORABLE," eBay, 18 December 2006 ⟨http://cgi.ebay.com/HOMEMADE-BLACK-DOLL-CLOTH-24-LONG-ADORABLE_W0QQitemZ180065700145QQihZ008QQcategoryZ35797QQrdZ1QQcmdZViewItem⟩.

111. poobelle, "BLACK AMERICANA RAG DOLL, CA.1920,Ex-collection," eBay, 8 July 2006 ⟨http://cgi.ebay.com/BLACK-AMERICANA-RAG-DOLL-CA-1920-Ex-collection_W0QQitemZ110006435418QQihZ001QQcategoryZ35797QQrdZ1QQcmdZViewItem⟩.

112. vintage.port, "BLACK BABY DOLL SO CUTE MINIATURE," eBay, 20 December 2006 ⟨http://cgi.ebay.com/BLACK-BABY-DOLL-SO-CUTE-MINIATURE_W0QQitemZ180066239663QQihZ008QQcategoryZ35797QQrdZ1QQcmdZViewItem⟩.

113. Gardner, "Fortune-Telling on eBay."

114. dolls*from*happier*times, "1950's Black Americana Ponytail Doll Made In Japan 5"," eBay, 31 July 2006 ⟨http://cgi.ebay.com/1950s-Black-Americana-Ponytail-Doll-Made-In-Japan-5_W0QQitemZ150017593802QQihZ005QQcategoryZ35797QQrdZ1QQcmdZViewItem⟩.

115. Motley et al., "Exploring Collective Memories Associated with African-American Advertising Memorabilia," 55.

116. sellinghistory, "Daddy's Long Legs Ticker Doll Excellent w/ tag," eBay, 29 July 2006 ⟨http://cgi.ebay.com/Daddys-Long-Legs-Ticker-Doll-Excellent-w-tag_W0QQitemZ260014507160QQihZ016QQcategoryZ35797QQrdZ1QQcmdZViewItem⟩.

117. delettao, "Vintage Black Americana Postcard Lot Mammy Tap Dancing," eBay, 31 July 2006 ⟨http://cgi.ebay.com/Vintage-Black-Americana-Postcard-Lot-Mammy-Tap-Dancing_W0QQitemZ330013604979QQihZ014QQcategoryZ36081QQrdZ1QQcmdZViewItem⟩.

118. sixandersons, "Black Americana Old South 16 views unfolding booklet," eBay,

1 August 2006 ⟨http://cgi.ebay.com/Black-Americana-Old-South-16-views-unfolding-booklet_W0QQitemZ190015535614QQihZ009QQcategoryZ36081QQrdZ1QQcmdZViewItem#ebayphotohosting⟩.

119. foothills, "Vintage BLACK MAMMY SOUVENIR BELL ~ NEW ORLEANS," eBay, 13 November 2006 ⟨http://cgi.ebay.com/Vintage-BLACK-MAMMY-SOUVENIR-BELL-NEW-ORLEANS_W0QQitemZ230051416489QQihZ013QQcategoryZ35797QQssPageNameZWDVWQQrdZ1QQcmdZViewItem⟩.

120. jayhawkme, "Vintage Souvenir New Orleans Black Cotton Picker Doll," 14 December 2006 ⟨http://cgi.ebay.com/Vintage-Souvenir-New-Orleans-Black-Cotton-Picker-Doll_W0QQitemZ110068813984QQihZ001QQcategoryZ35797QQssPageNameZWDVWQQrdZ1QQcmdZViewItem⟩.

121. Spain, "Race Relations and Residential Segregation in New Orleans."

122. sarcole, "VINTAGE AUNT JAMIMA SALT/PEPPER SHAKERS~NEW ORLEANS LA," eBay, 13 November 2006 ⟨http://cgi.ebay.com/VINTAGE-AUNT-JAMIMA-SALT-PEPPER-SHAKERS-NEW-ORLEANS-LA_W0QQitemZ250049733093QQihZ015QQcategoryZ394QQssPageNameZWDVWQQrdZ1QQcmdZViewItem⟩.

123. ceegeel, "Unusual Black Americana Salt & Pepper Shakers: Souvenier Set From New Orleans," eBay, 17 November 2006 ⟨http://cgi.ebay.com/Unusual-Black-Americana-Salt-Pepper-Shakers_W0QQitemZ300050421355QQihZ020QQcategoryZ29458QQrdZ1QQcmdZViewItem?hash=item300050421355⟩.

124. naillnh55, "Vintage Black Americana Post Card Adorable Collectible," eBay, 19 December 2006 ⟨http://cgi.ebay.com/Vintage-Black-Americana-Post-Card-Adorable-Collectible_W0QQitemZ150072876821QQihZ005QQcategoryZ35796QQrdZ1QQcmdZViewItem⟩.

125. Critical literature that addresses this work includes Catanese, "'How Do I Rent a Negro?'"; Elam, "Change Clothes and Go"; and Fusco, "All Too Real."

126. Mendi + Keith Obadike, "Keith Obadike's Blackness," 8 August 2001, 20 January 2011 ⟨http://obadike.tripod.com/ebay.html⟩.

127. Fusco, "All Too Real."

128. Mendi + Keith Obadike, "blackness for sale," 20 January 2011 ⟨http://www.blacknetart.com/index1_1.html⟩.

129. Keith Townsend Obadike, as quoted in Fusco, "All Too Real."

Afterword

1. craigslist, "craigslist | about ⟩ factsheet," 29 November 2010, 23 January 2011 ⟨http://www.craigslist.org/about/factsheet⟩.

2. Craig Newmark, as quoted in Philip Weiss, "A Guy Named Craig," *New York Magazine*, 8 January 2006, 23 January 2011 ⟨http://nymag.com/nymetro/news/media/internet/15500/index5.html⟩.

3. Oudshoorn et al., "Configuring the User as Everybody."

4. Newowl, "craigslist w4m issues," 2011, 23 January 2011 ⟨http://www.eskimo.com/ ~newowl/pages/Craigslist_W4M_Issues.htm⟩.

5. craigslist, "craigslist | about ⟩ mission and history," 15 September 2008, 23 January 2011 ⟨http://www.craigslist.org/about/mission_and_history⟩.

6. craigslist, "craigslist | about ⟩ craig newmark," 15 September 2008, 23 January 2011 ⟨http://www.craigslist.org/about/craig_newmark⟩; Craig Newmark, as quoted in "How to Succeed in 2007: Business 2.0," CNNMoney, 2006, 23 January 2011 ⟨http://money.cnn.com/popups/2006/biz2/howtosucceed/21.html⟩.

7. Craig Newmark, as quoted in "Craigslist Founder: I Won't Be Cashing In," MoneyNews.com, 28 September 2006, 23 January 2011 ⟨http://archive.news max.com/money/archives/st/2006/9/28/100253.cfm⟩.

8. Brad Stone, "Sex Ads Seen Adding Revenue to Craigslist," New York Times, 25 April 2010, 22 January 2011 ⟨http://www.nytimes.com/2010/04/26/tech nology/26craigslist.html?pagewanted=2&_r=1⟩; Peter M. Zollman, "Craigslist Revenue, Profits Soar," AIMGroup, 30 April 2010, 22 January 2011 ⟨http:// aimgroup.com/blog/2010/04/30/craigslist-revenue-profits-soar/⟩. Reporters also credited a large part of this increase to craigslist's fees in the adult services category, which is no longer available.

9. Craig Newmark, as quoted in Gillian Reagan, "Craig Newmark, Tech Genius, Is an Obama Man," New York Observer, 29 October 2008, 23 January 2011 ⟨http:// www.observer.com/2008/02/craig-newmark⟩.

10. Craig Newmark, "Obama's Schools Pick," KQED Radio, 16 December 2008, 23 January 2011 ⟨http://www.kqed.org/epArchive/R812160900⟩.

11. Barack Obama and Joe Biden, "National Service Plan Fact Sheet," BarackObama .com, 23 January 2011 ⟨http://www.barackobama.com/pdf/NationalService PlanFactSheet.pdf⟩; Michael Scherer, "Obama's Inaugural Internet Call to Service," Time, 15 January 2009, 23 January 2011 ⟨http://www.time.com/time/poli tics/article/0,8599,1872152,00.html⟩; USA Service, "Renew America Together," 6 February 2009 ⟨usaservice.org⟩.

12. Serve.gov, "Welcome to Serve.gov," 5 March 2010 ⟨http://serve.gov/⟩.

13. Adam Higginbotham, "Citizen Craig," Guardian, 18 August 2006, 23 January 2011 ⟨http://www.guardian.co.uk/theguardian/2006/aug/18/guardianweekly .guardianweekly11⟩; Nick Wingfield, "EBay Buys Stake in Craigslist," Wall Street Journal, 13 August 2004, 23 January 2011 ⟨http://www.craigslist.org/about/press/ ebay.stake.html⟩.

14. For a discussion of this, see BBC News, "EBay Sues Craigslist Ad Website," 23 April 2008, 23 January 2011 ⟨http://news.bbc.co.uk/2/hi/business/7362221.stm⟩; Jon Fine, "craigslist Countersues eBay," BusinessWeek, 13 May 2008, 23 January 2011 ⟨http://www.businessweek.com/innovate/FineOnMedia/archives/2008/05/ craigslist_coun.html⟩.

15. Kim Rubey, as quoted in Wendy Tanaka "Craigslist Fires Back at eBay," *Forbes*, 13 May 2008, 23 January 2011 ⟨http://www.forbes.com/2008/05/13/craigs-list-ebay-tech-ebiz-cx_wt_0513ebay.html⟩.

16. Craig Newmark, "eBay and craigslist," cnewmark: craig from craigslist indulges himself, 13 August 2004, 2 August 2008 ⟨http://www.cnewmark.com/2004/08/ebay_and_craigs.html⟩.

17. craigslist, "craigslist | about ⟩ help ⟩ search," 7 November 2007, 23 January 2011 ⟨http://www.craigslist.org/about/help/search⟩.

18. craigslist, "craigslist | about ⟩ help ⟩ faq," 12 August 2010, 23 January 2011 ⟨http://www.craigslist.org/about/help/faq⟩.

19. Bill Swingle, as quoted in Jeff Atwood, "Search all Craigslist.org cities," Coding Horror, 10 July 2008 ⟨http://www.codinghorror.com/craigslist/⟩; aettinger, "Craigslist Global Search," 23 January 2011 ⟨http://clsearch.org/⟩.

20. Craig Newmark, as quoted in Livingston, *Founders at Work*, 248.

21. Livingston, *Founders at Work*, 247.

22. craigslist, "craigslist | about ⟩ factsheet," 29 November 2010, 22 January 2011 ⟨http://www.craigslist.org/about/factsheet⟩.

23. Adam Lashinsky, "Burning Sensation," *Fortune*, 12 December 2005, 23 January 2011 ⟨http://money.cnn.com/magazines/fortune/fortune_archive/2005/12/12/8363113/index.htm⟩.

24. Dominic Rusche, "Falling for Super-Geek," *TimesOnline*, 7 May 2006, 2 August 2008 ⟨http://www.timesonline.co.uk/tol/life_and_style/article710613.ece⟩.

25. Nick Farrell, "Craig Denies He Has Left CraigsList," *Enquirer*, 24 August 2007, 7 December 2011 ⟨http://www.theinquirer.net/inquirer/news/1046562/craig-denies-he-has-left-craigslist⟩.

26. Rusche, "Falling for Super-Geek."

27. Craig Newmark, as quoted in Jeremy Pepper, "PR Face2Face: Craig Newmark, Founder, Craigslist," POP! PR Jots, 26 July 2005, 22 January 2011 ⟨http://pop-pr.blogspot.com/2005/07/pr-face2facecraig-newmark-founder.html⟩.

28. Kevin Dolak, "Not 'Adult Services,' but Apparent Prostitution Ads Still on Craigslist," ABC News, 5 September 2010, 22 January 2011 ⟨http://abcnews.go.com/Technology/craigslist-hosting-adult-services-ads/story?id=11565631⟩; Evan Hansen, "Censored! Craigslist Adult Services Blocked in U.S.," *Wired*, 4 September 2010, 22 January 2011 ⟨http://www.wired.com/epicenter/2010/09/censored-craigslist-adult-services-blocked-in-u-s/⟩; Lisa Kelly and Heidi Matthews, "Sex, Sin, and Craigslist," *Globe and Mail*, 31 December 2010, 22 January 2011 ⟨http://www.theglobeandmail.com/news/opinions/opinion/sex-sin-and-craigslist/article1852470/⟩.

29. Chris Matyszczyk, "Craigslist Censored: Adult Section Removed," CNET, 4 September 2010, 7 December 2011 ⟨http://news.cnet.com/8301-17852_3-20015629-71.html?tag=contentMain;contentBody;2n⟩.

30. For instance, auroracw is informed that her personal ad was flagged because she

did not provide enough personal information. She argues that this behavior is "rude," that it "amounts to censorship," and that she is "not going to cater to the needs of men looking at the ads so they can determine whether or not" she is "fat or thin enough for them." When Edna_K posted "looking for a man who's interested in feminism," "looking for women . . . to start a women's consciousness group," and "looking for a man with respect for women," she was flagged. This is because she is "a feminist and men on this site are threatened by that and flag" as "a way of shutting" her "up." auroracw, "Run of the mill personal ad w4m San Francisco," craigslist, 19 December 2008, 23 January 2011 ⟨http:// losangeles.craigslist.org/forums/?ID=110911910⟩; Edna_K, "I keep getting flagged because I'm a feminist," craigslist, 16 July 2008, 23 January 2011 ⟨http:// losangeles.craigslist.org/forums/?ID=96312690⟩.

31. craigslist, "craigslist | personals," 23 January 2011 ⟨http://neworleans.craigslist .org/cgi-bin/personals.cgi?category=w4w⟩.

32. Richardson, "Locating Sexualities," 392.

33. Craig Newmark, as quoted in Patrick Phillips, "Craig Newmark: Craigslist Isn't a Media Menace," *I Want Media*, 20 April 2007, 23 January 2011 ⟨http://www .iwantmedia.com/people/people66.html⟩.

34. Newowl, "Should I flag ads?" 14 January 2011 ⟨http://www.eskimo.com/~new owl/pages/shouldflag.htm⟩.

35. Craig Newmark, as quoted in Lidija Davis, "Craig Newmark's Keynote Unlocks the Secrets to Building a Community," ReadWriteWeb, 10 February 2009, 23 January 2011 ⟨http://www.readwriteweb.com/archives/craig_newmarks_key note_unlocks_the_secrets_to_building_a_community.php⟩.

36. craigslist, "craigslist | about ⟩ help ⟩ faq," 12 August 2010, 23 January 2011 ⟨http:// www.craigslist.org/about/help/faq⟩.

37. Newowl, "Flags Faq," 22 June 2008 ⟨http://www.eskimo.com/~newowl/Flagged_ FAQ.htm⟩.

38. craigslist, "help ⟩ flags and community moderation," 30 January 2009 ⟨http:// www.craigslist.org/about/help/flags_and_community_moderation⟩.

39. Newowl, "flagged," 14 January 2011 ⟨http://www.eskimo.com/~newowl/pages/ flagged.htm⟩.

40. rdd_guy, "If having your free personal ad flagged down," craigslist, 2 July 2008, 23 January 2011 ⟨http://phoenix.craigslist.org/forums/?ID=95244872⟩.

41. Craigslist Flagger Wars, "Open Letter to Craig," 1 February 2009 ⟨http://www .stopabusivecraigslistflaggers.com/Open_Letter_To_Craig.php⟩.

42. craigslist, "help ⟩ flags and community moderation," 30 January 2009 ⟨http:// www.craigslist.org/about/help/flags_and_community_moderation⟩.

43. -, "Why does the w4m section get so many more flags," craigslist, 21 June 2008, 23 January 2011 ⟨http://losangeles.craigslist.org/forums/?ID=94316748⟩. Many people post anonymously to the flag help forum and use a dash as their member name. Since people can post without signing in, craigslist uses a black and

green color system to differentiate between anonymous and more stable participants.

44. -, "Men flag more. Men get more scams." craigslist, 21 June 2008, 23 January 2011 ⟨http://losangeles.craigslist.org/forums/?ID=94316824⟩.

45. lovesleo, "Women just don't seem to flag the men's ads," craigslist, 2 July 2008, 23 January 2011 ⟨http://sfbay.craigslist.org/forums/?ID=95213582⟩.

46. FunkyshoeZ, "We don't flag ads here. We just look at," craigslist, 21 June 2008, 7 December 2011 ⟨https://forums.craigslist.org/?ID=94338027&areaID=7⟩.

47. no_spammers, "No. We are telling you what YOUR COMMUNITY," craigslist, 22 June 2008, 24 November 2011 ⟨http://losangeles.craigslist.org/forums/?ID=94386347⟩.

48. West and Zimmerman, "Doing Gender," 126.

49. MissAnthropy2009, "Why??" craigslist, 23 June 2008, 23 January 2011 ⟨http://losangeles.craigslist.org/forums/?ID=94383922⟩; ellememe, "why is this being flagged?" craigslist, 23 June 2008, 23 January 2011 ⟨http://losangeles.craigslist.org/forums/?ID=94407007⟩.

50. karakicks, "ok thanks," craigslist, 23 June 2008, 23 January 2011 ⟨http://losangeles.craigslist.org/forums/?ID=94401571⟩.

51. imakittykitty, "still doesn't make sense...," craigslist, 22 June 2008, 23 January 2011 ⟨http://losangeles.craigslist.org/forums/?ID=94367873⟩.

52. MissAnthropy2009, "Once Again," craigslist, 22 June 2008, 23 January 2011 ⟨http://losangeles.craigslist.org/forums/?ID=94387577⟩.

53. has_some_shred, "Sounds like your community," craigslist, 25 January 2009, 7 December 2011 ⟨https://forums.craigslist.org/?ID=114246064&areaID=31⟩.

54. Gail54321, "Innocuous Posting Removed? Why?" craigslist, 26 June 2008, 23 January 2011 ⟨http://ithaca.craigslist.org/forums/?ID=94790014⟩.

55. paul_baumer, "If you post as married unhappily," craigslist, 26 June 2008, 23 January 2011 ⟨http://ithaca.craigslist.org/forums/?ID=94790400⟩.

56. paul_baumer, "Of course it's fine for people to flag if they," craigslist, 26 June 2008, 23 January 2011 ⟨http://ithaca.craigslist.org/forums/?ID=94790400⟩.

57. Gail54321, "Married? What does that mean??" craigslist, 26 June 2008, 23 January 2011 ⟨http://ithaca.craigslist.org/forums/?ID=94790249⟩; Gail54321, "Ridiculous!" craigslist, 26 June 2008, 23 January 2011 ⟨http://ithaca.craigslist.org/forums/?ID=94790683⟩.

58. and_maybe_he, "let's ask him then," craigslist, 25 January 2009, 23 January 2011 ⟨http://neworleans.craigslist.org/forums/?ID=114246064⟩.

59. touia, "flagged my ad for no reason," craigslist, 21 July 2009, 23 January 2011 ⟨http://neworleans.craigslist.org/forums/?ID=131035211⟩; AvgWeirdo, "95% of w4m ads are either spam or hookers...," craigslist, 21 July 2009, 23 January 2011 ⟨http://neworleans.craigslist.org/forums/?ID=131035211⟩.

60. curves82_la, "3 times? what the hell? i posted before....," craigslist, 20 November 2008, 7 December 2011 ⟨https://forums.craigslist.org/?ID=108385237>.& amp;areaID=31⟩; -elsewhere-, "Good bye. peddle your gold diggin' whore ass," craigslist, 20 November 2008, 23 January 2011 ⟨http://neworleans.craigslist.org/forums/?ID=108385237⟩.

61. -, "whore §," craigslist, 30 January 2009, 23 January 2011 ⟨http://neworleans.craigslist.org/forums/?ID=114765581⟩; -ET-, "Your ad is prohibited, penis breath," craigslist, 30 January 2009, 23 January 2011 ⟨http://neworleans.craigslist.org/forums/?ID=114765581⟩; chez_moi, "You are advertisng your prostitution," craigslist, 30 January 2009, 23 January 2011 ⟨http://neworleans.craigslist.org/forums/?ID=114765581⟩.

62. Cant-think, "How can you not understand........," craigslist, 28 August 2008, 24 January 2011 ⟨http://neworleans.craigslist.org/forums/?ID=100135234⟩.

63. Kristeva, *The Powers of Horror*, 4.

64. AppleCure, "Wow," craigslist, 28 April 2008, 24 January 2011 ⟨http://neworleans.craigslist.org/forums/?ID=89943177⟩.

65. FunkyshoeZ, "We don't flag ads here. We just look at," 21 June 2008, 24 January 2011 ⟨http://losangeles.craigslist.org/forums/?ID=94338027⟩; TennCavs, "BBW is the kiss of death in W4M," craigslist, 21 June 2008, 24 January 2011 ⟨http://losangeles.craigslist.org/forums/?ID=94338027⟩.

66. hazelcat, "Don't put BBW?!" craigslist, 21 June 2008, 7 December 2011 ⟨https://forums.craigslist.org/?ID=94338027&areaID=7⟩.

67. Jane1010, "my point exactly!" craigslist, 1 August 2008, 7 December 2011 ⟨https://forums.craigslist.org/?ID=97723351&areaID=7⟩.

68. _change_, "complain all you want, but that's not going to §," craigslist, 4 August 2008, 24 January 2011 ⟨http://losangeles.craigslist.org/forums/?ID=97723351⟩; corvids, "Like I said below, it's human nature," craigslist, 1 August 2008, 24 January 2011 ⟨http://losangeles.craigslist.org/forums/?ID=97723351⟩.

69. -, "Yeah... I'd flag that in a heartbeat," craigslist, 21 June 2008, 24 January 2011 ⟨http://losangeles.craigslist.org/forums/?ID=94319074⟩; -----------------,"CL personals is a tough crowd sometimes," craigslist, 28 June 2008, 24 January 2011 ⟨http://sfbay.craigslist.org/forums/?ID=94921064⟩; -, "You STILL don't get it," craigslist, 21 June 2008, 24 January 2011 ⟨http://losangeles.craigslist.org/forums/?ID=94319470⟩.

70. -, "I completely understand why she said," craigslist, 17 January 2009, 24 January 2011 ⟨http://neworleans.craigslist.org/forums/?ID=113461406⟩; addanew handle, "too negative...," craigslist, 1 July 2008, 13 February 2011 ⟨http://sfbay.craigslist.org/forums/?ID=95127047⟩.

71. SexySingleSweetie, "Any help or suggestions?" craigslist, 26 January 2009, 24 January 2011 ⟨http://neworleans.craigslist.org/forums/?ID=114311184⟩.

72. karakicks, "flagging issues," craigslist, 23 June 2008, 24 January 2011 ⟨http://losangeles.craigslist.org/forums/?ID=94401232⟩.

73. myadbeingflagged, "my ad being flagged," craigslist, 23 June 2008, 24 January 2011 ⟨http://losangeles.craigslist.org/forums/?ID=94401463⟩.

74. Snappy_Comeback, "you got threadjacked by yet another person," craigslist, 23 June 2008, 24 January 2011 ⟨http://losangeles.craigslist.org/forums/?ID=94401596⟩.

75. --, "Threadjacking troll! Flagged! §" craigslist, 26 June 2008, 24 January 2011 ⟨http://ithaca.craigslist.org/forums/?ID=94791396⟩.

76. -, "Gail54321, please ignore Loku_v7," craigslist, 26 June 2008, 24 January 2011 ⟨http://ithaca.craigslist.org/forums/?ID=94791272⟩.

77. karakicks, "flagging issues," craigslist, 23 June 2008, 24 January 2011 ⟨http://losangeles.craigslist.org/forums/?ID=94401232⟩.

78. -x-, "1 Negativity draws flags. Seriously, think about," craigslist, 27 June 2008, 7 March 2012 ⟨https://forums.craigslist.org/?ID=94801111%C3%AC&areaID=201⟩; jpoqalot, "Excuse me...," craigslist, 27 June 2008, 24 January 2011 ⟨http://ithaca.craigslist.org/forums/?ID=94801111⟩.

79. yasuragi, "Do YOU flag the cock shots?" craigslist, 27 June 2008, 24 January 2011 ⟨http://ithaca.craigslist.org/forums/?ID=94801201⟩.

80. Craig Newmark, as quoted in Katharine Kieszkowski, "Are You on Craig's List?" Fast Company, 30 November 2000, 24 January 2011 ⟨http://www.fastcompany.com/magazine/nc02/026.html?page=0%2C3⟩.

81. Newmark, as quoted in Reagan, "Craig Newmark, Tech Genius, Is an Obama Man."

82. BusinessWeek, "The 25 Most Influential People on the Web," September 2008, 24 January 2011 ⟨http://images.businessweek.com/ss/08/09/0929_most_influential/16.htm⟩.

83. MIT World, "A Few Things Learned from Craigslist," 14 November 2008, 24 January 2011 ⟨http://mitworld.mit.edu/video/636⟩.

84. Barack Obama, "MEMORANDUM FOR THE HEADS OF EXECUTIVE DEPARTMENTS AND AGENCIES," White House, 24 January 2011 ⟨http://www.whitehouse.gov/the_press_office/TransparencyandOpenGovernment/⟩.

85. Kenneth Corbin, "Will e-Gov Get Its Day in Obama Administration?" InternetNews, 12 January 2009, 24 January 2011 ⟨http://www.internetnews.com/government/article.php/3795471/Will+eGov+Get+Its+Day+in+Obama+Administration.htm⟩.

WORKS CITED

Abelove, Henry, Michèle Aina Barale, and David M. Halperin, eds. *The Lesbian and Gay Studies Reader*. New York: Routledge, 1993.

Acker, Joan. "Hierarchies, Jobs, Bodies: A Theory of Gendered Organizations." *Gender and Society* 4, no. 2 (June 1990): 139–58.

Algesheimer, René, Utpal M. Dholakia, and Andreas Herrmann. "The Social Influence of Brand Community: Evidence from European Car Clubs." *Journal of Marketing* 69 (July 2005): 19–34.

Allison, Anne. "Portable Monsters and Commodity Cuteness: Pokémon as Japan's New Global Power." *Postcolonial Studies* 6, no. 3 (2003): 381–95.

Andersen, Poul Houman. "Relationship Marketing and Brand Involvement of Professionals through Web-Enhanced Brand Communities: The Case of Coloplast." *Industrial Marketing Management* 34 (2005): 285–97.

Anderson, Benedict. *Imagined Communities: Reflections on the Origin and Spread of Nationalism*. London: Verso, 1991.

Andrejevic, Mark. "Watching Television without Pity: The Productivity of Online Fans." *Television and New Media* 9, no. 1 (January 2008): 24–46.

Arvidsson, Adam. "Brands: A Critical Perspective." *Journal of Consumer Culture* 5, no. 2 (2005): 235–58.

Babuscio, Jack. "Camp and Gay Sensibility." In *Camp Grounds: Style and Homosexuality*, edited by David Bergman, 19–38. Amherst: University of Massachusetts Press, 1993.

Bacon-Smith, Camille. *Science Fiction Culture*. Philadelphia: University of Pennsylvania Press, 2000.

Bajari, P., and A. Hortacsu. "Winner's Curse, Reserve Prices, and Endogenous Entry: Empirical Insights from eBay Auctions." *Rand Journal of Economics* 34, no. 2 (Summer 2003): 329–55.

Baker, Stacey Menzel, Carol M. Motley, and Geraldine R. Henderson. "From Despicable to Collectible: The Evolution of Collective Memories for and the Value of Black Advertising Memorabilia." *Journal of Advertising* 33, no. 3 (Fall 2004): 37–50.

Banet-Weiser, Sarah. *Kids Rule! Nickelodeon and Consumer Citizenship.* Durham, N.C.: Duke University Press, 2007.

Barthes, Roland. *Camera Lucida: Reflections on Photography*, translated by Richard Howard. New York: Hill and Wang, 1981.

———. *The Pleasure of the Text*, translated by Richard Miller. New York: Hill and Wang, 1995.

Baym, Nancy. *Tune In, Log On: Soaps, Fandom, and Online Community.* Thousand Oaks, Calif.: Sage, 2000.

Becker, Edith, Michelle Citron, Julia Lesage, and B. Ruby Rich. "Lesbians and Film." In *Out in Culture: Gay, Lesbian, and Queer Essays on Popular Culture*, edited by Corey K. Creekmur and Alexander Doty, 25–43. Durham, N.C.: Duke University Press, 1995.

Belk, Russell W. *Collecting in a Consumer Society.* London: Routledge, 1995.

Belk, Russell W., Joon Yong Seo, and Eric Li. "Dirty Little Secret: Home Chaos and Professional Organizers." *Consumption, Markets, and Culture* 10, no. 2 (June 2007): 133–40.

Bell, David. "Pleasure and Danger: The Paradoxical Spaces of Sexual Citizenship." *Political Geography* 14, no. 2 (1995): 139–53.

Bell, David, and Jon Binnie. *The Sexual Citizen: Queer Politics and Beyond.* Malden, Mass.: Blackwell, 2000.

Benjamin, Walter. "The Work of Art in the Age of Mechanical Reproduction." In *Illuminations*, edited by Hannah Arendt, translated by John Zohn, 217–51. New York: Schocken Books, 1969.

Benkler, Yochai. *The Wealth of Networks: How Social Production Transforms Markets and Freedom.* New Haven, Conn.: Yale University Press, 2006.

Bennett, W. Lance. "Communicating Global Activism: Strengths and Vulnerabilities of Networked Politics." *Information, Communication and Society* 6, no. 2 (2003): 143–68.

Berger, Max. "American Slavery as Seen by British Visitors, 1836–1860." *Journal of Negro History* 30, no. 2 (April 1945): 181–202.

Bergman, David. Introduction to *Camp Grounds: Style and Homosexuality*, edited by David Bergman, 3–16. Amherst: University of Massachusetts Press, 1993.

Berlant, Lauren. "Nearly Utopian, Nearly Normal: Post-Fordist Affect in *La Promesse* and *Rosetta*." *Public Culture* 19, no. 2 (2007): 273–301.

Berlin, Ira. "American Slavery in History and Memory and the Search for Social Justice." *Journal of American History* 90, no. 4 (March 2004): 1251–68.

Best, Amy L. "The Production of Heterosexuality at the High School Prom." In *Think-*

ing *Straight: The Power, the Promise, and the Paradox of Heterosexuality*, edited
by Chrys Ingraham, 193–213. New York: Routledge, 2005.

Bielby, Denise D., C. Lee Harrington, and William T. Bielby. "Whose Stories Are
They? Fans' Engagement with Soap Opera Narratives in Three Sites of Fan
Activity." *Journal of Broadcasting and Electronic Media* 43, no. 1 (1999): 35–51.

Binnie, Jon, and Beverley Skeggs. "Cosmopolitan Knowledge and the Production and
Consumption of Sexualized Space: Manchester's Gay Village." *Sociological Review*
52, no. 1 (2004): 39–61.

Blackwell, Roger, and Tina Stephan. *Brands That Rock: What Business Leaders Can
Learn from the World of Rock and Roll*. Hoboken: John Wiley and Sons, 2004.

Blais, André, Elisabeth Gidengil, Neil Nevitte, and Richard Nadeau. "Where Does
Turnout Decline Come From?" *European Journal of Political Research* 43 (2004):
221–36.

Blanchot, Maurice. *The Unavowable Community*. Barrytown, N.Y.: Station Hill, 1988.

Bloch, Peter H., and Grady D. Bruce. "Product Involvement as Leisure Behavior."
Advances in Consumer Research 11, no. 1 (1984): 197–202.

Bogle, Donald. *Toms, Coons, Mulattoes, Mammies, and Bucks: An Interpretive History
of Blacks in American Films*. New York: Viking, 1973.

Bolter, Jay David. *Writing Space: The Computer, Hypertext, and the History of Writing*.
Hillsdale, N.J.: Lawrence Erlbaum Associates, 1991.

Bond, Julian. Introduction to *Black Americana Price Guide*, edited by Kyle Husfloen,
vi–ix. Iola, Wisc.: Antique Trader Books, 1996.

Bordo, Susan. "Gay Men's Revenge." *Journal of Aesthetics and Art Criticism* 57, no. 1
(Winter 1999): 21–25.

———. *The Male Body: A New Look at Men in Public and in Private*. New York:
Farrar, Straus and Giroux, 1999.

———. "Reading the Male Body." In *Building Bodies*, edited by Pamela L. Moore,
31–73. New Brunswick: Rutgers University Press, 1997.

Boyd, Josh. "In Community We Trust: Online Security Communication at eBay."
Journal of Computer-Mediated Communication 7, no. 3 (April 2002), 5 February
2011 ⟨http://jcmc.indiana.edu/vol7/issue3/boyd.html⟩.

Bradley, Stephen P., and Kelly A. Porter. "eBay Inc.: Case Study." *Journal of Interactive
Media* 14, no. 4 (Autumn 2000): 73–97.

Breen, T. H. *The Marketplace of Revolution: How Consumer Politics Shaped American
Independence*. New York: Oxford University Press, 2004.

Britton, Dana M. "Gendered Organizational Logic: Policy and Practice in Men's and
Women's Prisons." *Gender and Society* 11, no. 6 (December 1997): 796–818.

Brown, Jennifer, and John Morgan. "Reputation in Online Auctions: The Market for
Trust." *California Management Review* 49, no. 1 (Fall 2006): 61–81.

Bruckman, Amy, "Ethical Guidelines for Research Online." 4 April 2002, 5 February
2011 ⟨http://www.cc.gatech.edu/~asb/ethics⟩.

Buchanan, Elizabeth A., ed. *Readings in Virtual Research Ethics: Issues and Controversies*. Hershey: Idea Group, 2004.

Burton, David. "Collectible Aesthetics." *Art Education* 42, no. 6 (November 1989): 42–45.

Butler, Judith. *Gender Trouble: Feminism and the Subversion of Identity*. New York: Routledge, 1990.

Caffentzis, George. "Crystals and Analytic Engines: Historical and Conceptual Preliminaries to a New Theory of Machines." *ephemera: theory and politics in organization* 7, no. 1 (2007): 24–45.

Calkins, Mary M. "My Reputation Always Had More Fun Than Me: The Failure of eBay's Feedback Model to Effectively Prevent Online Auction Fraud." *Richmond Journal of Law and Technology* 7, no. 4 (Spring 2001), 5 February 2011 ⟨http://law .richmond.edu/jolt/v7i4/note1.html⟩.

Camille, Michael. "Editor's Introduction: Other Objects of Desire." *Art History* 24, no. 2 (April 2001): 163–68.

Canclini, Néstor García. *Consumers and Citizens: Globalization and Multicultural Conflicts*, translated by George Yúdice. Minneapolis: University of Minnesota Press, 2001.

Carducci, Vince. "Culture Jamming: A Sociological Perspective." *Journal of Consumer Culture* 6, no. 1 (2006): 116–38.

Cartwright, Lisa. "Film and the Digital in Visual Studies: Film Studies in the Era of Convergence." *Journal of Visual Culture* 1, no. 1 (2002): 7–23.

Case, Sue-Ellen. "Toward a Butch-Femme Aesthetic." In *The Lesbian and Gay Studies Reader*, edited by Henry Abelove, Michèle Aina Barale, and David M. Halperin, 294–306. New York: Routledge, 1993.

Casey, Catherine. "'Come, Join Our Family': Discipline and Integration in Corporate Organizational Culture." *Human Relations* 52, no. 2 (1999): 155–78.

Castille, George Pierre. "The Commodification of Indian Identity." *American Anthropologist* 98 (December 1996): 743–49.

Catanese, Brandi Wilkins. "'How Do I Rent a Negro?': Racialized Subjectivity and Digital Performance Art." *Theatre Journal* 57 (December 2005): 699–714.

Chasin, Alexandra. *Selling Out: The Gay and Lesbian Movement Goes to Market*. New York: Palgrave Macmillan, 2001.

Chrisman, Nicholas. "Full Circle: More than Just Social Implications of GIS." *Cartographica: The International Journal for Geographic Information and Geovisualization* 40, no. 4 (Winter 2005): 23–35.

Clark, Danae. "Commodity Lesbianism." In *The Lesbian and Gay Studies Reader*, edited by Henry Abelove, Michèle Aina Barale, and David M. Halperin, 186–201. New York: Routledge, 1993.

Cohen, Adam. *The Perfect Store: Inside eBay*. New York: Little, Brown and Company, 2002.

Collins, Patricia Hill. *Black Feminist Thought: Knowledge, Consciousness, and the Politics of Empowerment*. New York: Routledge, 1991.

———. "New Commodities, New Consumers." *Ethnicities* 6, no. 3 (2006): 297–317.

Colls, Rachel. "Outsize/Outside: Bodily Bignesses and the Emotional Experiences of British Women Shopping for Clothes." *Gender, Place and Culture* 13 (October 2006): 529–45.

Connell, R. W. "A Very Straight Gay: Masculinity, Homosexual Experience, and the Dynamics of Gender." *American Sociological Review* 57 (1992): 735–51.

Cook, Scott. "The Contribution Revolution: Letting Volunteers Build Your Business." *Harvard Business Review* 60 (October 2008): 60–69.

Cooley, Heidi Rae. "It's All about the Fit: The Hand, the Mobile Screenic Device, and Tactile Vision." *Journal of Visual Culture* 3, no. 2 (2004): 135–55.

Corrado, Marisa. "Teaching Wedding Rules: How Bridal Workers Negotiate Control over Their Customers." *Journal of Contemporary Ethnography* 31, no. 1 (2002): 33–67.

Coté, Mark, and Jennifer Pybus. "Learning to Immaterial Labour 2.0: MySpace and Social Networks." *ephemera: theory and politics in organization* 7, no. 1 (2007): 88–106.

Cova, Bernard, and Daniele Dalli. "Working Consumers: The Next Step in Marketing Theory?" *Marketing Theory* 9, no. 3 (2009): 315–39.

Cova, Bernard, and Stefano Pace. "Brand Community of Convenience Products: New Forms of Customer Empowerment—The Case 'My Nutella the Community.'" *European Journal of Marketing* 40, nos. 9/10 (2006): 1087–105.

Cova, Bernard, Stefano Pace, and David J. Park. "Global Brand Communities across Borders: The Warhammer Case Study." *International Marketing Review* 24, no. 3 (2007): 313–29.

Cowan, Ruth Schwartz. "The Consumption Junction: A Proposal for Research Strategies in the Sociology of Technology." In *Social Construction of Technological Systems: New Directions in the Sociology and History of Technology*, edited by Wiebe Bijker, Thomas P. Hughes, and Trevor Pinch, 261–80. Cambridge, Mass.: MIT Press, 1989.

Crocker, David A., and Toby Linden. *Ethics of Consumption: The Good Life, Justice, and Global Stewardship*. Lanham, Md.: Rowman and Littlefield, 1998.

Culbertson, Philip. "Designing Men: Reading the Male Body as Text." *Journal of Textual Reasoning* 7 (1998), 5 February 2011 ⟨http://etext.virginia.edu/journals/tr/archive/volume7/Culbertson1.html⟩.

Curien, Nicolas, Emmanuelle F. Auchart, Gilbert L. Affond, and Francois M. Oreau. "Online Consumer Communities: Escaping the Tragedy of the Digital Commons." In *Internet and Digital Economics: Methods and Applications*, edited by Eric Brousseau and Nicolas Curien, 201–19. Cambridge: Cambridge University Press, 2007.

Currie, Dawn H. "'Here Comes the Bride': The Making of a 'Modern Traditional' Wedding in Western Culture." *Journal of Comparative Family Studies* 24, no. 3 (Autumn 1993): 403–21.

Dalton, Russell J., Susan E. Scarrow, and Bruce E. Cain. "Advanced Democracies and the New Politics." *Journal of Democracy* 15, no. 1 (January 2004): 124–38.

Danet, Brenda, and Tamar Katriel. "No Two Alike: Play and Aesthetics in Collecting." *Play and Culture* 2 (1989): 253–77.

Daunton, Martin J., and Matthew Hilton, eds. *The Politics of Consumption: Material Culture and Citizenship in Europe and America*. Oxford: Berg, 2001.

Davis, Joseph E. "The Commodification of Self." *Hedgehog Review* (Summer 2003): 41–49.

Davis, Lisa E. "The Butch as Drag Artiste: Greenwich Village in the Roaring Forties." In *The Persistent Desire: A Femme-Butch Reader*, edited by Joan Nestle, 45–53. Boston: Alyson, 1992.

de Chernatony, Leslie. "Brand Management through Narrowing the Gap between Brand Identity and Brand Reputation." *Journal of Marketing Management* 15, nos. 1–3 (January–April 1999): 157–79.

Dean, Carolyn. "Boys and Girls and 'Boys': Popular Depictions of African-American Children and Childlike Adults in the United States, 1850–1930." *Journal of American Culture* 23, no. 3 (Fall 2000): 17–35.

Dellarocas, Chrysanthos. "The Digitization of Word of Mouth: Promise and Challenges of Online Feedback Mechanisms." *Management Science* 49, no. 10 (October 2003): 1407–24.

Denegri-Knott, Janice, and Mike Molesworth. "'Love It. Buy It. Sell It': Consumer Desire and the Social Drama of eBay." *Journal of Consumer Culture* 10, no. 1 (2010): 56–79.

Desrochers, Robert E., Jr. "Slave-for-Sale Advertisements and Slavery in Massachusetts, 1704–1781." *William and Mary Quarterly* 59, no. 3 (July 2002): 623–64.

Doane, Mary Ann. *The Desire to Desire: The Woman's Film of the 1940s*. Bloomington: Indiana University Press, 1987.

Douglas, Mary. *Implicit Meanings: Selected Essays in Anthropology*. London: Routledge, 1999.

Driskell, R. B., and L. Lyon. "Are Virtual Communities True Communities? Examining the Environments and Elements of Community." *City and Community* 1, no. 4 (2002): 373–90.

Drummond, Murray J. N. "Men's Bodies: Listening to the Voices of Young Gay Men." *Men and Masculinities* 7, no. 3 (2005): 270–90.

Duncan, Carol. "The MoMA's Hot Mamas." In *The Expanding Discourse: Feminism and Art History*, edited by Norma Broude and Mary D. Garrard, 347–58. New York: Harper Collins, 1992.

Dyer, Richard. "Don't Look Now: The Instability of Male Pin-Ups." *Screen* 23, nos. 3/4 (1982): 61–72.

Earl, Jennifer, and Alan Schussman. "Contesting Cultural Control: Youth Culture and Online Petitioning." In *Civic Life Online: Learning How Digital Media Can Engage Youth*, edited by W. Lance Bennett, 71–96. Cambridge, Mass.: MIT Press, 2007.

Elam, Harry J., Jr. "Change Clothes and Go: A Postscript to Postblackness." In *Black Cultural Traffic: Crossroads in Global Performance and Popular Culture*, edited by Harry Justin Elam Jr. and Kennell Jackson, 379–88. Ann Arbor: University of Michigan Press, 2005.

Elliott, Mary Jane Suero. "Postcolonial Experience in a Domestic Context: Commodified Subjectivity in Toni Morrison's *Beloved*." *MELUS* 25, nos. 3/4 (Fall/Winter 2000): 181–202.

Ellis, Rebecca M., and Anna Haywood. "Virtual_radiophile (163): eBay and the Changing Collecting Practices of the U.K. Vintage Radio Community." In *Everyday eBay: Culture, Collecting, and Desire*, edited by Ken Hillis, Michael Petit, and Nathan Scott Epley, 45–62. New York: Routledge, 2006.

Elsner, John, and Roger Cardinal. Introduction to *The Cultures of Collecting*, edited by John Elsner and Roger Cardinal, 1–6. Cambridge, Mass.: Harvard University Press, 1994.

Ess, Charles, and the AoIR Ethics Working Committee. "Ethical Decision-Making and Internet Research: Recommendations from the AoIR Ethics Working Committee." 27 November 2002, 5 February 2011 ⟨http://www.aoir.org/reports/ethics.pdf⟩.

Etzioni, Amitai. "Is Bowling Together Sociologically Lite?" *Sociological Review* 30, no. 3 (May 2001): 223–24.

Evans, David Trevor. *Sexual Citizenship: The Material Construction of Sexualities*. London: Routledge, 1993.

Fausto-Sterling, Anne. *Sexing the Body: Gender Politics and the Construction of Sexuality*. New York: Basic Books, 2000.

Fayard, Anne-Laure, and Gerardine DeSanctis. "Evolution of an Online Forum for Knowledge Management Professionals: A Language Game Analysis." *Journal of Computer-Mediated Communication* 10, no. 4 (2005), 5 February 2011 ⟨http://jcmc.indiana.edu/vol10/issue4/fayard.html⟩.

Fiske, John. "The Cultural Economy of Fandom." In *The Adoring Audience: Fan Culture and Popular Media*, edited by Lisa A. Lewis, 30–48. London: Routledge, 1992.

Ford, Robert C., Frank S. McLaughlin, and John W. Newstrom. "Questions and Answers about Fun at Work." *Human Resource Planning* 26, no. 4 (2003): 18–33.

Formanek-Brunell, Miriam. *Made to Play House: Dolls and the Commercialization of American Girlhood, 1830–1930*. New Haven, Conn.: Yale University Press, 1993.

Frankel, Mark S., and Sanyin Siang. "Ethical and Legal Aspects of Human Subjects in Cyberspace." American Association for the Advancement of Science, 1999, 5 February 2011 ⟨http://www.aaas.org/spp/dspp/sfrl/projects/intres/main.htm⟩.

Friese, Susanne. "The Wedding Dress: From Use Value to Sacred Object." In *Through* the Wardrobe: Women's Relationships with Their Clothes, edited by Ali Guy, Maura Banim, and Eileen Green, 53–69. Oxford: Berg, 2001.

Fusco, Coco. "All Too Real: The Tale of an On-Line Black Sale." 24 September 2001, 5 February 2011 ⟨http://www.blacknetart.com/coco.html⟩.

Gardner, Eric. "Fortune-Telling on eBay: Early African American Textual Artifacts and the Marketplace." In Everyday eBay: Culture, Collecting, and Desire, edited by Ken Hillis, Michael Petit, and Nathan Scott Epley, 63–75. New York: Routledge, 2006.

Gerson, Judith. "There Is No Sex without Gender." Sociological Forum 20, no. 1 (March 2005): 179–81.

Gilkeson, James H., and Kristy Reynolds. "Determinants of Internet Auction Success and Closing Price: An Explanatory Study." Psychology and Marketing 20, no. 6 (2003): 537–66.

Gill, Rosalind, Karen Henwood, and Carl McLean. "Body Projects and the Regulation of Normative Masculinity." Body and Society 11, no. 1 (2005): 37–62.

Gilman, Sander L. "Black Bodies, White Bodies: Toward an Iconography of Female Sexuality in Late Nineteenth-Century Art, Medicine, and Literature." Critical Inquiry 12, no. 1 (Autumn 1985): 204–42.

Goings, Kenneth W. Mammy and Uncle Mose: Black Collectibles and American Stereotyping. Bloomington: Indiana University Press, 1994.

Gordon, Stacey King. Buying and Selling Jewelry on eBay. Boston: Thomson Course Technology, 2005.

Gotham, Kevin Fox. "Marketing Mardi Gras: Commodification, Spectacle and the Political Economy of Tourism in New Orleans." Urban Studies 39, no. 10 (2002): 1735–56.

Gray, Herman. "Black Masculinity and Visual Culture." Callaloo 18, no. 2 (Spring 1995): 401–5.

Gray, Jonathan. "Antifandom and the Moral Text: Television without Pity and Textual Dislike." American Behavioral Scientist 48, no. 7 (March 2005): 840–58.

Gray, Jonathan, Cornel Sandvoss, and C. Lee Harrington. "Introduction: Why Study Fans?" In Fandom: Identities and Communities in a Mediated World, edited by Jonathan Gray, Cornel Sandvoss, and C. Lee Harrington, 1–16. New York: New York University Press, 2007.

Gregson, Nicky, Kate Brooks, and Louise Crewe. "Narratives of Consumption and the Body in the Space of the Charity/Shop." In Commercial Cultures: Economies, Practices, Spaces, edited by Peter Jackson, Michelle Lowe, Daniel Miller, and Frank Mort, 101–21. Oxford: Berg, 2000.

Grewal, Inderpal. Transnational America: Feminisms, Diasporas, Neoliberalisms. Durham, N.C.: Duke University Press, 2005.

Griffith, Jim. The Official eBay Bible. 2nd ed. New York: Gotham Books, 2005.

Grosz, Elizabeth. Volatile Bodies: Toward a Corporeal Feminism. Bloomington: Indiana University Press, 1994.

Hagel, John, and Arthur Armstrong. *Net Gain: Expanding Markets through Virtual Communities*. Boston: Harvard Business School Press, 1997.

Halberstam, Judith. *Female Masculinity*. Durham, N.C.: Duke University Press, 1998.

Hale, Grace Elizabeth. *Making Whiteness: The Culture of Segregation in the South, 1890–1940*. New York: Pantheon Books, 1998.

Hardt, Michael, and Antonio Negri. *Multitude: War and Democracy in the Age of Empire*. New York: Penguin, 2004.

Harris, Laura, and Liz Crocker. "An Introduction to Sustaining Femme Gender." In *Femme: Feminists, Lesbians, and Bad Girls*, edited by Laura Harris and Elizabeth Crocker, 1–12. New York: Routledge, 1997.

———. "Mysteries, Mothers, and Cops: An Interview with Mabel Maney." In *Femme: Feminists, Lesbians, and Bad Girls*, edited by Laura Harris and Elizabeth Crocker, 68–81. New York: Routledge, 1997.

Hauben, Michael, and Ronda Hauben. *Netizens: On the History and Impact of Usenet and the Internet*. Los Alamitas, Calif.: IEEE Computer Society Press, 1997.

Havens, Timothy J. "Exhibiting Global Television: On the Business and Cultural Functions of Global Television Fairs." *Journal of Broadcasting and Electronic Media* 47, no. 1 (2003): 18–35.

Hayles, N. Katherine. *How We Became Posthuman: Virtual Bodies in Cybernetics, Literature, and Informatics*. Chicago: University of Chicago Press, 1999.

Herring, Susan. "Critical Analysis of Language Use in Computer-Mediated Contexts: Some Ethical and Scholarly Considerations." *Information Society* 12, no. 2 (June 1996): 153–68.

Herring, Susan C., Inna Kouper, Lois Ann Scheidt, and Elijah L. Wright. "Women and Children Last: The Discursive Construction of Weblogs." In *Into the Blogosphere: Rhetoric, Community, and Culture of Weblogs*, edited by Laura J. Gurak, Smiljana Antonijevic, Laurie Johnson, Clancy Ratliff, and Jessica Reyman, June 2004, 5 February 2011 ⟨http://blog.lib.umn.edu/blogosphere/women_and_children .html⟩.

Herrmann, Gretchen M. "Gift or Commodity: What Changes Hands in the U.S. Garage Sale?" *American Ethnologist* 24, no. 4 (November 1997): 910–30.

———. "Women's Exchange in the U.S. Garage Sale: Giving Gifts and Creating Community." *Gender and Society* 10, no. 6 (December 1996): 703–28.

Hickman, Thomas, and James Ward. "The Dark Side of Brand Community: Inter-Group Stereotyping, Trash Talk, and Schadenfreude." *Advances in Consumer Research* 34 (2007): 314–19.

Hillis, Ken. "A Space for the Trace: Memorable eBay and Narrative Effect." *Space and Culture* 9, no. 2 (May 2006): 140–56.

Hillis, Ken, Michael Petit, and Nathan Scott Epley, eds. *Everyday eBay: Culture, Collecting, and Desire*. New York: Routledge, 2006.

Hills, Matt. "Patterns of Surprise: The 'Aleatory Object' in Psychoanalytic Ethnography and Cyclical Fandom." *American Behavioral Scientist* 48, no. 7 (March 2005): 801–21.

Hine, Christine. *Virtual Methods: Issues in Social Research on the Internet*. Oxford: Berg, 2005.

Hollenbeck, Candice R., and George M. Zinkhan. "Consumer Activism on the Internet: The Role of Anti-brand Communities." *Advances in Consumer Research* 33 (2006): 479–85.

Hollinger, Karen. "Theorizing Mainstream Female Spectatorship: The Case of the Popular Lesbian Film." *Cinema Journal* 37, no. 2 (Winter 1998): 3–17.

Holt, Douglas B. "Why Do Brands Cause Trouble? A Dialectical Theory of Consumer Culture and Branding." *Journal of Consumer Research* 29 (June 2002): 70–90.

Hongladarom, Soraj, and Charles Ess, eds. *Information Technology Ethics: Cultural Perspectives*. Hershey: Idea Group Reference, 2007.

hooks, bell. *Ain't I a Woman: Black Women and Feminism*. Boston: South End, 1981.

———. "Naked without Shame: A Counter-Hegemonic Body Politic." In *Talking Visions: Multicultural Feminism in a Transnational Age*, edited by Ella Shohat, 65–67. Cambridge, Mass.: MIT Press, 1998.

Houser, Daniel, and John Wooders. "Reputation in Auctions: Theory, and Evidence from eBay." *Journal of Economics and Management Strategy* 15, no. 2 (Summer 2006): 353–69.

Ibson, John. *Picturing Men: A Century of Male Relationships in Everyday American Photography*. Washington: Smithsonian Institution Press, 2002.

Ihator, Augustine S. "Communication Style in the Information Age." *Corporate Communications: An International Journal* 6, no. 4 (2001): 199–204.

Ingraham, Chrys. "The Heterosexual Imaginary: Feminist Sociology and Theories of Gender." *Sociological Theory* 12, no. 2 (July 1994): 203–19.

———. *White Weddings: Romancing Heterosexuality in Popular Culture*. London: Routledge, 1999.

Jackson, Stevi. "Gender, Sexuality and Heterosexuality: The Complexity (and Limits) of Heteronormativity." *Feminist Theory* 7, no. 1 (2006): 105–21.

Jang, Heehyoung, Lorne Olfman, Ilsang Ko, Joon Koh, and Kyungtae Kim. "The Influence of On-Line Brand Community Characteristics on Community Commitment and Brand Loyalty." *International Journal of Electronic Commerce* 12, no. 3 (Spring 2008): 57–80.

Jarrett, Kylie. "The Perfect Community: Disciplining the eBay User." In *Everyday eBay: Culture, Collecting, and Desire*, edited by Ken Hillis, Michael Petit, and Nathan Scott Epley, 107–21. New York: Routledge, 2006.

Jenkins, Henry, ed. *The Children's Culture Reader*. New York: New York University Press, 1998.

———. *Fans, Bloggers, and Gamers: Exploring Participatory Culture*. New York: New York University Press, 2002.

————. "Interactive Audiences?" In *The New Media Book*, edited by Dan Harries, 157–70. London: British Film Institute Publishing, 2002.

Jenkins, Richard. "Categorization: Identity, Social Process, and Epistemology." *Current Sociology* 48, no. 3 (July 2000): 7–25.

Johnson, Derek. "Fan-tagonism: Factions, Institutions, and Constitutive Hegemonies of Fandom." In *Fandom: Identities and Communities in a Mediated World*, edited by Jonathan Gray, Cornel Sandvoss, and C. Lee Harrington, 285–300. New York: New York University Press, 2007.

Jones, Amelia, ed. *The Feminism and Visual Culture Reader*. London: Routledge, 2003.

Jones, John Philip, and Jan S. Slater. *What's in a Name? Advertising and the Concept of Brands*. Armonk, N.Y.: M. E. Sharpe, 2003.

Jowett, Donna. "Origins, Occupation, and the Proximity of the Neighbour." In *Who Is This "We"?* edited by Eleanor M. Godway and Geraldine Finn, 11–30. Montreal: Black Rose Books, 1994.

Joyrich, Lynn. *Re-viewing Reception: Television, Gender, and Postmodern Culture*. Bloomington: Indiana University Press, 1996.

Kahn, Richard, and Douglas Kellner. "New Media and Internet Activism: From the 'Battle of Seattle' to Blogging." *New Media and Society* 6, no. 1 (2004): 87–95.

Kaplan, Caren. "'A World without Boundaries': The Body Shop's Trans/National Geographics." *Social Text* no. 43 (Autumn 1995): 45–66.

Kaplan, E. Ann. "Is the Gaze Male?" In *Powers of Desire: The Politics of Sexuality*, edited by Ann Snitow, C. Stansell, and S. Thompson, 309–27. New York: Monthly Review Press, 1983.

Kates, Steven M. "The Protean Quality of Subcultural Consumption: An Ethnographic Account of Gay Consumers." *Journal of Consumer Research* 9 (2002): 383–99.

Kennedy, Elizabeth Lapovsky, and Madeline Davis. *Boots of Leather, Slippers of Gold: History of a Lesbian Community*. New York: Routledge, 1993.

————. "'They Was No One to Mess With': The Construction of the Butch Role in the Lesbian Community of the 1940s and 1950s." In *The Persistent Desire: A Femme-Butch Reader*, edited by Joan Nestle, 62–79. Boston: Alyson, 1992.

Kerin, Roger A., and William L. Cron. "Assessing Trade Show Functions and Performance: An Exploratory Study." *Journal of Marketing* 51 (July 1987): 87–94.

Kern-Foxworth, Marilyn. *Aunt Jemima, Uncle Ben, and Rastus: Blacks in Advertising, Yesterday, Today, and Tomorrow*. Westport, Conn.: Greenwood, 1994.

Kessler, Suzanne J., and Wendy McKenna. *Gender: An Ethnomethodological Approach*. Chicago: University of Chicago Press, 1978.

Kibby, Marjorie, and Brigid Costello. "Displaying the Phallus: Masculinity and the Performance of Sexuality on the Internet." *Men and Masculinities* 1, no. 4 (April 1999): 352–64.

Kinsella, Sharon. "Cuties in Japan." In *Women, Media, and Consumption in Japan*, edited by Lise Skov and Brian Moeran, 220–54. Honolulu: University of Hawai'i Press, 1995.

————. "Minstrelized Girls: Male Performers of Japan's Lolita Complex." *Japan Forum* 18, no. 1 (2006): 65–87.

Kjus, Yngvar. "Idolizing and Monetizing the Public: The Production of Celebrities and Fans, Representatives and Citizens in Reality TV." *International Journal of Communication* 3 (2009): 277–300.

Kofman, Eleonore. "Citizenship for Some but Not for Others." *Political Geography* 14, no. 2 (1995): 121–37.

Korsgaard, Christine. "The Authority of Reflection." In *The Sources of Normativity*, edited by Onora O'Neill, 90–130. Cambridge: Cambridge University Press, 1996.

————. "The Normative Question." In *The Sources of Normativity*, edited by Onora O'Neill, 7–48. Cambridge: Cambridge University Press, 1996.

Kozinets, Robert V. "E-Tribalized Marketing? The Strategic Implications of Virtual Communities of Consumption." *European Management Journal* 17, no. 3 (1999): 252–64.

Krauss, Rosalind E. "Reinventing the Medium." *Critical Inquiry* (Winter 1999): 289–305.

Kristeva, Julia. *Powers of Horror: An Essay on Abjection.* New York: Columbia University Press, 1982.

Kücklich, Julian. "Precarious Playbour: Modders and the Digital Games Industry." *FibreCulture* 5, no. 17 (2005), 5 February 2011 ⟨http://www.journal.fibreculture.org/issue5/kucklich.html⟩.

Lægran, Anne Sofie, and James Stewart. "Nerdy, Trendy, or Healthy? Configuring the Internet Café." *New Media and Society* 5, no. 3 (2003): 357–77.

Landman, Ruth H. "Washington's Yard Sales: Women's Work but Not for the Money." *City and Society* 1, no. 2 (December 1987): 148–61.

Lasusa, Danielle M. "Eiffel Tower Key Chains and Other Pieces of Reality: The Philosophy of Souvenirs." *Philosophical Forum* 38, no. 3 (Fall 2007): 271–87.

Laughey, Dan. "User Authority through Mediated Interaction: A Case of eBay-in-Use." *Journal of Consumer Culture* 10, no. 1 (2010): 105–28.

Lazzarato, Maurizio. "Towards an Inquiry into Immaterial Labour." *Makeworlds* 4 (August 2004), 5 February 2011 ⟨http://makeworlds.org/node/141⟩.

Lehman, Peter. "You and Voyeurweb: Illustrating the Shifting Representation of the Penis on the Internet with User-Generated Content." *Cinema Journal* 46, no. 4 (Summer 2007): 108–16.

Lewallen, Avis. "Lace: Pornography for Women?" In *The Female Gaze: Women as Viewers of Popular Culture*, edited by Lorraine Gamman and Margaret Marshment, 86–101. Seattle: Real Comet, 1989.

Lewis, Charles. "Working the Ritual: Professional Wedding Photography and the American Middle Class." *Journal of Communication Inquiry* 22, no. 1 (January 1998): 72–92.

Lewis, Michael. *Twenty Questions to Ask before Buying on eBay.* Franklin Lakes, N.J.: Career Press, 2006.

Lillie, Jon. "Immaterial Labor in the eBay Community: The Work of Consumption in the 'Network Society.'" In *Everyday eBay: Culture, Collecting, and Desire*, edited by Ken Hillis, Michael Petit, and Nathan Scott Epley, 91–106. New York: Routledge, 2006.

Lindsay, Christina. "From the Shadows: Users as Designers, Producers, Marketers, Distributors, and Technical Support." In *How Users Matter: The Co-construction of Users and Technology*, edited by Nelly Oudshoorn and Trevor Pinch, 29–50. Cambridge, Mass.: MIT Press, 2003.

Lingis, Alphonso. *The Community of Those Who Have Nothing in Common*. Bloomington: Indiana University Press, 1991.

———. "New Walls in the Information Age." *Social Identities* 11, no. 3 (2005): 271–82.

Lipsitz, George. "Mardi Gras Indians: Carnival and Counter-Narrative in Black New Orleans." *Cultural Critique* 10 (Autumn 1998): 99–121.

Livingston, Jeffrey A. "How Valuable Is a Good Reputation? A Sample Selection Model of Internet Auctions." *Review of Economics and Statistics* 87, no. 5 (2005): 453–65.

Livingston, Jessica. *Founders at Work: Stories of Startups' Early Days*. Berkeley, Calif.: Apress, 2007.

Livingstone, Sonia, and Peter Lunt. "Representing Citizens and Consumers in Media and Communications Regulation." *Annals of the American Academy of Political and Social Science* 611 (May 2007): 51–65.

Loe, Meika. "Fixing Broken Masculinity: Viagra as a Technology for the Production of Gender and Sexuality." *Sexuality and Culture* 5, no. 3 (Summer 2001): 97–125.

Lott, Eric. *Love and Theft: Blackface Minstrelsy and the American Working Class*. New York: Oxford University Press, 1993.

Lyotard, Jean-François. *Postmodern Fables*, translated by Georges Van Den Abbeele. Minneapolis: University of Minnesota Press, 1997.

Madge, Clare. "Developing a Geographers' Agenda for Online Research Ethics." *Progress in Human Geography* 31, no. 5 (2007): 654–74.

Manning, Toby. "Gay Culture: Who Needs It?" In *Anti-gay*, edited by Mark Simpson, 98–117. London: Freedom Editions, 1997.

Manring, M. M. *Slave in a Box: The Strange Career of Aunt Jemima*. Charlottesville: University Press of Virginia, 1998.

Markham, Annette N., and Nancy K. Baym, eds. *Internet Inquiry: Conversations about Method*. Thousand Oaks, Calif.: Sage, 2009.

Martin, Emily. *The Woman in the Body: A Cultural Analysis of Reproduction*. Boston: Beacon, 2001.

McDonald, Cynthia G., and Carlos Slawson Jr. "Reputation in an Internet Auction Market." *Economic Inquiry* 40, no. 3 (October 2002): 633–50.

McIntosh, William D., and Brandon Schmeichel. "Collectors and Collecting: A Social Psychological Perspective." *Leisure Sciences* 26 (2004): 85–97.

McPherson, Tara. *Reconstructing Dixie: Race, Gender, and Nostalgia in the Imagined South*. Durham, N.C.: Duke University Press, 2003.

Melnik, Mikhail, and James Alm. "Does a Seller's Reputation Matter? Evidence from eBay Auctions." *Journal of Industrial Economics* 50, no. 3 (2002): 337–50.

Metz, Christian. *The Imaginary Signifier: Psychoanalysis and the Cinema*, translated by Celia Britton, Annwyl Williams, Ben Brewster, and Alfred Guzzetti. Bloomington: Indiana University Press, 1982.

Miami Theory Collective, eds. *Community at Loose Ends*. Minneapolis: University of Minnesota Press, 1991.

Micheletti, Michele, and Dietlind Stolle. "Fashioning Social Justice through Political Consumerism, Capitalism, and the Internet." *Cultural Studies* 22, no. 5 (September 2008): 749–69.

Miller, Toby. *Cultural Citizenship: Cosmopolitanism, Consumerism, and Television in a Neoliberal Age*. Philadelphia: Temple University Press, 2007.

————. "A Short History of the Penis." *Social Text* 43 (Autumn 1995): 1–26.

Minichiello, Victor, Jan Browne, and Hal Kendig. "Perceptions and Consequences of Ageism: Views of Older People." *Ageing and Society* 20 (2000): 253–78.

Mirzoeff, Nicholas. *An Introduction to Visual Culture*. New York: Routledge, 1999.

————, ed. *The Visual Culture Reader*. London: Routledge, 1998.

Mitchell, W. J. T. "Showing Seeing: A Critique of Visual Culture." *Journal of Visual Culture* 1, no. 2 (2002): 165–81.

Möllenberg, Antje, "Internet Auctions in Marketing: The Consumer Perspective." *Electronic Markets* 14, no. 4 (2004): 360–71.

Montfort, Nick. "Continuous Paper: The Early Materiality and Workings of Electronic Literature." 28 December 2004, 5 February 2011 ⟨http://nickm.com/writing/essays/continuous_paper_mla.html⟩.

Morgan, Jo-Ann. "Mammy the Huckster: Selling the Old South for the New Century." *American Art* 9, no. 1 (Spring 1995): 86–109.

Motley, Carol M., Geraldine R. Henderson, and Stacey Menzel Baker. "Exploring Collective Memories Associated with African-American Advertising Memorabilia." *Journal of Advertising* 32, no. 1 (Spring 2003): 47–57.

Mulvey, Laura. *Visual and Other Pleasures*. Bloomington: Indiana University Press, 1989.

Muñiz, Albert M., Jr., and Thomas C. O'Guinn. "Brand Community." *Journal of Consumer Research* 27, no. 4 (March 2001): 412–32.

Muñiz, Albert M., Jr., and Hope Jensen Schau. "Religiosity in the Abandoned Apple Newton Brand Community." *Journal of Consumer Research* 31 (March 2005): 737–47.

————. "Vigilante Marketing and Consumer-Created Communications." *Journal of Advertising* 36, no. 3 (Fall 2007): 35–50.

Murphy, Tom. *Web Rules: How the Internet Is Changing the Way Consumers Make Choices*. Dearborn, Ill.: A Kaplan Professional Company, 2000.

Nancy, Jean-Luc. *The Inoperative Community*, edited by Peter Connor. Minneapolis: University of Minnesota Press, 1991.

Nelson, Michelle R., Mark A. Rademacher, and Hye-Jin Paek. "Freecycle Community Downshifting Consumer = Upshifting Citizen? An Examination of a Local Freecycle Community." *Annals of the American Academy of Political and Social Science* 611 (2007): 141–56.

Nelson, Todd D. "Ageism: Prejudice against Our Feared Future Self." *Journal of Social Issues* 61, no. 2 (2005): 207–21.

Nestle, Joan. "Flamboyance and Fortitude: An Introduction." In *The Persistent Desire: A Femme-Butch Reader*, edited by Joan Nestle, 13–22. Boston: Alyson, 1992.

Ngai, Sianne. "The Cuteness of the Avant-garde." *Critical Inquiry* 31 (Summer 2005): 812–47.

Nissanoff, Daniel. *FutureShop: How the New Auction Culture Will Revolutionize the Way We Buy, Sell, and Get the Things We Really Want.* New York: Penguin, 2006.

Noveck, Beth Simone. "Trademark Law and the Social Construction of Trust: Creating the Legal Framework for On-Line Identity." 2005, 5 February 2011 〈http://www.infosci.cornell.edu/about/colloquiumFA05/sept30.doc〉.

Obst, Patricia, Lucy Zinkiewicz, and Sandy G. Smith. "Sense of Community in Science Fiction Fandom, Part 1: Understanding Sense of Community in an International Community of Interest." *Journal of Community Psychology* 30, no. 1 (2002): 87–103.

O'Neill, Onora. Introduction to *The Sources of Normativity*, edited by Onora O'Neill, xi–xv. Cambridge: Cambridge University Press, 1996.

Oppermann, Martin, and Kye-Sung Chon. "Convention Participation Decision-Making Process." *Annals of Tourism Research* 24, no. 1 (1996): 178–91.

Örnebring, Henrik. "Alternate Reality Gaming and Convergence Culture." *International Journal of Cultural Studies* 10, no. 4 (2007): 445–62.

Oswald, Ramona Faith. "A Member of the Wedding? Heterosexism and Family Ritual." In *Lesbian Rites: Symbolic Acts and the Power of Community*, edited by Ramona Faith Oswald, 107–31. New York: Harrington Park, 2003.

Otnes, Cele, and Tina M. Lowrey. "'Til Debt Do Us Part: The Selection and Meaning of Artifacts in the American Wedding." *Advances in Consumer Research* 20 (1993): 325–29.

Otnes, Cele, and Elizabeth Hafkin Pleck. *Cinderella Dreams: The Allure of the Lavish Wedding.* Berkeley: University of California Press, 2003.

Oudshoorn, Nelly, Els Rommes, and Marcelle Stienstra. "Configuring the User as Everybody: Gender and Design Cultures in Information and Communication Technologies." *Science, Technology and Human Values* 29, no. 1 (Winter 2004): 30–63.

Ozanne, Julie L., and Jeff B. Murray. "Uniting Critical Theory and Public Policy to Create the Reflexively Defiant Consumer." *American Behavioral Scientist* 38, no. 4 (February 1995): 516–25.

Panek, Elliott. "Who Are Wii? The Study of Console Fandom." *FlowTV* 5, no. 9, February 2007, 5 February 2011 〈http://flowtv.org/?p=55〉.

Parthasarathy, Shobita. *Building Genetic Medicine: Breast Cancer, Technology, and the Comparative Politics of Health Care*. Cambridge, Mass.: MIT Press, 2007.

Patterson, Laura Sloan. "Why Are All the Fat Brides Smiling? Body Image and the American Bridal Industry." *Feminist Media Studies* 5, no. 2 (July 2005): 237–60.

Perrin, Sarah. "A Serious Business." *Accountancy* 121, no. 1254 (February 1998): 40.

Petit, Michael. "'Cleaned to eBay Standards': Sex Panic, eBay, and the Moral Economy of Underwear." In *Everyday eBay: Culture, Collecting, and Desire*, edited by Ken Hillis, Michael Petit, and Nathan Scott Epley, 267–82. New York: Routledge, 2006.

Pigg, Kenneth E. "Applications of Community Informatics for Building Community and Enhancing Civic Society." *Information, Communication and Society* 4, no. 4 (2001): 507–27.

Pilgrim, David. "The Garbage Man: Why I Collect Racist Objects." Jim Crow Museum of Racist Memorabilia, Ferris State University, Big Rapids, Mich., February 2005, 5 February 2011 ⟨http://www.ferris.edu/news/jimcrow/collect/⟩.

Poster, Mark. "Visual Studies as Media Studies." *Journal of Visual Culture* 1, no. 1 (2002): 67–70.

Postigo, Hector. "From Pong to Planet Quake: Post-industrial Transitions from Leisure to Work." *Information, Communication and Society* 6, no. 4 (2003): 593–607.

Potts, Annie. "The Essence of the Hard On: Hegemonic Masculinity and the Cultural Construction of 'Erectile Dysfunction.'" *Men and Masculinities* 3, no. 1 (July 2000): 85–103.

Prahalad, C. K., and Venkat Ramaswamy. "Co-creation Experiences: The Next Practice in Value Creation." *Journal of Interactive Marketing* 18, no. 3 (Summer 2004): 5–14.

Prince, Dennis L., Sarah Manongdo, and Dan Joya. *How to Buy Everything for Your Wedding on eBay . . . and Save a Fortune!* New York: McGraw-Hill, 2005.

Putnam, Robert D. *Bowling Alone: The Collapse and Revival of American Community*. New York: Simon and Schuster, 2000.

———, ed. *Democracies in Flux*. Oxford: Oxford University Press, 2002.

Rafaeli, S., and A. Noy. "Online Auctions, Messaging, Communication, and Social Facilitation: A Simulation and Experimental Evidence." *European Journal of Information Systems* 11 (2002): 196–207.

Resnick, Paul, Richard Zeckhauser, John Swanson, and Kate Lockwood. "The Value of Reputation on eBay: A Controlled Experiment." *Experimental Economics* 9, no. 2 (June 2006): 79–101.

Rheingold, Howard. *The Virtual Community: Homesteading on the Electronic Frontier*. Reading, Mass.: Addison-Wesley, 1993.

Rice, Gillian. "Using the Interaction Approach to Understand Trade Shows." *International Marketing Review* 9, no. 4 (1992): 32–45.

Richardson, Diane. "Locating Sexualities: From Here to Normality." *Sexualities* 7, no. 4 (2004): 391–411.

Rietjens, Bob. "Trust and Reputation on eBay: Towards a Legal Framework for Feedback Intermediaries." *Information and Communications Technology Law* 15, no. 1 (March 2006): 55–78.

Riviere, Joan. "Womanliness as Masquerade." *International Journal of Psychoanalysis* 10 (1929): 303–13.

Roach, Joseph. "Carnival and the Law in New Orleans." *Drama Review* 37, no. 3 (Autumn 1993): 42–75.

Rohlinger, Deanna A. "Eroticizing Men: Cultural Influences on Advertising and Male Objectification." *Sex Roles* 46, nos. 3/4 (February 2002): 61–74.

Rubin, Gayle. "Thinking Sex: Notes for a Radical Theory of the Politics of Sexuality." In *The Lesbian and Gay Studies Reader*, edited by Henry Abelove, Michèle Aina Barale, and David M. Halperin, 3–44. New York: Routledge, 1993.

Ruggeri, Kevin. "Not for Sale: Liberation and Commodified Identity in Ellison's *Invisible Man*." *Concept: An Interdisciplinary Journal of Graduate Studies* (2007), 5 February 2011 ⟨http://www.publications.villanova.edu/Concept/2007.html⟩.

St. John, Maria. "'It Ain't Fittin''": Cinematic and Fantasmatic Contours of Mammy in *Gone with the Wind* and Beyond." *Studies in Gender and Sexuality* 2, no. 2 (2001): 129–62.

Sartelle, Joe. "As If We Were a Community: The Odd Experience of Attending Both the Lesbian and Gay Freedom Day Parade in San Francisco and the '25 Year Mission Tour' Star Trek Convention in San Mateo." *Bad Subjects* 1 (September 1992), 5 February 2011 ⟨http://bad.eserver.org/issues/1992/01/sartelle.html⟩.

Scammell, Margaret. "The Internet and Civic Engagement: The Age of the Citizen-Consumer." *Political Communication* 17, no. 4 (2000): 351–55.

Schild, Verónica. "Empowering 'Consumer-Citizens' or Governing Poor Female Subjects? The Institutionalization of 'Self-Development' in the Chilean Social Field." *Journal of Consumer Culture* 7, no. 2 (2007): 179–203.

Schot, Johan, and Adri Albert de la Bruheze. "The Mediated Design of Products, Consumption, and Consumers in the Twentieth Century." In *How Users Matter: The Co-construction of Users and Technology*, edited by Nelly Oudshoorn and Trevor Pinch, 229–45. Cambridge, Mass.: MIT Press, 2003.

Schudson, Michael. "Citizens, Consumers, and the Good Society." *Annals of the American Academy of Political and Social Science* 611 (May 2007): 236–49.

Schuster, Sherril Horowitz. "Here Comes the Bride: Wedding Announcements and Bridal Norms." *Sociological Focus* 30, no. 3 (August 1997): 279–94.

Secomb, Linnell, "Fractured Community." *Hypatia* 15, no. 2 (2000): 133–50.

Seidman, Steven. "From Identity to Queer Politics: Shifts in Normative Heterosexuality and the Meaning of Citizenship." *Citizenship Studies* 5, no. 3 (2001): 321–28.

Sender, Katherine. "Selling Sexual Subjectivities: Audiences Respond to Gay Window Advertising." *Critical Studies in Mass Communication* 16 (1999): 172–96.

———. "Sex Sells: Sex Class, and Taste in Commercial Gay and Lesbian Media." *GLQ: A Journal of Lesbian and Gay Studies* 9, no. 3 (2003): 331–65.

Shah, Dhavan V., Douglas M. McLeod, Eunkyung Kim, Sun Young Lee, Melissa R. Gottlieb, Shirley S. Ho, and Hilde Breivik. "Political Consumerism: How Communication and Consumption Orientations Drive 'Lifestyle Politics.'" *Annals of the American Academy of Political and Social Science* 611 (May 2007): 217–35.

Shea, Virginia. *Netiquette*. San Francisco: Albion Books, 1994.

Sicilia, Maria, and Mariola Palazón. "Brand Communities on the Internet: A Case Study of Coca-Cola's Spanish Virtual Community." *Corporate Communication* 13, no. 3 (2008): 255–70.

Simpson, Mark, "Gay Dream Believer: Inside the Gay Underwear Cult." In *Anti-gay*, edited by Mark Simpson, 1–12. London: Freedom Editions, 1997.

Slater, Don. "Trading Sexpics on IRC: Embodiment and Authenticity on the Internet." *Body and Society* 4, no. 4 (1998): 91–117.

Slater, Jan S. "Collecting The Real Thing: A Case Study Exploration of Brand Loyalty Enhancement among Coca-Cola Brand Collectors." *Advances in Consumer Research* 27 (2000): 202–8.

Smith, Herbert. "Buttons, T-Shirts, and Bumperstickers: The Semiotics of Some Recursive Systems." *Journal of Popular Culture* 21, no. 4 (Spring 1988): 141–49.

Smith, Shawn Michelle. "'Baby's Picture Is Always Treasured': Eugenics and the Reproduction of Whiteness in the Family Photograph Album." *Yale Journal of Criticism* 11, no. 1 (1998): 197–220.

Sobal, Jeffery, Caron Bove, and Barbara Rauschenbach. "Weight and Weddings: The Social Construction of Beautiful Brides." In *Interpreting Weight: The Social Management of Fatness and Thinness*, edited by Jeffery Sobal and Donna Maurer, 113–35. New York: Aldine de Gruyter, 1999.

Solomon, Alisa. "Not Just a Passing Fantasy: Notes on Butch." In *The Passionate Camera: Photography and Bodies of Desire*, edited by Deborah Bright, 263–75. London: Routledge, 1998.

Sontag, Susan. *On Photography*. New York: Penguin, 1977.

Spain, Daphne. "Race Relations and Residential Segregation in New Orleans: Two Centuries of Paradox." *Annals of the American Academy of Political and Social Science* 441 (January 1979): 82–96.

Stephens, Elizabeth. "Looking-Class Heroes: Dykes on Bikes Cruising Calendar Girls." In *The Passionate Camera: Photography and Bodies of Desire*, edited by Deborah Bright, 276–87. London: Routledge, 1998.

Stewart, Susan. *On Longing: Narratives of the Miniature, the Gigantic, the Souvenir, and the Collection*. Baltimore: Johns Hopkins University Press, 1984.

Stolle, Dietlind, Marc Hooghe, and Michele Micheletti, "Politics in the Supermarket: Political Consumerism as a Form of Political Participation." *International Political Science Review* 26, no. 3 (2005): 245–69.

Straayer, Chris. *Deviant Eyes, Deviant Bodies*. New York: Columbia University Press, 1996.

Suhr, Hiesun Cecilia. "Underpinning the Paradoxes in the Artistic Fields of MySpace:

The Problematization of Values and Popularity in Convergence Culture." *New Media and Society* 11, nos. 1/2 (2009): 179–98.

Swanberg, Jennifer E. "Illuminating Gendered Assumptions: An Important Step in Creating a Family-Friendly Organization: A Case Study." *Community, Work and Family* 7, no. 1 (April 2004): 3–28.

Terranova, Tiziana. "Free Labor: Producing Culture for the Digital Economy." *Social Text* 63, 18, no. 2 (Summer 2000): 33–58.

———. *Network Culture: Politics for the Information Age*. London: Pluto, 2004.

Thrift, Nigel. "Closer to the Machine? Intelligent Environments, New Forms of Possession and the Rise of the Supertoy." *Cultural Geographies* 10 (2003): 389–407.

Tiefer, Leonore. "The Medicalization of Impotence: Normalizing Phallocentrism." *Gender and Society* 8, no. 3 (September 1994): 363–77.

Trodd, Zoe. "Reading eBay: Hidden Stories, Subjective Stories, and a People's History of the Archive." In *Everyday eBay: Culture, Collecting, and Desire*, edited by Ken Hillis, Michael Petit, and Nathan Scott Epley, 77–90. New York: Routledge, 2006.

Turner, Patricia A. *Ceramic Uncles and Celluloid Mammies: Black Images and Their Influence on Culture*. New York: Anchor, 1994.

van Oost, Ellen. "Materialized Gender: How Shavers Configure the Users' Femininity and Masculinity." In *How Users Matter: The Co-construction of Users and Technology*, edited by Nelly Oudshoorn and Trevor Pinch, 193–208. Cambridge, Mass.: MIT Press, 2003.

Venman, Barbara. "Boundary Face-Off: New Orleans Civil Rights Law and Carnival Tradition." *TDR* 37, no. 3 (Autumn 1993): 76–109.

Wakeford, Nina. "Developing Methodological Frameworks for Studying the World Wide Web." In *Web Studies*, edited by David Gauntlett and Ross Horsley, 34–50. 2nd ed. London: Arnold, 2004.

Walton, Kenneth. *Forgery, Lies, and eBay*. New York: Simon Spotlight Entertainment, 2006.

Ward, Graham. "Hung Like a Horse: Male Stripping in Recent Films." *Journal of Textual Reasoning* 7 (1998), 5 February 2011 ⟨http://etext.virginia.edu/journals/tr/archive/volume7/ward.html⟩.

Wellman, Barry. "From Little Boxes to Loosely Bound Networks: The Privatization and Domestication of Community." In *Sociology for the Twenty-First Century: Continuities and Cutting Edges*, edited by Janet L. Abu-Lughod, 94–114. Chicago: University of Chicago Press, 2000.

West, Candace, and Don H. Zimmerman. "Doing Gender." *Gender and Society* 1, no. 2 (June 1987): 125–51.

White, Michele. "Babies Who Touch You: Reborn Dolls, Artists, and the Emotive Display of Bodies on eBay." In *Political Emotions*, edited by Janet Staiger, Ann Cvetkovich, and Ann Reynolds, 66–89. London: Routledge, 2010.

———. *The Body and the Screen: Theories of Internet Spectatorship*. Cambridge, Mass.: MIT Press, 2006.

————. "Engaged with eBay: How Heterosexual Unions and Traditional Gender Roles Are Rendered by the Site and Members." *Feminist Media Studies* 11, no. 3 (September 2011): 1–17.

————. "Listing eBay Masculinity: Erotic Exchanges and Regulation in 'Gay' and 'Gay Interest' Underwear and Swimwear Auctions." *Journal of Gender Studies* 19, no. 1 (March 2010): 43–58.

————. "My Queer eBay: 'Gay Interest' Photographic Images and the Visual Culture of Buying." In *Everyday eBay: Culture, Collecting, and Desire*, edited by Ken Hillis, Michael Petit, and Nathan Scott Epley, 245–65. New York: Routledge, 2006.

————. "Regulating Research: The Problem of Theorizing Community on LambdaMOO." *Ethics and Information Technology* 4, no. 1 (2002): 55–70.

————. "Representations or People." *Ethics and Information Technology* 4, no. 3 (2002): 249–66.

————. "What a Mess: eBay's Narratives about Personalization, Heterosexuality, and Disordered Homes." *Journal of Consumer Culture* 10, no. 1 (2010): 80–104.

Wilcox, Ronald T. "Experts and Amateurs: The Role of Experience in Internet Auctions." *Marketing Letters* 11, no. 4 (November 2000): 363–74.

Williams, Linda. "Second Thoughts on *Hard Core*: American Obscenity Law and the Scapegoating of Deviance." In *Dirty Looks: Women, Pornography, Power*, edited by Pamela Church Gibson and Roma Gibson, 176–91. London: British Film Institute Publishing, 1993.

Wood, Mitchell J. "The Gay Male Gaze: Body Image Disturbance and Gender Oppression among Gay Men." *Journal of Gay and Lesbian Social Services* 17, no. 2 (2004): 43–62.

Woolgar, Steve. "Configuring the User: The Case of Usability Trials." In *A Sociology of Monsters: Essays on Power, Technology and Domination*, edited by John Law, 58–99. London: Routledge, 1991.

Woolgar, Steve, Janet Vaux, Paula Gomes, Jean-Noel Ezingeard, and Robert Grieve. "Abilities and Competencies Required, Particularly by Small Firms, to Identify and Acquire New Technology." *Technovation* 18, nos. 8/9 (1998): 575–84.

Yee, Nick. "The Labor of Fun: How Video Games Blur the Boundaries of Work and Play." *Games and Culture* 1, no. 1 (January 2006): 68–71.

Yetman, Norman R. "The Background of the Slave Narrative Collection." *American Quarterly* 19, no. 3 (Autumn 1967): 534–53.

Young, Iris Marion. *On Female Body Experience: "Throwing Like a Girl" and Other Essays*. New York: Oxford University Press, 2005.

Zwick, Detlev, Samuel K. Bonsu, and Aron Darmody. "Putting Consumers to Work: 'Co-creation' and New Marketing Govern-Mentality." *Journal of Consumer Culture* 8, no. 2 (2008): 163–96.

INDEX

Abject, 20, 86, 98, 101–4, 189, 213

About Me, 35, 37, 58, 61, 80, 131, 145, 149, 156

Acker, Joan, 8, 85

Adesso, 91–92, 94–95

Adult Only category, 10, 112, 121, 132

Ageism, 62–64

Anderson, Benedict, 30, 67

Anti-brand communities, 80–83, 182

Anti-fans, 79–83, 138, 182

Apple computer, 4, 28, 37

Archive, 148; gay and lesbian, 132, 149–50

Aspling, Brad, 88, 96, 108

AuctionWeb, 9, 26

auntjennysbox, 149–50

Authentic: body as, 133, 164; community as, 80; crafting and, 185; experience of, 16, 49, 99; objects as, 186; photography as, 15–16, 113; troubling of, 15–16, 184–86

Authorship, 4–7, 10, 23, 25, 34, 46, 55–56, 125, 132, 150, 176, 200–202, 207, 216

Avatars, 78, 117, 167, 169, 184

Bakker, Conrad, ix

bamajl, 70–71

Barbie doll, 1–2, 141

Barthes, Roland, 15, 123, 161

Baym, Nancy, 58, 64

beachbadge, 60–61, 69, 70

Benjamin, Walter, 15, 184

Black Americana category, 21, 170–71; Asian products in, 180–82, 199; collecting of, 168, 173, 182–85; commodification in, 169, 172, 177–78, 183, 187–89, 197, 200; community and, 169, 185, 197; cuteness in, 172, 191–93; eBay's policy on, 174–75; history in, 171, 182, 198; oversize features in, 190–91, 194, 199; racism in, 168, 171, 173, 177–78, 186–87, 189, 194, 199; resistance to, 182–84, 186–87, 199–202; sexuality in, 179, 180, 188–89, 195; slavery and, 178–80, 182, 187, 194–95; stereotypes in, 169, 180, 182, 186, 193–94, 199; women and, 175–76, 178, 187–89, 195

Blogging, 13, 22, 33

bobal, 66, 69–71

Bodies: construction of, 3, 9, 133–34, 163–64, 166–67, 188; control of, 1, 20, 22, 51, 84, 98, 196; gay identities and, 79, 110–11, 113–14, 118–31, 135–36; masculinity and, 20, 134, 140; technology and, 91; unruly forms of, 107, 162–64; view-

Dress advertisement, 88–89
Duncan, Carol, 155, 157
Dyer, Richard, 111, 125

eBay-ana, 17, 50–51, 52, 56, 70, 122; advent of, 76–77; collecting of, 19, 27, 70, 72–80, 82; employees and, 74–75, 77; prices of, 77, 79–80; values and, 53, 75–76
eBay branded items, 3, 19–20, 37, 52–53, 55, 60, 67–68, 70, 72–74, 80
eBay Developers Conference, 17, 36, 40
eBay forums, 17, 19, 20, 26–28, 32, 35–36, 38, 43, 56–71, 76, 113, 121, 149
eBay gift finders, 7, 9, 13–14, 86
eBay headquarters, 40, 101
eBay Live! community conference board, 58–60, 62–71
eBay Live! conference, 17, 24–25, 36, 37, 45, 47, 50–51, 52–54, 71–72, 74; age at, 62–63; cancellation of, 52, 70, 82–83; clothing at, 67–68, 72–73; executives and employees at, 5, 49, 60, 72, 79; family at, 62, 66–67; friendship at, 24–25, 52–53, 62, 69–70, 75; gender at, 61–62; illicit activities at, 75–76; race at, 61; seasonal aspects of, 82–83; sexuality at, 62–65; values and, 60, 75, 81, 88, 96; weddings at, 25, 88
eBay: On Location conference, 52–53, 58, 59, 70, 77, 82
eBay's community values, 5, 6, 37–40, 42, 174
eBay's founding mythos, 9–11, 13, 85, 86, 88, 92, 137
eBay's history, 5, 12–13, 19, 32, 56, 60, 85, 86, 104, 106; gay and lesbian transformations of, 110, 149
eBay's policies, 7, 12–13, 41–43, 46, 47–48, 59, 82, 109, 111–12, 116, 118, 123, 174–75, 178, 186, 187, 194
eBay's values, 2–6, 13, 16, 19–20, 25, 27–30, 38, 40–41, 44, 55, 57, 60–61, 66–67, 70–71, 83, 109, 205, 208; black Ameri-

cana and, 174, 181; challenging of, 49, 75, 109, 161, 202; community and, 2–6, 19, 29, 37, 40, 42; gay and lesbian interests and, 20, 64–65, 114, 141; gender and, 64–65, 94, 107; heteronormativity and, 20, 63–64, 84, 95, 102
ebulges, 131–33
ecommerce, 30–31, 113
eGay, 41–42, 122, 137, 232 n. 90
elegantharlot, 170–71
elfie, 35–36
Elsner, John, and Roger Cardinal, 139, 141
Empowerment: brand communities and, 4, 33, 49–50, 66; consumers and, 31; craigslist's narratives about, 207; eBay's narratives about, 4, 19, 24, 27–29, 49–50, 90–91, 99, 107, 176; technologies and, 7, 61, 91, 205, 207, 217
endymian, 135, 137, 139
Engagements, marriage: eBay's use of, 85–89, 104, 110, 146, 149, 160, 167, 187
Engagement rings: eBay's use of, 13, 20, 84–85, 87–89, 101, 141, 173
Erotica, 148, 150, 188; eBay and, 10, 20, 47, 118, 132; gay interest uses of, 20, 42, 113–18, 121, 123, 131–32, 136–37, 139, 142; gender and, 147, 150, 157, 159, 165, 172, 188; lesbian interest uses of, 20–21, 143–48, 150–57, 165, 167, 172
Essentialism: black culture and, 177; gay interest as, 139–40, 153
Everyone, 29; craigslist's narratives about, 38, 211; eBay's narratives about, 2–5, 7, 9, 25, 37, 49, 59, 61, 66, 83, 85, 90, 93, 95, 111; identity implications of, 7, 9, 61, 83, 85, 89–95, 111, 124, 211; technologies' narratives about, 61, 85, 91–94, 204, 217
Experiential shopping, 16, 36

Facebook, 167, 206
Failures: site promises and, 38, 43, 174–75, 210, 214; technologies and, 16–17, 33, 50, 108–9, 137, 148, 166, 179
Families: corporations' use of, 66–67; eBay

Live! and, 62, 66, 69–71, 76; eBay's use of, 1–2, 9, 10, 29, 49–50, 62, 70, 87, 132, 185; gay and lesbian interest reformations of, 111, 113, 135, 145, 148–49, 161; technology's use of, 91–94; weddings and, 95–97, 100

Fans, 49, 76; brand community members as, 4, 13, 20, 25, 51, 53, 55–56, 59, 67, 69–70, 73–76, 82–83, 121–22, 131, 174, 182; branded objects and, 53, 67–68, 73, 77–79, 82, 115; emotions and, 56–57, 65–66, 72, 79, 80–81, 98–99; free labor of, 35, 58, 72. *See also* Anti-fans

Fan studies, 7, 53, 55–56, 80, 82, 216

Fat, 98; craigslist's control of, 22, 214; weddings and, 20, 86, 97–98, 160

Fayard, Anne-Laure, and Gerardine DeSanctis, 57, 66

Feedback system, 8, 18, 28, 34, 43–46, 48, 58, 66, 80–81, 84, 131, 156, 159

fellowes1964, 129–30

Femininity, 124, 157–58; challenges to, 65, 104–6, 129, 146, 153, 156, 165, 214; instructions in, 21, 22, 210–15; masculinity and, 1, 89–90, 106, 125–31, 135, 142, 160, 207; traditional forms of, 60–62, 85, 156, 161, 191, 211–12; weddings and, 85, 96–97, 104; work and, 7, 33, 35

Feminists: eBay sellers as, 107; politics and, 33; regulation of, 22, 107, 216; research and, 6, 23, 63, 85, 147, 149, 154, 158, 159, 167, 188

Femmes, 160–62, 165

fiberwireguy, 64–65, 80–81

Film theory, 147–49, 154–66, 158–59, 188

FireMeg.com, 47–48, 111

Flickering signifiers, 111, 119, 123, 133, 136, 167

Flickr, 93–94

Flipping, 149

Freecycle, 39–40, 43

Free labor, 1–2, 4, 7, 12, 19, 25–27, 31–36, 49, 50, 59, 68–71, 131–32, 203, 206–10, 215

Fun: eBay Live! as, 62, 68, 71; eBay's site as, 36–37; work rather than, 36

Game modders, 34–35

Garage sales, 39, 107, 238 n. 36

gargantua, 138, 140

Gay and lesbian visibility, 111, 115–17, 123, 136, 138, 146, 150

Gay closet, 79, 123, 138–39

Gay interest listings, x; collecting and, 113–14, 120, 131, 135, 141–42, 173; community in, 40, 114–15, 120, 124, 149; consumer critique in, 110; eBay's regulation of, 2, 10, 12, 104, 110–12, 115, 117–19, 175, 187, 194, 201; eroticism in, 42, 109, 117, 119–20, 123, 125, 127, 131, 135–37; gaze in, 124, 131; history in, 112–13, 135, 149; homophobia and, 137–38; oppositional strategies of, 20, 109, 111, 128, 131, 142, 146, 163; photography and, 134–37; politics of, 10, 137–38; pricing in, 42, 112, 118, 132–33, 149; sexual citizenship in, 10–11, 42, 204; unconventional masculinity and, 110–11, 120, 124–31, 135, 140, 142; underwear, swimwear, and, 119–21, 125, 128–31; visibility in, 62, 111, 115, 123, 163

Gay marketing niche, 119

Gay window ads, 138

Gaze: consumerist forms of, 124, 159; female forms of, 157, 159; gay interest listings and, 121, 124, 130, 142; heterosexuality and, 158; men as object of, 79, 124–26, 131, 158–59; women as object of, 125, 151, 154–56, 159. *See also* Lesbian look; Male gaze

Geni, 93

Genitals, 21, 37, 65, 110–12, 116–20, 122–23, 125, 127–36, 140, 142, 149, 161–64, 166–67, 179, 186, 215. *See also* Cultural genitals; Penises; Visible penis lines

Gift finders, 7, 9, 14

Goings, Kenneth W., 172, 182, 186, 189, 191

Good, 38–39, 208; bad behavior and, 38, 41, 44, 49, 81, 104, 107–9, 168, 174, 177,

Mardi Gras, 73, 180–81

Marriage, 7, 100, 107; consumerism and, 88, 95; critiques of, 85, 94, 104–7, 166–67; eBay's use of, 2, 84–88, 96, 102, 146; members and, 20, 63, 69, 86; Omidyar and Wesley's, 2, 9–10, 13, 86, 96, 146; sexual citizenship and, 10; Wolfe and Aspling's, 88, 96, 108

Marriage engagements: eBay's use of, 85–87, 104, 110, 146, 149, 160, 167, 187

Masculinity: body and, 113–14, 125, 130–31; challenges to, 1, 21, 23, 90, 120, 125, 128, 130, 133–34, 140, 142, 157, 159, 163, 177; feminine forms of, 90, 125–30; gay identities and, 111, 125; gaze and, 120–21, 124–26, 131, 142, 154–59, 162; technologies and, 7; traditional forms of, 85, 89, 105, 113, 125, 157; women's performances of, 143–44, 147, 159, 163, 165

Maze advertisement, 90–91

McCain, John, 11–13

Media fans, 55, 67, 82

Mess, x, 2–3, 86, 98, 101–4

Microsoft, 6–7

Mock weddings, 146–47, 160–61, 163

Modding, 34–35

Mothers, 27, 93; eBay's use of, 90; link to values, 41–43, 100, 222 n. 42; Whitman's references to, 12, 60–61, 85–86

mscljocko, 117, 119, 121, 131

Mulvey, Laura, 147, 154–55

Muscles, 112, 113, 116, 119–20, 125–26, 129, 135

My eBay, 26

My World, 58, 156

Nancy, Jean-Luc, 30, 67

Netiquette, 91 .

Newmark, Craig, 203, 205–10, 214, 216–17

New media studies, 3, 7, 11, 22, 23, 26, 31, 34, 147, 204, 216, 217

New Orleans, 52, 73–74, 181–82, 189, 190, 198–200

Ngai, Sianne, 172, 191, 192

Normative citizens, 25, 41, 88–89, 110, 131, 144

Nostalgia, 100–102, 149; black Americana as, 172–73, 178, 180–81, 184–87

Obadike, Mendi + Keith, 200–202

Obama, Barack, 11, 205, 217

Omidyar, Pierre, 2, 5–7, 9–10, 13, 26–28, 30–34, 37, 39–41, 43–44, 56–58, 60, 79–80, 86–87, 95–96, 108, 146, 205–8

OnlineAuction, 50

Organizational logic, 3, 7–9, 13, 20–23, 37, 61, 64–65, 84–88, 93–95, 102, 109–10, 122, 131–32, 137, 142, 144, 146, 148, 165, 167, 202, 204–5

Penises; butches' possession of, 161–62; elision of, 123, 128–31, 136; erect forms of, 119, 125, 130–31, 134, 136, 163; flaccid forms of, 110–12, 119, 130–31, 134, 142, 264 n. 102; gay interest featuring of, 112, 117, 119, 125, 127, 134–35; simulation of, 133, 162–63; troubling of, 133–34, 136, 142, 163–64, 215. *See also* Cultural genitals; Genitals; Visible penis lines

People are basically good slogan, 5, 31, 37, 44, 49, 60, 70, 107, 208

Petit, Michael, 116

Pez dispensers, 9, 13, 14, 57, 86, 146

Phanfare, 94

Photography: collecting of, 93, 121, 135, 149–50, 156–57; copies and, 15–16; digital technologies and, 15–16, 93–94, 133, 167; failure of, 16, 108, 137, 185; family and, 29, 93–97, 101, 113, 135, 149, 167; gay interest listings and, 42, 113, 118, 121, 124, 126, 134, 135–42; gender and, 84, 96–97, 140, 142, 146, 155–57, 160–65, 195–96; heterosexuality and, 21, 84, 94, 101; history and, 94, 113, 135, 149, 161; lesbian interest listings and, 20–21, 143–67; referential aspects of, 14–17, 68, 113, 137, 147, 161, 165–67; reordering context through, 29, 134, 143–44, 146, 160–61;

Stewart, Susan, 78, 100
Straayer, Chris, 147, 158–59

Technological failures, 16, 33, 108–9, 137, 214
Technologies, 119, 123, 129, 169; configuration through, 6–7, 23, 50, 85; co-production of, 7, 25; effacement of, 27, 185; empowerment and, 61, 85; gender and, 9–10, 23, 61, 92–94, 134, 194, 204, 207; politics and, 7, 11–13, 205, 217; race and, 23, 61; sexuality and, 9, 92–94, 129; work and, 33, 72
Terranova, Tiziana, 34–35
thana0, 129–30
tomscoolcollectibles, 154–55
Toy Boat advertisement, 29, 101, 173
Trading cards, 70, 73, 74, 76, 78–80, 104–6
Trust, 44; craigslist's production of, 203, 206, 208; eBay's production of, 18, 19, 29, 43, 46, 66, 95, 206; erosion of, 46–51, 186; feedback system and, 26, 43–46, 131; images and, 14, 17
Turner, Patricia, 172, 178, 183, 194
twingles33, 1–2
Typographical errors, ix, 1, 18, 219 n. 1

unclecrickey, 139, 150
Uncle Griff, 14, 57, 70, 78–79
unique–find, 24, 27, 52, 53
unique_finds93, 64–65
Unwashed clothing, 20, 86, 101–4, 116–17
Up-skirt photography, 195
Usenet, 27, 30

Virtual, 33, 59–61, 70, 78, 96, 121, 124, 158, 187
Virtual community, 3, 7, 19, 26, 28–31, 38, 40, 55, 59, 87
Visible penis lines, 42, 111, 112, 116, 117, 119, 123, 129, 132–33, 135–36
Visual culture studies, 13–14, 17, 139

Visually accessible bodies, 120–21, 135, 154–58, 165, 195 98, 204

Walsh, Joan, 22, 23
Wedding dresses: breakups and, 104–5, 107; collecting of, 100, 102; dirt on, 100–104; drag and, 146, 160; eBay's use of, 20, 84, 96, 99; fandom for, 98–99; memories of, 97, 149; pricing of, 99; selling of, 84–86, 96–105, 107–9; treasuring of, 100; weight and, 96–99; whiteness and, 101, 103
Wedding dress guy, 104–5, 108
Weddings, 85–86, 95; companies' use of, 91–92, 94; consumerism in, 95, 160; drag and, 21, 146–47, 160–61, 163; eBay's use of, 10, 13, 20, 25, 84–88, 96–104, 116, 160, 187; members' use of, 20, 25, 63, 65, 83, 96–110; Omidyar, Wesley, and, 2, 13, 86, 96, 146; photographs of, 96–97, 101, 102, 104, 108–9; traditional values and, 85–86, 94–101, 107, 146, 149, 160–61; troubling of, 20, 104–9, 160–61; Wolfe, Aspling, and, 87–88, 96, 108
Welcome messages, 3, 90
Wesley, Pam, 2, 9–10, 13, 57, 86, 146, 205, 207
Whatever it is, you can get it on eBay campaign, 2, 220 n. 4; confusion and, 16, 64, 90; everything and, 2, 85, 93, 153; sexuality and, 2, 10–11, 88–89, 93, 109, 142, 153
Whitman, Meg: eBay and, 5, 27, 72; fans of, 5, 41, 49, 62, 79; gender and, 5, 62, 86; motherhood and, 12, 60, 86; politics and, 11–13, 25, 50, 84, 87, 205
Wolfe, Maggy, 88, 96, 108
Woolgar, Steve, 6, 85, 221 n. 24
WorldofGood.com, 2, 11, 38

Yahoo! 61, 148, 174
YouTube, 27, 217

Michele White is an associate professor in the Department
of Communication at Tulane University. She is the author of
The Body and the Screen: Theories of Internet Spectatorship (2006).

Library of Congress Cataloging-in-Publication Data
White, Michele, 1962–
Buy it now : lessons from eBay / Michele White.
p. cm.
Includes bibliographical references and index.
ISBN 978-0-8223-5226-6 (cloth : alk. paper)
ISBN 978-0-8223-5240-2 (pbk. : alk. paper)
1. Internet—Social aspects. 2. eBay (Firm). 3. Electronic
commerce—Social aspects. 4. Internet and women. 5. Online
identities. I. Title.
HM851.W455 2012
381′.177—dc23   2011053341